Cultural Atlas of
CHINA

Editor Graham Speake
Art editor Andrew Lawson
Map editors Nicholas Harris, Zoë
  Goodwin
Text editors Jennifer Drake-
  Brockman, Robert Peberdy
Picture research Diana Morris,
  Mel Cooper
Index Jennifer Drake-Brockman
Design Adrian Hodgkins
Production Clive Sparling

AN EQUINOX BOOK
Published in North America by
Facts On File, Inc., 460 Park
Avenue South, New York, N.Y.
10016

Planned and produced by
Equinox (Oxford) Ltd,
Musterlin House,
Jordan Hill, Oxford
England OX2 8DP

Copyright © Equinox (Oxford)
Ltd, 1983
Text copyright © Caroline
Blunden and Mark Elvin, 1983
Reprinted 1988, 1989

Library of Congress
Cataloging in Publication Data
Blunden, Caroline.
  Cultural Atlas of China.
  Includes index.
  1. China—Maps. 2. China—
  Historical geography.
  I. Title.
G2305.B56   1983
912′.51   82-675304
ISBN 0–87196–132–6

Origination by Alpha
Reprographics, Harefield,
Middlesex; Siviter Smith Ltd,
Birmingham; Fotographics Ltd,
London · Hong Kong

Maps drawn and originated by
Lovell Johns Ltd, Oxford;
Thames Cartographic Services,
Maidenhead; Mais Map Services,
Hornchurch.

Filmset by Keyspools Ltd,
Golborne, Lancs., England

Printed in Spain by Heraclio
Fournier SA, Vitoria

Frontispiece A traditional Chinese
shadow puppet. Sticks attached
to its joints can be manipulated
to make it capable of a wide
variety of lively movements.

Cultural Atlas of
CHINA

by Caroline Blunden
and Mark Elvin

Facts On File®
New York • Oxford

CONTENTS

List of Maps

List of Tables

CHRONOLOGICAL TABLE

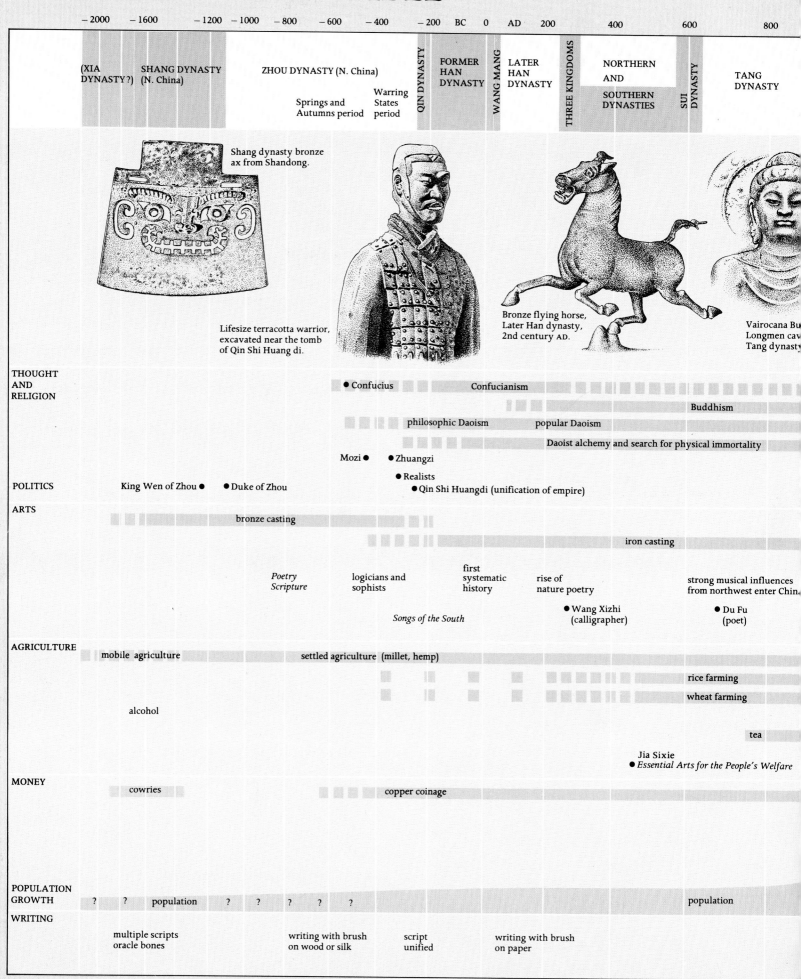

| | −2000 | −1600 | −1200 | −1000 | −800 | −600 | −400 | −200 | BC | 0 | AD | 200 | 400 | 600 | 800 |

(XIA DYNASTY?) | SHANG DYNASTY (N. China) | ZHOU DYNASTY (N. China) | QIN DYNASTY | FORMER HAN DYNASTY | WANG MANG | LATER HAN DYNASTY | THREE KINGDOMS | NORTHERN AND SOUTHERN DYNASTIES | SUI DYNASTY | TANG DYNASTY

Springs and Autumns period — Warring States period

Shang dynasty bronze ax from Shandong.

Lifesize terracotta warrior, excavated near the tomb of Qin Shi Huang di.

Bronze flying horse, Later Han dynasty, 2nd century AD.

Vairocana Bu
Longmen cave
Tang dynasty

THOUGHT AND RELIGION

● Confucius   Confucianism

Buddhism

philosophic Daoism   popular Daoism

Daoist alchemy and search for physical immortality

Mozi ●   ● Zhuangzi

● Realists

POLITICS

King Wen of Zhou ●   ● Duke of Zhou   ● Qin Shi Huangdi (unification of empire)

ARTS

bronze casting

iron casting

Poetry Scripture   logicians and sophists   first systematic history   rise of nature poetry   strong musical influences from northwest enter China

Songs of the South   ● Wang Xizhi (calligrapher)   ● Du Fu (poet)

AGRICULTURE

mobile agriculture   settled agriculture (millet, hemp)

rice farming

wheat farming

alcohol

tea

Jia Sixie
● Essential Arts for the People's Welfare

MONEY

cowries   copper coinage

POPULATION GROWTH

? ? population ? ? ? ? ?   population

WRITING

multiple scripts oracle bones   writing with brush on wood or silk   script unified   writing with brush on paper

JIN
(RUZHEN)

YUAN
(MONGOL)
DYNASTY

MING DYNASTY

QING (MANCHU) DYNASTY

REPUBLIC
OF
CHINA

PEOPLE'S
REPUBLIC
OF
CHINA

SONG DYNASTY

GDOMS

(Taiwan)

The Great Wall.

Yuan dynasty porcelain vase
with underglaze decoration.

Marble barge,
Summer Palace, Beijing.

The great leader,
Chairman Mao.

millions
1000

Neo-Confucianism   Neo-Confucianism   Communism

Buddhism

popular Daoism   popular Daoism

● Wang Anshi   Nestorianism   Catholicism   and Protestantism
(Reformer)   ● Zhu Xi (synthesizes Neo-Confucianism)   ● Wang Yangming   Kang Youwei ●   ● Mao Zedong
Regular civil-service examinations   Maritime Interdict   (politician-philosopher)   Opening of China

750

rise of   firearms
landscape
painting   rise of drama   rise of novel   creation of a
      "national language"
Confucian   ● Shen Gua (scientist)   ● Cao Xueqin (novelist)
Scriptures   *Dreampool Jottings*   *Story of the Stone*
printed

500

cotton

tea widely drunk

tobacco, potatoes, peanuts, corn

opium addiction

250

copper coinage

hyperinflation

paper money

influx of silver from Japan and Americas

copper imports

Yunnan copper mines

population   major epidemics   cholera epidemic

0

movable
types

color
printing

modern printing,
typewriters, romanization,
simplified characters

odblock
inting

9

Note on Transcription and Pronunciation

This volume uses the new *pinyin* system of romanizing Chinese, as the nearest to an international standard. The older Wade-Giles forms and, where appropriate for the place-names, the Post Office forms as well, are entered in the Gazetteer and Index to facilitate cross-reference to other books and to library catalogs, most of which are currently Wade-Giles. Thus, typical entries begin:

Zhuang Zhou/Chuang Chou . . .,

and

Beijing/Pei-ching/Peking . . .,

for the philosopher and capital city respectively. While "Canton" here has its standard *pinyin* form "Guangzhou," we have felt obliged to retain the use of "Cantonese" to describe the people, language and cuisine.

Readers who do not speak Mandarin Chinese can produce a recognizable pronunciation of the romanized words apart from the tones, by following these rules:

Consonants: much as in English, except for
  c which sounds like *ts* in "ca*ts*,"
  q which sounds like *ch* in "*ch*eek,"
  x which sounds like *sh* in "*sh*een,"
  z which sounds like *dz* in "a*dz*e" and
  zh which sounds like *j* in "*j*ar."

Vowels: much as in Italian, except for
  ian and yan which sound like "*yen*,"
  e and i after c, s, z, and ch, sh and zh, which have a neutral sound, as in "s*e*rve" and "sh*i*rk" and
  ui which sounds like "*way*."

An apostrophe separates syllables in cases where confusion can occur. Thus *xian* contains a single syllable (meaning "county," etc.) and *Xi'an* (the place-name) contains two.

Tones in the Mandarin dialect are marked, where necessary, by accents. Thus

  mā, má, mǎ and *mà*

show the level, rising, dipping and falling tones respectively.

PREFACE

Do even the Chinese have much idea of what China has been in times past? It is the world's oldest living civilization, in terms of a continuity of culture, yet its past has been endlessly re-edited rather than actually preserved. Compared with the Mediterranean world there are few Chinese ancient monuments or buildings still above ground. Chinese wood and soft brick have perished swiftly compared with Western stone.

Nor are there many original Chinese documents. Mostly there are only copies of copies. (And this is sometimes true even of paintings.) Chinese archives seem to have been kept no longer than was administratively necessary; then essential items were excerpted and abstracted, and the rest destroyed. And paper – the writing material of the Chinese for close on two thousand years – has lacked the durability of parchment or papyrus.

As regards the earliest times, the last two generations have seen exciting developments. The thin stock of inscriptions on bronze, that were previously our only wholly authentic records, has been supplemented by the excavation of oracles scratched on bone or shell, a handful of silk manuscripts, some of the wooden strips that formed the earliest Chinese books, and many often visually dazzling artifacts. Compared with the wealth of information on which the reconstruction of the pre-classical Middle East has been based, it is still a meager store; but archaic China is visible now with a clarity that would hardly have been thinkable a lifetime ago. One of the purposes of the present work is to make this strange and recently discovered world accessible to the general reader.

It is paradoxical that the very continuity of Chinese history has often served to obscure their own past to the Chinese. Thus ancient Chinese texts, perpetually reinterpreted, have been only too easy to understand in the terms provided by the present. Until not many decades ago, for example, the love songs in the *Scripture of Poetry*, a product of the first half of the first millennium BC, were conventionally understood by Chinese scholars as allegories referring to the relationship of ruler and minister.

In general, the awareness of the different character of remote times has been muted in China compared with the West. There have been few sharp divides, of which people have remained conscious, comparable with the coming of an all-pervading Christianity or Islam, with the arrival or departure of empires such as Rome's, or with the total forgetting of the meaning of scripts such as the Egyptian hieroglyphs that remained for millennia as a visible reminder to later generations of other ideas and values, of another inner world.

Perhaps this is where the Western scholar has a useful role to play. Far less well attuned than his Chinese colleagues to nuances of meaning, he is freer from the taboos, inhibitions and assumptions of the Chinese present. In some ways it is psychologically easier for him to respond to the otherness of the Chinese past, for historically continuity has not meant that – cumulatively – there have not been great changes. There have, and at all times. It is one of the primary purposes

of this cultural atlas to bring them as vividly before the reader's consciousness as possible.

A sharply focused understanding of China's past is essential for making sense of China's complex present. We have made every effort to avoid the distortions arising from emotional and ideological bias (of all kinds) that disfigure so much contemporary writing on the country. It is important, for example, not to allow admiration for the greatness of China's civilization, nor sympathy with her humiliations between 1840 and 1950, or the difficulties of her present situation, economic, cultural and political, to prevent a realistic appraisal of her as being, over the longer run, a highly successful imperializing and colonializing power. We hope that Chinese friends, who will not always agree with what we have written, will not misunderstand our motive, which is to be as truthful as possible, given the need for often sweeping generalizations imposed by the scale of our subject.

A word is perhaps in order about the division of labor in what is a two-author volume. In general, Caroline Blunden has been responsible for everything pertaining to the arts, including archaeology, and the selection of illustrations. Mark Elvin has written the historical text and designed the maps. We are grateful to Professor Colin Mackerras of Griffith University, Brisbane, for contributing the special feature entitled ''Music in Society.'' It should be stressed, though, that the book is a collective endeavor in a much wider sense. It would have been impossible without the editorial, artistic, cartographic and research skills of the team at Equinox whose names appear on page 2. We are deeply grateful and indebted to them. Other obligations are too diffuse and numerous to list one by one (though this in no way lessens the obligation), with two exceptions. Without the facilities of the Bodleian and the library of the Oriental Institute of the University of Oxford, and the unfailingly helpful attitude of the librarians, Mr David Helliwell and Mr Anthony Hyder, the work would have been much slower and much more difficult. Our heartfelt thanks.

Inevitably there is much more to say than is possible within a volume of this size. We hope that those whose interest has been whetted but not satisfied by the relatively brief treatment of poetry, painting and philosophy will soon be able to read in a separate book the longer surveys that we originally prepared. For the specialist it is also planned to produce a Chinese-character index for the gazetteer. Any reader who needs one should write in the first place to Mark Elvin at the Oriental Institute, Oxford University.

At the present moment Chinese studies, which take for their domain the ideas and actions of about a quarter of the human race, are almost wholly neglected even at our greater universities. We should feel more than rewarded for our own efforts if these pages help to bring home how profoundly both a general personal culture, whether artistic or historical, and a practical political realism require an understanding of one of the greatest civilizations of antiquity and the Middle Ages that is also one of the great international powers of today.

PART ONE
SPACE

THE LAND AND ITS PEOPLES

There are many ways of dividing up the space that we think of – too simply – as "China." It may be imagined in terms of its geology and geomorphology, or of the distribution of plants, animals and human populations, or of functional regions bound together by transport, trade and communications. In considering these spatial patterns it is necessary to remember that both the natural and the human landscapes have been continually changing. The Yellow River has not flowed in one but in several major channels during recorded history. Much of southern China and parts of the north were once covered with forests, now stripped by human activity. The mean annual temperature has risen and fallen over the centuries. The area that is now Shanghai was under the sea a thousand years ago, before the Yangzi River had deposited all the alluvium on which it is now built. Different Great Walls and Grand Canals have followed different alignments. The areas of Chinese culture and settlement, and of Chinese political domination, have both extended greatly over the span of 40 centuries from their original core in the middle of the valley of the Yellow River, but in some cases the greatest expansion has been surprisingly recent. The "China" that we think of today has actually not been in existence for very long.

Inner and Outer China

The most fundamental distinction of all is that between the two regions that may be called Inner and Outer China. The boundary between them is defined in terms of the contrast between a settled, and frequently irrigated, intensive farming, and a pastoral economy, sometimes combined with marginal dry-farming, or with complementary agricultural enclaves like the oases of the northwestern deserts. For most of history this frontier, which has never been stable, ran westwards from the Gulf of Bohai, more or less along the line of the present Great Wall, until reaching the lower slopes of the Tibetan plateau, where it turned sharply southwards. Until the present century Manchuria is best thought of as having been a part of Outer China, except for a small area along the lower reaches of the Liao River. With the heavy Han Chinese immigration and agricultural development of the last 70 years, it has now clearly become incorporated into Inner China. The boundary line now runs northwards along the lower eastern slopes of the

Daxing'an range (the Greater Khingan mountains). This change of status is reflected in the present Chinese preference for the name "The Three Northeastern Provinces" instead of the historically more appropriate "Manchuria." The far southwestern end of the dividing line has also long been somewhat unclear, as the jungle that dominates this corner of the subcontinent has only begun to be extensively cleared and farmed in the Chinese fashion since the later 18th century.

The two basic regions are of roughly comparable area, but hardly more than 5 per cent of the population live in Outer China. Some areas are effectively uninhabited, and in the greater part of it population density does not exceed one person per square kilometer. It is as empty as most of Inner China is crowded. The physical differences are also worthy of note. Outer China has spectacular, if often inhospitable, scenery. It includes the world's highest mountain, Qomolangma (Zhumulangma) or Mount Everest, 8848 meters above sea level, and the second lowest place on dry land, the Turfan Depression, which is 154 meters below sea level. It also contains some of the world's fiercest deserts in the Gobi and the Takla Makan, huge swamps like those of the Qaidam basin, virgin forests and endless, grass-covered steppes. Inner China, by way of contrast, is a gentler land of alluvial plains, river valleys and rolling hills, but worn bare by centuries of human occupancy, and so monotonous with its browns and greens and grays that the eye develops a hunger for bright colors.

Much of the "outback" that constitutes Outer China is a region of inland drainage. In essence this is the result of the upthrusting of central Asia caused by the collision about 15 million years ago of the crustal plate carrying India with the southern edge of Tibet. Around the edges the rivers flow away from China. Thus the Heilongjiang (the "Black Dragon River" or Amur) turns sharply northwards into the subarctic Pacific, and the Yarlung Zangbo River (Yaluzangbujiang), after flowing from west to east not far from Lhasa, plunges south through unnavigable gorges and reappears in India as the Brahmaputra. For these reasons Outer China was cut off from the extensive system of inland waterways that underpinned the high level of premodern economic integration achieved in much of Inner China. The one great route across Outer China was of course the so-called Silk Road which once took

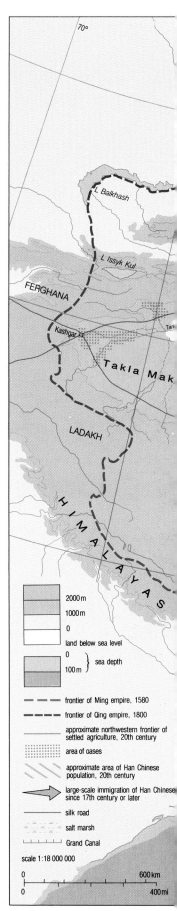

2000m
1000m
0
land below sea level

0
100 m } sea depth

– – – frontier of Ming empire, 1580

▬ ▬ ▬ frontier of Qing empire, 1800

approximate northwestern frontier of settled agriculture, 20th century

area of oases

approximate area of Han Chinese population, 20th century

large-scale immigration of Han Chinese since 17th century or later

silk road

salt marsh

Grand Canal

scale 1:18 000 000

0 ———— 600 km
0 ———— 400 mi

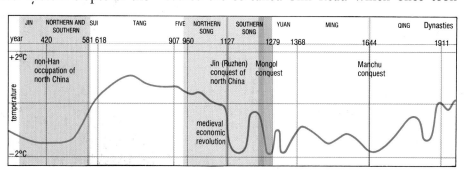

Changes in mean annual temperature
Zhu Kezhen's phenological studies (in other words, the comparison of the northern and southern ranges of various types of plants at different times) suggest that the medieval economic revolution was associated with a period of relatively high mean temperature, and maximum activity among the northern barbarians with relative cold.

Inner and Outer China
Present-day China falls into two main divisions. Inner China is relatively low-lying, agricultural, densely populated and inhabited by the Han Chinese. It is the core of the historical Chinese empire up to and including the Ming dynasty (1368–1644), whose frontiers are shown on the map. Outer China is a vast, sparsely populated and elevated region whose people are not ethnic Chinese, but of Mongol, Turkish, Tibetan or other stock. Its economy depends mostly on large herds of animals, with farming in a secondary place except for the oasis cities of the northwest. The rivers here either flow out of China or die away into basins of inland drainage, in contrast to those of Inner China which serve, together with the coastal shipping routes, as a complex network of water transportation. Apart from a few short-lived extensions of imperial suzerainty, Outer and Inner China were only joined together politically under the Manchu (or Qing) dynasty, mostly in the course of the 18th century. It was this process that accounts for the huge size of the People's Republic today. During the last two centuries movements of Han Chinese migrants have considerably extended Inner China, in particular by converting much of Manchuria from forest and pasture into farmland.

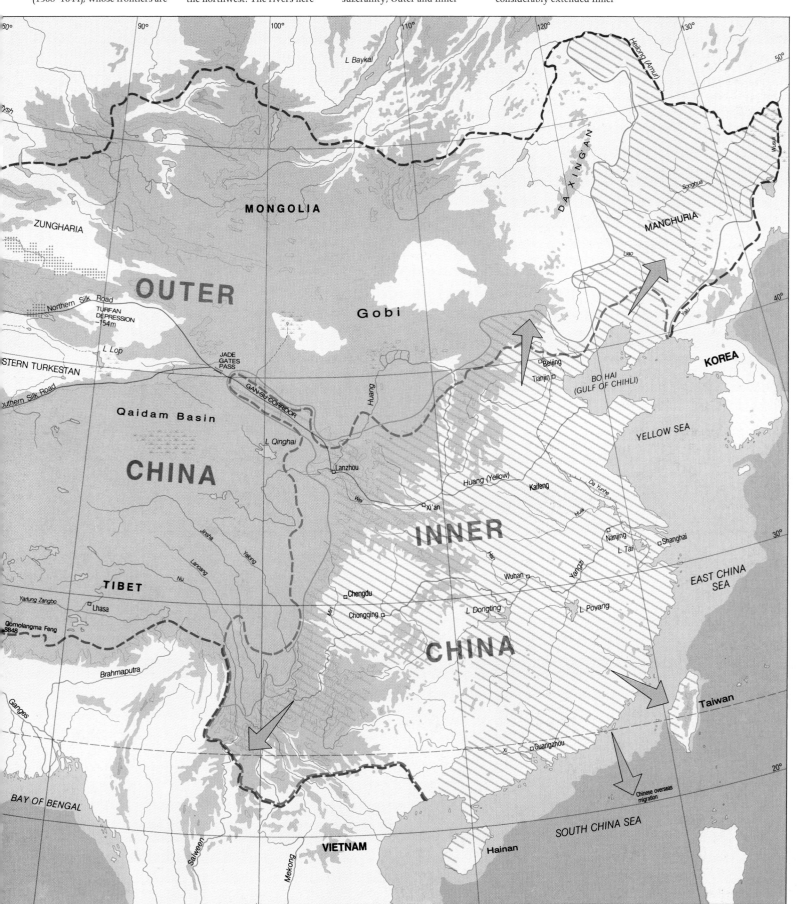

Chinese silks to the Roman empire. It ran northwest along the Gansu corridor and through the Jade Gates pass, beyond which – in Chinese folklore – spring was said never to go. From the Jade Gates the two main routes ran along the north and south rims of the Tarim basin, and thence over the mountains either north into Ferghana (now in the Soviet Union) or south into Bactria (now in Afghanistan). Until the 9th century AD the peoples of the oases along the Silk Road spoke Indo-European languages, and were the one direct contact between China and the Indo-European world.

About a thousand years ago there was still quite extensive pasturage in the northern parts of Inner China, but since then large-scale stockraising has been confined to Outer China. A sharper distinction between the cuisines of the two worlds also dates from this time, as the milk-based dishes that had been quite common in early medieval Han Chinese cooking increasingly passed out of use in Inner China. Herds of sheep, goats, cows, horses, camels and yaks have been the economic basis of most of Manchuria, Mongolia, Eastern Turkestan and Tibet until early modern times. Inner China, in contrast, has long been short of animal power and manures. Its typical livestock are scavengers like ducks, poultry and pigs. For transportation, the operation of machinery and the provision of fertilizer, humans have often supplied what, under other circumstances, could have been had more easily or cheaply from animals.

To speak in loose terms, the population of Inner China has long been overwhelmingly Han, the term commonly used for ethnic Chinese. That of Outer China, at least until recent migrations into Manchuria and the far northwest, has been predominantly non-Han. Much of this difference is probably cultural, as repeated historical invasions and occupation of the north China plain by northern and western "barbarians" have led to much intermixing. Satisfactory specification of physical racial characteristics is notoriously difficult, but the vast majority of the inhabitants of Inner and Outer China alike can be plausibly grouped together as "Mongolids." Among their distinguishing features with respect to non-Mongolids are very little body and facial hair, yellow to yellow-brown skin, dark brown eyes, a tendency to possess the epicanthic fold above the eyes and the near absence of odor-bearing sweat-glands under the armpits. The finer distinction made here between "Han" and "non-Han" corresponds roughly to the contrast sometimes made between two subgroups, namely the southern "Sinids" and the more northern "Tungids" or Mongols. The latter tend to have flatter faces, narrower eyes, shorter and squatter stature and a more pronounced eye-fold. The only important exceptions to these generalizations are the Tibetans and the original populations of the southern coastal regions (now largely vanished in pure form), neither of whom are Mongolids.

The political union of Inner and Outer China was only achieved in the 18th century. This was the work of the Manchu (Qing) dynasty, which had a dual character, part Chinese and part "barbarian." After the unification, the bureaucratic system of government used for two millennia in Inner China was not extended to Outer China, which was ruled instead under a variety of jurisdictions, some feudal, some military, some little more than a nominal supervision as in Tibet. All of the latter were ultimately answerable to the Office for the Management of the Frontiers, and did not come under the authority of the traditional six ministries. Eastern Turkestan was only made into a province in 1884, under the name of Xinjiang, which means "New Region." The political map of the People's Republic still reflects this duality. Almost all of

Right: Autonomous Regions and Autonomous Districts
The government of the People's Republic of China has set up so-called "Autonomous Regions" and smaller "Autonomous Districts" in areas where the non-Han population predominates. Although some important concessions are made to the non-Han (such as the non-imposition of the policy of the single-child family), there is no meaningful autonomy. At times the policy of destroying non-Chinese cultures has been pursued by violent means, most notably in Tibet during the Cultural Revolution when most of the Buddhist monasteries were pulled down and the monks returned to the lay life. Among the Kazakhs the traditional highly skilled art of hunting animals with trained birds (such as eagles) was outlawed, presumably because it was not amenable to collectivist economic control. In more recent years the gentler but probably more lastingly effective weapon of education has been used by the Beijing government to spread Chinese and Communist values. Anti-Chinese liberation movements have flared up from time to time (notably that of the Kham in eastern Tibet in 1959), but recurrences look increasingly less likely at the present.

Left: The changing courses of the Yellow River
The upper course of the Yellow River has followed slightly different lines in different eras, particularly where it breaks into multiple channels near present-day Ningxia and at the northwestern corner of its hairpin bend, but has remained essentially stable. The lower course, east of Mount Hua and the Sanmen (or "Three Gate") Gorges, has varied dramatically in historical times.

During the second millennium BC the lower course ran almost northwards just below the mountains of present-day Shanxi province. In the next two millennia it swung around little by little like the hand of a clock until, from 1289 to 1324, it was flowing in a southeasterly direction into the middle reaches of the Huai River, which in turn emptied into the lower Yangzi. Since 1324 it has moved back and forth in an irregular fashion, and at present again debouches north of the Shandong peninsula.

The primary cause of these rapid shifts of course has been the uniquely heavy load of silt carried by the Yellow River. As the current slackens near the sea, much of this is redeposited, building up the riverbed and sooner or later forcing the water to run elsewhere. The present multi-exit system seeks to avoid this by the regular dredging of channels temporarily taken out of use.

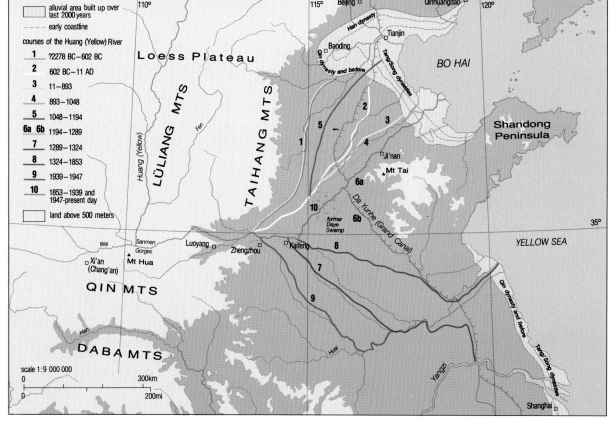

▭	alluvial area built up over last 2000 years
– – –	early coastline

courses of the Huang (Yellow) River

1	??2278 BC–602 BC
2	602 BC–11 AD
3	11–893
4	893–1048
5	1048–1194
6a 6b	1194–1289
7	1289–1324
8	1324–1853
9	1939–1947
10	1853–1939 and 1947–present day
▭	land above 500 meters

scale 1:9 000 000
0 — 300km
0 — 200mi

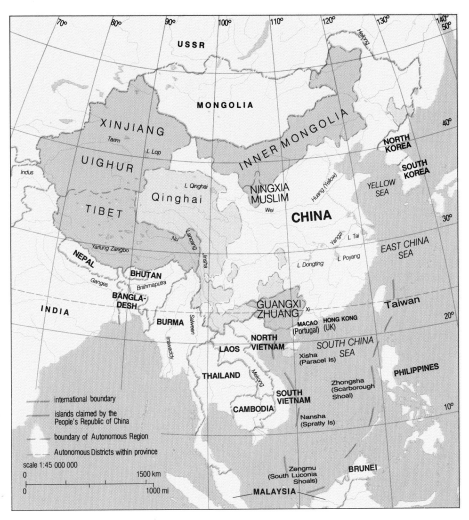

the Qinling and Daba ranges. These form a barrier that divides Inner China into two, at a latitude of about 35 degrees north. South of the Qinling and Daba the annual rainfall is 1295 millimeters heavier on average than to the north. Precipitation is quite variable in both regions, but especially so in the north, where the average deviation from the mean is about 30 per cent. Both drought and flooding are commoner in the north. The comparative stability of the south must also be in part attributed to the different natures of the two great rivers that dominate each region, the Huanghe, or "Yellow River," and the Changjiang, or "Long River," usually known in the West as the Yangzi. The Yellow River flows through the loess or "yellow earth" regions of fine wind-blown soil for much of its upper course and so becomes the most silt-laden of all the great rivers in the world. Much of this silt is then dropped in its more sluggish lower reaches, building up the height of the river bed, and making its course unstable. In many places the dikes have been built higher and higher until the river flows above the level of the surrounding countryside, a recipe for trouble. The Yangzi discharges a greater volume of water, but is much more stable. In part this is because the two great lakes on its middle course, Dongting and Poyang, act as overflow basins that store water in times of flooding and release it in times of shortage.

North China has historically been a land of dry-field farming, mostly wheat and millet. South China has been the home of wet-field rice farming. The general nature of the soils is also different, being more alkaline in the north and more acidic in the south. Much of south China is crisscrossed with navigable rivers and canals; travel and transport-ation have for more than a millennium made great use of boats. Intensive coastal shipping also developed early up and down the southeastern littoral, making use of the convenient seasonal alternation of the monsoon winds. In north China, however, one went on horseback in imperial times if one was in a hurry, otherwise by two-wheeled cart or on foot. Loess does not allow the easy construc-tion of good roads and becomes an almost im-passable mud when wet. The building of railroads since the end of the 19th century has had only a limited impact on transportation in south China, but a dramatic one in north China, especially Manchuria, where the best "roads" of earlier times were the ice-bound rivers in winter.

South China is a land of Han in-migration, but once the migrants had arrived there the hilly valleys seem to have limited further mixing and to have preserved a great variety of subcultures and different dialects. By contrast, the language of the north is relatively homogeneous; almost everyone speaks some form of what is commonly, if not entirely accurately, called "Mandarin" after the former lingua franca of the imperial officials. The physical appearance of northerners and southerners is also different: the northerners are on average more than five centimeters taller, and more solidly and heavily built. In vulgar speech, northerners sometimes refer slightingly to the southerners as "monkeys" and the southerners respond in kind by calling the northerners "steamed bread." Making sweeping cultural contrasts is too hazardous, especially given the many changes over time and the

historic Outer China is divided into so-called "Autonomous Regions." These are as follows: Nei-Menggu Zizhiqu (Inner Mongolian Autonomous Region); Ningxia Huizu Zizhiqu (Ningxia Muslim Autonomous Region); Xinjiang Weiwuer Zizhiqu (Xinjiang Uighur People's Autonomous Region); Guangxi Zhuangzu Zizhiqu (Guangxi Zhuang People's Autonomous Region); and Xizang Zizhiqu (Tibetan Autonomous Region). To these should be added most of the province of Qinghai or "Blue Sea," named for the lake of Kokonor, which is part of the Tibetan region and almost wholly under a regime of "Autonomous Districts." Some few small areas of Inner China inhabited by minority nation-alities are likewise under the rule of "Autonomous Districts," which are smaller than the Regions and, unlike them, under a provincial government.

Not all of the Qing domain has been inherited by the People's Republic. The northernmost parts were lost to Czarist Russia in the middle of the 19th century. Outer Mongolia achieved virtual inde-pendence in 1912, and became a People's Republic and satellite of the Soviet Union in 1924.

Finally, Inner and Outer China have historically had different religions. The traditional faiths of Inner China were Confucianism, Daoism, Mahayana Buddhism and an amalgam of local cults. In Outer China people gave their allegiance to Lamaist Buddhism, Islam or the remnants of older indigen-ous systems of belief such as the Tibetan Bon.

North and south

The Kunlun mountains that run along the north edge of Tibet extend into Inner China in two prongs,

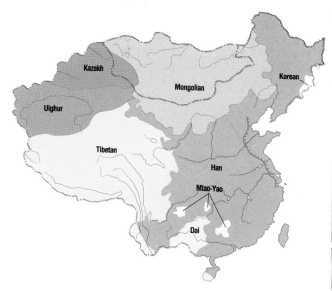

Ethnic Chinese (Han) constitute approximately 94 per cent of China's population. The remainder consists of over 50 ethnic groups, the main types being the Japano-Korean, Altaic, Indo-European, Tibeto-Burman, Austro-Asiatic, Dai, Miao-Yao and Malayo-Polynesian. Physically the majority share with the Han variations of the Mongolid race-type. The most notable differences are seen in Xinjiang where Caucasian and central Asiatic features mix, producing fair-haired children with Mongolid features. Typical Mongolid features include coarse, straight black hair, flat face accentuated by a low nasal root and a fold of skin over the inner end of the eye-opening, covering part of the upper lid.

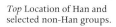

Top Location of Han and selected non-Han groups.

Below map A blue-eyed, long-bearded Russian of Indo-European stock, one of a small group of some 600 Russians living in Xinjiang.

Above The Miao minority originate mainly from southern Guangxi, near China's border with Vietnam.

Center right These Hani women and children belong to a small minority group in Yunnan which is part of the Tibeto-Burman family.

Right A Tibetan family in Lhasa.

Center left Han faces in Shanxi province in central China. Note the typical facial flattening, eyefold and low-bridged noses.

Left A girl of the Dai ethnic group from southern Yunnan, near the border with Burma.

Below A young Mongolian couple in national dress.

Above Both Uighurs and Kazakhs are Muslims. This horse-herding Kazakh from Xinjiang, like his fellow Turkic-speakers, is a nomad.

Left This Uighur of Islamic faith comes from Xinjiang, and is of Turkic stock.

extent of more local variations. It would seem, though, that the southerners have long had a stronger sense of the numinous quality of the landscape. They are the originators both of earth magic or geomancy, and of the first purely landscape poetry in the Chinese tradition, during the middle third of the first millennium AD. The southern economy has also for many centuries been richer than that of the north, and the south, especially the lower Yangzi valley, has been more inclined to extravagance, ostentation and sensuality. In recent times, but before the Communist revolution in the economic and social institutions in the countryside, south China was distinguished for its powerful lineages or ''clans,'' and for its relatively high levels of tenancy. North China, by way of contrast, was a land of small owner-operator farmers for the most part, and strong lineages were much less in evidence.

The historic links between north and south China were the various Grand Canals. The first of these was built with conscripted labor, including many women, early in the 7th century under the Sui dynasty. As can be seen from the map on page 105, its two main arms followed the nearly level ground used by the courses of the Yellow River at various times. Its basic purpose was to bring the plentiful rice of the south to the Sui capital in the northwest at Daxingcheng (present-day Xi'an) and to the armies stationed in the northeast. When the Mongol (Yuan) dynasty located their capital at Dadu, on the site of modern Beijing, much of the canal was rebuilt on a shorter route that took it over the western spurs of the Shandong hills. This led to engineering difficulties, and use was also made of both a sea route and a combination of a sea route and a subsidiary canal cut across the middle of the Shandong peninsula, the so-called Jiao-Lai Canal.

It was only in the 15th century, under the Ming dynasty, that the problem of keeping enough water in the higher parts of the canal was solved. Although the Chinese had invented the double-gate or pound lock in the 11th century, they did not use it on this part of the waterway, preferring immovable solid barriers that retained water, while the boats were hauled around them on slipways. This of course limited the size of vessel that could be used. In its final form, the state grain transportation system (see map p. 104) sometimes employed up to 150 000 soldiers to man its fleet, and required compulsory labor-services of many more civilians to dredge and maintain the channels. Boats belonging to commoners were also entitled to use the Grand Canal, and it thus served as a commercial artery linking the north and the south. Its scale was stupendous for the Middle Ages, being over 1000 kilometers in length. Canals of a comparable scale only began to be cut in Europe, notably in France, in the 18th century.

In this way there developed a sort of complementary relationship between the north and the south. The economic center of gravity was in the south, but the political center was almost always in the north. This split had not existed at the beginning of the empire. The earliest imperial capital, late in the 3rd century BC, was that of the Qin at Xianyang, near Xi'an in the area known as Guannei (''Within the Passes''). It was more fertile than it is today, and there was a local system of irrigation and transpor-

tation canals. The principal capitals of both the Han and Tang dynasties were on essentially the same site, at Chang'an, the name of which means ''Everlasting Peace.'' Guannei was a strategically well-protected location, but its remoteness made it difficult to supply from outside. As the local economy deteriorated, probably through climatic desiccation, and the size of the capital grew, the Han and the Tang both established a secondary capital in the north China plain at Luoyang.

It was during the Tang that the south first began to challenge the north for economic supremacy, and the split of which we have spoken began to appear. The capital of the Northern Song from the late 10th to the early 12th century AD was at Kaifeng, on the last safe high ground to the east and close to the point where the Yellow River has historically shifted its course either north or south. Kaifeng was also the nearest of the northern capitals to the southern granaries, and the easiest to supply by waterway. In its heyday the official transportation brought it six million Chinese bushels of rice annually, or a quantity of the order of a third of a million tons (the exact conversion ratio is uncertain).

The Mongol (Yuan) in the 13th century had their capital near modern Beijing, deliberately straddling the divide between Inner and Outer China. They were the first dynasty to rule over both these areas. The original Ming capital was at Nanjing (''Southern Capital''), but they soon turned to a double capital system with the substantive administrative center in the north at Beijing and a more ceremonial center in the south. The reason for this shift was presumably strategic: to make the capital, in conjunction with the rebuilt Great Wall, a massive obstacle in the way of any would-be invader from Mongolia or Manchuria. Both the Manchu (Qing) and the People's Republic have kept the capital at Beijing, presumably partly out of respect for tradition, and partly because it remains close to the meeting-point of Han and non-Han domains.

There have been only two other southern capitals belonging to regimes that have had some claim to speak for China as a whole. These were the Southern Song metropolis at Hangzhou in the 12th and 13th centuries, the single seaport in imperial history to be a capital, and the Nationalist center at Nanjing from 1927 to 1937. The sole western city to be a national capital was the wartime headquarters of the Nationalist government at Chongqing on the upper Yangzi between 1937 and 1945, a time when most of eastern China was occupied by the Japanese.

Patterns of unity and disunity

The two-fold division between north and south China found an approximate political expression during the 12th and 13th centuries. China south of the Yangzi valley was ruled by the Southern Song and the north China plain by the Jin dynasty of the Ruzhen (or Jurjen) people, ancestors of the Manchus, and then later by the Mongols between 1234 and their conquest of the south in the 1270s.

A three-fold division can be seen during the Three Kingdoms period in the 3rd century AD. China was split between Wei, which dominated the valley of the Yellow River, Chu, which controlled the Yangzi and some areas further south, and Shu, a landlocked domain upriver from the Yangzi gorges.

An economic counterpart of this tripartite political division appeared under the unified rule of the Tang dynasty in the 7th to 9th centuries, and of the Northern Song in the later 10th and 11th. As may be seen from the map (p. 98), there were three separate regional marketing areas, firmly linked by only three routes that were all partly man-made. The west and the north were joined by the Gallery Road, named for the wooden walkways driven into the mountainsides. The west and the south were connected by the Yangzi gorges, up which boats could go only when hauled by trackers on a precarious towing-path cut through the cliffs along the bank. The south and the north were tied together by the Grand Canal.

In some periods China was even more fragmented. The earliest of these patterns of subdivision that is still of some general interest is that of the Warring States in the 4th and 3rd centuries BC. Many of the names of these states continued to be used in literary contexts in later times, although they had long vanished from the official maps. Not too much significance should be attached to the precise boundaries shown on the map (p. 71); with one exception, the states of the 4th century were accretions made up from a larger number of preexisting smaller states, and their frontiers were in continual flux as they fought each other. The exception was the central core of Zhao, Wei and Han, which were the fragments left by the break-up of the state of Jin in the 5th century. They sat astride the center of the north China plain. Around this core was a ring of larger states. To the west lay Qin, based in the valley of the Wei River, and enriched by its two southwestern conquests. These were Shu on the plain of the Min River, and the home of large-scale irrigated agriculture in China, and Ba, on the Yangzi above the gorges, and centered on what is today the city of Chongqing. To the immediate south was Chu, occupying the Han River valley and the central Yangzi region, much of which was then untamed lakelands and the famous "Cloud Dream Swamp." To the east was Qi, the most urbanized and civilized, incorporating Lu, the little state where Confucius had been born several centuries earlier. Outside this ring were the peripheral states of Yan in the far northeast, and Yue in the lower Yangzi valley and part of the southeastern seacoast. Yue, which had absorbed its arch-rival Wu early in the 5th century BC, was the home of Chinese seafaring, in contrast to the other states, whose people were firmly orientated towards the land.

In the last historical period of thoroughgoing political fragmentation, that of the Five Dynasties and Ten Kingdoms in the 10th century AD, a somewhat different pattern emerged (see map p. 25). The core composed of Zhao, Wei and Han (that is the fragments of Jin) now joined together with Qin and Qi to constitute a relatively large state dominating north China. Around it lay a ring of smaller states, some of which approximated to those of Warring States times, others of which were new. There was, as before, a Yan in the northeast, and a Shu in the west, corresponding to the former Shu and Ba. Chu in the central Yangzi and Wu (Southern Tang) divided most of the ancient domain of Chu between them; Wu-Yue was what its name implies, the geographical successor to the Wu and Yue of the past. There were two new states. Min was on the lower

southeast coast, populated by recent Chinese migrants and famous for its gold-roofed Buddhist temples which could be seen by travelers far out at sea. Southern Han occupied the present-day Canton basin. At this time the scale of Chinese states such as these, and their international relations based on a shared culture but riven with military and mercantile rivalry, in many ways resembled those of early modern Europe.

The administrative units that appear at first sight to have corresponded most closely to the independent states of the periods when the empire was fragmented were the provinces. Most provincial boundaries, however, have been extremely unstable over the longer historical run, and thinking about China in terms of its provinces can sometimes be more confusing than helpful.

True provinces, in the sense of small-scale systems of centralized administration, did not appear until the later 13th century, when they were called "administrative chancelleries" (xingsheng, or simply sheng). They had predecessors, however, in the regions called "circuits" (dao) by the Tang and demarcated for military and strategic purposes. The map of the early Tang circuits (p. 26) shows the prosaically straightforward descriptive names given to them, so characteristic of Chinese bureaucratic tradition. This simple and logical pattern became complicated in the last years of the Tang dynasty, when the northern part of the country fell under the rule of military commissioners who had charge of rather smaller areas than the original circuits.

The Northern Song provinces were known as "routes" (lu). Besides Tang-style location names they were in quite a number of cases identified in terms of one or more of the most important prefectures that they contained. The provinces of the Mongol (Yuan) dynasty were the simplest of all, but they had a pattern surprisingly different from that of the Song. A new and confusing feature of the naming system is that three of the names contain abbreviated references to the names of former provinces, and the geographical meaning is no longer evident at first sight. It is only with the provinces of the Ming dynasty that something like the present-day pattern begins to appear.

There were only a few changes under the Manchu (Qing) dynasty that came to power in 1645. As may be seen by comparing the maps on pp. 26–27, the Southern Area of Direct Rule was converted into the provinces of An-Hui (that is, Anqing and Huizhou prefectures), and Jiang-Su (that is, the part of South-of-the-Yangzi containing Suzhou prefecture). Gansu reappeared in the northwest, and at the very end of the dynasty Xinjiang ("New Region") and the island of Taiwan ("Tower Bay") acquired provincial status.

It is clear from the kaleidoscope presented in the maps that most of China's administrative provinces have not been based on deeply rooted natural regions. One or two scholars have even thought that the government may in some cases have deliberately split a natural economic and social region into two politically so as to weaken its sense of identity and to prevent too great a growth of regional power.

In general, the historical provinces are not the most suitable units to use for thinking about China in spatial terms. There are rather too many of them,

Top Terracing has provided the best use of land in mountainous areas. Today terraces are being releveled where possible to allow for farm machinery.

Above The karst limestone peaks of Guilin unfold like the mountainous scenery of a traditional Chinese painting.

and their relevance to social life is limited. The tendency under the present Communist regime to allow the province very considerable powers in matters of economic administration, and the general "cellularization" of the economy since the 1950s, may however have gone some way to making them more authentic units than they have ever been in the past.

Instead of using provinces, some approach based on functional regions is necessary. Such a region may be defined as an area whose core has a high density of population compared to an interregional margin, and being marked off fairly sharply from other areas by its high level of internal inter-communication and economic interdependence. The map of the regional structure of 19th- and 20th-century China (p. 24) shows two possible schemes of regional subdivision. One is a practical scheme used by the former imperial administration for the sale of government monopoly salt, and the other is a theoretical solution recently devised by G. W. Skinner. In both cases the natural compartmentaliz-ation created by mountain ranges and by the concentration of the population in the river valleys are the foundations of the systems of demarcation; this gives the two patterns much in common.

Some of the differences are of less importance than they appear at first sight to be. The salt-system corridor that runs from the eastern seacoast to the Huainan sale zone is obviously an administrative artifact designed to facilitate the transportation of salt from the salterns to the interior. The fragmen-tation of the north China region into three salt sale zones is not of great significance either, since their outer boundaries coincide closely with Skinner's regional boundaries. It is also easy to explain why the northwestern frontier of the Hedong salt zone runs along the Yellow River: there was so much naturally occurring salt in the interior of the northwest, principally in the form of brine lakes, that maintaining a state monopoly to the west of the river was too difficult to be worth attempting.

There is, in general, a good case for thinking of Chinese history not in national terms, nor in provincial terms, but in terms of these ten large regions. Over the centuries their fortunes rose and fell to some extent independently of each other; and they remain to some degree distinctive worlds even today. On the other hand, it is important not to forget that the complexities and caprices of political fortune have sometimes led to the Chinese domain being cut up in ways that seem to ignore regional boundaries. As an illustration of this, the map on page 25 shows the approximate limits of the territories ruled by the major warlords and their allies around the beginning of 1926. Regional analysis is not an infallible key.

In contrast to the functional regions, a different sort of subdivision arises when we define areas in terms of shared similar characteristics. The most obvious of these are the climatic zones (see map p. 28). The general pattern is one of transition from tropical and moderate climates with hot summers and mild winters in the southeast through a cooler intermediate belt to arid and high-mountain climates in the northwest. Two other features of importance are the lines marking the northern limits at which 200 and 300 days a year free of frost may be relied on. The first is the limit up to which some sort

of double-cropping is usually possible; the second is the limit for the double-cropping of rice with rice. As may be seen from the numerals on the map, the growing season in the far south is more than twice as long as that in Manchuria.

The movement of the springtime from south to north is delightfully exemplified in Zhu Kezhen's map (p. 29) of the dates at which peach blossoms open in different parts of the country. This pattern of horizontal layers is typical of winter climates in China; in the high summer the center of Inner China becomes almost uniformly hot from north to south, with the seacoasts and higher mountains providing a relatively cooler periphery. The complexity of the climatic pattern leads to schedules for farmwork that are quite different in different parts of the country. This is suggested in the two maps (p. 28) showing the dates at which wheat is sown and harvested across the country. It is evident that there is a major division between the area of spring wheat, approximately north of the Great Wall, and the area of winter wheat south of it. Northern winter wheat requires more than eight months to ripen, whereas southern spring wheat takes little more than three. South of the Yangzi wheat is of course only a subsidiary crop.

The agricultural economist J. L. Buck, who organized a large-scale survey of the Chinese farm economy in the late 1920s and early 1930s, defined eight major agricultural regions for Inner China, excluding Manchuria and Taiwan. His main crite-rion was the clustering of characteristic groups of food plants, but he also used other determinants, such as groups of typical village trees. These farming regions are shown in the four maps on page 29, together with measures of the intensity of land use, productivity per worker, total regional farm population, and the density of farm population relative to cropland. The patterns that they reveal are probably still broadly valid today, though there are certain to have been some changes in addition to the growth in the number of farmers, who are now about twice as numerous as when Buck did his work. It is evident that the winter wheat and gaoliang region and the core of the Sichuan rice region are by far the most heavily farmed. The winter wheat and gaoliang region also has much the largest population. The productivity of farm labor in the southwestern rice region is more than twice as high as that in the spring wheat region. More than three times as many farmers are supported on a square kilometer of cropland in the southwest as in the northwest. As is indicated on the map of north and south China (p. 22), these regions may also be used to express the varying incidence of tenancy for pre-Communist times, landlordism being high-est in the Sichuan rice area, the Yangzi rice and wheat area, the rice and tea area, and the double-cropping rice area. This makes the point that the productivity of the land, and not of the workforce, was probably the main inducement to landlordism. The exception, the southwest, where land was highly productive, presumably had a lowish rate of tenancy because it had only been recently settled.

text continues on page 37

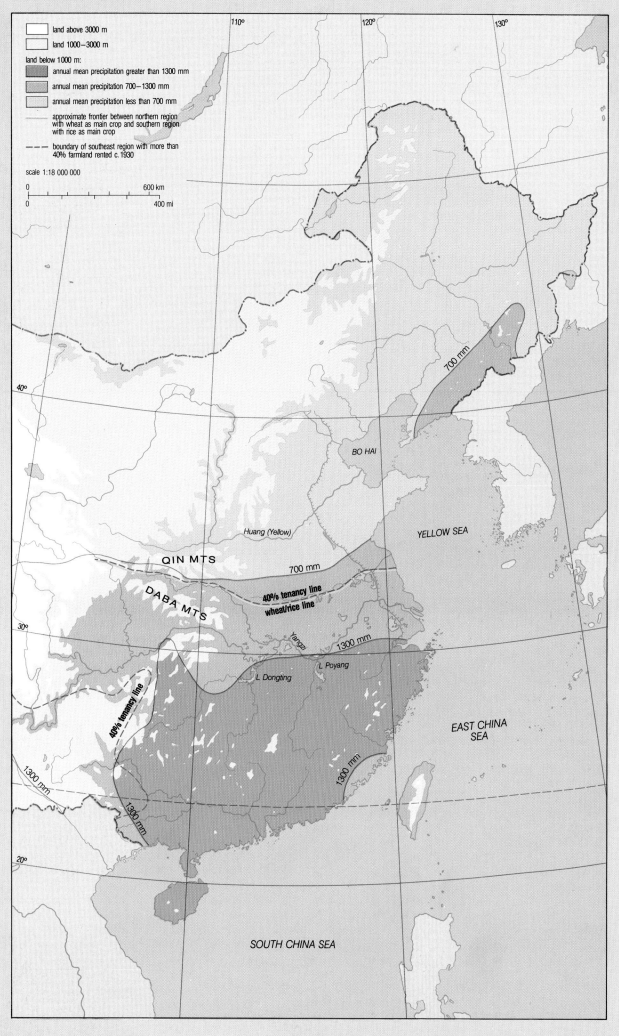

land above 3000 m

land 1000–3000 m

land below 1000 m:

annual mean precipitation greater than 1300 mm

annual mean precipitation 700–1300 mm

annual mean precipitation less than 700 mm

approximate frontier between northern region with wheat as main crop and southern region with rice as main crop

boundary of southeast region with more than 40% farmland rented c.1930

scale 1:18 000 000

0   600 km

0   400 mi

700 mm

BO HAI

Huang (Yellow)

YELLOW SEA

QIN MTS

DABA MTS

700 mm

40% tenancy line

wheat/rice line

Yangzi

1300 mm

L Poyang

L Dongting

40% tenancy line

EAST CHINA SEA

1300 mm

1300 mm

1300 mm

1300 mm

SOUTH CHINA SEA

North and south China   1
This map brings out in striking fashion the late-traditional contrast between the dry-farming north, with its predominantly owner-operator peasants, and the wet-field-farming south, where a substantial proportion of farmers rented their lands from landlords. The collectivist system imposed by the People's Republic has of course obliterated these organizational differences, and the recent northward extension of irrigation has also to a limited extent modified the technical contrast.

North and south China   2

Historical north China is the land of loess. This fine, wind-borne yellow dust has a top layer that forms an easily cultivated soil, and it thus facilitated the early appearance of agriculture here. It is striking how close the last of the Great Walls—that built under the Ming from the late 14th century to the 16th—runs along the northern edge of the loess deposits, separating the Chinese from the non-Chinese world. Apart from the artificially constructed Grand Canal, however, the north has lacked a satisfactory system of inland waterway transportation, and the seas off its shores are often difficult and dangerous.

The south, in contrast, has long had both an interconnecting network of inland water routes and easy coastal navigation based on the seasonal alternation of the monsoon winds, as well as numerous excellent harbors. A safe and regular sea connection with the north was only established in the later 18th century. Although the official grain transportation sailed from the Yangzi delta to the site of present-day Tianjin at various times under both the Mongols and the Ming, it was still in those days a hazardous undertaking.

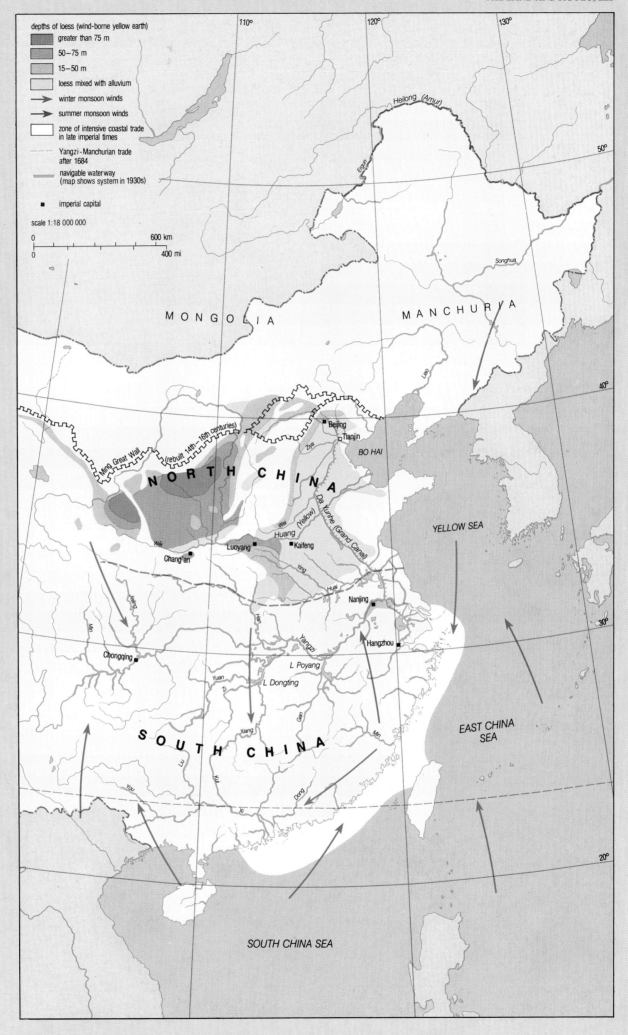

depths of loess (wind-borne yellow earth)
- greater than 75 m
- 50–75 m
- 15–50 m
- loess mixed with alluvium
- → winter monsoon winds
- → summer monsoon winds
- zone of intensive coastal trade in late imperial times
- Yangzi-Manchurian trade after 1684
- navigable waterway (map shows system in 1930s)
- ■ imperial capital

scale 1:18 000 000

0 ___ 600 km
0 ___ 400 mi

MONGOLIA

MANCHURIA

Heilong (Amur)

Ergun

Songhua

Liao

Ming Great Wall

(rebuilt 14th–16th centuries)

■ Beijing
Tianjin

BO HAI

NORTH CHINA

YELLOW SEA

Wei

Huang (Yellow)

Da Yunhe (Grand Canal)

Wei
● Chang'an

● Luoyang   ■ Kaifeng

Yong

Huai

Nanjing ■

Min

Jialing

Han

Hangzhou ■

Chongqing ■

Yangzi

L Poyang

Yuan

L Dongting

Zi

Gan

Xiang

SOUTH CHINA

Min

EAST CHINA SEA

Lu

Gui

Dong

You

Xi

SOUTH CHINA SEA

110°   120°   130°

50°

40°

30°

20°

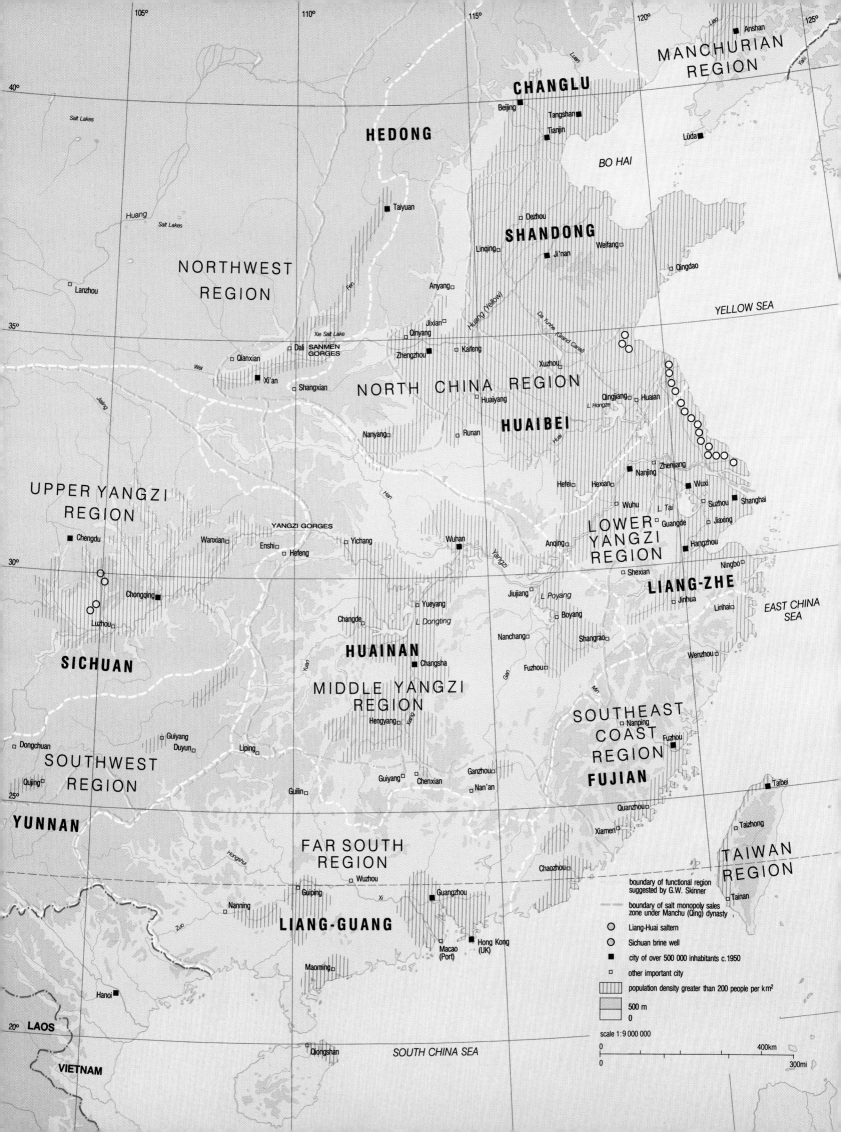

MANCHURIAN
REGION

CHANGLU

HEDONG

Anshan

Beijing
Tangshan
Tianjin

Lüda

BO HAI

NORTHWEST
REGION

Lanzhou

Salt Lakes

Huang   Salt Lakes

Taiyuan

Dezhou

SHANDONG

Linqing   Ji'nan   Weifang

Qingdao

YELLOW SEA

Fen

Xie Salt Lake

Qianxian   Dali   SANMEN
GORGES

Qinyang   Jixian

Anyang

Huang (Yellow)

Da Yunhe (Grand Canal)

Wei

Zhengzhou   Kaifeng

Xuzhou

Shangxian

NORTH CHINA REGION

Huaiyang

Qingjiang   Huaian

L Hongze

Xi'an

HUAIBEI

UPPER YANGZI
REGION

Jialing

Nanyang

Runan

Hui

Hefei   Hexian   Nanjing

Zhenjiang

Wuxi

Han

Chengdu

Wanxian   Enshi   Hefeng   Yichang

YANGZI GORGES

Wuhan

Wuhu   L Tai   Suzhou   Shanghai

Guangde   Jiaxing

LOWER
YANGZI
REGION

Anqing

Hangzhou

Yangzi

Shexian

Ningbo

Chongqing

Luzhou

Jiujiang   L Poyang

LIANG-ZHE

SICHUAN

Yueyang

Changde   L Dongting

Boyang

Jinhua

Linhai

EAST CHINA
SEA

Dongchuan

Guiyang   Duyun

HUAINAN

Yuan   Changsha

Nanchang   Shangrao

Wenzhou

Qujing

SOUTHWEST
REGION

Liping

MIDDLE YANGZI
REGION

Gan   Fuzhou

SOUTHEAST
COAST
REGION

Nanping

Fuzhou

YUNNAN

Qujing

Hengyang   Kang

FUJIAN

Guiyang   Chenxian   Ganzhou

Guilin   Nan'an

Min

Taibei

FAR SOUTH
REGION

Wuzhou

Chaozhou

TAIWAN
REGION

Guiping

Nanning

Xi

Guangzhou

Quanzhou

Tainan

Hongshu

Xiamen

Taizhong

LIANG-GUANG

Zuo

Macao
(Port)

Hong Kong
(UK)

Maoming

Hanoi

boundary of functional region
suggested by G.W. Skinner

boundary of salt monopoly sales
zone under Manchu (Qing) dynasty

○ Liang-Huai saltern

○ Sichuan brine well

■ city of over 500 000 inhabitants c.1950

□ other important city

population density greater than 200 people per km²

500 m

0

scale 1:9 000 000

LAOS

Qiongshan

SOUTH CHINA SEA

VIETNAM

0   400km

0   300mi

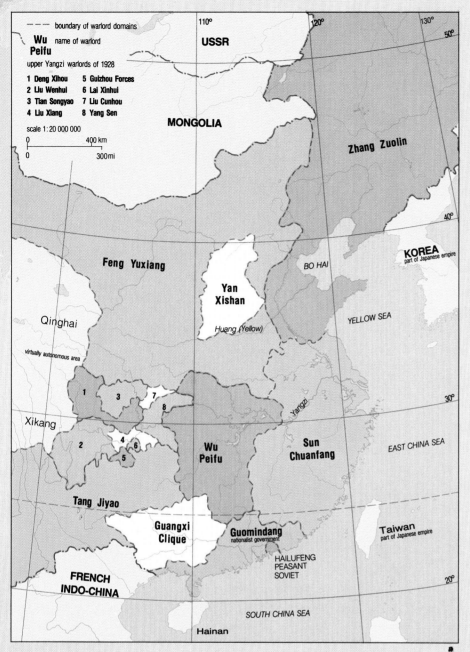

--- boundary of warlord domains

Wu Peifu name of warlord

upper Yangzi warlords of 1928

1 Deng Xihou 5 Guizhou Forces
2 Liu Wenhui 6 Lai Xinhui
3 Tian Songyao 7 Liu Cunhou
4 Liu Xiang 8 Yang Sen

scale 1:20 000 000

Far left: The regional structure of 19th- and 20th-century China
Topography and density of population together provide general indications of the way in which late traditional and early modern China may plausibly be subdivided into functional regions. The details of any scheme depend, however, on which aspects are stressed and there is no unique solution. The map shows one operational set of regions (the Qing dynasty marketing zones for state monopoly salt) and one theoretical set (devised by G. W. Skinner). There is a large measure of agreement between the schemes if the subdivision of Skinner's North China region into the three salt zones of Shandong, Changlu and Huaibei is disregarded. The only conflict of importance is over Skinner's Southwest region, which is bisected by a salt zone boundary, and is in any case suspect on other grounds as being something of a "residual" area. The salt system corridor from the Liang-Huai salterns on the east coast to the Huainan salt zone in the interior was clearly an administrative artifact for ease of supervision, and should not be taken as implying a regional frontier. The multiplicity of linkages possessed by certain intermediate areas is especially evident along the southeast coast, where the salt zones and the Skinner regions follow different lines of demarcation. That these regions were partially self-contained arenas of social and economic development is evident, but their autonomy should not be exaggerated.

Below: China early in the period known as the "Five Dynasties and Ten Kingdoms" (c. 920 AD)
During the first 60 years of the 10th century AD the political map of China briefly took on almost the appearance of early modern Europe. There were initially ten kingdoms, later eight, that might easily have grown into nation-states, constantly in conflict with each other but sharing the same underlying cultural values. Each of these realms had its own currency, and the rulers – in mercantilist fashion – often tried to manipulate interstate trade so as to accumulate reserves of copper, the major monetary metal. During these 60 years five dynasties followed one another in rapid succession in the central plain, including one Shatuo Turk ruling house (the Later Tang). The borders of the southern states remained fairly stable, although Min was eventually absorbed by Wuyue amd the Southern Tang (formerly Wu).

Above: Warlords 1926
The checkerboard of warlord satrapies was constantly changing, except for the domains of one or two long-term experts at survival such as Yan Xishan, who ruled Shanxi from 1912 to 1949 with only one brief interruption. The present map, which shows the division of territories around 1926, is intended mainly as an antidote to any excessive faith in functional regions as the dominant arenas in which Chinese history was enacted below the national level. Under the warlords a region might be fragmented, as in the case of Sichuan. Alternatively parts of it might be amalgamated into domains composed of one or more other regions, as happened at this time to the piece of the North China region controlled by the Manchurian warlord Zhang Zuolin.

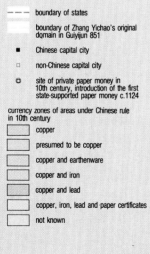

boundary of states

boundary of Zhang Yichao's original domain in Guiyijun 851

■ Chinese capital city

□ non-Chinese capital city

⊡ site of private paper money in 10th century, introduction of the first state-supported paper money c.1124

currency zones of areas under Chinese rule in 10th century

copper
presumed to be copper
copper and earthenware
copper and iron
copper and lead
copper, iron, lead and paper certificates
not known

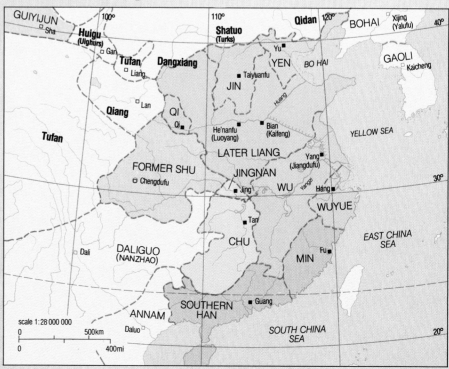

scale 1:28 000 000

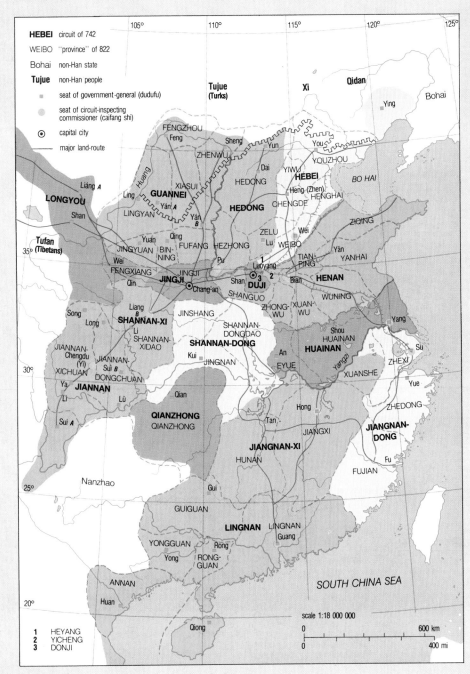

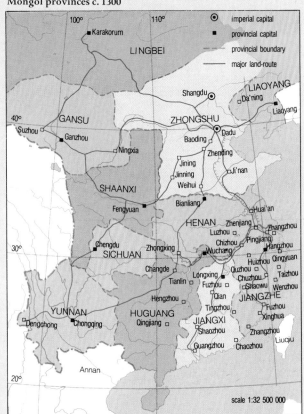

Mongol provinces c. 1300

Zhongshu	[province of] the Central Chancellery [i.e. the capital at Dadu or Khanbalik]
Liaoyang	North Bank of the River Liao [which was also the name of the provincial capital]
Gan-Su	Ganzhou and Suzhou [prefectures]
Shaanxi	West of Shaan [the ancient imperial domain of the Zhou dynasty]
Henan	South of the Yellow River
Sichuan	The Four Rivers [namely, the Min, Luo, Lu and Ba]
Yunnan	South of the Clouds
Hu-Guang	Lake Region and Cantonese Region
Jiangxi	Western [South-of-the-] Yangzi
Jiang-Zhe	The [Two] Zhe part of [South-of-the] Yangzi

Above: The circuits of Tang China in 742 and the "provinces" of 822
The circuits (dao) of early Tang China had no structural administrative significance. They were the domains of inspecting commissioners who merely supervised the administration of the prefectures. After the rebellion of An Lushan in 755 the empire split up into approximately 40 domains ruled by military governors, many of whom were effectively independent. The dramatic fragmentation of the empire that resulted is clear from the map. The court pursued a campaign for the reimposition of imperial control, and this was comparatively successful for a brief period around 820. After the Huang Chao rebellion (874–84), however, the collapse of central authority in the "provinces" was all but total.

Left: Tang circuits c. 742 AD

Jingji	[Chang'an] Metropolitan District
Duji	[Luoyang] Metropolitan District
Guannei	Within the Passes
Hedong	East of the Yellow River
Hebei	North of the Yellow River
Henan	South of the Yellow River
Longyou	West of Mount Long
Jiannan	South of the Gallery Road through Jianmen Pass
Qianzhong	[Name of a kingdom in the Warring States period]
Shannan	South of the [Qinling] Mountains
Huainan	South of the Huai River
Jiangnan	South of the Yangzi River
Lingnan	South of the [Southern] Ranges

Shannan and Jiangnan were both subdivided into western and eastern sections.

Right: Provincial boundaries under the Ming dynasty c. 1550, with major changes made under the Qing
The Ming pattern of provincial subdivision was taken over with relatively few alterations by the Qing. The Southern Metropolitan region (Nanzhili) was split to form Anhui and Jiangsu; Huguang was partitioned into Hubei and Hunan; Shaanxi lost its western half to the province of Gansu. Apart from these changes, there were a number of net additions to Inner China: the island of Taiwan, which for most of the Qing was a prefecture of adjacent Fujian, and tracts of extra territory in the north, northwest and west. The map also shows the distribution of Ming military administrations, which points to the dynasty's overriding concern with the northern frontier. The seats of the Qing governors-general, who had overall supervision of more than one province in most cases, are also indicated.

Left: Mongol provinces c. 1300
It was under the Mongols that the first true provinces (*sheng*) appeared, in the sense of scaled-down regional replicas of the central administration. The new provincial units were large by present standards and in most cases of a shape quite unlike any modern province.

Below left: Northern Song routes c. 1100
The "routes" (*lu*) of the Northern Song were still supervisory units without major administrative substance. The pattern of subdivision was, in several respects, strikingly different from that of the present-day provinces of Inner China. Note, in particular, the area covered by Liang-Zhe, which corresponded much more closely to an organic regional unit than the later artificial division into the southern part of Jiangsu and Zhejiang.

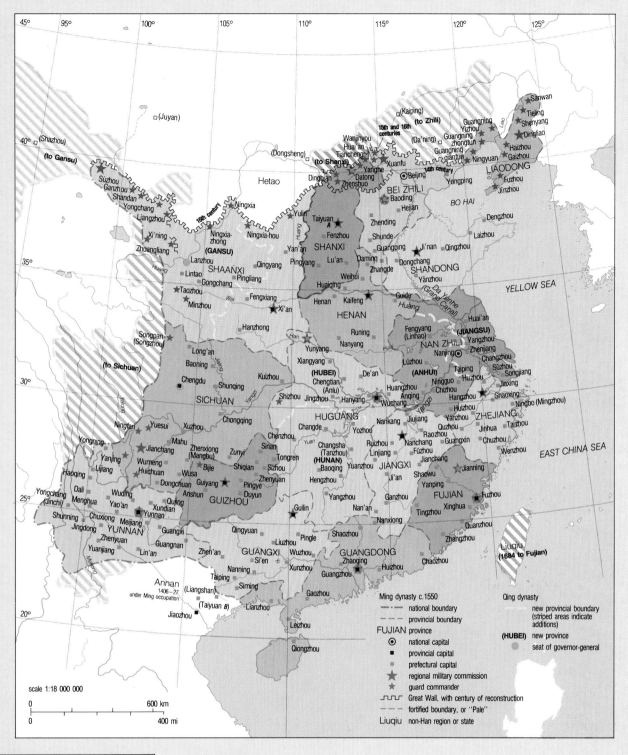

Map legend:

Ming dynasty c.1550
- ——— national boundary
- – – – provincial boundary
- FUJIAN province
- ⊙ national capital
- ■ provincial capital
- □ prefectural capital
- ★ regional military commission
- ✦ guard commander
- ⌐⌐⌐ Great Wall, with century of reconstruction
- – – – fortified boundary, or "Pale"
- Liuqiu non-Han region or state

Qing dynasty
- new provincial boundary (striped areas indicate additions)
- (HUBEI) new province
- ● seat of governor-general

scale 1:18 000 000

0 — 600 km
0 — 400 mi

Jingdong-xi	Western East-of-the-Capital
Jingdong-dong	Eastern East-of-the-Capital
Jingxi-bei	Northern West-of-the-Capital
Jingxi-nan	Southern West-of-the-Capital
Hebei-dong	Eastern North-of-the-Yellow-River
Hebei-xi	Western North-of-the-Yellow-River
Huainan-dong	Eastern South-of-the-Huai River
Yongxing-jun	Yongxing Military Route
Qin-Feng	Qinzhou and Fengxiang [prefectures]
Lizhou	Lizhou [prefecture]
Chengdu	Chengdu [prefecture]
Zizhou	Zizhou [prefecture]
Guizhou	Guizhou [prefecture]
Jinghu-bei	North of the Lake of Jing [an ancient state]
Jinghu-nan	South of the Lake of Jing
Liang-Zhe	The Two Zhe [Zigzag] River regions. [These were West and East, north and south respectively of the Qiantang River.]
Jiangnan-dong	Eastern South-of-the-Yangzi
Jiangnan-xi	Western South-of-the-Yangzi
Fu-Jian	Fuzhou and Jianzhou [prefectures]
Guangnan-dong	Eastern Cantonese Southern Region [Canton was Guangzhou]
Guangnan-xi	Western Cantonese Southern Region

Left: Northern Song routes c. 1100

Ming provinces c. 1600

Jingshi or Bei Zhili	The Capital or Northern Area of Direct Rule
Nanjing or Nan Zhili	The Southern Capital or Southern Area of Direct Rule
Shandong	Mountainous East
Shanxi	Mountainous West
Shaanxi	West of Shaan
Henan	South of the Yellow River
Sichuan	The Four Rivers
Yunnan	South of the Clouds
Guizhou	[probably named after the Mongol-Yuan prefecture of this name]
Hu-Guang	The Lake and Cantonese Region [but, in fact, the latter had now been separated, and the name was therefore a misnomer]
Jiangxi	Western [South-of-the-] Yangzi
Zhe-Jiang	The [Two] Zhe Part of [South-of-the-] Yangzi
Guangxi	Western Cantonese Area
Guangdong	Eastern Cantonese Area
Fu-Jian	Fuzhou and Jianzhou prefectures

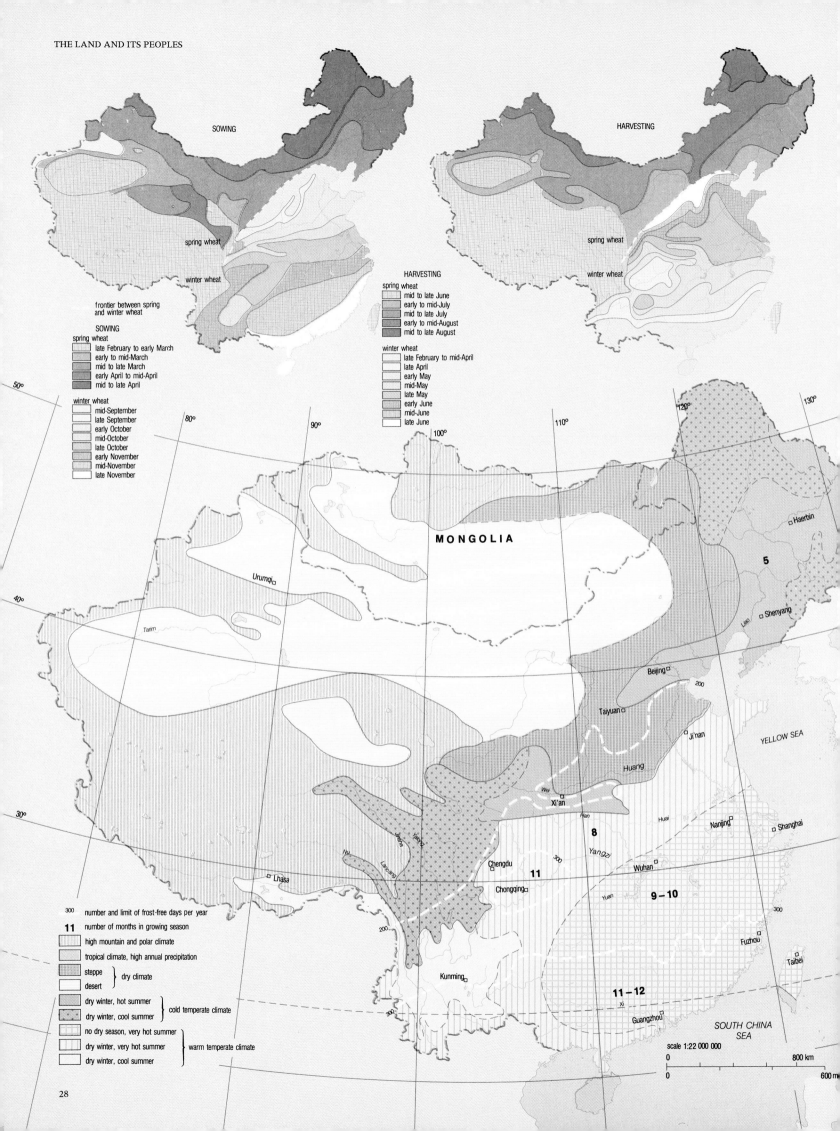

SOWING

HARVESTING

spring wheat

winter wheat

HARVESTING

spring wheat

winter wheat

frontier between spring
and winter wheat

SOWING

spring wheat

	late February to early March
	early to mid-March
	mid to late March
	early April to mid-April
	mid to late April

winter wheat

	mid-September
	late September
	early October
	mid-October
	late October
	early November
	mid-November
	late November

HARVESTING

spring wheat

	mid to late June
	early to mid-July
	mid to late July
	early to mid-August
	mid to late August

winter wheat

	late February to mid-April
	late April
	early May
	mid-May
	late May
	early June
	mid-June
	late June

50°

40°

30°

80°

90°

100°

110°

120°

130°

MONGOLIA

Urumqi

Tarim

Haerbin

5

Liao

Shenyang

Beijing

200

Taiyuan

Ji'nan

YELLOW SEA

Huang

Wei

Xi'an

Han

Huai

Nanjing

Shanghai

8

Yangzi

Jinsha

Yalong

Lancang

Chengdu

11

300

Wuhan

Nu

Lhasa

Chongqing

Yuan

9–10

Han

300

300

number and limit of frost-free days per year

11

number of months in growing season

	high mountain and polar climate
	tropical climate, high annual precipitation
	steppe
	desert

} dry climate

| | dry winter, hot summer |
| | dry winter, cool summer |

} cold temperate climate

	no dry season, very hot summer
	dry winter, very hot summer
	dry winter, cool summer

} warm temperate climate

Kunming

Fuzhou

Taibei

11–12

Xi

Guangzhou

SOUTH CHINA
SEA

scale 1:22 000 000

0   800 km

0   600 m

200

300

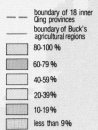

boundary of 18 inner
Qing provinces
boundary of Buck's
agricultural regions

80-100 %
60-79 %
40-59 %
20-39%
10-19 %
less than 9%

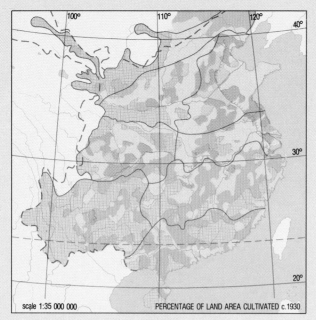

scale 1:35 000 000

PERCENTAGE OF LAND AREA CULTIVATED c.1930

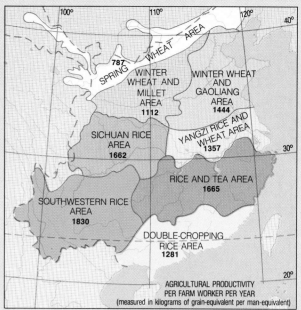

WHEAT AREA
787
SPRING
WINTER
WHEAT AND
MILLET
AREA
1112

WINTER WHEAT
AND
GAOLIANG
AREA
1444

SICHUAN RICE
AREA
1662

YANGZI RICE AND
WHEAT AREA
1357

RICE AND TEA AREA
1665

SOUTHWESTERN RICE
AREA
1830

DOUBLE-CROPPING
RICE AREA
1281

AGRICULTURAL PRODUCTIVITY
PER FARM WORKER PER YEAR
(measured in kilograms of grain-equivalent per man-equivalent)

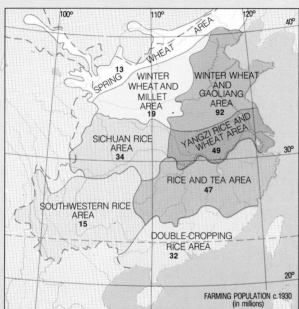

WHEAT AREA
13
SPRING
WINTER
WHEAT AND
MILLET
AREA
19

WINTER WHEAT
AND
GAOLIANG
AREA
92

SICHUAN RICE
AREA
34

YANGZI RICE AND
WHEAT AREA
49

RICE AND TEA AREA
47

SOUTHWESTERN RICE
AREA
15

DOUBLE-CROPPING
RICE AREA
32

FARMING POPULATION c.1930
(in millions)

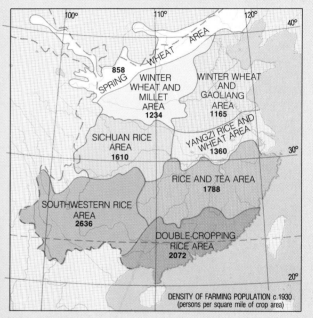

WHEAT AREA
858
SPRING
WINTER
WHEAT AND
MILLET
AREA
1234

WINTER WHEAT
AND
GAOLIANG
AREA
1165

SICHUAN RICE
AREA
1610

YANGZI RICE AND
WHEAT AREA
1360

RICE AND TEA AREA
1788

SOUTHWESTERN
RICE AREA
2636

DOUBLE-CROPPING
RICE AREA
2072

DENSITY OF FARMING POPULATION c.1930
(persons per square mile of crop area)

Left: Climatic zones
China's climatic zones may be
thought of as running along a
gradient from the southeast to
the northwest. Tropical climates
with rainfall all the year swiftly
give way to two types of
moderate climate: the first with
long hot summers and mild
winters, the second with short
summers and severe winters. In
general there is a season of rain
or at least drizzle in the summer
in these zones, contrasting with a
rain-free winter. The next
climatic zone is that of the dry to
arid climates, including steppe
land and deserts. Finally, along
the western and northwestern
rims, there are high mountains
and polar climates. The growing
season for crops varies from as
little as three months in the
northernmost parts of Manchuria
to year-round cultivation in the
far south.

**Above: Agricultural regions
in the 1930s according to the
survey conducted by J. L.
Buck**
The exact figures in these maps
should be treated with some
caution. Thus the total farming
population of internal China in
the 1930s was clearly well above
the 301 millions indicated in the
third map. But the composite
picture they give of regional
variations in the last peacetime
period of Chinese agriculture
under the family-farm system is
accurate enough. Used with
imagination they can summon to
the mind's eye the great
differences in wealth and in
settlement patterns among the
peasants in different parts of the
Republic.

**Below: Peach blossom
opening times**
This charming map, based on the
work of Zhu Kezhen, shows the
advance of spring from south to

north in terms of the dates when
peach blossoms first open. The
south in particular displays the
characteristic layered pattern of
regional temperatures in winter.

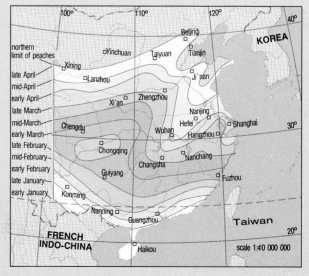

KOREA
northern
limit of peaches
late April
mid-April
early April
late March
mid-March
early March
late February
mid-February
early February
late January
early January

Beijing
Yinchuan
Taiyuan
Tianjin
Xining
Ji'nan
Lanzhou
Zhengzhou
Xi'an
Nanjing
Shanghai
Chengdu
Hefei
Wuhan
Hangzhou
Chongqing
Nanchang
Changsha
Fuzhou
Guiyang
Kunming
Taiwan
Nanning
Guangzhou

FRENCH
INDO-CHINA
Haikou
scale 1:40 000 000

29

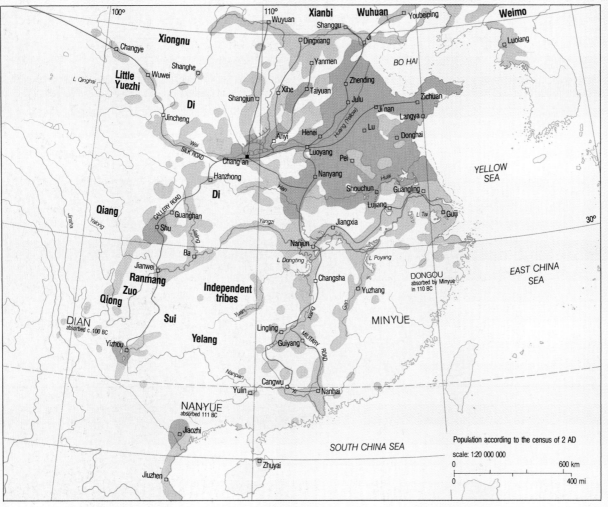

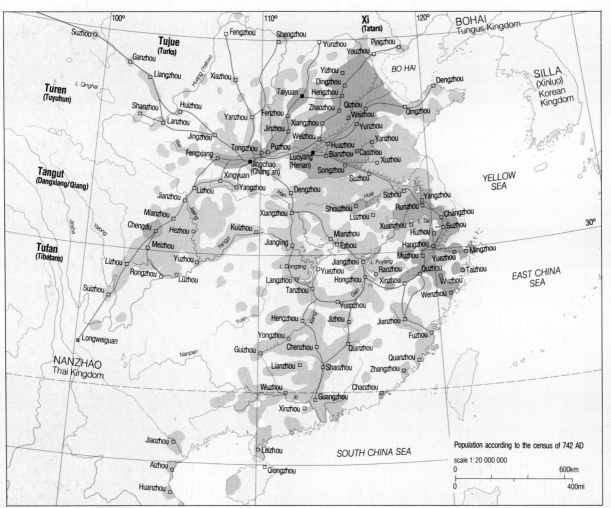

The distribution of population under the Former Han (above left), Tang (below left) and Northern Song (right) dynasties

Outside the great concentration in the north China plain, the ethnic Han Chinese population under the early empire was distributed along the river valleys. The higher ground was left mostly to non-Han peoples and non-Han states, many of which acknowledged Chinese suzerainty in some fashion, and some of which were even ruled by Chinese refugees who had "gone native." The maps show officially registered citizens, and while the overwhelming majority were ethnic Chinese this should not be assumed to have been so in every case, especially for the areas that are today parts of Vietnam and North Korea.

Under the Tang dynasty the south has begun to fill up, and the lower Yangzi is beginning to rival the north in economic importance.

The Northern Song dynasty map shows the consequences of the continuation of this process, and the enormous increase in demographic density and urbanization is immediately apparent.

All these maps emphasize settlement patterns, and national frontiers have been purposely omitted. It is evident how dramatically the "real" China at these three epochs differed from that depicted in the familiar historical maps based on political boundaries.

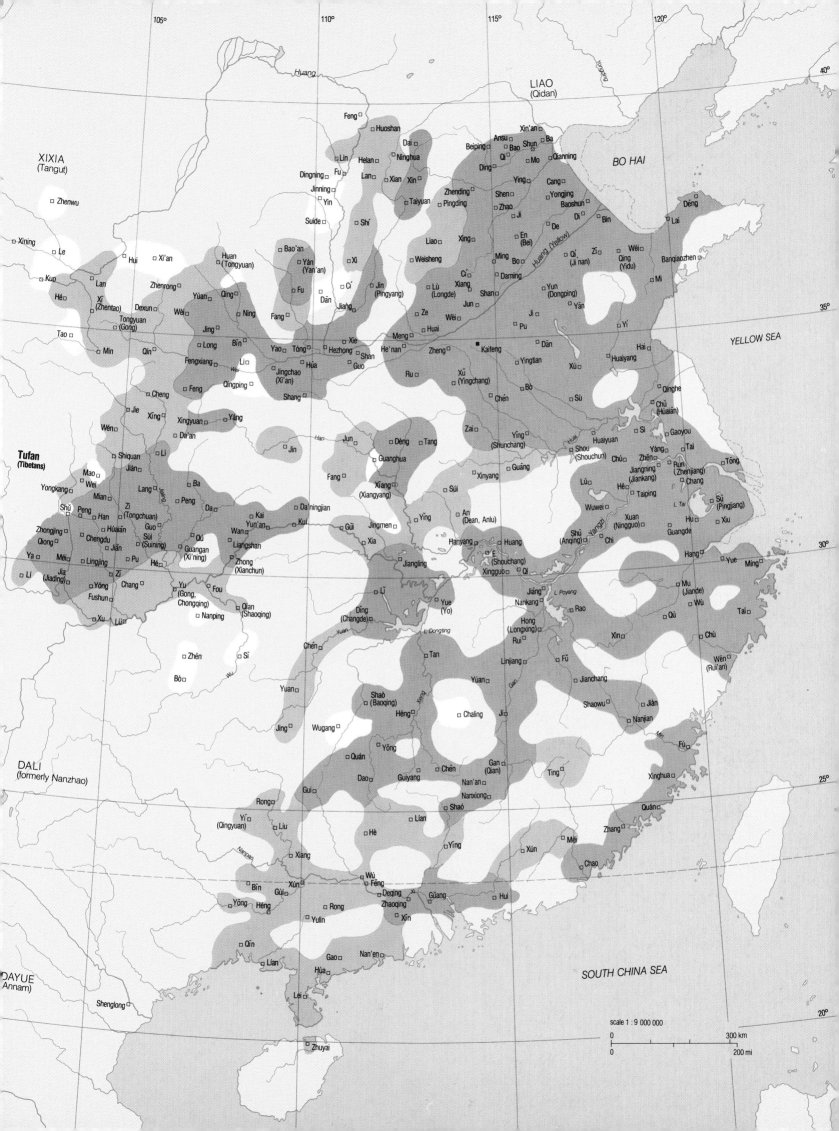

40°

XIXIA
(Tangut)

LIAO
(Qidan)

BO HAI

Huang

Zhenwu

Xining

Le

Kuo

Hé

Lan

Hui

Xi'an

Huan
(Tongyuan)

Zhenrong

Dexun

Tongyuan
(Gong)

Tao

Min

Qin

Wén

Xíng

Xingyuan

Da'an

Jin

Fengxiang

Li

Feng

Cheng

Jie

Long

Jing

Bin

Yao

Tóng

Hezhong

Shan

Guo

He'nan

Zheng

Kaifeng

Yingtian

Shí

Yin

Suide

Feng

Huoshan

Dai

Ninghua

Lin

Helan

Lan

Xian

Xin

Taiyuan

Pingding

Zhending

Shen

Zhao

Ji

Xing

Liao

Ming

Weisheng

Bo

Daming

Ci

Xiang

Lù
(Longde)

Shan

Jun

Wèi

Ze

Huai

Meng

YELLOW SEA

Dingning

Fu

Jinning

Yán
(Yan'an)

Fu

Cí

Dān

Jiàng

Xie

Xi

Jin
(Pingyang)

Yúan

Qing

Ning

Bao'an

Wèi

Fang

Hùa

Jingchao
(Xi'an)

Shang

Qingping

Yáng

Ru

Xin'an

Beiping

Ansu

Bao

Qi

Ding

Shun

Ba

Mo

Qianning

Ying

Cang

Yongjing

Baoshun

De

Di

Bin

Qì
(Ji'nan)

Zi

Wèi

Qing
(Yidu)

Déng

Lai

Banqiaozhen

Mi

Huang (Yellow)

Yun
(Dongping)

Yǎn

Ji

Pu

Yí

Hai

Huaiyang

Dàn

Xú

Bò

Sù

Qinghe

Chén

Zai

Ying
(Shunchang)

Hua

Huaiyuan

Si

Gaoyou

Chù
(Huaian)

Shou
(Shouchun)

Chú

Zhèn

Yáng

Tai

Tong

Jiangning
(Jiankang)

Run
(Zhenjiang)

Chang

Tufan
(Tibetans)

Shiquan

Jiàn

Li

Da'an

Jin

Jun

Dèng

Tang

Guanghua

Fang

Xiang
(Xiangyang)

Súi

Guāng

Xinyang

An
(Dean, Anlu)

Lú

Hé

Taiping

Wuwei

Xuan
(Ningguo)

Hu

Guangde

Sù
(Pingjiang)

Xiu

Mao

Wéi

Mian

Lang

Ba

Peng

Da

Kai

Yun'an

Kui

Gǔi

Xia

Jingmen

Yíng

Hanyang

Huang

E
(Shouchang)

Xingguo

Qi

Chi

Shù
(Anqing)

Yongkang

Shǔ

Peng

Han

Zi
(Tongchuan)

Guo

Sùi
(Suining)

Qú

Wan

Liangshan

Zhong
(Xianchun)

Jiangling

Lì

Ding
(Changde)

Yue
(Yo)

Jiàng

Nankang

L Poyang

Rao

Qù

Hang

Yue

Ming

Zhongjing

Qiong

Chengdu

Jiàn

Pu

Hé

Guangan
(Xi'ning)

Hong
(Longxing)

Rui

Xin

Mu
(Jiande)

Wú

Tai

Ya

Měi

Lingjing

Zǐ

Chang

Yu
(Gong,
Chongqing)

Fou

Qian
(Shaoqing)

Nanping

Linjiang

Fú

Jianchang

Chú

Wén
(Rui'an)

Li

Jia
(Jiading)

Fushun

Xu

Lü

Zhēn

Sī

Bò

Yuan

Chén

Tan

Yúan

Shaowu

Jiàn

Nanjian

Fù

DALI
(formerly Nanzhao)

Jing

Wugang

Shaò
(Baoqing)

Héng

Chaling

Ji

Jianchang

Yǒng

Quán

Dao

Guiyang

Chén

Gan
(Qian)

Ting

Xinghua

Rong

Gǔi

Lián

Shaó

Nan'an

Nanxiong

Quán

Zhang

Yí
(Qingyuan)

Liu

Hè

Yíng

Xún

Měi

Chao

Xiang

Nanjiang

Bìn

Gǔi

Xún

Wú

Fēng

Deqing
Zhaoqing

Xi

Gǔang

Hui

Yǒng

Héng

Rong

Yulin

Xīn

Qìn

Lán

Gao

Hùa

Nan'en

Lei

SOUTH CHINA SEA

Shenglong

Zhuyai

DAYUE
(Annam)

scale 1 : 9 000 000

0   300 km

0   200 mi

35°

30°

25°

20°

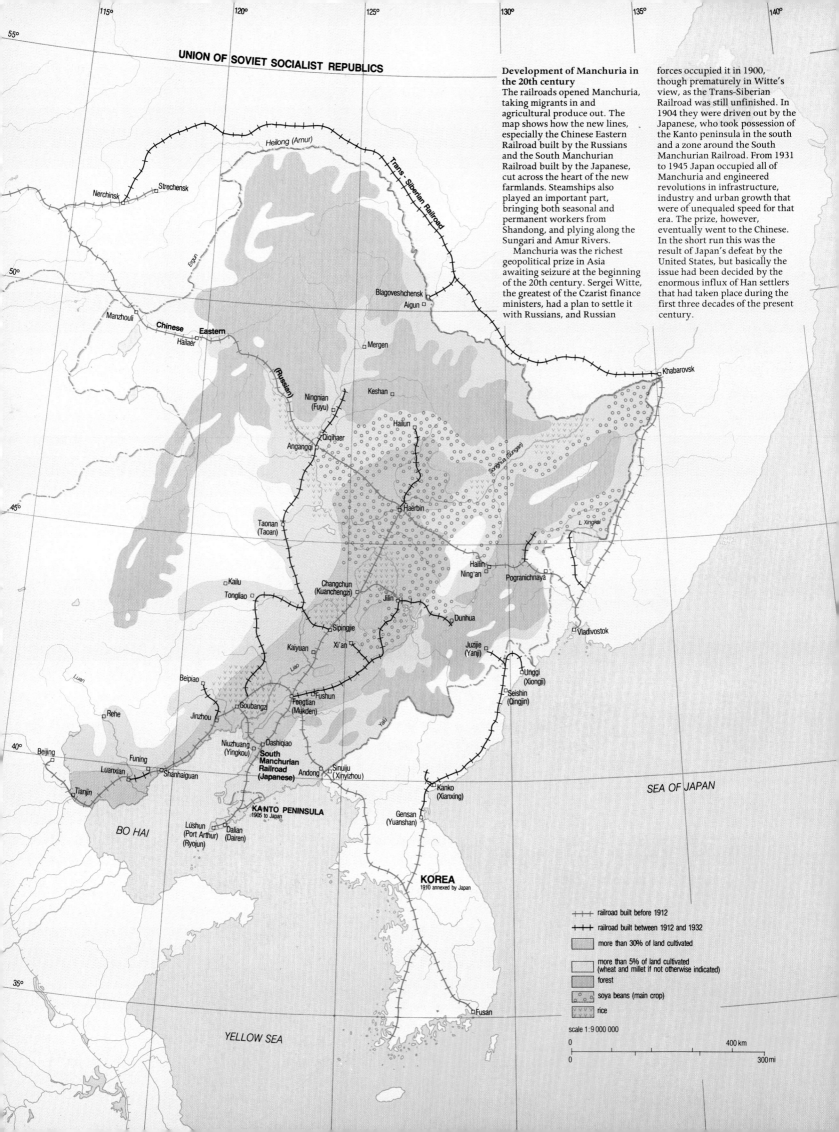

UNION OF SOVIET SOCIALIST REPUBLICS

Development of Manchuria in the 20th century

The railroads opened Manchuria, taking migrants in and agricultural produce out. The map shows how the new lines, especially the Chinese Eastern Railroad built by the Russians and the South Manchurian Railroad built by the Japanese, cut across the heart of the new farmlands. Steamships also played an important part, bringing both seasonal and permanent workers from Shandong, and plying along the Sungari and Amur Rivers.

Manchuria was the richest geopolitical prize in Asia awaiting seizure at the beginning of the 20th century. Sergei Witte, the greatest of the Czarist finance ministers, had a plan to settle it with Russians, and Russian

forces occupied it in 1900, though prematurely in Witte's view, as the Trans-Siberian Railroad was still unfinished. In 1904 they were driven out by the Japanese, who took possession of the Kanto peninsula in the south and a zone around the South Manchurian Railroad. From 1931 to 1945 Japan occupied all of Manchuria and engineered revolutions in infrastructure, industry and urban growth that were of unequaled speed for that era. The prize, however, eventually went to the Chinese. In the short run this was the result of Japan's defeat by the United States, but basically the issue had been decided by the enormous influx of Han settlers that had taken place during the first three decades of the present century.

Heilong (Amur)

Trans - Siberian Railroad

Nerchinsk   Strechensk

Manzhouli   Chinese   Eastern

Hailaér

(Russian)

Blagoveshchensk
Aigun

Mergen

Khabarovsk

Ningnian (Fuyu)   Keshan

Hailun

Qiqihaer

Anganqqi

Sorghua (Sungari)

L. Xingkai

Haёrbin

Taonan (Taoan)

Hailin
Ning'an   Pogranichnaya

Kailu

Changchun (Kuanchengzi)

Tongliao

Jilin

Dunhua

Vladivostok

Sipingjie

Xi'an

Juzijie (Yanji)

Kaiyuan

Unggi (Xiongji)

Beipiao

Liao

Seishin (Qingjin)

Fengtian (Mukden)   Fushun

Goubangzi

Rehe

Jinzhou

Niuzhuang (Yingkou)   Dashiqiao

South Manchurian Railroad (Japanese)

Yalu

Andong   Sinuiju (Xinyizhou)

Kanko (Xianxing)

SEA OF JAPAN

Beijing

Funing

Luanxian   Shanhaiguan

Tianjin

KANTO PENINSULA
1905 to Japan

Gensan (Yuanshan)

Lüshun (Port Arthur) (Ryojun)   Dalian (Dairen)

BO HAI

KOREA
1910 annexed by Japan

YELLOW SEA

Fusan

railroad built before 1912

railroad built between 1912 and 1932

more than 30% of land cultivated

more than 5% of land cultivated (wheat and millet if not otherwise indicated)

forest

soya beans (main crop)

rice

scale 1:9 000 000

0   400 km

0   300 mi

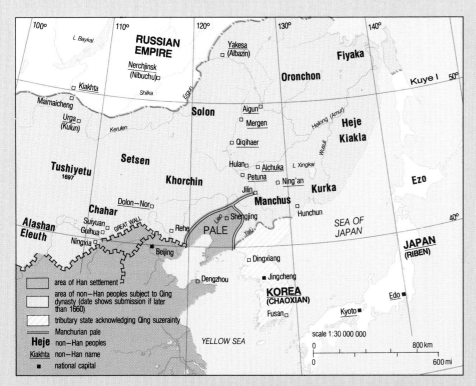

Left: Position of the Chinese Pale in Manchuria c. 1660
There was a wall beyond the Wall. Under the Ming the Chinese settlers in the valley of the Liao River were protected by a continuous wooden palisade, with gate towers, that ran in a loop from a little way north of Shanhaiguan to the banks of the lower Yalü River on the Korean frontier.

Below: The Manchurian Pale before 1859
The Manchu dynasty retained the Pale, on a slightly different alignment, but with the altered purpose of keeping the Chinese in. This policy of preserving a racially pure Manchu homeland was never wholly successful, and the ban on Chinese colonization was lifted in 1859 to permit new settlements that could serve as a barrier to Russian encroachment from the north.

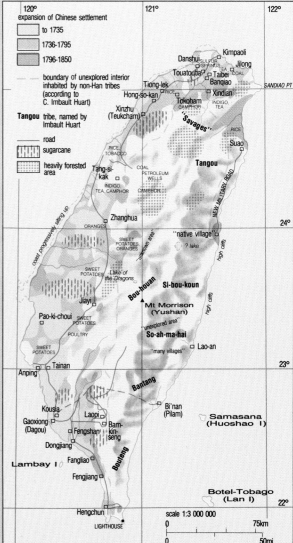

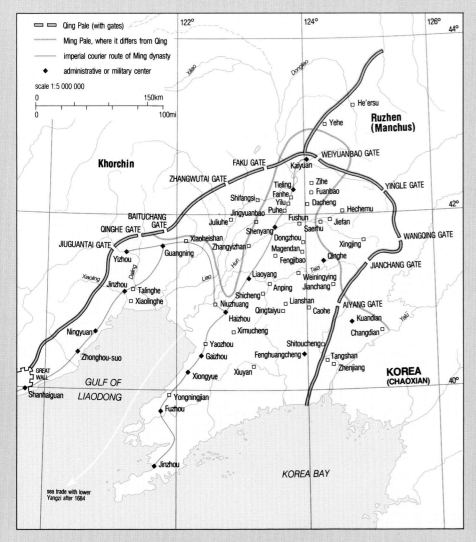

Taiwan in the 19th century
The Chinese colonization of Taiwan has been a slow and difficult process. The map shows how from the middle of the 17th century until the middle of the 19th Chinese settlers from the province of Fujian across the straits displaced the aboriginal inhabitants from the coastal plains in the west, and confined them to the mountainous eastern half of the island. Even by the end of the 19th century large parts of the hinterland remained unexplored, as the comments quoted here from a map made by the then French consul-general vividly indicate. In the first half of the present century, under Japanese rule, the Chinese began the colonization of the eastern seaboard, a savage coastline that has been the graveyard of ships over many centuries. The absence of good natural deep-water harbors, not only here but to the west as well, was a major reason in times past for the slowness of the island's economic development.

Helsinki

Arkhangelsk

SIBERIA

10°

20°

30°

40°

50°

60°

70°

80°

90°

100°

St Petersburg

Warsaw

Vienna
Budapest
1721

Moscow

Smolensk

Nizhniy
Novgorod

Perm

Tyumen

Angara

Tomsk

50°

Belgrade
1878

1678

Kiev

Kharkov

Omsk

Irtysh

Ob

1913

1908

1830

Odessa

Rostov

Tsaritsyn

Volga

Ural

CZARIST RUSSIAN EMPIRE

Istanbul

BLACK SEA

Astrakhan

Semipalatinsk

40°

Athens

Ankara

GEORGIA

ARMENIA

Tbilisi

Yerevan

KIRGIZSTAN

CASPIAN
SEA

ARAL
SEA

TURKESTAN

KAZAKHSTAN

L. Balkhash

Alma Ata

Ürümqi

Hami

Crete

MEDITERRANEAN SEA

Cyprus

OTTOMAN

KURDISTAN

Tabriz

Khiva

Syr Darya

Tashkent

L. Issyk Kul

Aksu

XINJIANG
(EASTERN TURKESTAN)

30°

Jerusalem

Damascus

Amman

TURKMENISTAN

Bukhara

Amu Darya

Samarkand

Kāshgar

Tarim

L. Lop

Cairo

EMPIRE

Baghdad

Tigris

Euphrates

Tehran

**PERSIA
(Iran)**

Khotan

Nile

AFGHANISTAN

Kabul

TIBET
1912–50

Islamabad

20°

RED
SEA

Riyadh

Lahore

Sutlej

PAKISTAN
1947

Delhi

NEPAL

Kathmandu

Thimbu

Lhasa

BHUTAN

Brahmaputra

Mecca

Indus

BANGLADES
1971

Dacca

ARABIA

Karachi

INDIA
1947

Ganges

Calcutta

ARABIAN SEA

10°

Aden
1524 Portuguese, 1839 British,
1937 British crown colony

Bombay

Hyderabad

BAY OF BENGAL

**BRITISH INDIAN
AND
MALAY EMPIRE**

Socotra
1507–11 Portuguese,
1886 British,
1967 to Yemen

Goa
1510–1961 Portuguese,

Madras

Laccadive Is
1956 to India, previously British

Calicut

Pondicherry
1674–1954 French

Karikal
1738–1954 French

Andaman Is -
1789–1947 British

0°

INDIAN OCEAN

Colombo

Kandy

Ceylon
1948

Nicobar
1756 Danish
1869 British
1947 to Ind

10°

Maldive Is
1815–1965 British

scale 1:28 000 000

Seychelles
1794–1976 British

0   1000 km

0   800 mi

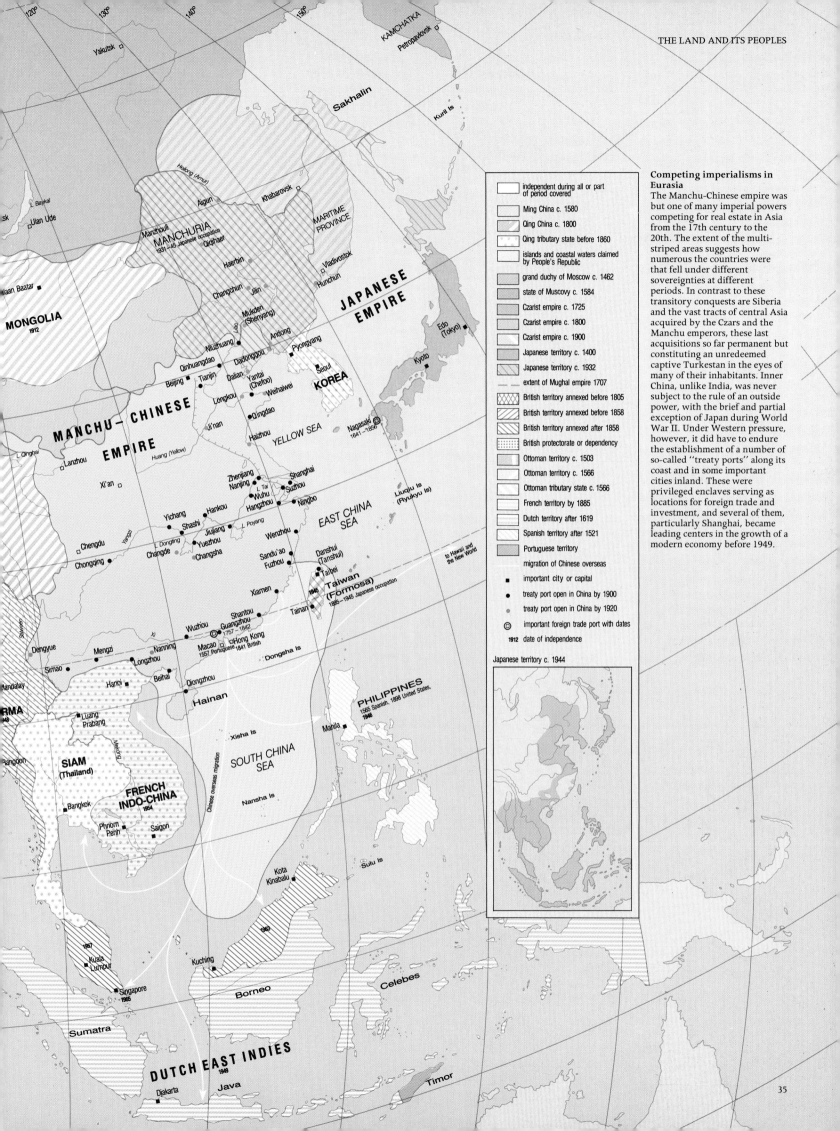

Legend

- independent during all or part of period covered
- Ming China c. 1580
- Qing China c. 1800
- Qing tributary state before 1860
- islands and coastal waters claimed by People's Republic
- grand duchy of Moscow c. 1462
- state of Muscovy c. 1584
- Czarist empire c. 1725
- Czarist empire c. 1800
- Czarist empire c. 1900
- Japanese territory c. 1400
- Japanese territory c. 1932
- extent of Mughal empire 1707
- British territory annexed before 1805
- British territory annexed before 1858
- British territory annexed after 1858
- British protectorate or dependency
- Ottoman territory c. 1503
- Ottoman territory c. 1566
- Ottoman tributary state c. 1566
- French territory by 1885
- Dutch territory after 1619
- Spanish territory after 1521
- Portuguese territory
- migration of Chinese overseas
- ■ important city or capital
- ● treaty port open in China by 1900
- ● treaty port open in China by 1920
- ◎ important foreign trade port with dates
- 1912 date of independence

Japanese territory c. 1944

Competing imperialisms in Eurasia

The Manchu-Chinese empire was but one of many imperial powers competing for real estate in Asia from the 17th century to the 20th. The extent of the multi-striped areas suggests how numerous the countries were that fell under different sovereignties at different periods. In contrast to these transitory conquests are Siberia and the vast tracts of central Asia acquired by the Czars and the Manchu emperors, these last acquisitions so far permanent but constituting an unredeemed captive Turkestan in the eyes of many of their inhabitants. Inner China, unlike India, was never subject to the rule of an outside power, with the brief and partial exception of Japan during World War II. Under Western pressure, however, it did have to endure the establishment of a number of so-called "treaty ports" along its coast and in some important cities inland. These were privileged enclaves serving as locations for foreign trade and investment, and several of them, particularly Shanghai, became leading centers in the growth of a modern economy before 1949.

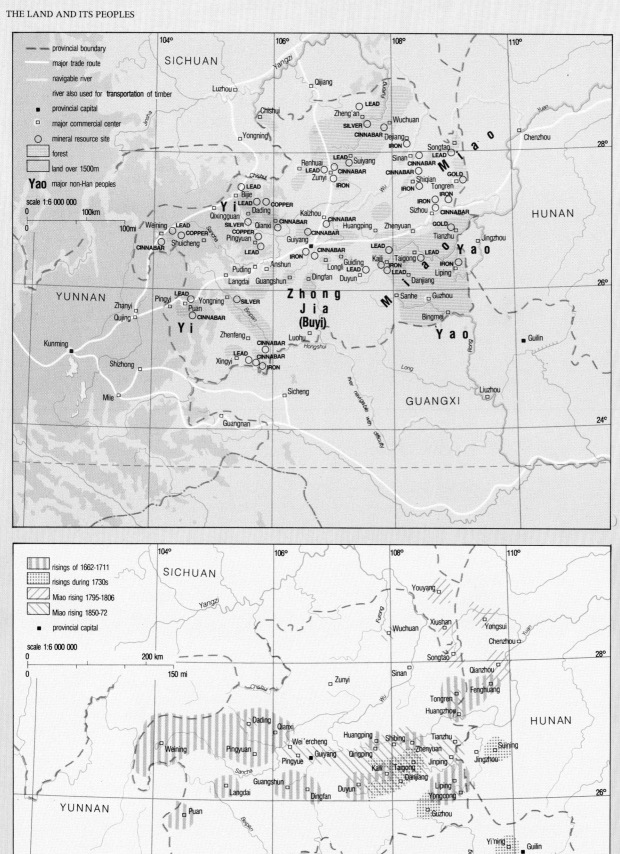

Map 1 (top) — Guizhou in the 18th century

Legend:
- – – – provincial boundary
- —— major trade route
- —— navigable river
- river also used for transportation of timber
- ■ provincial capital
- ▫ major commercial center
- ○ mineral resource site
- forest
- land over 1500m
- **Yao** major non-Han peoples

scale 1:6 000 000

0 100km
0 100mi

SICHUAN
Luzhou
Qijiang
Chishui
Zheng'an
Wuchuan
Chenzhou
LEAD
SILVER
CINNABAR
Dejiang
Songtao
Yongning
Renhuai
LEAD Suiyang
Sinan
LEAD
M i a o
LEAD
CINNABAR
Bijie
LEAD
CINNABAR
Zunyi
IRON
Shiqian
Tongren
GOLD
LEAD
Yi
Dading
COPPER
Kaizhou
CINNABAR
IRON
IRON
HUNAN
Qixingguan
SILVER
Qianxi
CINNABAR
Huangping
IRON
Sizhou
CINNABAR
Weining LEAD
COPPER
COPPER
Pingyuan
Guiyang
CINNABAR
Zhenyuan
GOLD
Jingzhou
CINNABAR
Shuicheng
LEAD
Tianzhu
Yao
Puding
IRON
CINNABAR
Anshun
Longli
Guiding
LEAD
Kaili
Taigong
LEAD
IRON
Langdai Guangshun
Dingfan
Duyun
IRON
Liping
Danjiang
M
Sanhe
Guzhou
Pingyi LEAD
Yongning
SILVER
Bingmei
Yao
Zhanyi
Puan
CINNABAR
Zhong
Jia
(Buyi)
Qujing
Yi
Luohu
Hongshui
Guilin
Kunming
Zhenfeng
CINNABAR
river navigable with difficulty
Shizhong
LEAD
CINNABAR
Xingyi
IRON
Liuzhou
Mile
Sicheng
GUANGXI
Guangnan

(rivers labelled: Yangzi, Jinsha, Furong, Yuan, Wu, Chishui, Sancha, Beipan, Long)

Map 2 (bottom) — Anti-Chinese resistance movements in Guizhou during the Qing dynasty

Legend:
- risings of 1662–1711
- risings during 1730s
- Miao rising 1795–1806
- Miao rising 1850–72
- ■ provincial capital

scale 1:6 000 000

0 200 km
0 150 mi

SICHUAN
Yangzi
Youyang
Wuchuan
Xiushan
Yongsui
Chenzhou
Zunyi
Sinan
Songtao
Qianzhou
Dading
Qianxi
Tongren
Fenghuang
Wei'ercheng
Huangzhou
HUNAN
Weining
Pingyuan
Huangping
Shibing
Tianzhu
Guiyang
Qingping
Zhenyuan
Suining
Pingyue
Kaili
Jinping
Jingzhou
Guangshun
Taigong
Liping
Langdai
Dingfan
Danjiang
Duyun
Yongcong
YUNNAN
Puan
Guzhou
Yi'ning
Guilin
Liuzhou
GUANGXI

(rivers labelled: Furong, Wu, Chishui, Sancha, Beipan, Hongshui, Rong, Long, Yuan)

Left: Guizhou in the 18th century
Guizhou was one of the classical territories of Han Chinese colonial penetration and settlement. It was rich in timber and material resources that proved irresistible lures in spite of the hostility of the Miao, Yi and other non-Han peoples indigenous to the area.

Left below: Anti-Chinese resistance movements in Guizhou during the Qing dynasty
Chinese repression of the Miao, and attempts to destroy or subvert their culture, provoked a series of resistance movements. The largest of these was probably that in the middle of the 19th century, which lasted for close to 20 years.

The growth of Han China across time

The present-day Han Chinese domination of the ethnic minorities in Outer and Inner China (see map p. 15) is the end-product of a colonialist and sometimes imperialist expansion that has continued through more than three millennia and is still going on. By "colonialism" is meant the settling of territory that is either empty or inhabited by other peoples; by "imperialism" the establishing of political control over peoples whose cultures are different from that of the rulers.

A glance at the map of the distribution of the registered population under the Han dynasty (p 30) shows that, outside the northern plain, the real China of 2000 years ago consisted of thin arms of settlement along river valleys. The higher ground in between was occupied by non-Han peoples, the more advanced of whom were organized into simple states. The picture given by the map is however slightly misleading in that it is certain that not all the areas shown as settled by the registered population were predominantly Han Chinese in nature. This is particularly so for what are today northern Korea and northern Vietnam.

In the period that followed the fall of the Han empire, and its successor the Western Jin, early in the 4th century AD, there was both an absolute and a relative decline in the Han Chinese population in the more northerly parts of China. The plain was overrun by Xiongnu (who are often identified with the Huns) and by the Xianbi (who were of Tungusic stock), and extensive interracial mixing must have resulted. At the same time the Han Chinese population pushed further into the southeast and south, driving out or absorbing people of Yue (Viet), Thai (Zhuang) and other stocks. Several of the non-Han states that emerged in the south and southwest now and later were also led by Chinese emigrés who had "gone native." The new pattern that emerged may be seen from the map showing the distribution of the population under the Tang dynasty in 742 AD (p. 30). The lower Yangzi has become a new center of dense settlement, and the sinification of the area that is today Fujian province has begun; but it is also evident how long drawn out was the process of the spreading of Chinese colonial settlement and cultural assimilation.

The map on page 30 shows that under the Northern Song dynasty the movement had gone further. Apart from the southwest and Manchuria, Inner China had acquired a settlement pattern of which the general features are close to those of today. The total population in the 11th century was also at least double the maximum attained in the Han and the Tang, the most recent estimate suggesting that it may have been as high as 140 million, in contrast to the 65 million reached by the two previous dynasties at their greatest. Urbanization was also more intense. The Tang capital at Chang'an may have had more than a million residents; under the Song there were several great cities that probably reached this total; and accounts of smaller cities bursting out of the confines of their walls are common.

The southward shift of the demographic center of gravity continued under the Mongol dynasty, but the data are too uncertain to make the details worth showing on a map. The Huai valley had been depopulated by the frontier warfare between the

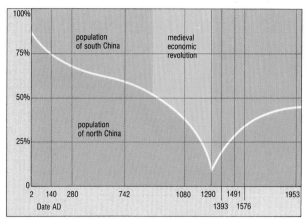

Jin (or Ruzhen) and the Southern Song; and the Mongol occupation of the north seems to have brought further decline in the population, though under-registration makes it hard to know how much. In the later 14th century the recolonization of the north from the south under the Ming began a long-term trend that has now brought north China back into approximate parity in terms of numbers with south China. The accompanying chart shows the shifting balance over the last two millennia.

The rise of southern China should not be allowed to obscure the fact that, as is obvious from the three population maps, the north China plain remained throughout by far the largest *single* region in terms of numbers. This meant that whoever controlled the plain was bound to have an advantage over political rivals who disposed only of the more limited resources of one of the southern or western regions. These other regions were too separated geographically, and hence to some extent also culturally, for it to be easy for them to be welded together politically into a unit capable of challenging the north. This is one reason why the Chinese empire stayed together over the long run, in spite of periods of fragmentation. The Roman empire conspicuously lacked a comparable consolidated dominant region. The resistance of the Chinese empire to attempts at conquest from outside, or its failure to offer effective resistance to such attempts, of course involves other factors besides the geopolitical. In particular, the outflow of military and organizational technology to China's semi-barbarian enemies and the variable capacity of the empire under varying circumstances to mobilize its own resources for administration and warfare can be shown to have been critical, as is explained in Part Two of this volume. But the demographic preponderance of the north China region was the crucial obstacle to permanent internal disintegration.

The three major colonizing thrusts of the Han Chinese since Ming times have been: (1) the expansion into the jungle lands of the southwest; (2) overseas migration from south and southeast China into Taiwan, the Nanyang or "Southern Seas" region and many other parts of both the Old and New Worlds; and (3) the settlement of Manchuria since the end of the 19th century. The first and third have been based on opening land to the Chinese style of intensive farming; the second has been a mixture, agricultural in Taiwan, mostly commercial elsewhere.

This colonial expansion was accompanied by much bloody warfare. The table lists the tribal

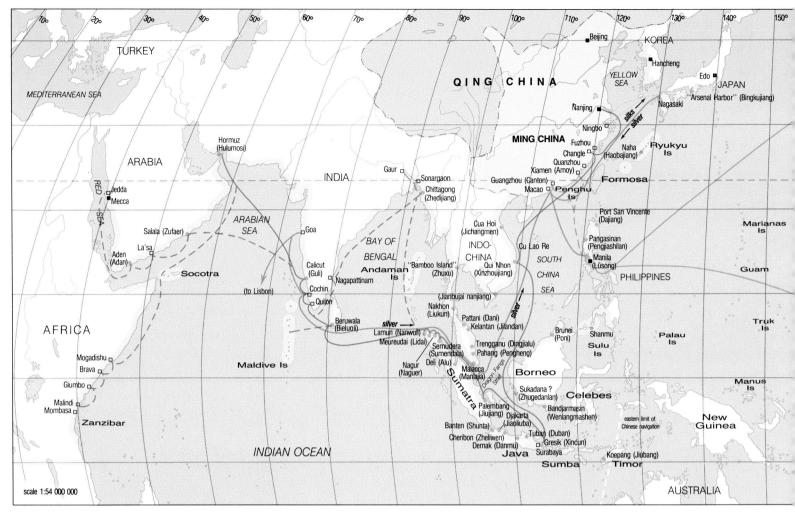

uprisings against the Han Chinese in the southwest from the 7th to the 17th century. The rising intensity of resistance to Han occupation is evident in the increase in the frequency of revolts from about one in every four years under the Tang to more than one a year under the Ming. Refusals to submit to the pressures of Han colonial settlement and Han political overlordship continued under the Manchu (Qing) dynasty, and were suppressed in some cases with wholesale massacres of the utmost ferocity.

One of the basic motives of the Han Chinese push into the southwest was the desire to exploit untapped natural resources. Thus Guizhou (see map p. 36) yielded wood that was floated out on the rivers, and had mines that produced lead, copper, iron, silver, cinnabar (from which mercury is made) and gold. The policies pursued by the Qing government to secure this rich and underdeveloped area included summary justice, limitations on the freedom of movement of the non-Chinese, the building of walled towns, implanting military colonies, confiscating tribal lands and giving them to Chinese, and a deliberate attempt to smash up tribal cultures. Thus the religious festivals of the Miao people were forbidden, the men were forced to abandon their traditional costumes and hair-styles, and Chinese education was promoted, especially for the children of collaborators. There were three large-scale Miao attempts at liberation, two in the course of the 18th century and one in the middle of the 19th, all of them unsuccessful. The Muslims of Yunnan also made efforts to free themselves, the most spectacular being the kingdom of Dali set up

by Du Wenxiu or "Sultan Suleiman" in Yunnan from 1855 to 1872. After many years of mutual killing by both sides, it ended with the slaughter of perhaps 30 000 Muslims by the troops of Cen Yuying. The colonization of the island of Taiwan in the 17th and 18th centuries followed a somewhat similar pattern (see map p. 33). The Chinese settlers, a turbulent and lawless frontier society, in which the cultural subgroup known as the Kejia (or Hakka) bore the main brunt of the constant daily harassment of the native population, gradually drove the Malayan-Polynesian aborigines off the fertile western plains and into the inhospitable mountains of the east.

The Chinese settlement of Manchuria beyond the "Pale" in the Liao River valley seems to have been peaceful in comparison (see maps pp. 32–33). The Pale was a wall of wooden stakes, the southern

Below: Tribal uprisings against Han Chinese rule from the 7th century to the 17th.

Province	AD 618–959	AD 960–1279	AD 1280–1367	AD 1368–1644
Yunnan	53	0	7	2
Guanxi	14	51	5	218
Hunan	10	112	6	16
Sichuan	0	46	0	3
Guangdong	5	23	17	52
Guizhou	0	0	0	91
Total	82	232	35	382

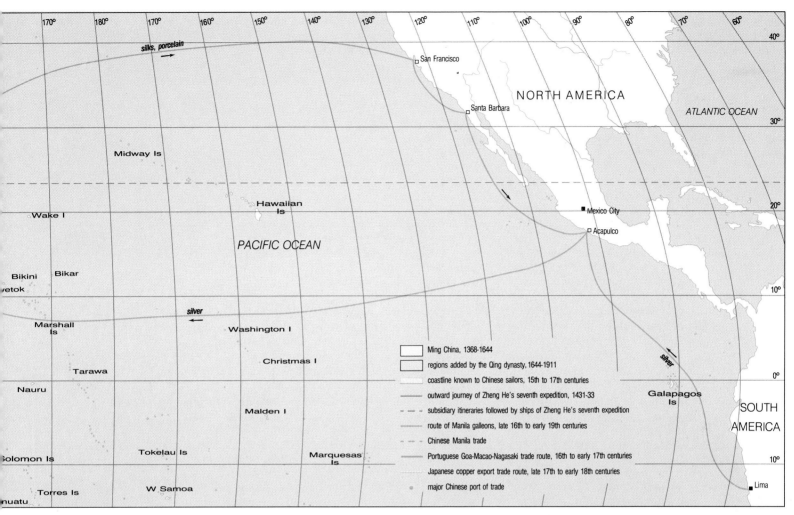

Map legend:

- Ming China, 1368-1644
- regions added by the Qing dynasty, 1644-1911
- coastline known to Chinese sailors, 15th to 17th centuries
- outward journey of Zheng He's seventh expedition, 1431-33
- subsidiary itineraries followed by ships of Zheng He's seventh expedition
- route of Manila galleons, late 16th to early 19th centuries
- Chinese Manila trade
- Portuguese Goa-Macao-Nagasaki trade route, 16th to early 17th centuries
- Japanese copper export trade route, late 17th to early 18th centuries
- major Chinese port of trade

Above: China's relations with the world overseas
China is so often thought of as having been an economically and psychologically landlocked country that the extent and importance of its relations with the world overseas are easily overlooked. Surviving Chinese maps and manuals for navigators show that between the 15th and 17th centuries Chinese sailors knew the Asian seas from the East African littoral to Timor, and from the straits of Hormuz to the port of Kobe. Chinese merchants were particularly active in southeast Asia (including, incidentally, the local slave trade). The famous westward voyages of the Ming admiral Zheng He in the early 15th century went for the most part along routes long familiar to his compatriots in the years before the imposition of the Maritime Interdict.

While the southeast Asian trade, and even that with Japan, was of limited importance for the Chinese mainland economy, the trans-Pacific voyages of the Spanish galleons from Acapulco supplied the vast quantities of New World silver (in return for Chinese silks and porcelain) that underpinned the economic revival of later Ming times. Without this silver, and smaller but still important amounts from the Portuguese at Macao and from Japan, the Chinese trading system, deeply distrustful of imposed paper currencies, would have suffered a severe liquidity crisis.

extremity of which linked onto the Great Wall where it comes down to the sea at Shanhaiguan. Under the middle and later Ming it served to protect the Han Chinese. Rebuilt by the Manchu (Qing) along a slightly different alignment, it served to keep the Chinese in. For most of the Qing dynasty, the Manchu authorities, well aware of the capacity of their Han subjects for settling sparsely inhabited lands, deliberately placed Manchuria out of bounds to Chinese migrants, their object being to preserve a base to which they could retreat if ever they lost control of the rest of the empire. The need to contain Russian expansion along the Amur River valley in the middle of the 19th century changed this policy. At first, however, there was only a trickle of migrants until the building of railroads began around the turn of the 19th and 20th centuries, initially by the Russians, and then by the Japanese and the Chinese themselves. The migrants traveling on these railroads, and on the steamships sailing from the Shandong peninsula, turned the trickle into a flood. For a few years in the mid-1920s almost a million new inhabitants a year may have made their way into Manchuria. Between 1905 and 1940 the population doubled, and the cultivated area more than doubled. The map shows clearly how the new lines ran through the heart of the new farming areas, from which they carried out a huge quantity of agricultural exports, especially soybeans. The Japanese, who occupied Manchuria in 1931, imposed severe limitations on further Chinese in-migration, but too late to alter the demographic transformation that had occurred.

The imperialist aspect of the Chinese state, in the sense of the political control of peoples of non-Han race, was comparatively limited in ancient and medieval times. When the empire was strong it usually governed an outer fringe of non-Chinese. The Han dynasty, as may be seen from the population map for this period (p. 30), ruled over a sizable part of the areas that are today Korea and Vietnam. When the empire was weak, or the Chinese heartland fragmented, the reverse often happened, and barbarian states ruled over considerable numbers of Chinese. Under the Northern Song, in the early 11th century AD, Chinese authority did not extend much beyond the regions inhabited by the Han people, and its non-Chinese neighbors possessed powerful independent states of their own: the Qidan (or Liao) in southern Manchuria, the Xixia in the near northwest, the Tufan (Tibetans) in the west, the state of Dali of the southwestern tribes and the Dayue of the Vietnamese. In this multistate world the Chinese practiced a pragmatic diplomacy which tacitly accepted that they were dealing with equals. The mystique of a cultural-political world suzerainty for which the Chinese empire was rightly renowned was merely a useful weapon, then as later, to be brought out when convenient, rather than a doctrine deeply believed in.

The transition came in the 17th century. For more than 2000 years Inner and Outer China had been at war, especially along the northern frontier. The main line of division was that marked by the successive Great Walls (see maps pp. 26, 27, 71, 123); these indicate how the Chinese had fallen back southwards since the days of the early empire under the Qin and Han. (The Wall that visitors see today dates from the Ming and was built at various times between the late 14th and the middle 16th century.) When the Manchus took over China in the 17th century – it would be too much to say that they "conquered" it, given the extent of the help they received from renegade Chinese generals on the frontier – they began to bring this conflict to an end. During the next hundred years the campaigns of the Manchu emperors brought Mongolia, Zungharia, Eastern Turkestan and Tibet under their sway, though the last-mentioned was no more than a protectorate enjoying virtually total internal autonomy. Thus the western frontiers of the People's Republic today are the inheritance of a Manchu empire that is relatively recent in historical terms.

The map (p. 34) depicting the various imperialisms that have competed with each other in Eurasia since the 17th century makes the general case for seeing the Manchu-Chinese empire as just one imperialism among many. Not long after the Ottoman sultans had extended their dominion over the eastern Mediterranean and Mesopotamia, and the Dutch had begun their conquest of the East Indies, and at about the same time as the British were dismembering Mughal India, the Manchu-Chinese state was carving up central Asia with the Russians. The end result of this process was that the two empires, the core areas of which were over 4800 kilometers apart, had established a common frontier from the Pamirs to the Pacific that also ran for over 4800 kilometers. There are numerous fracture zones, where the various powers clashed directly, shown in multiple colored stripes on the map. The classic case of such a fracture zone is Manchuria, which was occupied by Czarist Russia from 1900 to 1904, and by Japan from 1931 to 1945, before passing back into Chinese hands in 1946 after another brief Russian occupation. Many of the states that paid "tribute" to the Manchu (Qing) also became the temporary possessions of European powers or of Japan. Annam, Burma and Korea are examples. How seriously the tributaries took their status is open to some question. For some, like Sulu, it was probably merely a useful cover for trading; for others, like the Vietnamese, little more than a means of humoring a large and powerful neighbor.

The transitory humiliations of China at the hands of the Western powers in the 19th century (symbolized on the map by the so-called treaty ports, cities forcibly opened to international trade) and later at the hands of the Japanese in the 1930s and 1940s, should not be allowed to obscure the fact that China has managed to hold on to the greater part of its imperial possessions. The chief exception is Mongolia, which achieved a measure of independence in 1912, and then became a virtual protectorate of the Soviet Union in 1924. Tibet enjoyed effective autonomy, under a distant British supervision, from 1912 to 1947, but passed back under Chinese control in 1950.

Broadly speaking, the Chinese position in the period of the greatest Western expansion had a dual character: even as China was obliged to make concessions to the force of arms wielded by these increasingly modern and industrial nations, it was buying and imitating their weapons to subdue the non-Han in the interior, and many Chinese were migrating from the southern ports to Spanish, French, British and Dutch colonial territories. Here their commercial and entrepreneurial skills were eventually to earn them the unflattering description of "second-class imperialists." In the Philippines they were called "Sangleys," which means in the Xiamen dialect "[those who] do business." Integration has been difficult, except among the sophisticated and accommodating Thais. In many regions and at many times Chinese migrants have been the subject of murderous attacks by resentful and apprehensive rival or host communities. Such occurrences go back to the early 17th century in Manila, when the Spaniards killed 23 000 Chinese in retaliation for an attempted Chinese uprising that left half the Spanish garrison dead. After the Chinese rebellion of 1857 in what is now Sarawak, James Brooke (the first of the "White Rajahs") had almost every Chinese hunted out of the country, though of course they later returned. A partial modern parallel is the massacre and maltreatment of the Chinese in Indonesia in the 1960s. The existence of the Chinese state of Singapore is likewise an illustration of the difficulty that Malays and Chinese have found in getting on together politically.

China's historical relations with the world overseas have been much less important than those it has had along its land frontiers. They should not, however, be overlooked on this account. From around the end of the first millennium AD improvements in the Chinese techniques of shipbuilding allowed Chinese merchantmen to take over much of the southeast Asian trade that had till then been mostly in the hands of Persians, Arabs and the local inhabitants. The climax of these developments was the powerful early Ming navy, one of whose chief tasks was to safeguard from pirates the ships carrying northwards the tax-grain from the Yangzi valley, and the great voyages made to India and the east coast of Africa in the 1420s and early 1430s by fleets under the command of Zheng He, the so-called "Three-Jewel Eunuch." This maritime expansion was cut short early in the 15th century. The rebuilding of an effective Grand Canal made the navy largely unnecessary, and the westward voyages brought little tangible commercial or strategic benefit. The Ming withdrew from the sea, and even banned Chinese coastal shipping altogether for more than 150 years. Possibly they feared the politically destabilizing effects of vigorous peripheral societies under some measure of foreign influence. Chinese seagoing shipping of course continued illegally, often in the form of piracy, which was usually (but mostly inaccurately) attributed to the Japanese. In the second half of the 16th century most of the bans were removed, and Chinese links with the world of international ocean trade revived. The most spectacular and important link was with Manila, where junks from Xiamen (Amoy), Ningbo and other ports took silks and porcelains to exchange for New World silver shipped in the trans-Pacific galleons from Acapulco. In some years late in the 16th century the net inflow of silver into China exceeded a million Chinese ounces. The effects of this bullion in providing a money supply for the expanding late Ming and Qing economy were comparable to those of Spanish treasure in Western Europe. In the following century there were also large imports of copper from Japan. Chinese pirates were a menace in

The 19th-century Muslim independence movements Muslims in northwestern China rested uneasily under Chinese rule, many of them not accepting the general premises of a Chinese type of political order, differing in this from Han Chinese rebels in the main part of the empire. The 1860s saw the outbreak of extensive communal strife between Muslims and non-Muslims in Shaanxi and Gansu provinces, and in some cases fighting between traditional Muslims and the adherents of the so-called "New Faith," which was probably some form of Wahabism. The center of the New Faith was at Jinjibao, in the Ningxia area, under the leadership of Ma Hualong. The area became for a decade or so a small theocratic state, defended by hundreds of forts constructed in the surrounding countryside.

A partially competing Muslim

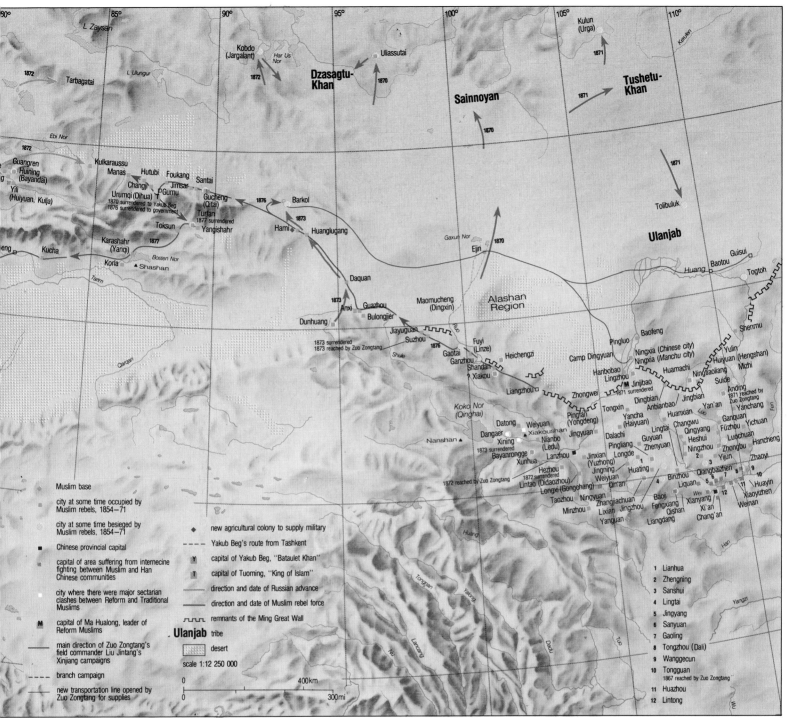

Muslim base

- ● city at some time occupied by Muslim rebels, 1854–71
- ● city at some time besieged by Muslim rebels, 1854–71
- ■ Chinese provincial capital
- ■ capital of area suffering from internecine fighting between Muslim and Han Chinese communities
- ● city where there were major sectarian clashes between Reform and Traditional Muslims
- M capital of Ma Hualong, leader of Reform Muslims
- —— main direction of Zuo Zongtang's field commander Liu Jintang's Xinjiang campaigns
- - - - branch campaign
- —— new transportation line opened by Zuo Zongtang for supplies

- ◆ new agricultural colony to supply military
- - - - Yakub Beg's route from Tashkent
- Y capital of Yakub Beg, "Bataulet Khan"
- T capital of Tuoming, "King of Islam"
- —— direction and date of Russian advance
- —— direction and date of Muslim rebel force
- ◠◠◠◠ remnants of the Ming Great Wall
- **Ulanjab** tribe
- ▒ desert

scale 1:12 250 000

0 ———————— 400km

0 ———————— 300mi

1 Lianhua
2 Zhengning
3 Sanshui
4 Lingtai
5 Jingyang
6 Sanyuan
7 Gaoling
8 Tongzhou (Dali)
9 Wanggecun
10 Tongguan
11 Huazhou
12 Lintong

rebel movement appeared about the same time in Urumqi under Tuolonga, who assumed the title of "Pure and Correct King," which carried the implication of "Monarch of Islam." Slightly later a third rebel regime came into being in the far west under a military adventurer from Tashkent called Yakub Beg, and originally chief of staff of a leader of the Khoja family. Yakub extended his dominion over the oasis cities of the Tarim basin, and then over the Urumqi region as well, maneuvering for diplomatic support from both Britain and Russia.

Suppression of the revolts by the Chinese imperial forces was the achievement of the strategist Zuo Zongtang and had a decisive effect on the map of the People's Republic today by keeping Xinjiang within the Chinese sphere of political control.

eastern waters at this time, and had the successors of the freebooter and Ming loyalist Zheng Chenggong (or "Koxinga") succeeded in maintaining the independent kingdom that he set up in Taiwan in 1661 (it fell in 1683), a maritime Chinese state might conceivably have come into being.

The strong conviction of almost every Chinese today that the non-Han regions of the People's Republic are inalienable parts of "China" makes it difficult to apply the same straightforward standards to them that are used in other similar cases without arousing a considerable hostility among all but the most fairminded Chinese. Yet this belief was not always so solid. After the massive Muslim independence movements of the 1860s in Shaanxi and Gansu, which were put down by the Qing with the most appalling loss of life, there appeared new risings in what is now western Xinjiang. These led to a shortlived state under Yakub Beg, who also styled himself the "Good Luck Khan." Several

weary officials at court at this point proposed abandoning Xinjiang as simply too much trouble, and these views might have carried the day but for the opposition of Zuo Zongtang, whose subsequent slow methodical campaigning (using Western-style breech-loading rifles manufactured at Lanzhou) brought Yakub Beg's rule to an end in 1878. Both the Nationalists and the Communists, before they obtained power, at least considered the idea of offering the major non-Han peoples their independence, only to discard these notions after victory.

There remains today a persistent uncertainty as to the answer to the question: "Who is a Chinese?" Is it someone who lives in the People's Republic, or is it someone of Han race and culture? The two definitions do not overlap, and, as the Kham uprising in 1959 in eastern Tibet and the expulsion of the Chinese from Vietnam after 1978 indicate, the ambiguities that surround this question may continue to give rise to conflicts in the future.

Left The Tianshan ("Mountains of Heaven"). The scenery is Alpine and nomadic herdsmen set up their yurts (campsites or tents) and graze their sheep and goats here in summer.

Below The sandy-colored arid scenery near Turfan along the ancient Silk Road lies below sea-level. Where irrigation is possible, excellent vines and delicious melons are grown in autumn.

Right The characteristic feature of the area centered on Shanxi is the loess, sandy soil deposited by wind thousands of years ago. This area was a center of the Chinese culture for centuries.

Left The loess beside the Yellow River in Gansu province is extremely fertile and fields of rape abound. Wheat is grown in the less fertile mountainous areas to the north and south.

Below Mt Everest (Qomolangma Feng) seen from Tibet.

Below right Goods are transported by horse and cart across the central plain of Shanxi province where cereal crops are grown in the light sandy soil.

Above Herds of camel and sheep graze on the grasslands of the Mongolian plain where pastoral nomadism is the way of life.

Left The sparsely vegetated stony plains of the Gobi stretch as far as the eye can see. The elusive wild horse known as the Przewalski Horse and other rare animals come from this area.

Right Until the development of hauling-ways through the gorges of the Yangzi during the Tang dynasty, communications between Sichuan and the rest of China depended on precarious ''gallery'' roads.

Previous page The karst limestone mountains of Guilin rise like a series of jade hairpins from the river valley.

Above This lush, productive valley lies to the south of Sichuan in Guizhou. Many of China's national minority groups live in this area.

Right These strange rock formations of Shilin ("Stone Forest") stand outside the city of Kunming in Yunnan.

Below An industrial complex at Anshan in Manchuria. Like most industrial installations in this part of China it was begun in the 1930s by the Japanese and symbolizes China's continuing debt to the period of occupation.

Below right The pine-clad peaks of Huangshan ("Yellow Mountain") in Anhui have long inspired artists in China. Mountain peaks appear as in a traditional Chinese landscape painting.

PART TWO
TIME

THE
ARCHAIC
WORLD

THE FOUNDATION OF A CULTURE

Prehistory

In the last million years the area we now know as China has experienced dramatic changes in climate. There were four ice ages, during which the higher ground was covered by glaciers. In the lowlands the weather was cold and wet. Much of the seawater was locked up in the ice, with the result that landbridges joined islands such as Taiwan with the mainland. At its lowest, the mean annual temperature may have been 8 degrees centigrade below the present level. Typical animals of these cold periods were the woolly rhinoceros in the north and the mammoth in the south. The three interglacial intervals were relatively milder; and the immediately postglacial age that began between 12 and 10 thousand years ago had an average temperature 2 degrees higher than today. Animals found in north China at this time included the elephant, the water buffalo, the porcupine, the tapir, the water deer, the tiger and the bamboo rat, all of which only thrive in warmer conditions than obtain at present. Much of the north China plain was a marsh, and the Shandong peninsula probably an island. In later times the temperature has fallen again. The north of east Asia has become cooler and drier. The forest cover had diminished; the former inland lakes that were dotted across Mongolia have dried up; and the desert has spread.

Man, in ecological terms, is an opportunist who can adapt to a variety of habitats. Throughout these changes, which altered the animal populations, he – almost alone – survived and evolved physically and culturally.

It is usual to distinguish three main epochs in early human development: (1) the Paleolithic, which ended with the last of the ice ages; (2) the Mesolithic, broadly defined by the use of more skillfully worked stone tools, but not a very distinct stage in China; and (3) the Neolithic, which opened with the appearance of agriculture in the fourth millennium BC and came to an end with the rise of bronze early in the second millennium BC. As different regions differed greatly in the pace of their development, these epochs overlapped and coexisted in China considered as a whole.

During the Paleolithic north China was inhabited by huge anthropoid apes such as *Gigantopithecus blacki* and various species of *Homo erectus*. The most primitive of these was Lantian Man, and the most famous Beijing Man, whose brain was about two-thirds the size of ours. These people were hunters of wild game, much of it large and dangerous, like saber-toothed tigers, wild boars and elephants, and requiring social organization on the part of the hunters for successful capture. They knew how to make fires and, to judge from split human marrow-bones, also practiced cannibalism. By the beginning of the last of the ice ages, however, a modern man – *Homo sapiens* – had appeared, with recognizably Mongolid features, and begun to displace them.

At the very end of the glacial period, when the weather was dry and cold, the northwest of China was gradually covered with a fine, yellow, wind-blown dust from the central Asian deserts. In some places it accumulated up to several tens of meters deep. The soil that results from this so-called loess is easy to work and very fertile if watered. It is also treacherous, quickly turning to impassable mud, and constantly changes the shape of the landscape as it is picked up in the form of silt by rivers and dropped again as their current slackens. Most of the north China plain is made of redeposited loess mixed with sands and gravels. It was in this fruitful but precarious environment that the nucleus of Chinese civilization was later to emerge.

There was no sharp dividing-line in the Yellow River valley between the Paleolithic and the Mesolithic. In the north, including present-day Mongolia, there were advances in the making of small stone blades and composite tools and in the use of pressure-flaking techniques. In the south there was a quite separate group of settlements where the earliest surviving pottery appeared, simple types of ware on which cord-mark patterns were impressed.

Perhaps the most significant development in this period was the gradual differentiation of two cultural spheres: the steppe and the desert north, spotted with inland lakes, and the wooded south of Inner China. It was the confrontation between these two worlds that was later, in the imperial age, to be at the heart of the conflict of the Chinese and the northern barbarians along the lines of the various Great Walls.

The Neolithic, by definition, saw the beginning of farming. The staple cereal was millet, but wheat and rice were also known. The technique of cultivation came in relatively rapidly. It may therefore have been imported from the Near East, but an indigenous invention seems equally likely. Among the animals domesticated at this time were dogs, pigs, goats, sheep, cattle and possibly horses. Houses were sturdy structures, half underground, thatched, provided with stoves and ovens and floored with plaster. Settlements grew larger,

Previous page This Shang dynasty bronze ax was found on the entrance ramp of a cruciform tomb at Sufutun, Yidu, in Shandong, where 48 sacrificial victims were buried. The punched-out face depicted on the ax is suitably powerful, and executed with painstaking precision using the piece-mold technique of bronze casting.

Right Excavations in the Yangshao area show that the leader of the village in Neolithic times was female, and suggest that the tribal system was run on matriarchal lines. Dogs and pigs were the main domesticated animals. Tombs were set apart from the village, as were kilns. Males and females were buried separately. Females' tombs were richer in content, containing jade decorative objects, and in one case 8577 small bone balls. These were used for body decoration, and a ring of bones supported a topknot hairstyle.

Patterns of fish and deer appear on Yangshao pottery and were reduced to geometric designs. On some vessels more than 20 different vertical, hook-like and arrow-headed designs are drawn; these might constitute the original Chinese characters.

The houses had floors of beaten earth, and walls made of wattle and mud. The large conical roof with overhanging eaves was supported by wooden posts inside. The men of the village spent their time fishing and hunting, using implements, while the women looked after their homes.

sometimes covering a greater area than the modern villages near the old sites. Pottery became common, decorated with swirling geometric designs, and much of it in shapes that can already be recognized as characteristic of later Chinese tradition. It was important in economic life for the storage and preparation of food and for the transportation of water. Stone whorls found in Neolithic sites fairly certainly served as primitive spindles and indicate the production of cloth. The remains of cut silkworm cocoons show that sericulture was known.

Here for the first time too we can sense the presence of religious beliefs in the carefully performed burials, and in the shoulderblades of oxen and deer fractured into cracks with a hot-pointed implement, probably a stick, for the purpose of divination. The first simple figurines showing the human face stare out at us from this period with their curiously self-confident expressions, and the earliest drawings of fish, birds and domestic animals appear.

The detailed analysis of this more complex age leads straight into one of the major fields of scholarly controversy. It is generally agreed that there were two main Neolithic cultures in north China, known as the Yangshao and the Longshan. Some authorities would distinguish a third from the last mentioned, namely the early Xiaotun, a forerunner of the later Shang culture in its pre-bronze phase. The main criterion used to define these cultures is pottery, and they are often associated respectively with their characteristic red, black and gray wares. The arguments arise over how much weight should be put on the differences in geographical distribution between the two cultures and how much on their separation in time. The Yangshao is found primarily but not exclusively in the northwestern part of the north China plain, while the Longshan is in the east and northeast. The Xiaotun is associated with the lower course of the Yellow River. In the quite numerous sites where all three appear together, they tend to form a stratified sequence: (1) Yangshao; (2) Longshan; (3) Xiaotun. There are also mixed deposits, however, and sequences in which one of the three is absent. A second set of difficulties arises from the lack of a precise correspondence in the pattern of variation of artifacts other than pottery (such as stone sickles, for instance) with the variations in the pottery remains.

Some of the technological differences between the Yangshao and the Longshan indicate a progression from less to more advanced methods. Yangshao pots are coiled or molded; much Longshan pottery is made on a wheel. Longshan sites show the domestication of sheep and cattle; Yangshao sites do not. Other distinguishing features suggest more deep-seated differences. Many Yangshao settlements, for example, buried their dead some way away from the houses of the living, but in Longshan villages burial in the midst of the settlement was commoner. One plausible but not entirely satisfactory solution is that there was a central focus from which the Yangshao and Longshan radiated out at different times and in different directions; and other, more peripheral, cultures such as the Qingliangang in Jiangsu and the Qiujialing in Hubei can be fitted into this scheme.

Neolithic Art

Above This mask-like face is one of the earliest prehistoric clay images of a human being. It forms the knob and lid of a painted pottery vessel of the Yangshao culture.

Right: Yangshao and Longshan sites
The two main Neolithic groups of central and northwestern China and of the east coast have been identified by their pottery types as Yangshao (painted pottery) and Longshan (black pottery) respectively. These names have been applied to the groups living in these areas from the fifth millennium BC. The map shows the main sites. The remains of Banpo, one of the best-preserved Neolithic settlements in the world, were excavated in the 1950s and belong to the Yangshao culture. The site includes the foundations of houses, kilns, pits and tombs

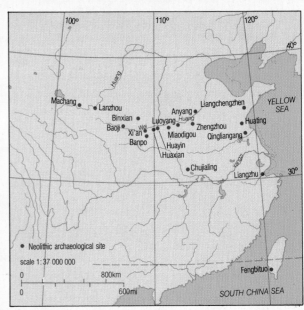

Right and below The patterns on Yangshao pottery are thought to have developed from realistic depictions to abstract geometric designs. Fish caught with finely made bone hooks provided some of the most popular decorative motifs.

Below Longshan burnished black pottery of c. 2000–1500 BC was turned to an incredible thinness. It is distinguished by an absence of decoration.

Bottom left This demonic creature on a jar from Gansu (3rd millennium BC) may reflect the beliefs of the Yangshao people. It may also be the earliest surviving representation of the dragon of Chinese myth.

Bottom right Yangshao earthenware pots of c. 4000–3500 BC seem to be primarily mortuary items. Sweeping lines and geometric designs decorate the upper part; the lower is nearly always left undecorated, possibly because they were set in sandy soil to prevent them overturning while being painted.

The peoples of the Neolithic cultures left no written records or names. We are therefore dealing with a people described by their surviving pottery, kilns, stone tools and buildings. The question of relative chronology is difficult. Countless Neolithic sites have been excavated dating from about 6000 to about 1500 BC. The Bronze Age site at Anyang, the last capital of the Shang dynasty, in Henan, revealed Longshan material above that of Yangshao, and succeeded by bronze remains of the Shang period. However, this does not necessarily mean that the entire Longshan culture succeeded that of Yangshao.

Yangshao culture is best seen at the excavated site of Banpo in Shaanxi. The inhabitants lived in rectangular round or square houses with reed roofs supported by wooden beams. The floor was dug some feet below the surrounding area, and near the center was a shallow round hearth-pit. Many had storage niches carved out of the sunken walls. Cemeteries and kilns were set apart from the living area. The cemetery reveals that corpses were buried on their backs, with their heads to the northwest.

Yangshao pottery consists of two distinct types. The first is of coarse gray earthenware built up by hand with coils of clay, and smoothed over to conceal the joins. The pots are decorated with cord, mat or basket impressions. The second type is superior in quality and appears to have been used for mortuary purposes. It consists of fine-grained ware with a lightly burnished surface decorated with painted designs in black, red, maroon and brown. The designs are of simple geometric patterns, or of fish, animal or human faces, and vary from region to region. Banpo is characteristic of the central area.

In northwest China the so-called Gansu-Yangshao culture is generally thought to be later than that of the central area. The designs consist of branching spirals and curvilinear designs painted in loose fluid strokes. Black is the main color, and brown and maroon are also used. In the eastern area the Yangshao culture overlaps with the Longshan culture, and the red pottery when painted uses a white slip as ground for other colors. The designs are not as well organized as in the west, and the shapes also differ, being generally smaller at the base.

Longshan culture of the east coast is best known for its black pottery. The very fine particles of clay in black pottery made it possible to use the potter's wheel to turn the shapes to incredible thinness. This could not have been achieved with coarser clays. The wheel was also used to finish hand-made earthenware, judging from the rims which show signs of finishing on the wheel. Kiln designs were improved, and firing temperatures could be more easily regulated and controlled. There was a greater diversity of clays used along the east coast, including reddish-brown clay and gray clay. The everyday ware was decorated with impressed patterns of geometric designs. The fine thin-walled black ware has little surface decoration; apart from simple incised geometric designs and the occasional bands raised in relief, the surfaces remain plain. However the shapes are much more varied than those of the Yangshao culture. The slender shapes of some of the vessels suggest that they were more likely to have been used for ritual than for practical purposes.

The Shang empire

The earliest of the dynasties mentioned by the traditional Chinese historical sources is the Xia. Its founder is said to have been Yu the Great (2205–2197 BC), minister to and successor of the sage-emperors Yao and Shun. If this dynasty is to be identified with any level in the sequence of archaeological remains it has to be with the Yangshao and Longshan complex. So far not the tiniest scrap of evidence has emerged to justify any such association. Nonetheless, the conservatism and faithfulness of ancient Chinese record-keeping make it unwise to dismiss the Xia as entirely mythical. Perhaps the earliest records were written with a brush, in the way that pottery was painted, and kept only on materials like wood strips that have now perished, unlike the texts on bones, shell and bronze from slightly later times.

Chinese prehistory ends some time in the second quarter of the second millennium BC with the rise of the Shang dynasty. The heartland of the new kingdom was that part of the present-day province of Henan where the higher ground slopes down to the flood-plain of the Yellow River. At its zenith its influence radiated as far as Mongolia in the north,

Gansu in the northwest and the Yangzi valley in the south. Its trade for the commodities that it especially valued, such as tin and mother-of-pearl, reached even further afield.

The Shang was an aristocratic culture, brilliant, luxurious and savage, resting on a still largely Neolithic agricultural base. One new economic feature was the taming of the water buffalo, large herds of which flourished in the warm, flooded conditions found at this time in the north China plain. Remains of irrigation ditches and harvest records also suggest that rice cultivation was now of importance. The leaders of the Shang clans were addicted to warfare, hunting, wine, and human and animal sacrifices on an enormous scale. The distinctive characteristics of their civilization were the use of bronze for weapons and ritual vessels, the mastery of writing, the horse-drawn chariot, a coherent administrative structure, the ability to mobilize the human labor needed to build massive walls of rammed earth and great tombs, cities, a relatively accurate calendar, money in the form of strings of cowrie shells, a pantheon of gods, a complex lineage structure and the worship of ancestors. We also meet for the first time with

The Shang empire c. 1300 BC
There are three main sources of information about the geography of the Shang dynasty. These are the traditional histories, archaeological excavations and places mentioned on the oracle bones recording the results of royal divinations. Each of them reveals a slightly different picture. In particular it is interesting to contrast, on the one hand, the relatively compact area covered by the archaeological sites and centered on the lower course of the Yellow River and western Shandong and, on the other, the locations mentioned on the oracle bones which show a comparatively strong bias in the direction of the southeast, perhaps because of the importance of royal hunts and campaigns in this region. Very few of the oracle-bone places shown here have been directly identified, and in most cases even the pronunciation of the graph representing them is unknown; but their relative positions and the distances in time required for travel between them have been reasonably firmly established thanks to the

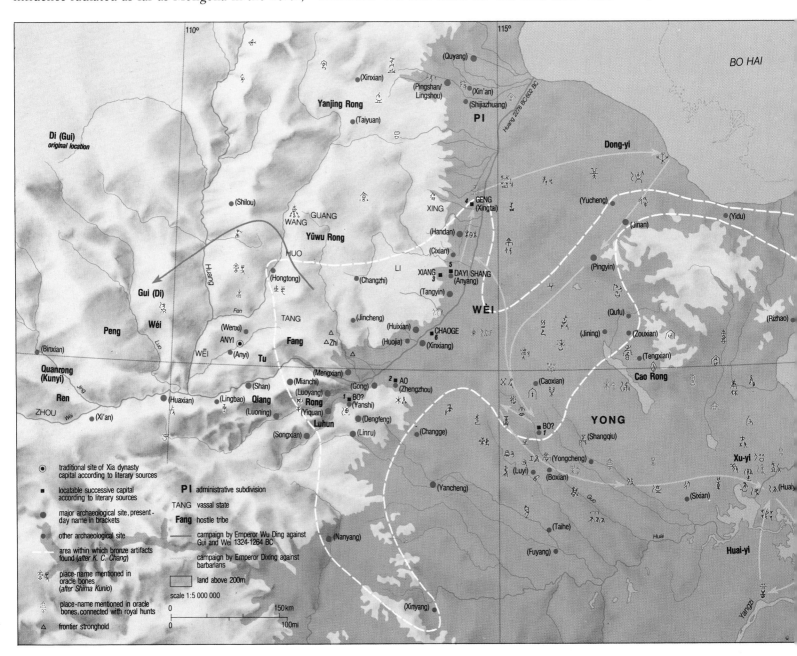

labors of the Japanese scholar Shima Kunio. It has likewise been impossible to locate more than a few of the known Shang vassal states. When future research eventually makes available the full picture, it will be even more of a mosaic than that shown here.

Right above These Shang dynasty pictographic emblems give a lively depiction of everyday activities. The same methods of carrying grain can be seen in China today.

Right The cracks produced by the application of a heated point to the undershell of a tortoise formed the basis for divination in Shang times. The answers to the questions asked were then recorded on the shell with a sharp stylus.

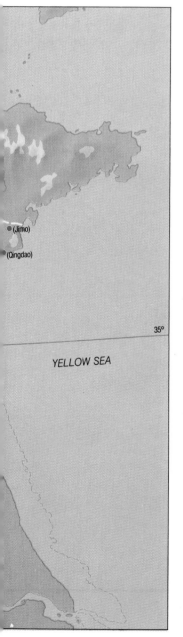

musical instruments: drums, bells, chiming stones and ocarinas. The melodies have vanished, but we know they used a tritonic and a pentatonic scale. In contrast to the geometric decoration of the preceding age, Shang art is dominated by animal motifs, most of them highly stylized. But some are naturalistic, and a few are of imaginary composite monsters.

There are also a few representations of human beings, garbed in the belted dressing-gown garment, with turned-over collar, characteristic of archaic China. The usual sitting posture seems to have been to kneel and then rest on the heels, as the Japanese still do today; and this continued to be the "correct sitting" position in China until early in the first millennium AD. Shang architecture was based on rectangular wooden frameworks, without diagonal bracing. The slope of the thatched roofs was straight, unlike the gently sagging curves that came in after the Tang dynasty. Grandeur was given to these rather simple structures by siting them on top of platforms approached by long flights of stone steps. This conception has lain at the foundation of Chinese palace-type buildings throughout traditional times, and can still be seen today in, for example, the imposing memorial museum built for President Jiang Jieshi (Chiang Kai-shek) in Taibei.

Thus the cultural style was already unmistakably Chinese. Nowhere is this more evident than in the language and the script of the Shang inscriptions. For all their obscurity, both are clearly the direct ancestors of the modern tongue and the modern written characters.

Dates in the records of the oracles consulted by the kings of the period from the 14th to the 12th century BC have been linked with the standard Scaliger sequence of numbered days used by astronomers, but reconstructing Shang chronology is still problematic. Using round numbers, it is reasonable to take 1750 BC as the date of the foundation of the dynasty by King Tang. He is said by the traditional historical texts to have ousted the morally degraded last emperor of the Xia, whose chief source of pleasure, it is alleged, was sailing with his queen in a barge on a lake of wine watching thousands of naked men and women eating and copulating. It was probably about 1600 BC that the dynasty moved to the last of its seven capitals, near present-day Anyang. Finally, around 1100 BC, Di-xin, the last of the Shang rulers, was destroyed by the state of Zhou, an overmighty vassal-kingdom whose center of power lay to the west in the valley of the Wei River.

There are two obvious problems concerning Shang culture. First, how did it emerge with such relative suddenness? And second, how did the political power of its rulers endure with such apparent stability for two-thirds of a millennium?

To some extent the swift rise of the Shang may be an illusion, due to our ignorance of its antecedents. Thus until quite recently it was thought that bronze-casting had appeared in China in a mature and technically perfect form. This was taken to be compelling grounds for believing that it was derived from elsewhere, presumably the ancient Near East. But recently a few early bronzes of a crude nature, probably of the 18th century BC, have been unearthed. Likewise the script used for recording oracle consultations and other matters is clearly a simplified version of an older and more overtly pictographic form of writing found occasionally on Shang bronzes. Scholars who think that the Shang culture had a more-or-less wholly Chinese origin stress, quite correctly, the unique character of its bronze-casting techniques. These make use (on the whole) of piece-molds rather than the "lost-wax" process usual elsewhere. Archaeologists point to the continuity of Shang culture with that of the early Xiaotun pottery. But the discontinuities are so evident, and cluster together in such a marked fashion, that it is hard not to believe in influence from earlier centers of Old World culture. The chariot, in particular, is unlikely to have been invented twice. The forms of certain tools and pottery vessels also indisputably indicate the existence of some contacts between China, the Near

East and the Indus valley. An example is the type of jar cover with a phallic-shaped handle standing upright in the center of the pot.

The second question, about the durability of the Shang, obliges us to try to reconstruct in our minds its social, political and religious structures and their environment. Shang society was probably based on two or three hundred clans, concentrated in particular localities, each with its particular emblem, and serving as the focus of its members' affiliations, loyalties and observances. The possession of bronze weapons, notably the "dagger-ax" or Chinese halberd, bronze arrow- and spear-heads and bronze helmets, gave those who were privileged to have them a nearly decisive superiority in the use of force. We may surmise that this ensured both the dominance of a warrior nobility of clan leaders over their commoners, and of the Shang people as a whole over the less advanced tribes who lived around and among them. The Shang kings engaged in continual military expeditions. Plunder and tribute were part of the royal economy. Captives taken in war were either slaughtered as sacrificial victims or enslaved.

The new weapons may also have been part of the explanation of the passion of the Shang aristocrats for hunting. The kings maintained a huge hunting-ground on the western skirts of the Tai and Meng mountains in the southern part of what is now Shandong province. Excavations of Shang sites have yielded the bones of elephants, rhinoceroses, bears, tigers, leopards, deer, monkeys, foxes and badgers. The hunting-meet was also the best training for battle. Individuals could practice the use of weapons, and groups the art of moving in coordination. But while warfare was now based on metal, ordinary economic life continued to make do with stone, wood and bone.

The new power of coercion was the foundation of new political and administrative structures. At the center was the royal clan, whose members seem to have taken their principal wives, though not their secondary wives, from among their own number. The clan was divided into ten groups, labeled by characters corresponding to our "A, B, C, ... J"; and the succession shifted among them according to rules that are no longer clear. Commonly, but not invariably, the throne passed to one of the dead king's brothers, and from the youngest brother to his son (see chart). The ultimate source of political power was thought to be the royal ancestors, with the spirits of deceased ministers also wielding some influence over events. The dead were believed to go to Heaven, over which presided *Shangdi*, the Lord on High. There they could intercede on behalf of their descendants. The ritual life of the Shang court was therefore a continual sequence of sacrifices to these ancestors. Furthermore, no action of any importance was undertaken without first having recourse to divination. As in Longshan times, the under-shell (or plastron) of a tortoise, or the shoulderblade of an animal, was cracked with a hot point, and the resulting pattern of lines subjected to interpretation. The most commonly asked questions concerned the appropriateness of the ancestral sacrifices, warfare and hunting, rainfall and harvests, and inauspicious events. The verdicts were recorded and form our chief source of information about Shang life.

Right: The succession of the Shang kings
How to reconstruct the rules governing the succession of the Shang kings has been a topic of recent scholarly debate. The controversy centers on whether or not there was one main line of descent, or multiple lineages within the royal clan, each line designated by one of the cyclical characters that serve as the second half of all the royal posthumous names used here. This table may therefore be interpreted in two ways. "Paternity" and "fraternity" can be understood in a merely classificatory sense indicating respectively membership of the immediately preceding and of the same generation within the clan, or in their usual modern sense.

Other topics of debate are the rationale behind the ordering of the cyclical characters (*jia, yi, bing* etc.), none of which occurs twice in the same generation, the unequal representation of these characters, and why *Da*, meaning "great," is restricted to the main line of descent.

Left This bronze wine vessel (*yu*) with a swinging handle shows the terrified face of a human figure frozen in the jaws of a devouring monster, reflecting the power and terror of the social order. Human faces seldom appear on Shang dynasty bronzes, and when they do they probably represent the victims of human sacrifice. This face is similar to one on the side of a *ding* vessel excavated in 1965 at Ningxiang in Henan. The elaborate surface decoration seen here embodies much of the late Shang style of the 11th century BC.

Right below Charioteers have been found buried with their horses and chariots in the Shang dynasty royal tombs at Anyang. Chariots were not known in China until the Anyang period of the Shang dynasty, c. 1300 BC. They resemble those found in burials in the Caucasus, having similar low open-fronted bodies, large wheels, with many spokes, and wheel rims made of two bent pieces of wood.

Previous page According to chariot burials in the Shang royal tombs, the most important position in the low open-fronted chariot was on the left-hand side. The right side was occupied by an attendant and the charioteer stood in front. The headdress of the king in the reconstructed drawing is designed after that on a small figure excavated from a Shang dynasty tomb, thought to be the ruler of heaven. The attendant soldiers wear bronze helmets and round-necked armor after excavated Shang dynasty examples. The vehicle was drawn by either two or four horses and was made of wood, with fittings and fixtures of bronze. Hunting expeditions were carried out like military exercises and animals and enemy were killed alike.

Note: The names used here are posthumous names. Kings placed in the same generation line are "brothers," at least in a classificatory sense. Those enclosed in square brackets have not yet been found on oracle bone inscriptions.

→ Royal succession.

Indicates "paternity," at least in a classificatory sense.

Older to younger siblings in each generation →

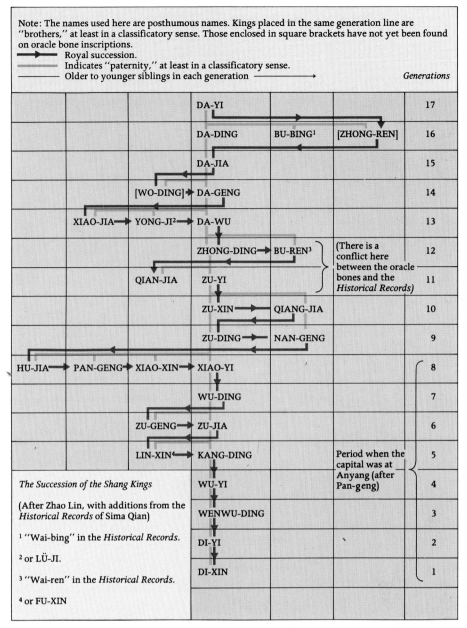

Generations

	17 DA-YI
	16 DA-DING, BU-BING[1], [ZHONG-REN]
	15 DA-JIA
	14 [WO-DING] DA-GENG
	13 XIAO-JIA YONG-JI[2] DA-WU
	12 ZHONG-DING BU-REN[3]
	11 QIAN-JIA ZU-YI
	10 ZU-XIN QIANG-JIA
	9 ZU-DING NAN-GENG
	8 HU-JIA PAN-GENG XIAO-XIN XIAO-YI
	7 WU-DING
	6 ZU-GENG ZU-JIA
	5 LIN-XIN[4] KANG-DING
	4 WU-YI
	3 WENWU-DING
	2 DI-YI
	1 DI-XIN

(There is a conflict here between the oracle bones and the *Historical Records*)

Period when the capital was at Anyang (after Pan-geng)

The Succession of the Shang Kings

(After Zhao Lin, with additions from the *Historical Records* of Sima Qian)

[1] "Wai-bing" in the *Historical Records*.

[2] or LÜ-JI.

[3] "Wai-ren" in the *Historical Records*.

[4] or FU-XIN

The spirit of central control and standardization was already at work in the Shang state. A decimal system of measurement was defined for public use, using a unit of 1·7 centimeters. The calendar had 12 months of 30 and 29 days in alternation, with seven extra months intercalated every 19 years by the royal astronomers. Within the king's domain, farm labor was organized under official superintendents. Tools were issued and stored by the authorities, and the harvests kept in the royal granaries. Outside the central area there seem to have been fiefs, some of them bestowed on queens and princes, others on deserving generals and office-holders. Their obligations were to provide military help, present tribute and supply manpower for public works.

The gods and spirits of the Shang were of two kinds: those in Heaven, who did not receive sacrifices, and those of the earth, divinities of particular places, who did, as also did ancestors. Life after death was probably thought of as a continuation of life in this world. Such a belief would explain the massacres of human beings and animals that accompanied the burials of rulers and great men. Tens or even hundreds of companions, women, servants and pets were slaughtered to follow their masters into the afterworld. The bronze, stone and jade objects found beside some of these skeletons suggest that they cannot all have been common folk, but many of the bodies of those sacrificed were mutilated before being interred, which does not indicate companionship. Others were equipped with halberds, and their positioning shows that they were guards, there to protect their lord against evil spirits below the earth. Both men and animals were also immolated to consecrate new buildings and in the honor of various deities.

The Zhou empire

Towards the end of the 12th century BC King Wu of the Zhou rebelled against the Shang emperor Di-xin. Wu took advantage of the depletion of the Shang ruler's forces because of his campaigns against the eastern tribes, and destroyed him at the battle of Chaoge (or Muye). The new dynasty that he set up, the Zhou, was to be the longest lived and the most revered of all the ruling houses in Chinese history. The first 200 years of its dominion, in particular, were looked back on as a golden age of good government and prosperity.

There is no doubt that the rise of the Zhou was the work of a succession of unusually gifted leaders. During the days when the new state was a dependency of the Shang, its strength was built up by King Wen, whose name in Chinese is literally synonymous with "culture" or "civilization." Wen is remembered for his piety towards gods and ancestors, his concern for the well-being of his people and his skill is forging alliances. King Wu, the "Martial King," was his son. He was noted for his hatred of the alcoholic excesses of the Shang, and for his attempt to impose the death penalty for any collective drinking of wine except at the ritual sacrifices. (The ancestral spirits liked to get drunk.) Wu also stressed the impartial administration of justice, and the importance of proper family relations. Unlike later Chinese rulers and philosophers who spoke only of the need for the subordination of juniors to seniors, Wu threatened to punish fathers and elder brothers, as well as sons

and younger brothers, if they did not fulfill their familial duties. The new state was consolidated by Wu's younger brother, the duke of Zhou, who governed as regent during the minority of Wu's son. The duke, who was well acquainted with the Shang nobility from his many years as a young man at the Shang court, suppressed a counterrebellion launched by the remnants of the old regime who had allied themselves with certain members of the Zhou royal family. Confucius later regarded him as the exemplar of the loyal minister, and in his young days saw him frequently in his dreams.

That there was internal tranquillity in the early centuries of Zhou rule seems beyond doubt. Apart from that, there is reason to be skeptical about many aspects of the rosy traditional picture. The Zhou were the first masters of political propaganda in China. They probably destroyed the literature of the Shang (none of which has survived in a form that is certainly authentic), lest it support a view of history different from their own. They certainly set about preaching an ingenious and persuasive doctrine to reconcile the conquered Shang to their subjection. This was the theory of the "Mandate of Heaven." According to this theory, the emperor is the "Son of Heaven," *Tian*, the Zhou supreme deity. The entire world, "All under Heaven," is his lawful domain. He receives the right to rule as long as he does so justly and with a proper concern for the welfare of his subjects. King Wu quoted with approval the old saying: "Men should not mirror themselves in water, but in the people." If, however, the ruler was unjust, or immoral, then Heaven, after warning him, would take away his mandate to rule and give it to another. The last ruler of the Xia had been depraved (and was required by the theory to have been). Heaven had therefore given his realm to Tang, founder of the Shang. Likewise, Di-xin had been morally unfit, and in particular he was alleged to have been a sadist who had invented new tortures. Heaven had therefore conferred the right to rule upon the Zhou. The victory at Chaoge had been a divine judgment. Several of the pieces in the collection called the *Songs*, later canonized as one of the Confucian scriptures, are homilies on this theme addressed to the Shang, which indicate that *Shangdi*, the Lord on High, was the same as *Tian*, Heaven. It seems to have been a successful, if dishonest, justification for what

can be shown to have been a rebellion plotted over several generations.

There were only a few immediate cultural discontinuities between Shang and Zhou. Tortoiseshell divination was no longer used routinely at court, but only when special problems arose. The use of "A, B, . . ."-type markers for clan sub-groups in posthumous royal names came to an end. This was probably because the Zhou had shifted to a simple inheritance of the throne from father to son. The extravagance of the Shang, its great hunts and sacrificial murders, gave way to a relative restraint, though both of these practices continued. The motifs of the bronze-caster's art, notably the stylized animal mask called *taotie*, hardly changed until the mid-10th century BC.

The early Zhou realm was a family empire. It was decentralized into fiefs given to the relatives of the ruler and his most valued helpers. These lands were in theory revocable, but in practice most of them became hereditary possessions. The emperors had a central proto-bureaucratic administration, in which appointments were not inherited. The general spirit of the system, however, was to emphasize the man rather than the office, and titles and functions were not closely related. The emperors also maintained under their direct control a number of standing armies stationed at various points in the country. Wars against the barbarians were fought by these troops in combination with forces contributed by the fiefs.

The bronze halberd and the walled city remained the chief techniques for attack and defense, but there is evidence to suggest that both metalworking and city-building were becoming increasingly known to the barbarians, and that the supremacy of the Zhou ultimately rested on superior organization. The region under imperial rule covered modern southern Shaanxi, Shanxi, Henan, Hebei and Shandong. Imperial influence was wider still, if we may judge from the distribution of early Zhou bronze vessels, which range from Rehe in the north to Jiangsu province in the south. King Zhao (1052–1002 BC) made several military expeditions to the Han River, on the last of which he died. His successor, King Mu (1001–947 BC), was transformed by later legends into the archetype of the world traveler, which may perhaps be taken as symbolizing the expansion of royal power at this time.

Above The monster mask (known as *taotie*) appears as one of the main decorative motifs on bronzes in different shapes and forms throughout the Shang and Zhou periods. Its principal elements are horns, protruding eyes and ferocious upper jaw. At times it merges into the background decoration and is only identifiable by its eyes; at other times its elements are totally dismembered. It is thought to have averted evil, and could be a symbol of gluttony or simply of terror.

Right Most bronzes of the Shang period were either three- or one-footed vessels. The form of the vessels continued or further developed ceramic types of the Neolithic period. The lightweight shape of the early Shang three- or four-legged vessel (*ding*) gave way to a heavy ponderous shape with increased decoration. The *ding* was used for both ritual and practical purposes and could be placed over the fire.

Above This bronze vessel (*yu*) of early Zhou date from Anhui illustrates the more restrained and classic style of 10th-century bronzes in comparison with the elaborate style of the monster vessel of the late Shang period (page 58).

Early Shang

Late Shang

Early Zhou

Late Zhou

The first sign that Zhou rule was faltering occurred at the beginning of the 9th century BC when King Yi was placed on the throne by an alliance of vassals. In the reign that followed, that of King Li (878–828 BC), the dynasty was nearly toppled by the revolt of the marquis of E, who had allied himself with some sinicized barbarians. Finally, in 771 BC, King You was killed when the Rong barbarians and the marquis of Shen and his allies assaulted his capital at Hao on the Wei River. One of his sons, whom the rebels favored, was put on the throne and acknowledged by most of the feudal lords. For safety's sake he moved his capital east, near to modern Luoyang. The power of the monarch progressively diminished until it was eventually little more than a ritually recognized suzerainty without substance.

Historians usually divide the dynasty into the periods before and after 770 BC. The former, when the kings had real and effective power, is known as the Western Zhou. The latter, during which the emperor became an increasing irrelevance in a fragmented world of rival states emerging from former fiefs, is called the Eastern Zhou, with reference to the shift of the capital.

The processes underlying this political destabilization are obscure. The underlying cause of change was probably the steady spread of advanced technology, military and economic, from the center to the outlying areas. The manufacture of good bronze weapons was no longer the monopoly of a small handful of artisans and powerholders. The number of cities with rammed-earth fortifications grew rapidly towards the end of the Western Zhou. The once vulnerable islands of urban-agricultural development, surrounded by hostile and less civilized peoples, that had formed the early Zhou domain had expanded their areas of cultivation and settlement, a process celebrated in the *Songs*.

At the same time as the bonds of kinship and the memories of mutual support between the fiefs and the dynasty were weakening, the fiefs were growing stronger and better able to resist the barbarians without help from the center. They were also better able to resist the center itself. On the other hand, the so-called "barbarians" within what is now Inner China (as opposed to those coming in from outside) were also becoming more menacing for similar technical reasons: farming, metalworking and the construction of cities. Some of them even had chariots. The gap between "Chinese" and "barbarians" at this time was less than these terms suggest. Intermarriage was common at the personal level, and alliances at the political level.

In this world of new competing states the old clan system seems to have gradually disintegrated. At the upper levels of society it was replaced by an aristocratic culture based on a more narrowly familial kinship system, and priding itself on its chivalry, courtesy, pageantry, genealogy and the correct observance of ritual. This age is known to traditional historians as "the Springs and Autumns period," after the title *Springs and Autumns* of the annals of the state of Lu, which cover these years. It is conventionally dated 770 BC to 481 BC, two years before the death of Confucius. Since it was the background against which the classical culture of China was formed, it deserves to be studied in some detail.

The Springs and Autumns period

At first it was a world of numerous small city-states. Towards the end of the 8th century BC one minister declared that "Capital cities of more than 3000 yards in circumference are harmful to the state." He thought that in the golden past even the largest subordinate cities had been only a third of the size of the capitals, and the smallest no more than a ninth, in other words, mere castles. This remark gives a vivid idea of the tiny scale of some of these polities.

Ceaseless warfare soon led to their destruction or absorption by larger political units that may be regarded as "states" in a sense not too different from the modern meaning of the word. They consisted, each one, of a people with a self-conscious identity and feeling of unity, associated with a specific, demarcated territory. In this last respect they clearly differed from the barbarian tribes to their north. Wei Jiang, prime minister of the state of Jin in the 6th century BC, said of them that "they live where the pastures are. They care greatly for goods, but little for land, which can be bought from them."

Each of these Chinese states had a well-defined system of superordination and subordination, that is of ranks, classes and civil and military positions. Their rulers felt, or were supposed to feel, a responsibility for the welfare of their people as a whole. This was expressed in fiscal and economic policies, in the promulgation of laws and in religious rituals to promote prosperity and avert disasters. The sense of a coherent and comprehensive system, at least in theory, is unmistakable in the traditional account of the state of Chu under its prime minister Zi Mu in the middle of the 6th century BC. He had the minister of war "list the cultivable land in a register, survey the mountains and forests, group together marshes and water-meadows, distinguish between the heights and the hillocks, mark out the salterns, measure the frontiers and flooded areas, trace the dikes and divide the areas between the dikes into small fields, make pastures of the banks beside the water, and fields for eight-family groups in the fertile places, calculate the quotas of the contributions to be paid in, the numbers of horses and chariots to be supplied, and those of soldiers mounted in chariots and on foot, and of body-armor and shields."

Internally, these states were often the scenes of ferocious power-struggles between the great families, but it is significant that in some of them at least the ruler had the power to approve or disapprove the selection of a new head of the family when the former head had died. Regicide was not uncommon, either by an angry populace or disgruntled nobles. But to deny these polities the title of "state" (as some scholars have done) creates the almost insurmountable problem of defining what a state is, if these were not.

Three centuries of tangled history may be simplified into nine phases:

1 Towards the end of the 8th century BC Duke Zhuang of the state of Zheng emerged as the first of the hegemons, that is to say, dominant rulers who exercised a general primacy over the other states in the name, at least, of the Zhou emperor. Zheng was located just south of the elbow of the Yellow River, where it turns sharply eastwards towards the sea. It

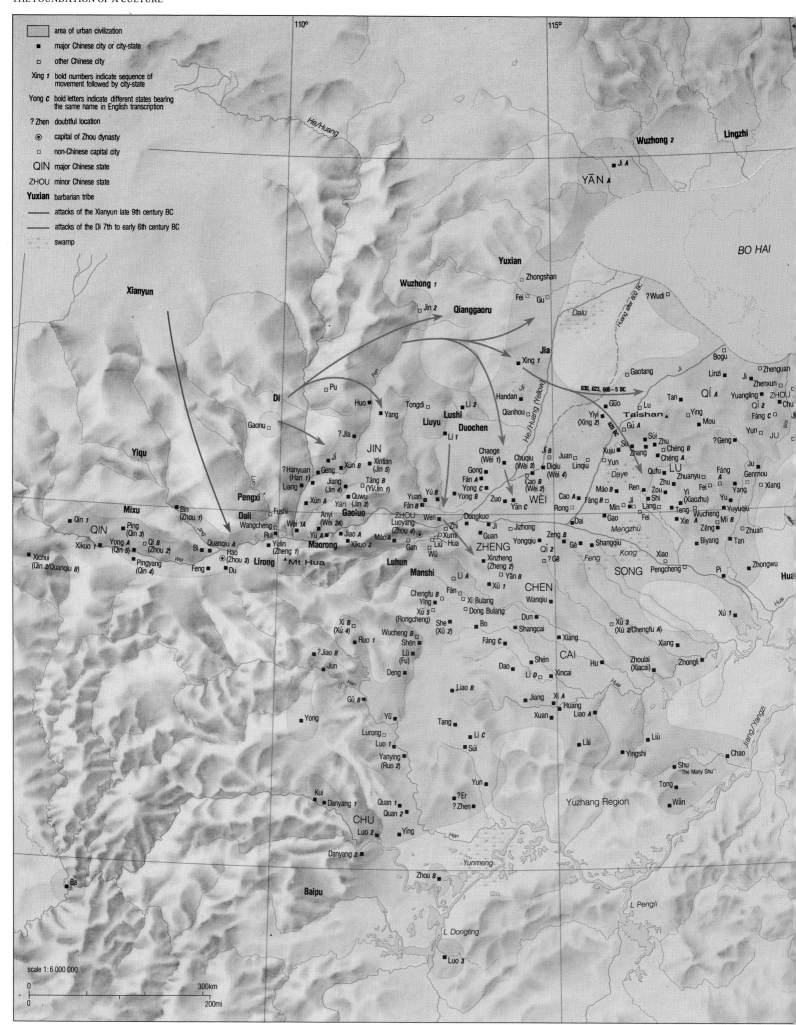

area of urban civilization
■ major Chinese city or city-state
□ other Chinese city
Xing 1 bold numbers indicate sequence of movement followed by city-state
Yong c bold letters indicate different states bearing the same name in English transcription
? Zhen doubtful location
◉ capital of Zhou dynasty
□ non-Chinese capital city
QIN major Chinese state
ZHOU minor Chinese state
Yuxian barbarian tribe
—— attacks of the Xianyun late 9th century BC
—— attacks of the Di 7th to early 6th century BC
⋯⋯ swamp

scale 1:6 000 000

0   300km
0   200mi

had a central location, near to the imperial domain, that was perhaps an advantage at first. Later this became a source of difficulties as strong neighbors pressed upon it from all sides.

Zheng was the earliest of the new states described above, and it coordinated its northern allies to resist a growing menace from the south. This was the state of Chu in the central Yangzi valley, with "mountains for its ramparts and the Han River for its moat." From the end of the 8th century BC Chu pressed northwards, destroying the lesser powers that stood in its way. There thus developed an antagonism between the north and the south that was to be a central theme of diplomacy and warfare for the next 500 years.

2 In the first half of the 7th century BC it was the turn of Duke Huan of Qi, and his famous minister Guan Zhong, to assume the role of hegemon. Qi was in the northeast and owed its primacy in part to leadership of the Chinese against the barbarians. Its economic strength was founded on a salt monopoly, the state-supervised manufacture of iron farm tools, the casting of coins and the control of prices. Guan Zhong developed the institution of the Oath of Alliance which bound the Chinese states together under the hegemon's ascendancy. Although he stressed that "one uses ritual to attract those who are estranged, and charismatic virtue to cherish those who are far away," he had Qi attack states that did not take part in the Oath.

3 Qi's power collapsed in the middle of the 7th century BC when Duke Huan's death led to struggles over the succession. This induced Duke Xiang of Song to try to become hegemon, inspired by delusions of reviving the greatness of the Shang imperial family, of which he was a descendant. Song was a relatively small state between the Yellow River and the upper reaches of the Huai, and too weak to support such an ambitious enterprise. The duke also lost a critical battle with Chu, that he might otherwise have won, because of his quixotic insistence on chivalrous behavior in war.

4 Duke Wen of Jin became hegemon in the later 7th century BC. Jin covered the southern part of what is now the province of Shanxi. Wen had spent 15 years wandering around the rest of China after having refused to fight the army sent against him by his father. He might not have returned had he not been urged on by one of his wives who told him that "to have affections and to live in peace is to destroy your hopes of making a reputation." He came to power with the help of the ruler of Qin, a state lying to the west in the valley of the Wei River.

The spread of cities in China during the Springs and Autumns period
The first half of the first millennium BC saw a dramatic extension of the urban way of life in northern China. Most of the cities marked here as "major" were at some time or another independent city-states, often in the period not long after the turn of the millennium when Western Zhou hegemony began to weaken. As the centuries passed, the majority of them were then absorbed into one or another of the emerging major states.

A characteristic of this early period of urbanization was the geographical mobility of city-states and state capitals. Sometimes this was the result of pressure from powerful Chinese neighbors, as with the southward move of Xǔ to She, its original location having been too close to Zheng for comfort. Sometimes it was designed to evade barbarian attack. Thus in the 7th century BC Wèi moved its capital eastwards from Chaoge to Cao in the hope of escaping from the marauding Di.

Duke Wen was famous for keeping his pledged word, for educating his people and for inflicting exemplary punishment upon aristocrats, "after which the people were submissive." The Zhou emperor formally recognized him as the first of the feudal lords. One of his ministers described Wen's conception of hegemony as "to repay good deeds, to give aid to those threatened with disaster and by so doing to obtain authority." He inflicted a heavy defeat on Chu at the battle of Chengpu.

At about the same time, and slightly later, Duke Mu of Qin exercised a partial hegemony in the west, mostly as a result of his campaigns against the Rong barbarians. Towards the end of his reign, he broke his alliance with Jin as the result of the persuasiveness of the diplomats of Zheng, who had induced him to fear the rising power of his reinvigorated neighbor. In consequence, the north was less able to resist the south than it had been before.

5 The next hegemon was thus King Zhuang of Chu. He flourished around the turn of the 7th and 6th centuries BC. Zheng was conquered, and its duke came out to meet him dressed like a slave, with his shoulders bare. But Zhuang did not follow the counsel of his advisers that "when one captures a state, one shows it no mercy," and allowed Zheng to continue to exist.

Apologists who presented the better side of Chu — often, of course, to buttress some argument of the moment — described it as governed under particularly tight control. When the Chu army was mobilized, it was said, "merchants, artisans, farmers, and storekeepers were not disrupted in the pursuit of their occupations." The king filled high offices with a judicious mixture of his own kinsmen and members of long-established families. He was kind to the old and to strangers. The status divisions in society were carefully observed. It was a matter of fact, too, that the military leaders of Chu were unusually patriotic and imbued with a spirit of self-sacrifice.

King Zhuang was a cautious man. One of his maxims was: "Victory can never be guaranteed. The last king of the Shang conquered a hundred times, but left no heirs," having been beaten — once — by the Zhou. Another of his favorite sayings was: "The people's livelihood depends on their diligence. If they are diligent, they will not be in want." He was also self-critical and modest. One of his ministers once proposed that they should erect a huge mound over a pile of enemy corpses. "I have heard it said," the minister explained, "that if we are to overcome our foes, such things must be displayed to our sons and grandsons, so that they do not forget our military achievements." King Zhuang would have none of this. "To be truly martial," he said, "is to repress violence and put away weapons." He expressed the feeling that, despite his prowess on the field of battle, he had in a deeper sense failed, by not giving the people the peace that they wanted. "What is there," he concluded, "to show our sons and grandsons?"

6 Early in the 6th century BC Jin began to reassert its claim to hegemony. The first duke to try to do so was Jing, and he was not entirely successful. He is chiefly remembered for the terms that he vainly tried to impose on Qi after a victory against that

state. All the furrows in the Qi fields were to be plowed in an east–west direction, presumably to make access easier for the Jin chariots, and the duke of Qi's mother was to be given as a hostage. The Qi diplomatists made Duke Jing look somewhat foolish by pointing out that the kings of former times had always paid attention to the lie of the land as regards plowing, and that surrendering one's mother as a surety was contrary to filial piety. "To act in a fashion different from that of the ancient rulers," they said, "is not righteous. How are you going to become lord of the Oath of Alliance?"

His successor was Duke Diao, who flourished in the second quarter of the 6th century BC. Under the guidance of his minister Wei Jiang, he opened his reign as a model ruler. By acts of grace he remitted debts owed to the state, lightened taxes, showed indulgence to criminals, helped the distressed, reduced state expenditures and only asked the people for labor-services when the heavy farmwork had been done. From the duke downwards, those who had stored goods "gave them out" (how is not quite clear), "so that there was no stagnant accumulation in the state, and no more people in distress."

There was a conservationist and conservative character to Diao's administration. For a time at least, no new bronze vessels were cast, and the existing supply of chariots and clothing (perhaps of the ceremonial sort) was regarded as sufficient. Officials were not promoted beyond what their position in the order of precedence allowed.

Duke Diao's chief weakness was hunting. This earned him a magisterial historical sermon from Wei Jiang on the danger of this passion in rulers. He moderated his indulgence.

As hegemon he used force to make Zheng transfer its allegiance from Chu to Jin, an action that was much criticized. The Zheng diplomatists asserted that "an Oath of Alliance imposed by force has no substance. The spirits do not preside over it." Even some of his own officials were unhappy about it, declaring that "without ritually correct behavior, how can we be the lord of the Oath of Alliance?"

7 By the middle of the 6th century the endless wars between Jin and Chu and their allies had caused a great deal of suffering, and it had become clear that neither side was going to win. Moves in the direction of peace sponsored by the state of Song gained effectiveness as the two chief antagonists increasingly encountered new difficulties. Jin was rent by strife among its great families. Chu was busy fending off the attacks of Wu, a state that had newly risen to power on its flank downstream in the lower Yangzi valley. What in fact emerged from the peace movement was a sort of dual hegemony of Jin and Chu; this proved quite burdensome in terms of tribute for the smaller states.

There were even various proposals for what amounted to disarmament. Zi Han of Song was skeptical of the possibility of any such thing.

It is through the force of arms that Jin and Chu overawe the lords of territories and the lesser states. It is through fear that goodwill and harmony reign between superiors and inferiors. . . . Without fear, there is arrogance. From arrogance disorder is born. . . . Heaven

created the five elements, and the people make use of all of them. It is not possible to do away with one [that is to say, with metal]. Who can abolish the weapons of war? They are an institution of long standing. They are the means by which the lawless are filled with fear, and civilization and virtue able to display themselves. . . . The rise and fall of states, their survival and their extinction, fame and obscurity, all depend on the weapons of war.

In these harsh words we hear the other, and equally authentic, voice of the Springs and Autumns period: a cold-blooded realism contemptuous of the pieties of religion and ritual, a practicality impatient of ethical aspirations not backed by power. An uneasy peace between Jin and Chu nonetheless lasted through most of the second half of the 6th century BC.

8 The outstanding statesman of the later 6th century, and probably of the entire Springs and Autumns period, was Zi Chan, prime minister of Zheng. Confucius, who was not easily moved to praise, said of him that he had some lingering remnant of the compassion that had, the sage believed, prevailed in ancient times.

Zi Chan was of a subtle and skeptical character. "Men's hearts," he once observed, "are no more alike than their faces." When fires broke out in the capital city, and there were demands for sacrifices to prevent their recurrence, he refused. "The ways of Heaven are remote," he said. "Those of men are close at hand. They do not meet. How can the ways of Heaven be known?" There were no more fires. On another occasion, when some dragons had been seen fighting, he again refused to have sacrifices made to them. "We demand nothing of dragons," was his answer, "and they likewise demand nothing of us." His political philosophy is summed up in his advice to his successor: "Only those who possess charismatic virtue can make the people submit by means of gentleness. For those who are less endowed, severity works best. Governing by means of gentleness is hard."

Zi Chan was an administrative innovator and systematizer. He organized farming families into groups, had the fields surveyed and imposed a tax on land (following in this the example of the state of Lu). People of different ranks were made to wear different sorts of clothing. Such policies were unpopular at first, but he persisted stubbornly. "If my measures are to the advantage of the state, I shall make use of them, regardless of whether I live or die in consequence," he said, and added, "It is not possible to make people happy in a self-indulgent way."

Zheng had a system of so-called "rural schools," where people met and sometimes criticized government policies. When it was suggested to Zi Chan that he should abolish them, he demurred. "They are our teachers," he told those who had put forward the proposal. "Why should we destroy them?" He explained that such severity only put a temporary end to grievances. It was like blocking a stream with a dam, behind which the pressure grew until it was swept away. It was better to make small breaches and to let the water trickle through.

He had the criminal laws of Zheng cast on the

Designs after hunting scenes and beasts from an inlaid bronze *hu* of the late Warring States period. The inlay surrounding these shapes on the bronze vessel is now missing so that they stand in slight relief.

surface of bronze caldrons, a procedure that amounted to publishing them. One critic from the state of Jin said that the rulers of ancient times had not promulgated specific criminal laws in this way, "fearing that the people would have a quarrelsome spirit." They had made their judgments on the basis of general principle. Furthermore, the critic added, "If the people know that there are specific laws, they do not feel a respectful awe towards their superiors." Zi Chan did not refute these arguments, merely answering, "I am lacking in talent and will be without influence on future generations. Saving the present age is my concern." Later on, Jin also cast its laws on iron caldrons, so incurring the censure of Confucius. Recent studies on the effects of introducing a written law in various countries around the world suggest that the critics had a better case than perhaps they knew. Written law lacks the flexibility and adaptability to changing circumstances of an oral tradition continuously reinterpreted by elders. It makes the present the prisoner of the past, and thus often creates injustice.

Zi Chan's most delicate task was preserving the independence and dignity of Zheng, which had by now become a relatively weak state. To this end he displayed a diplomatic virtuosity of the highest order, especially towards Jin, expressing a deference that was not subservient, and making a principled resistance to improper demands that was clearly differentiated from disloyalty.

9 The Springs and Autumns period came to a close with the rise of two southeastern states: Wu on the lower Yangzi, and Yue in what is today northern Zhejiang. Both of them were important naval powers, and Wu even used hydraulic warfare to flood cities and force their surrender. Wu's military skills had initially been learned from Jin, which had hoped thereby to cause trouble for Chu. Later, a political refugee from Chu, who wanted revenge, advised Wu to harass the Chu forces by semi-guerrilla tactics before closing for the main engagement. This proved highly successful. Wu also subdued Yue, but its ruler, Fu Chai, did not heed the advice he was given: "When you root out an evil, it is best to do it thoroughly." By allowing Gou Chian, king of Yue, to escape, he caused the eventual destruction of his own state. Fu Chai's aggressive foreign policy then weakened Wu, and it was said that he "regarded the people as his enemy," taxing them heavily to support his wars and personal pleasures. In 473 BC Gou Chian's army defeated him and made an end to his state.

The Springs and Autumns period was, in general, barbaric. Victors in war habitually presented the cut-off ears of their enemies at the temples and butchered living captives to smear their blood on the ceremonial drums. Life and limb were cheap. Geng Yu, lord of the petty state of Jiu, was a connoisseur of swords who enjoyed trying out his new blades on innocent people. Yu Quan of Chu was a devoted minister who forced his king at weapon-point to follow his advice, and then cut off his own feet as a self-inflicted punishment, so proving his loyalty. In the western state of Qin, and elsewhere too, the close political associates of a ruler often committed suicide to follow him in death, or were obliged to do so. Critics disapproved of this practice chiefly because it removed able men from the government. In 496 BC Gou Chian disrupted the tightly disciplined ranks of a Wu army by gruesome tactics. Three lines of convicted Yue criminals were sent forward to stand in front of the Wu lines, holding swords beneath their own necks. They then made the following announcement: "We have violated military discipline. We do not dare to flee from punishment. We do dare to go to our deaths." They then cut their own throats. While the attention of the Wu army was distracted by this macabre spectacle, the Yue forces fell on them suddenly and routed them.

The efforts of statesmen to bring about order, harmony and stability – whether by ritual, or by charismatic virtue, or by the systematic regimentation of civil and military life – have to be seen against this background of brutality. Most of their concepts, such as "charismatic virtue," later became the stock-in-trade of philosophers. They began, however, by being conceived as having a straightforward practical function in these violent and difficult times.

At the risk of anticipating the process of rationalization and the increasingly self-conscious clarification of ideas that only occurred between the 8th and the early 5th centuries BC, we may take as the central text expressing the ethos of the age a statement attributed to Zi Chan by a historical anthologist of the 4th century BC. In it he sets forth the view that morality is based upon nature, and that the ethically perfect society is one that lives in resonance with the regular workings of nature.

Ritual movement is in the constant tracks of the heavenly world. It is in the appropriate correctness of the earthly world. It is in the [proper] practices of the people. The people take as their model the constant tracks of the heavenly and earthly worlds. They take as their model the bright intelligence of Heaven and follow the inherent qualities of Earth. If ethers, elements, flavors, colors or sounds lose their proper proportions, then there is confusion and disorder; and the people lose their inherent qualities. It is for this reason that ritual actions are performed, in order respectfully to keep hold on them.

He then compared the relations of junior kinsmen with the head of their clan to the revolution of the constellations around the pole star. He pointed out that work and government regulations varied according to the seasons. Punishment resembled thunder and lightning. The emotions were the effects of the various ethers or atmospheres. He concluded that "if human joy and grief are felt only at the appropriate times, then it is possible for men to be in accord with the inherent qualities of the heavenly and earthly worlds."

A distinctive feature of this view of the universe was that man, and in particular the government, was an equal partner with heaven and earth. Thus it was possible for a colleague to say to Zhao Wenzi, the prime minister of Jin, "That heaven has not caused any great disasters is due to your efforts." The implications of this way of thinking may be made clearer by what appears to us as almost a caricature of it: the explanation allegedly given by the annalist Cai Mo of Jin as to why there were so few dragons around in China by the late 6th century BC. It had not always been so, he said. "The men of ancient times kept dragons as domestic animals." In general there had to be officials in charge of each sort of beast and devoted solely to it. "If the officials fulfill their duties, numerous animals arrive. If the post is abolished, the animals disappear and hide. Their reproduction stops, and they bring forth no more young." Rearing dragons needed special skills, and for various reasons the line of official dragon-herds had died out. All might still have been well had there been an official in charge of the right element, which was water (since Chinese dragons were aquatic, unlike their fiery Western cousins). But, he said, "because the post of the officer who presides over water has been abandoned, no more dragons are born." Given this human responsibility – or, more precisely, this governmental responsibility – it is easy to see why anomalies in the natural order, such as comets, were of such concern. They could be tokens of moral or ritual inadequacy in rulers, and so portents of disaster. More rarely, they reflected virtue and presaged good fortune.

There were also skeptics. One day in 644 BC five meteorites fell on Song and six birds were seen flying backwards over the capital, probably because of the wind. When the duke asked an annalist from Zhou what these events meant, he was given a political interpretation. Once away from the ducal presence, however, the annalist privately scoffed at such superstitition. "These are natural events," he commented, "and not produced by coming good or evil fortune. Good and evil fortune derive from human behavior." The most impressive example of this tension between ritualism and realism is provided by an exchange between the same duke, Xiang of Song, and his minister Zi Yu. The duke had lost the battle of Hong River in 638 BC because he had refused to attack the Chu army before they had finished crossing and had drawn up in their ranks. When he was criticized, he answered, "A man of lordly qualities does not wound twice. He does not take prisoner enemies with gray hair. Those who made war in ancient times did not ambush their foes in defiles. Although I am but the descendant of the ruined dynasty of Shang, I will not order an attack on troops not drawn up in formation." Zi Yu replied that the duke knew nothing of war. If an enemy was trapped in a defile, that was a gift from Heaven, and to be accepted. Elderly enemies were still enemies. If the first blow was not fatal, not to strike again was equivalent to not having struck at all. The purpose of armies was to be used, and for the state's advantage.

There was a comparable difference of opinion over the importance, in an age when betrayal was commonplace and casual, of keeping one's sworn word. Some saw trustworthiness, especially in international relationships, as "the treasure of the state, and the protection of the people." Others, like Zi Mu, prime minister of Chu, despised such sanctimony. "If we can get what we want," he said, "why should we worry about good faith?"

At the same time, we should not make too much of these conflicts. "Ritual" was seen, in quite mundane terms as the principles of hierarchy and appropriate behavior by which a state and society were ordered. A noble who willfully broke them in an arrogant way might be summarily executed. "Music," which meant dances representing historical events and a variety of celebrations, was both a cosmological magic created by the ruler to "spread harmony among things" and an exercise in applied psychology. It "gave peace to the people's hearts" and "made virtue firm." "Charismatic virtue" was a tangible political asset. A minister who possessed it in abundance was seen as impossible to resist. "Righteousness" was not just intrinsically desirable, but a protection against enmity. "Those who use their strength injustly will soon perish," said the conventional wisdom. The pay-off of these qualities was regarded as obvious. As one Jin statesman observed, "Charismatic virtue and righteousness are the foundations of advantage."

When we compare the Chinese culture of these times with its counterparts in the other regions of the Old World, what is most remarkable is the emphasis placed on human beings rather than on gods or God. There were scriptures, above all the *Songs* and the *Documents*, that were referred to as authorities, but they were "storehouses of righteousness," not divinely revealed instructions. The decisive force was the people, who offered sacrifices to the spirits and were therefore often described, in a striking phrase, as "the hosts of the spirits." It was this cliché that was used by Zi Yu of Song, the realist, to oppose the desire of the duke, a ritualist, for a human sacrifice. "Would there be any [divinities]," he asked, "who would enjoy such an offering?"

Heaven and the spirits could destroy a state with which they were displeased, but it was believed that "Heaven always follows what the people desire." This was a religious way of making a practical point. Yue Qi of Song gave the secular equivalent: "There never was a ruler who could accomplish his ambitions without having the people with him." Zi Chan put it in negative terms: "If one is alone in wanting something, it cannot be done. It is disastrous to oppose the multitude."

The Warring States

The last age of pre-imperial China is known to historical tradition as the "Warring States." The name refers to the unremitting struggles between the seven strongest countries, and above all between Qi in the northeast, Chu in the south and Qin in the northwest, for mastery over the Chinese world. There is no sharp line dividing the two and a half centuries from 480 BC to 221 BC and the preceding Springs and Autumns period, but the overall contrast is dramatic.

Above all, it is a question of scale. There were now cities with hundreds of thousands of inhabitants. One such was Linzi, the capital of Qi: "Linzi is so wealthy and well supplied that all of its inhabitants play the flute, strum the harp, pluck the zither or stroke the lyre. They match gamecocks, race their hounds, gamble and play ball. Its streets are so crammed that the carriages rub rims; and its populace so great that the people rub shoulders." This increase in numbers was based on an extension of the land under agriculture. In the state of Wei, it was said, "all the land between the cottages in the fields and the galleried houses is farmed. Not a foot is turned to pasture or grazing." The conscription of the people let states put huge armies in the field.

In 1978 64 bronze *bian*-bells of the Warring States period were excavated from the tomb of the Marquis Yi in Hubei province. They were discovered in their original position together with stone chimes and a large number of burial objects. Inscriptions on each bell indicate the notes. They are arranged in three rows on an L-shaped frame. The scale of the whole set is not unlike C major, and the range is five octaves. Ancient Chinese music must have sounded something like Balinese music today in which stone chimes and bells play an important part.

Totals of several hundreds of thousands are routinely mentioned in the sources. Even allowing for literary exaggeration, these were enormous forces for that age in the world's history.

War had become a conflict between entire societies. Here is how Su Qin, a semilegendary master of political rhetoric, described the economic burden of mobilization:

> When the sound of war is heard, personal wealth must be diminished to make soldiers rich. Food and drink are rationed to pamper suicide warriors. Carriages are smashed to make firewood. Oxen are slaughtered to feed the armies. . . . The citizens say prayers. The ruler makes offerings. From the most accessible city to the smallest district, altars appear everywhere. Every town big enough to hold a market stops its work in order to maintain the King. . . . [And after it is over] the families of the dead impoverish themselves to bury their kin. Households of the wounded exhaust their wealth to get them medicine, while those left sound drink so heavily and spend so wildly that as much is wasted by them as is spent on the dead and wounded.

Symptoms of this total social involvement were the long walls of pounded earth that, from the 5th century BC onwards, ran for hundreds of kilometers not only between the Chinese states and the northern barbarians, but between the Chinese states themselves, fruits of millions of man-years of conscripted labor.

The technological underpinnings of the new age were iron tools and weapons, cavalry, plow-oxen and more effective methods of warfare and administration. While wrought iron has been found in minute quantities in late Shang dynasty sites, cast-iron tools only became common in the 7th and 6th centuries BC. It was in this latter century that the iron sword replaced the bronze dagger-ax or halberd, and the crossbow was invented. Infantry wore iron armor, such as the face-masks of the foot soldiers of the state of Han. Under the influence of the steppe cultures, horses were now ridden instead of being used merely to pull chariots. The northern state of Zhao made compulsory the wearing of barbarian clothes, notably trousers, the reason being the needs of the military rider. Barbarian mounted archery became a skill delighted in by Chinese noblemen. Siege warfare also made its appearance, with assault towers and tunneling. It was Su Qin's view that "a siege that succeeds in a month or two is an exceedingly short one." Fighting

became a professionalized skill, and treatises were written on the art of war.

Farming was not only improved by iron tools and draft-oxen (these latter a Qin speciality), but also by irrigation systems and drainage canals. These were made possible by the same flair for mobilizing manpower that was apparent in the armies, and in the public roads that now began to crisscross the Chinese world.

The new spirit of government, the search for efficiency without regard for virtue or honor, can be seen in extreme form in the Qin reforms of the middle of the 4th century BC. They are traditionally associated with the name of Lord Shang, a native of Wei who became Qin's prime minister. Lord Shang abolished the ancient aristocracy and created a new military nobility with ranks based on the number of enemy heads cut off in battle. The country was subdivided into administrative districts. The lands formerly farmed by groups of families owing a joint

The armor of the cavalry differed from that of the infantry: tunics were laminated to the waist and large shin guards were worn over leather boots with clothing relatively close fitting. The horses' harness was made of leather straps and bronze rings and knobs.

levy to a fief-holder were converted into private property. The buying and selling of fields was permitted. Peasants who produced harvests above a specified level were exempted from labor-services. Families were formed into groups mutually responsible to the authorities for the good behavior of their members. Movement around the country was only permitted to those who possessed a permit to do so. Idlers, vagrants and criminals were made into state slaves. Weights and measures were standardized. Rewards and punishments were allocated with

a mechanical exactness. The scriptures that formed the basis of education in the other states were destroyed.

To other Chinese the Qin state that resulted from Lord Shang's measures was an object of both admiration and terror. Su Qin spoke of it as ''fat fields, flourishing people, ten thousand chariots, a million mettlesome troops, a thousand miles of rich fallow-land, and an abundance laid up within defensible borders – truly an arsenal of nature, the

most awesome state in the world!'' Zhang Yi, prime minister of Qin in the late 4th century BC, told its king: ''Men fly from the bosom of their parents, and though they have never in their lives seen an enemy, hearing the sounds of war they stamp their feet, bare their chests, and rush upon naked blades or across beds of coals, determined to die in the forefront. Such is the difference between Qin and the [anti-Qin] Alliance.'' But Lu-lian of Qi spoke for most Chinese when he declared that ''the country of Qin has abandoned morality. . . . It has managed its officers by power and its people by slavery.'' And Zhu Ji of Wei was even more savage in his condemnation. Qin, he said, ''shares customs with the barbarians. It has the morality of a tiger or a wolf. It delights in cruelty, is covetous of gain, and knows nothing of good faith, ritual righteousness or virtuous action.''

Qin was exceptional in its systematic approach. But statesmen in other states shared its concern with results, and even expressed a certain cynical pride in their own realism. Typical of this outlook are the words that Su Dai is said to have spoken to the king of Yan: "I am one who works for advance and advantage. I look on incorruptibility as holding no hope for personal success. I look on righteousness as incapable of sustaining my livelihood or securing me a position. Those who practice benevolence and righteousness seek only the way of their own self-fulfillment." And thus there was born, in this age, one of the most enduring tensions in the Chinese soul: the belief that while politics was in many ways the most honorable, desirable and socially praise-worthy calling for a man of ability, it was also of its nature irredeemably contaminating. Here, putting the dilemma very gently, is Yan Chu speaking to the king of Qi who has offered him a position: "Jade is found in the mountains. Only when worked does it flaw. The final product is still valuable, but its pristine wholeness is lost. A country squire comes from a simple life. If he is chosen and accepts emolument, though he is not dishonored, he loses some unity of spirit and person. I prefer to return to my old ways. To eat only when hungry is better than dining on meat. To walk in peace is better than riding in a state carriage."

One further new feature of the age deserves mention. This is the rise of commerce. Its importance can be sensed from the prevalence of metaphors and illustrations drawn from the market-place in literature, though we have little direct information about it. Merchants sometimes rose to high political office, like Lü Buwei in mid-3rd-century Qin. There were toll-barriers on the roads, taxes on traders, written contracts based on matching tallies and many forms of cast coinage issued by the different states. In the northern, western and central regions bronze spade-shaped coins were cast in mints of which 142 have so far been identified. In the east a knife-shaped coin of bronze was the dominant form. The south used cowrie-shaped pieces of bronze for small transactions and stamped bars of gold for larger ones. Towards the end of the Warring States period, round coins with holes in them were issued, the forerunners of the later imperial "cash" strung in strings of a thousand.

Our knowledge of the details of the history of the Warring States period is at best sketchy. Most of the records of the individual countries were destroyed by the First Emperor of Qin in the later 3rd century BC, to prevent them serving as a foundation for a possible renaissance of local patriotisms. Bearing in mind the fragmentary nature of our evidence, and the need to use semi-fictional sources as a supplement, it is possible to distinguish three main chronological phases:

1 The fragmentation of the north (480 BC to about 340 BC)

In the course of the 5th century BC the state of Jin broke into three parts: Zhao, Wei and Han. These states bore the names of three of the six great families that had little by little usurped the effective power of the dukes of Jin. A fourth family, and initially the most powerful, was that of the earl of Zhi. In 454 BC the earl led his own forces and those of the Wei and the Han to attack the Zhao in their stronghold of Jinyang (modern Taiyuan). The immediate cause was a quarrel over the sharing out of lands belonging to the other two great families,

who had been ruined. The real issue, though, was the earl's control of Jin. The siege lasted over a year. A river, deflected from its course to flood the city, came within two meters of the top of the walls. In the laconic formula of the traditional chroniclers, "people exchanged their children to eat." Eventually the leaders of the Wei and the Han realized that, if the Zhao were broken, they would be the earl of Zhi's likeliest next victims. They therefore assassinated him and made peace. The head of the Zhao family had the earl's skull varnished, and used it as a drinking cup.

The state of Wei had a brief moment of glory under Duke Wen, who reigned from 424 to 387 BC. Distinguished men frequented his court, such as Zi Xia, the disciple of Confucius. The duke's respectful attitude towards these worthies is evident in his comment on Duangan Mu: "He is in the first rank for virtue, just as I am in the first rank for power." It was during Duke Wen's reign that Li Ke drew up the Wei code of law that was later to serve as a model for the Han dynasty. Li also originated the idea that the government should buy up stocks of grain in times of plenty and sell them off in times of famine.

After Duke Wen's death Wei was weakened by a civil war and outside pressures. There was a revival in the 350s under King Hui (to give him his usual royal title), but this was halted by a severe defeat at the hands of the state of Qi in 341 BC. Though Wei only survived in an enfeebled condition, King Hui's court became the intellectual center of the age. Among its luminaries were Master Zhuang, the Daoist, and the logicians Master Hui and Gongsun Lun. Mencius, the most famous of the later Confucians, was a visitor.

Han was an even smaller state, but famous for the best crossbows in China and for excellent swords. Late in the 4th century BC Zhang Yi of Qin contemptuously described it to its ruler's face as "narrow, poor and mountainous." Its people, he said, "feed on beans and porridges of pulse. If a single harvest fails, your citizens are happy to fill their stomachs with dregs and lees." Its one major accomplishment was the conquest and absorption of the state of Zheng in 375 BC.

In the northeast the great state of Qi was dominated from the early 5th century BC by the Tian family. They took over formally much later, some time early in the 4th century BC. Their political style is shown by the coup staged by Tian Qi in 490 BC. Having disposed of a duke of whom he did not approve, he produced his chosen replacement from a sack at a banquet he was giving to the leading men of the realm. His son, Tian Chang, is remembered for the proposal that he made to the next duke: "What men desire are benefits. You should take charge of them, my prince. What men fear are punishments. Permit me to inflict them." The duke agreed, and real power fell into Tian Chang's hands. He cemented political loyalties by opening his celebrated harem, consisting of more than a hundred exceptionally tall beauties, to his guests and followers for their pleasure.

Of the rulers of the Tian line, the most remarkable was King Wei. For the first nine years of his reign he attended to none of his duties, lived a life of dissipation and let his ministers run the state as they pleased. Some time around 349 BC he suddenly sprang into political activity, boiled to death a

In the second millennium BC cowrie shells were used as tokens of value before the adoption of bronze as a medium of exchange with intrinsic value for tools and weapons. At Anyang 7000 cowries were found in the tomb of Fu Hao, one of the royal consorts of King Wu-ding of Shang. By the 7th century BC spade- and knife-shaped coins were cast in bronze, marking the introduction of official coinage. The disk coin perforated by a square hole was used in the 4th and 3rd centuries BC and remained the standard medium of small exchanges for the following 2000 years.

Right This representation of a general of the time of the Zhou dynasty is based on excavated material. His boots would have been made of leather with metal studs. The breastplate is bronze, decorated with a *taotie* monster mask. The helmet bears a remarkable resemblance to Roman types.

The Warring States and the rise of Qin, 350-249 BC
The rise of the western state of Qin to the point where it dominated the rest of the Chinese world took about a hundred years, from the middle of the 4th century BC to the middle of the 3rd. Apart from the inability of its victims to ally effectively against it, Qin's advance was based on three sources of strength: the administrative and social reforms of Shang Yang, the acquisition of a rich and secure hinterland in Shu, and the step-by-step seizure of key strategic locations that enabled it to dominate the entrances to the northern Han River valley and to the lower course of the Yellow River where it leaves the mountains. The swiftness of the subsequent seizure of the remaining Chinese states by the First Emperor was made possible by these efforts of his predecessors.

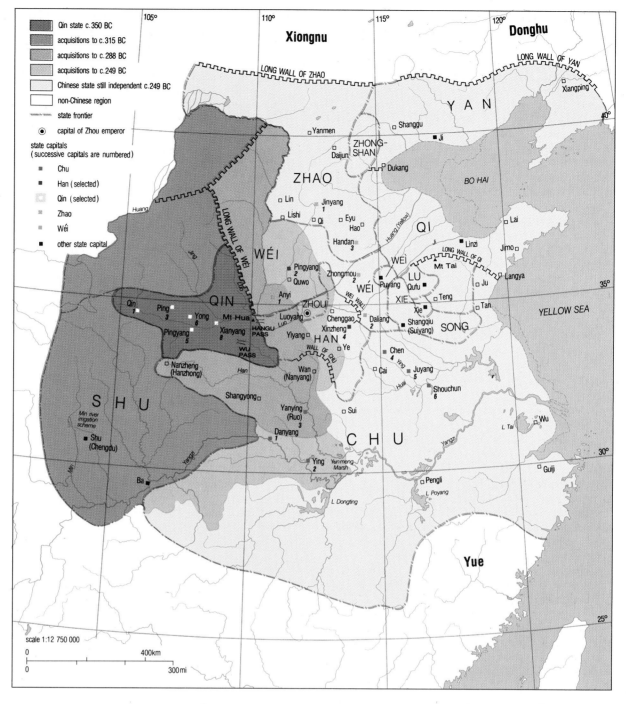

number of incompetent officials and waged a short victorious war against Zhao and Wei. Qi was respected as the most powerful of the states until his death in about 320 BC.

2 The rise of Qin and Chu and the creation of a triangular balance of power (340 BC to about 280 BC) During this period the western state of Qin grew dramatically in strength. This was partly the result of the internal reforms already discussed, and partly of the conquest, during the last years of the 4th century BC, of a large and productive hinterland in what is now the province of Sichuan. About the same time the southern state of Chu acquired a comparable hinterland in the lower Yangzi by destroying the state of Yue. For a time there was therefore a three-way balance of power between Qi, Qin and Chu.

Two series of disasters undermined the strength of Qi and Chu in the second decade of the 3rd century BC and destroyed this equilibrium. In 284

BC an alliance composed of Qin, Chu, Yan, Zhao, Wei and Han attacked Qi. The Yan general Yo Yi then overran the northeastern state with the exception of just two cities, and ruled it as an overlord for six years. In the south, during the last few years of the 4th century BC and the first few years of the 3rd, Qin had inflicted major defeats on Chu and broken into the upper part of the Han River valley, so breaching Chu's natural defenses. This assault was renewed in 280 BC, and two years later the cruel and brilliant Qin general Bo Qi took the Chu capital at Ying. Chu's power fell into a swift decline.

Qi was later reconstituted by the genius of the general Tian Dan, one of the most effective practitioners of disinformation, propaganda and psychological warfare in the history of China; but after about 349 BC there was no longer any political will to resist. Qi enjoyed peace at the price of offering no help to the other states that fell victim to Qin. In 221 BC it was itself to surrender without a fight.

Defeats at the hands of the reformed Qin also had a shock effect on King Wuling of Zhao. Searching for a strategy of survival in the year 307 BC, he ordered the introduction of barbarian clothes (especially trousers) and barbarian mounted archery, as has already been mentioned. Faced with violent criticism that he had betrayed Chinese values, Wuling told his detractors that ''the sage observes the place where he is, and conforms to what is necessary.'' ''As regards the advantage of the state,'' he added, ''it is not always necessary to model ourselves on antiquity.'' By 296 BC the newly strengthened Zhao had conquered the small state of Zhongshan that lay between it and Yan. Most of Zhao's new power was, however, dissipated by the faction fighting that followed King Wuling's ill-judged abdication; and its short-sighted alliance with Qin in the 280s caused it to fight states that were its best potential allies in resisting the growing menace from the west. Soon Zhao too was incapable of offering any serious opposition.

3 The triumph of Qin (280 BC to 221 BC)
As may be seen from the map showing the expansion of Qin after the absorption of the Sichuanese state of Shu in 316 BC, Qin had already made substantial advances beyond its original boundaries by 288 BC. Access both to the north China plain and to the Han River valley was firmly in its hands. The next 40 years witnessed further steady encroachments. It moved up the Fen River valley into present-day Shansi; it edged eastward beyond modern Luoyang; its southern extension, as has already been mentioned, led to the annexation of the historic Chu capital at Ying (present-day Jiangling). Thus by about 249 BC the material preponderance of Qin was becoming overwhelming; its territorial domains, though not all fully developed, were almost equal to all the rest of the Chinese states put together, and its population was probably larger than that of any other single state. Indeed, one of the indications of the depth of the resources available to Qin is that, although during the last 14 years of the conquest some severe military defeats were inflicted on Qin by Zhao and by Chu, these hardly interrupted at all the momentum of the Qin war-machine. During the 240s Qin's supplies of food were increased by two immense irrigation schemes. One was the Min River system on the Chengdu plain; the other was the Zheng Guo canal that ran north of the Wei River, parallel to it, and linking the Jing and the Luo. Iron was another key commodity; and the capture of Shu and then the commandery of Nanrang, just south of Luoyang, had given Qin two of the best ironworking centers in China. The reforms introduced by Shang Yang in the previous century enabled the Qin state to mobilize proportionately more tax-grain, more military manpower and more enslaved or conscripted labor for public works than any of its rivals. It was a crude but effective military-agrarian meritocracy. Significantly, many of Qin's greatest statesmen, such as Yang himself, Lü Buwei and Li Si, who became the most influential minister guiding the work of unification after Lü's fall in 237 BC, were not natives of Qin, and Qin's own aristocracy played a very limited part in government. When King Zheng, the future First Emperor, came to the throne in 246 BC as a boy of 12, he merely continued

through their final phase plans long since developed by his predecessors. The extraordinary rapidity of the conquest during the final decade, from 230 BC to 221 BC, when Han, Wei, Chu, Zhao, Yan and Qi were annexed in succession, should not be allowed to obscure the fact that the total process had taken almost a hundred years.

Looking back on the history of more than two millennia outlined in the preceding pages, we can say that it was during this period that, starting from a Neolithic base that was the common heritage of much of the Old World, the Chinese culture area developed its own distinctive civilization. This was achieved partly through borrowing and partly through original invention, the exact balance still being difficult to determine. The combination of elements was indisputably unique. This deepest characteristic cultural stratum has been eroded and sometimes metamorphosed in subsequent ages, as well as overlaid with other matter. But, to an extent that is probably unequaled elsewhere, it is the foundation of China's cultural landscape even today.

This intricate gold dagger handle was cast by the ''lost-wax'' method, allowing for the openwork style. The compact composition of writhing interlaced animals and scrolled figures abstracted from them is typical of decorative designs of the 5th to 3rd centuries BC.

KINSHIP AND KINGSHIP

Shang society

Chinese society in the Shang and Western Zhou periods can be defined in terms of kinship and kingship. The two institutions were related in several ways, most obviously through the particular pattern taken by the worship of ancestors. Under the Shang, for example, all the Shang people or tribe were regarded as the younger kinsmen of the monarch. He and his deputies alone had the right to sacrifice to all those ancestors – not just dead kings – whose power was believed to continue in existence. They did this as the representatives of the entire community. The Western Zhou sponsored or accepted a multiplicity of ancestral cults in the houses of their vassals, and the vassals in the houses of their subordinates. Their worship, unlike that of the Shang, was strictly limited to the direct line of ascent above the worshiper. In political terms this system corresponded to the decentralized feudalism of the later dynasty. Kin structures and the system of names given to individuals also became more complex. Eventually, in the middle and later Zhou, well-defined families and lineages appeared, organized in elaborate hierarchies of obligation for ancestor-worship and mourning.

Shang kin-groups were distinguished by emblems, halfway between pictures and writing, cast on their ritual bronze vessels to identify them. They show human beings performing various activities, weapons, tools like the double-pronged plowing-stick, buildings, graves and pens for sacrificial animals. These kin-groups were probably associated with particular occupations or obligations to the royal house.

The Shang had genealogies, but no surnames (*xing*). With distinctions between generations but little emphasis on descent from a particular father, there was no concern with the "filial piety" (*xiao*) that was later to be so important. Military units may also have been based on kinship bonds. One of the modern Chinese words for "family" (*zu*), the graph for which shows a flag and an arrow, is derived from a military unit of this time. Kin-groups were typically based in small cities of their own.

Shang kingship was the sacral and religious suzerainty of the royal kin-group. The king was the intermediary between the spirits and the human world. He was believed to be descended from God (*Di*), who ruled the spirits. The word *di* formed part of the posthumous names of the last two Shang monarchs, rulers who had attempted to elevate themselves above the rest of the royal kin-group by rejecting collateral succession in favor of father-to-son succession. A thousand years later it was part of the usual term for "emperor" (*huangdi*).

The importance of the king's religious role is apparent when we recall that, for the Shang, the spirits controlled everything that happened: a queen's headache, a kin-group's harvest, victory or defeat in battle. It was a vital and never-ending task to divine their intentions and wishes, to propitiate their malevolence and to win their favors. Even the weather was scrutinized for its purport. The rainbow, for example, was seen as a two-headed snake that drank the water of the rivers. Its appearance was thought to herald disaster. The winds were magical birds, the messengers of God. The once identical words for "wind" and "phoenix" (*feng*) were later separated by the Chinese when they forgot their common origin.

This sense of spirit-power pervading the universe can be felt in the numinous presence of the Shang bronze vessels used for religious ceremonies. Many of them carry the *taotie* mask, a baleful demon made into the guardian of boundaries, but interpreted by some scholars as the representation of the multiple beings of the world in a single symbol. It is said to have the horns of an ox, the ears of an elephant, the talons of a bird, the eye of a man and the crest of a dragon. Another symbol is the cicada pattern, which represents the return and renewal of life. In contrast, the bronzes of the middle and later Zhou have a secularized feeling, in spite of their use for ancestor-worship, and are decorated, rather than infused with a single vital design. They typically carry inscriptions recording royal gifts and appointments.

The Shang king's assertion of his unique right to sacrifice at certain sacred spots was equivalent to the assertion of his political supremacy. Sometimes embassies were sent out, under armed guard, to perform these rituals at places distant from the capital.

Outside the capital were the cities ruled by the king's relatives, his sons and sometimes his queens. Beyond these, or perhaps interspersed between them, were regions ruled by other powerful tribes who occupied a position between subordinates and allies. The pre-conquest Zhou were one such. Beyond these again were the non-Chinese such as the Jiang and the Nan, thought to be demons who had taken on the form of humans.

Until recently, archaeologists in the People's Republic have been obliged to describe the Shang as a "slave society" in order to conform with political orthodoxy. Most still do so. It is of course probable that some of the population were slaves. Captured Qiang barbarians were put to work tending animals, at which they were expert, or farming. One form or another of compulsion may be assumed. But it seems unlikely that the system of production as a whole was based on slavery. There is no evidence of any regular system of procurement, and war would have been too chancy a basis for an entire economy.

One common argument is that only slavery could have provided both the labor-power needed to build the huge Shang tombs and the victims for the large-scale human sacrifices. It is more likely, however, that the temporary conscription of subordinate kin-groups provided the labor for tomb construction, as it did for other services, and it is fairly certain that the majority of those murdered to accompany funerals were non-Chinese prisoners of war.

Other arguments turn on the interpretation of oracle texts, and notably on the word *jong*, which in later times can be translated as "the multitude" or "the masses." Some texts refer to them in connection with farming and construction works. That they were not slaves, however, is clear from the following considerations: (1) the *jong* were closely connected with the king's person; (2) they were involved in warfare, and sometimes went to frontier areas; (3) they were the subject of royal acts of divination, as were members of the royal household and some groups of officials; (4) they were linked with a school and training of some sort; and (5) the words describing what the king did to them are "assemble," "call," "collect together" and "take along," never "buy," "sell" or "give." They were possibly a military guard intermittently convened for a variety of purposes.

Under the Zhou, however, there are a number of inscriptions on bronzes that refer to royal gifts of cities, retainers, kin-groups, commoners, overseers and slaves, and servants and prisoners of war. There are also a few references to the sale of persons, and to the losers of lawsuits paying with people and lands as compensation. What seems in general to have happened is that a dynasty of conquest had imposed, on top of the old ordering of society by tribes and kin-groups, an aristocracy that was based on large holdings of land, enfeoffment and a mainly hereditary succession to government office. The result was a system that combined elements of collective feeling and action with elements of subordination and servility, probably in a great variety of ways.

This rural world of the early first millennium BC can be glimpsed in parts of the scripture called the *Songs*. We read of farmers weeding in "thousands of pairs," "in long, long rows" and "in crowds" to grow the grain from which alcohol was produced for ritual offering to the ancestors. There are clear indications of a hierarchy of authority, headed by "the descendant," who was presumably the chief of the clan. Other songs mention an "inspector of the fields," and describe the workers as "farm laborers," "our multitude" and even (if the translation is correct) as "dependants." One poem compares the possession, or at least the use, of human beings to that of land.

People have their lands and fields. . . .
People have their commoners.

That such subordination is unlikely to have been slavery is indicated by lines in another song that is a calendar of the year's activities.

In the second month is the hunting-meet,
Where we keep up *our skills in war.*

For ourselves we take the younger boars,
But offer the fully grown to *our lord.*

Slaves are not often fighting men. Further evidence of the collective life was the community feast, held in the public hall at the end of the farming year to honor the ancestors, and there were also community archery competitions.

A sense of the moral superiority of living together in this way remained with the Chinese throughout their history, though the number who practiced it became progressively fewer in later ages. Many dynasties, down to the Mongols in the 13th century, gave awards to lineages who lived together for many generations, holding their property in common and eating together. There may be here a thread of idealism that links the archaic past with the impulse to collectivization under the Communists, though Communism is of course hostile to kinship bonds.

This way of life largely disintegrated during the middle of the first millennium BC. The new basic social unit of the Springs and Autumns period, and of the Warring States, was the three-generation family. This sort of family functioned on the principle that a man's grown sons and their children continued to live with him until his death. It was evidently linked with the appearance of private property in land, its division and inheritance on the owner's death and the growing emphasis placed on filial piety and obedience.

In the state of Qin in the middle of the 4th century BC, Shang Yang tried to destroy the three-generation family. His object was to strengthen state power by weakening paternal authority and to increase state revenue by inducing the formation of more farms. He decreed that any commoner who had two or more grown-up sons, and who did not give the extra sons their share of the property so that they could leave him and set up on their own, was to have his taxes doubled. Later writers contrasted Qin unfavorably with other states where respect for the father was much stronger. In the 2nd century BC the statesman-philosopher Jia Yi wrote:

Lord Shang abandoned ritual and righteousness. He forsook human-heartedness and the sense of obligation. He set hearts upon advancement and advantage. After this policy had been pursued for 20 years, the customs of Qin were falling in ruin. If a Qin family were rich, it would send its grown sons off on their own with a share of the property. If it were poor, the grown sons would be sent off as superfluous. If sons lent their father even a tilth-spreader or a toothed cultivator, their faces would assume an expression of virtue. If their mothers took so much as a basket or a broom from them, they would immediately speak to them abusively. Their wives would hug their children and feed them, but towards their fathers-in-law they would be grasping and arrogant. Wives and mothers-in-law found no pleasure in each other's company, but would take stock of each other with their lips pursed. In caring only for their offspring, and in their enjoyment of profit, they were not far removed from animals.

From Jia Yi's condemnation of Qin it is possible to imagine, in contrast, something of the nature of the patriarchal family in the rest of China. It became and stayed the center of society. Nowhere is this more obvious than in Confucius' famous rebuke to the self-styled "duke" of She. The "duke" had boasted that in his domain there was a man called Upright Gong who was so honest that he had borne witness

Human and animal figures on a wooden musical instrument excavated from a Chu tomb in Xinyang, Henan, c. 4th–3rd century BC. There is a strong contrast between the arts of Chu and those of the northern states. The *Songs of the South* are a good source for Chu beliefs, and images of strange spirits of heaven and earth abound.

against his father for stealing a sheep. "In my country," said the sage, "the upright men are of quite another sort. A father will screen his son, and a son his father."

Zhou kingship: ritual and realism

The Zhou monarchy began as a dynasty of conquest, as we have seen. Perhaps for this reason it was both obliged to be more accommodating than the Shang towards those whom it ruled, and to work out a more explicit justification for its actions, as well as devising – in a more self-consciously aware fashion – a structure of government. The character of Zhou feudalism is well expressed in many of the bronze inscriptions recording the relationship of the recipients with the king. Thus the Great Tetrapod of Yu (which stands over a meter high) commemorates King Kang's gifts of lands, persons and regalia to a certain Yu on the occasion of his appointment to authority over the Rong barbarians, together with the following exhortation:

> Yu! The grand and illustrious King Wen received the great mandate of Heaven. King Wu succeeded him and created the state. He swept away evil, possessed the four quarters far and wide, and corrected their people. . . . Heaven watched over him and protected him. . . . I take as my model the upright virtue of King Wen, and wish to follow the principles ordained by him. I now command you, Yu, to be of assistance to me. Respectfully strengthen my virtue and correct action. Attend tirelessly morning and evening to offer your criticism. Give me your good offices, and be fearful with the fear of Heaven.

In addition to this feudal element there was also a measure of bureaucracy. This can be seen in the creation of officials whose titles at least expressed quite specific responsibilities, such as the minister for forests.

According to Western Zhou ideas, the king was the "counterpart" of Heaven or God. He was a "law," a "model" or a "pattern" to the people and states of the earth below. He was an exemplar to whose manifest virtue they responded, and a teacher. The king was also meant to be "accommodating" and "concordant" towards his subjects, "responding to the world," in the phrase of the *Songs*. He had to "keep good faith with the people" and to be "the one in whom the people find rest." He and his vassals were those who set the world in order, building walls and marking out and sharing out the fields for farming. He was also "the host to the hundred spirits," making them offerings and "obedient to the dead princes of the clan." These were the ancestors who watched over him, received his sacrifices and listened to the musical performances that he arranged, descending from Heaven in order to do so. There were many rituals

surrounding the monarchy, but their nature is now largely obscure. Perhaps the most important was the so-called *biyong*, which involved a sacred building surrounded by water, ritual fishing by the king from a boat and the sacrifice of fish, symbols of fertility.

In the course of the 9th century BC the Zhou kings began to have trouble controlling the aristocrats. Amid disorders and natural disasters, there was a feeling that the old society was crumbling. The rulers had a growing sense of their own failure, and there was a pervasive fear of Heaven's anger. This is very evident from both the bronzes and the songs of the time:

> To no spirit have we not offered sacrifice,
> Nor begrudged the killing of victims.
> Our ritual jades have all been given
> – Why does no spirit hear us?

After the 8th century and the decline of the power of the Zhou house, the political culture expressed in the ritual bronze vessels also weakened and then virtually disappeared. The high officials and then the independent rulers of the Springs and Autumns states took over many of the royal ceremonials. Thus there is a bronze recording how the count of Qi enfeoffed the commander of his armies with 300 districts, and horses, chariots, weapons and 350 families of serfs. From the late 6th century BC we have a bronze from the state of Qin that appropriates the doctrine of the Zhou kings on behalf of a nominally subordinate state:

> The duke of Qin said: Grand and illustrious are our august ancestors. They received the mandate of Heaven and dwelt in the tracks of [the sage-emperor] Yu. The 12 former dukes live in the place of God. They watch strictly over the mandate of Heaven, and protect their Qin, ruling in brilliant fashion over barbarians and Chinese. Though We are but a child [in comparison], We augustly wield our bright virtue . . . and correct the countless people. We nurture successive generations of knights. . . . We subdue states that do not come to court. We are reverent in the sacrifices, make ritual vessels for our ancestors and thus follow our august forebears.

By this time, however, the Zhou conception of kingship based on a culture of rituals was only a little more than a revered memory. The harsh pragmatism of the Warring States era was at hand.

The ideal of the true king, who rules not by force but by power of virtue and example, became deeply rooted in later Chinese thought. As the more complex historical reality faded from men's minds, it was in the ritually based kingship of the early Zhou that they sought their chief assurance that such rulers had in fact once existed, and could therefore perhaps do so again. Already in Confucius (551–479 BC) we find a restorationist fervor at odds with what was evidently a prevailing mood of skepticism: "If it is possible to make a state by means of rituals and deference, what more is there to be said on the matter? But if it is not possible to make a state by means of rituals and deference, of what use are rituals?"

Bronze Age Art

The Bronze Age

The earliest bronzes attributable to the Shang dynasty come from a site at Erlitou in Henan dating from the 19th century BC. They are thin walled, have narrow bands of sparse ornament using thread lines in relief, and were made in piece-molds. The Shang capital was moved several times and the last capital was at Anyang (c. 13th–12th century BC). In the present-day village of Xiaotun the ancient walled city of Anyang, south of the river, and a ritual site and many tombs on the north bank have been excavated. Among recently excavated tombs, that of Fu Hao, a royal consort of the early 12th century BC, was intact and included over 400 bronzes, weapons, many jades, stone and ivory carvings inlaid with turquoise, and 7000 cowrie shells (probably used as money). The bronze vessels were used for ritual purposes as containers for offering sacrifices to the ancestors. A set of cooking vessels is inscribed with the characters "Fu Hao"; judging by the soot stains on the legs and bottom of the range, these vessels were for daily use. The tomb also contained 16 human sacrifices.

The decoration of the Shang bronzes consisted of geometric and spiral motifs and imaginary beasts such as the *taotie* monster mask and *kui* dragon arranged in well-defined zones. In the later Shang bronzes the abstract elements forming the masks and dragons are often dismembered and set against squared spirals called *leiwen* or thunder pattern by the Song antiquaries. The seams caused by the joins in the piece-molds were turned into decorative flanges which reach their greatest elaboration in the Zhou period. A small number of bronzes have more realistic depictions of animals and in rare instances a human head survives.

The earliest of the Western Zhou bronzes were similar to those of late Shang, but certain new shapes such as the *gui* vessel were introduced and others discontinued. The proportions of the Shang vessels with their uplifted profiles became increasingly bottom-heavy in the Zhou period. Patterns were simple in some cases and elaborate in others, with exaggerated hooked flanges on the sides of vessels. Created bird designs became increasingly popular. By the late 10th century the abstract geometric elements of *taotie* mask break up into individual shapes, leaving the symbolic eye to indicate that the pattern was still zoomorphic. The patternizing tendency developed and subordinated individual motifs into an all-over pattern. The *taotie* mask was no longer the main feature of the design. Purely abstract designs replaced the birds, dragons and animal masks, and swept in restless movement, breaking free from the symmetrical rigidity of earlier Shang models. Large wave-like motifs undulated around the entire vessel, regardless of the divisions of the bronze created by the piece-mold which up to this period held the designs within well-defined boundaries.

The continuous wave pattern survived into the

8th century. Dragon motifs intertwine, replacing the interlacing ribbons of the earlier period, and units are reduced in size forming a unified surface pattern. The so-called Liyu style belongs to this type. It is named after a village in Shanxi where a bronze hoard was discovered. This contained bronzes showing animal forms reminiscent of the art of the steppes, together with the bronzes showing interlacing dragons in high relief against a plain ground. The Houma excavations in the southwest of Shanxi show bronzes of the Liyu style and also inlaid wares which were to dominate bronze decoration of the succeeding period. The bronze foundry excavated at Houma shows that stamps were used for repetitive designs; this had not been the case in Shang times when the most minute spirals were individually executed by hand.

The rise of the feudal kingdoms saw a greater diversity of bronze styles displaying eccentricities and individual characteristics of different areas. An important bronze culture developed in the south, centered on the Yangzi valley, with richly ornamen-

Above Among the sacrificial food vessels of the late Shang the *ding* holds pride of place. Its feet are said to symbolize the power, upright government and stability of the state—remove one and it topples. The flat legs take the form of *gui* dragons. This example is inscribed with the name of Fu Hao, a royal consort buried at Anyang in Henan province in the early 12th century BC.

Right Jade objects were highly prized in Shang times and aristocrats were buried with their most precious jade possessions. The practice continued in succeeding dynasties.

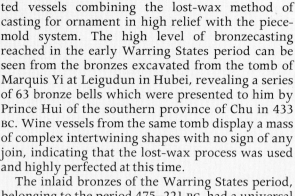

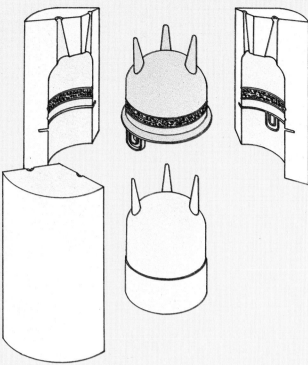

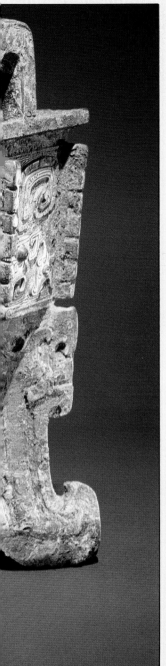

Above The great advantage of the piece-mold system was the clarity of decoration. This method, used elsewhere for implements, was unique to China for making large vessels. The lost-wax method was also used in which the model was made of wax, then surrounded with clay. When fired, the wax melted and flowed out, and molten metal replaced it. It seems that the piece-mold technique was the major method used in the pre-Shang and Shang dynasty bronzes, the lost-wax process being used possibly in combination with the piece-mold system for the more intricate interlace and overlapping designs and open work on bronze objects of the Eastern Zhou period.

The piece-mold method of bronze casting was as follows:
1 A mold for the bronze object was made by pressing clay to the surface of a model which included the broad elements of the pattern.
2 When dried the mold would be cut from the model and the fine details of the design carved into the leather-hard clay.
3 The mold and case were fired.
4 The pieces of the mold were then assembled upside down in a frame to receive the molten bronze.
5 After the cast had cooled the mold would be removed and the bronze polished and inlaid in some cases with pigment.

ted vessels combining the lost-wax method of casting for ornament in high relief with the piece-mold system. The high level of bronzecasting reached in the early Warring States period can be seen from the bronzes excavated from the tomb of Marquis Yi at Leigudun in Hubei, revealing a series of 63 bronze bells which were presented to him by Prince Hui of the southern province of Chu in 433 BC. Wine vessels from the same tomb display a mass of complex intertwining shapes with no sign of any join, indicating that the lost-wax process was used and highly perfected at this time.

The inlaid bronzes of the Warring States period, belonging to the period 475–221 BC, had a universal appeal which resulted in their stylistic dominance over a vast area, unifying and bringing together regions which had produced such a variety of styles during the early Eastern Zhou period. Although the art of inlay was practiced in the Shang Dynasty when turquoise was used, the inlay style did not become popular in China until the 6th century. Designs to receive inlay were cut into the piece-mold. It has also been suggested that the metal inlays were cast onto the surface of the vessels by fixing the silhouettes to the outer mold. Copper, gold and silver were used for pictorial inlaid bronzes depicting figures of gods, men, beasts, trees and buildings arranged in zones. The art of artificial patination to darken the gold surface of the bronze so that the inlay of gold and silver would stand out was probably known at this time. Malachite and turquoise were also used and color became the main decorative feature with dark green malachite set off against a background of red copper. From the mid-4th century BC to the beginning of the Former Han period in 206 BC inlaid bronzes may be divided into two main areas: metropolitan China and south China. Inlay patterns became increasingly light and gold curves in thin wiry lines take on a jewel-like quality. From this time onwards inlaid bronzes tend towards refinement and precision. In south China curvilinear designs have more in common with lacquered wooden objects and painted silks than with the geometric patterns of the metropolitan area.

Jade

Jade has been highly valued in China for its strength and purity from Neolithic times. The main source of the stone was Khotan in central Asia and the sources and technique of jade carving were passed from the Neolithic to the Shang period. It is an extremely hard stone and difficult to work. Craftsmen are said to have handled and studied a piece of stone for years before starting to work on it, by grinding it down with the aid of abrasive sand. Jade surviving from Shang and Zhou tombs is either white or yellowish in color and more rarely grayish green. It was used for ritual ornamental and funerary purposes, and decorated with superficial incisions that followed the general trends of bronze decoration. Due to the difficulties of carving, emphasis was placed on the shape and silhouette of the object. Small jade animals from the early 12th-century tomb of Fu Hao at Anyang are surprisingly life-like, though the main joints of the body are incised with abstract geometric ornament. By the Zhou period an increasing refinement was shown in textured surfaces and in the late Warring States period the quality of workmanship and skill required to form the openwork designs in jade were never surpassed.

Lacquer

Lacquer is the pure sap from the lac tree that grows in west China in Sichuan and Yunnan. It was mixed with color and painted in thin layers onto wooden objects. Lacquer may have been used as an adhesive for the turquoise inlaid bronzes of the Shang period and earlier impressions of lacquer have been discovered in Shang tombs, the wooden objects having decayed. Lacquer survives as painted decoration on wooden vessels in the Warring States period, and was highly valued. The tomb of the Marquis Yi at Leigudun in Hubei of the early Warring States period contains furniture, food vessels in the shape of animals and musical instruments decorated in lacquer. The inner coffin is painted in abstract designs of yellow, black and red, with horned monsters carrying halberds occupying the central panel either side. A stag is painted in a diaper pattern of feather and dots, and a lacquer food container imitates both bronze shape and decoration. These designs transform to the swirling lines more suited to the brush which in turn influenced the decoration of inlaid bronzes in the later Warring States period.

Inset right An inscription on this early Western Zhou bronze (c. 11th century BC) records attacks made on the Shang.

Inset center A ritual bronze vessel of the 5th century BC in the "Liyu style," characterized by the layers of interlaced dragons enlivened with geometric designs.

Inset left A monster (*taotie*) mask set over a ring is found on bronze vessels and wooden coffins of the

Warring States period. In the late 6th century the mask reappears, probably as a deliberate allusion to Shang ritual.

Right This rhinoceros, of the late 3rd century BC, discovered in Shaanxi province, was used as a wine-container. The decorative patterns were once inlaid.

Below A knee-high lacquer-stag excavated from the tomb of the Marquis Yi (c. 5th century BC) in Hubei province.

THE EMPIRE OF QIN

The mandate of Heaven

The Qin unification in 221 BC is customarily seen by historians as the beginning of a new age – the Chinese empire – that lasted until 1911 AD. Looking back on these two millennia from the present, when the empire has vanished and it seems that a long chapter of history has closed, there is some justification for this view. But in many ways the unification is better understood as the culmination of the ideas and institutions developed during late archaic times, as an end as much as a beginning.

The Qin state was more than 500 years old at the time of its triumph, and its rulers, in their own view, had long since received the mandate of Heaven. This is evident from the Qin bronze inscription quoted in a previous chapter. When King Zheng, posthumously called "First Emperor," and in his lifetime just "Emperor" (huangdi), gave thanks for his victory over the other six rival states, he spoke of having "relied upon the magical powers of our ancestors," and gave them the retrospective title of "August Exalted Sovereigns" (taishanghuang). It was only the Han emperors who followed the Qin, but had no such prestigious genealogy to invoke, who spoke instead of "relying on the magical powers of Heaven and Earth."

Later Han dynasty historians implied that Zheng had claimed a new mandate from Heaven, but this is unlikely to have been the case. To have done so would have been a slur upon his illustrious forebears. Nor is it likely, as the Han historians also asserted, that he saw his rise to world dominion as part of a cyclical process determined by the succession of the five elements or "phases" (wu xing), linked with particular colors and numbers. This too would have been an affront to the royal ancestors, by giving the credit to King Zheng alone. Worse still, it would have implied an eventual end to the sway of the Qin house, and the First Emperor stated explicitly that he expected his line to endure for ever.

The public conception of the awe-inspiring but far from universally welcomed achievement of unification that the First Emperor and his minister Li Si wished to propagate was set forth in a number of inscriptions that they had engraved, mostly on the summits of the mountains visited by the emperor during tours of his new domains. The earliest of them – that on Mount Yi in what had long before been the state of Zou – stressed the imperial gift of peace and the justification thereby of universal monarchy:

The state established by the emperor
Is the foremost since all ages past,
Descendant of a line of many kings.

He has rooted out disorder and rebellion,
With authority effective to the world's four
    bounds,
And military justice undeviating and exact.

When his soldiers and officials received his
    decrees,
Only the briefest time elapsed
Before they had smashed the six unruly powers.

In the six and twentieth year of his reign
He offered up announcement of his august title,
Making the way of filiality brilliant and
    manifest.

Since presenting them with the great
    accomplishment
And bestowing below the benefits of his
    complete devotion,
He has traveled in person to distant places.

Having climbed to the summit of Mount Yi,
The retinue of officials following him
All think on things far-off but once long-lasting.

They recall the age of disordered confusion
When the land was divided and separate states
    established,
So opening wide the fissures of strife,

When assaults and battles every day arose,
And blood flowed on the plains,
As it had since earliest antiquity.

For generations past all count
Till the time of the Five Emperors
None could forbid it or make it stop.

Not until now, when this our emperor
Has made the world one family,
And weapons of warfare are lifted up no longer.

Natural disasters and man-made hurts are gone,
The black-haired people live robust and
    peaceful,
Profits and rich resources last for ever. . . .

The inscription on Mount Tai describes the emperor's role as a giver of laws and instruction, and expresses the characteristic Chinese notion of kingship based upon charismatic virtue, both in the sense of an influential moral presence and as an all-pervading magical life-giving power:

The way of government proceeds and takes
    effect,
So all things born obtain what suits them best,
And each thing has its proper law and pattern. . . .

The norms of his instruction reach abroad,
Distant and close alike observe good order,
Accepting the sage-ruler's will.

The inscription on the terrace of Mount Langya in Shandong paints a portrait of the ideal sovereign, drawing on a mixture of Confucian, legalist and

Above The armor of the Qin dynasty was brightly colored according to traces of pigment painted on clay soldiers excavated near the tomb of Qin Shihuangdi ("First Emperor of Qin"). There were several color schemes for the infantry. One group wore bright green tunics with purple-edged collar and cuffs under black laminated armor with white studs, purple straps and yellow buckles together with dark blue trousers with black shoes and orange laces. Another group had short red coats with pale blue patterned collars and cuffs. Its armor was of dark brown plates with red or light green rivets and orange cords. The reconstructed drawing shows the elaborately colored armor of an infantry officer.

Right: Structure of the Qin government.

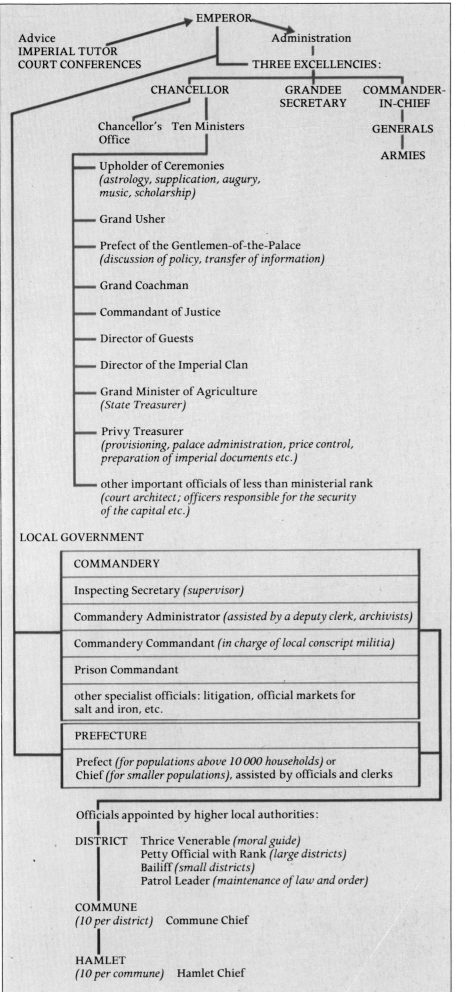

Advice
IMPERIAL TUTOR
COURT CONFERENCES

EMPEROR

Administration

THREE EXCELLENCIES:

CHANCELLOR

GRANDEE
SECRETARY

COMMANDER-
IN-CHIEF

GENERALS

ARMIES

Chancellor's Office   Ten Ministers

- Upholder of Ceremonies
  (astrology, supplication, augury, music, scholarship)

- Grand Usher

- Prefect of the Gentlemen-of-the-Palace
  (discussion of policy, transfer of information)

- Grand Coachman

- Commandant of Justice

- Director of Guests

- Director of the Imperial Clan

- Grand Minister of Agriculture
  (State Treasurer)

- Privy Treasurer
  (provisioning, palace administration, price control, preparation of imperial documents etc.)

- other important officials of less than ministerial rank
  (court architect; officers responsible for the security of the capital etc.)

LOCAL GOVERNMENT

COMMANDERY

Inspecting Secretary *(supervisor)*

Commandery Administrator *(assisted by a deputy clerk, archivists)*

Commandery Commandant *(in charge of local conscript militia)*

Prison Commandant

other specialist officials: litigation, official markets for salt and iron, etc.

PREFECTURE

Prefect *(for populations above 10 000 households)* or Chief *(for smaller populations)*, assisted by officials and clerks

Officials appointed by higher local authorities:

DISTRICT Thrice Venerable *(moral guide)*
          Petty Official with Rank *(large districts)*
          Bailiff *(small districts)*
          Patrol Leader *(maintenance of law and order)*

COMMUNE
(10 per district) Commune Chief

HAMLET
(10 per commune) Hamlet Chief

---

even Daoist ideas. The emperor is at the same time the wielder of magical moral powers, who vivifies both the human and the natural world, the supreme educator, and a hardworking disciplinarian giving precise, explicit shape to institutions and undertakings, his right to do so justified by the benefits that he confers on ordinary people. The passion for social uniformity is also evident and so is the belief in the importance of hard work and decorum:

> He makes rules and measures just and fair;
> He is the regulator of all beings.
> He thus illumines the affairs of men,
> And brings son and father together in concord.
> His sage's wisdom, altruism and justice
> Make bright and clear the principles of the Way.
>
> The merit of the emperor
> Is toiling diligently at basic matters.
> He exalts farming, ends derivative occupations;
> It is the black-haired folk whom he enriches. . . .
>
> Vessels and tools have identical measurements,
> Documents are written in a single script.
> Wherever sun and moon shine down,
> Wherever boats and carts proceed,
> Everyone lives out his allotted span,
> And there is no one but attains to his desires.

The other inscriptions add a few new emphases. The encomium on Mount Zhifu talks of the "emperor's sorrow for the masses" and how he had "been the salvation of the black-haired folk." That cut on the gates of the city of Jieshi depicts the sovereign as giving even its physical shape to the world, at least in some measure:

> He had both inner and outer walls pulled down,
> And waterways and dikes were opened;
> Leveled away were the dangerous defiles.
>
> Once the form of the land had been determined,
> The black-haired multitudes had no corvée labor,
> And all below Heaven were cherished.

The inscription carved on Mount Guiji in the southeast shows the ruler's right and duty to frame binding definitions.

> When the sage of Qin succeeded to the dynastic government
> He first determined punishments and categories,
> And clearly set forth the old standards.
>
> He first made equitable rules and model forms,
> Distinguishing, after inquiry, between each post and duty,
> So as to establish routine norms. . . .
>
> He sets into motion and regulates the multitude of things;
> He scrutinizes the substance of events,
> That each may bear its proper name. . . .

With only slight changes, this general conception of what a supreme ruler should be like has dominated the Chinese political imagination down to and including the time of Chairman Mao Zedong.

The way of government

This was the rhetoric. What were the distinctive features of the early Chinese empire considered as a working political system?

First and foremost, it was a bureaucracy. That is to say, it was a political, administrative and military machine the component parts of which were human beings assigned to perform particular functions and selected for their presumed ability to do so. It was paid for by compulsory taxes and labor-services levied from a registered population. In its essential conception it was therefore opposed to feudalism, considered as a system of power devolved from superiors to inferiors on the basis of lifelong and usually inherited loyalties and obligations that existed, or were supposed to exist, between individuals as individuals, typically lords and vassals. The major exception to the ban on the inheritance of political power was of course the imperial position itself; there were a few other minor privileges passed on from one generation to the next. The bureaucracy was likewise distinct from a household type of government in that specific functions were in principle the responsibility of specific functionaries. Lastly, it was systematized and formalized in that its business was done on the basis of written rules and through the medium of written documents.

Under the First Emperor the rejection of administrative feudalism was explicit. Previous Qin rulers had on occasion practiced various forms of enfeoffment both of high officials and of their own sons. Thus when Lü Buwei was prime minister he had been ennobled as the marquis of Wenxin and given 100 000 households in the Luoyang area "to eat," as the contemporary term so bluntly described what may be called a "revenue fief" (as opposed to one administered by the recipient). The experience of the pre-unification rulers with the institution of administrative feudalism had been far from comfortable. One royal prince who had been made marquis of Shu (in conquered Sichuan) had been executed for allegedly plotting rebellion. Early in King Zheng's own reign the newly elevated marquis of Changxin, of whom it was said that in his fief "all matters great and small were decided by him," rose in revolt and was put down with difficulty.

The moment of decision came in 221 BC, when Chancellor (or Prime Minister) Hang Wan and others proposed setting up the emperor's sons as "kings" in the far northeast, the east coast and the central Yangzi on the grounds that these places were far away and that there would otherwise be no means of controlling them. This suggestion was successfully attacked by Li Si in a famous speech:

The sons and younger brothers and other agnatic relatives to whom Kings Wen and Wu of the Zhou dynasty gave fiefs were extremely numerous. Subsequently the links between them grew loose and they became estranged, attacking each other as if they were enemies. Even more did the feudal lords [of the Springs and Autumns period] exterminate each other. The Zhou Son of Heaven was incapable of stopping them. Today, through your majesty's divine magical powers, the lands within the seas have been united, and all are commanderies of prefectures. The royal princes and

meritorious officials should have bestowed upon them rich rewards drawn from the state's tax revenues. Since they will then be easy to control, and there will be no divergent ideas in the empire, this is the way to secure peace. Setting up lordships will not lead to this end.

In 213 BC several Confucian scholars proposed that feudalism should be restored. They argued that the Shang and the Zhou dynasty had owed their long survival to their enfeoffing their junior relatives to serve as "props and cart-supports" of the royal house. They concluded, "We have never heard of anything lasting long that did not take antiquity as its teacher." Li Si countered by saying that times were continually changing, and that "if the scholars do not take the present as their teacher but instead study the past, using it to criticize the present age, they will confuse the black-haired people and throw them into disorder." This led to one of the barbaric acts of policy for which Li Si and the First Emperor have been hated ever since. With the exception of books on farming, medicine and divination, all writings on philosophy and all historical records except those of the state of Qin were systematically destroyed, and the execution was ordered of anyone who ventured to quote them.

This did not mean the end of feudal tendencies in Inner China. The Han dynasty, which was much weaker in its early years than the Qin had been, felt obliged to reintroduce a number of apanages for imperial relatives and supporters of the new house. Seven of these semi-independent kingdoms rose in revolt in 154 BC, and after they had been suppressed the bureaucratic principle was reimposed on the feudal areas. Much of Chinese political history for the next thousand years or so can be seen as a tug-of-war in practice between locally based, and often hereditary, powerholders and an administration trying to assert an effective central control. This struggle took many forms, and the fortunes of the sides varied greatly from time to time, while the basic superiority of the centralizing principle to some extent also remained open to doubt. As late as the early 9th century AD, a time when much of the country was dominated by semi-independent military governors, the philosopher Liu Zongyuan felt impelled to write an essay "On Feudalism," insisting on the value of a bureaucratic state. Even in 1052 a leading official could propose, though not successfully as it turned out, that official rank should be given to rich landlords who trained armies of private retainers.

The titles and functions of the officials of the Qin empire were, historically speaking, a composite formed of earlier Zhou practice, general Warring States practice and Qin innovation. There is not enough information to make clear the precise lines of authority, but the general structure of central government, of ministries and of local government is shown in the table on page 81. The system of army ranks was quite straightforward in principle: under the generals, each of whom had a chief clerk, there were colonels-in-chief, commandants, majors and captains.

As a distinctive system of local administration the prefecture or *xian* (a term which is probably related to the word meaning "suspended from") seems to have begun in areas newly acquired by the Chinese

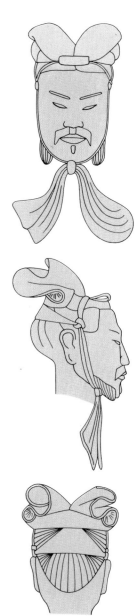

states from other Chinese states. The rather later beginnings of the larger commandery or *jun* (another old term, and cognate with that for "lordship") seem to have been in certain frontier regions facing non-Chinese barbarians. It was the Qin contribution to systematize and universalize these bureaucratic structures. The actual number of commanderies in the empire is controversial. A commonly quoted figure is 36 at the time of reunification, but it may have risen as high as 49 later in the dynasty.

Within three years of the First Emperor's death in 210 BC this remarkable system had collapsed. Revolts among conscripted laborers led to a short period of civil war between rival contenders for supremacy, and ended with the rise of the new dynasty of the Han in 206 BC. There were two main reasons for the downfall of the Qin. The first was the increasingly pathological nature of political life at the court, which crippled the formation of sensible policies and eventually the execution of policy as well. The second was economic overstrain. The resources of the early empire were not able to maintain the costs of the large-scale military campaigns, of building strategic roads and the Great Wall, and of other public works such as the First Emperor's palaces and his colossal mausoleum on which 700 000 conscripts are said to have labored and in which they were buried alive to guard its secrets.

The roots of the degradation of the political process may be traced to the First Emperor's megalomania, his growing intolerance of criticism and the side-effects of the superstitious credulity which inspired his search for the secrets of personal physical immortality. All these can be seen in his famous outburst of rage on learning of the flight of a scholar called Lu, whom he had put in charge of discovering the drugs that conferred eternal life, but who had decided – or so the Han dynasty *Records of the Grand Historian* say – that such an emperor was unfit for such a privilege.

> I destroyed all the useless books in the world [the emperor declared]. I summoned to court a multitude of scholars versed in literature and in magical techniques. I hoped thereby to bring about an age of great well-being. The alchemists I wished to purify themselves so that they might seek for magical drugs. Now I hear that Han Zhong and the others [who went with him on the quest for elixirs] have gone off without returning to report, and that Xu Fu's company [who set sail to find the islands of the immortals] have squandered vast sums of money, without in the end getting any magic drugs. Every day I hear of nothing but profits made by trickery and mutual denunciations. I have honored scholar Lu and his associates with rich gifts, but now they are slandering me. The burden of their complaint is that I am without charismatic virtue. As to the scholars in the capital, Xianyang, I have sent out people to investigate them, and some of them appear to be throwing the common folk into confusion with their weird and improper talk.

There was an inquiry conducted by the grandee secretary, during which these scholars tried to save themselves by denouncing each other. The emperor then had more than 460 of them buried alive and "caused the world to know of it, that it might be a warning to their successors." This was perhaps the first instance of a tendency that has resurfaced from time to time in China ever since, namely the temporary killing of cultural life by the central government through a mixture of monopoly, inquisition and purges. But the most serious immediate consequence for the Qin was that the able crown prince was banished to the frontier for protesting that dealing in this way with scholars, "all of whom praise and model themselves on Confucius," was not the right way to keep the newly conquered empire at peace. Once the First Emperor had died, this banishment made it possible for the eunuch Zhao Gao to contrive the crown prince's suicide, rig the succession and seize power. The consequence was the total corruption of the court, well symbolized by the famous story of the stag. Zhao Gao wanted to know which of the officials were his supporters and therefore presented the emperor with a stag that he declared was a horse. Those who spoke the truth, and insisted it was nonetheless a stag, he had punished. Shortly afterwards he forced the new emperor to commit suicide. The nervous third emperor then had the eunuch assassinated, but survived on the throne for a mere 46 days before the rebels broke into Xianyang.

Qin institutions had extended state income by creating and then taxing a free peasantry, the indispensable adjunct of the effective bureaucratic state. In the regions that Qin conquered the new rulers deliberately broke the power of the indigenous aristocracies by removing the peasants from their communities and setting them up as individual farmers who owed taxes, labor and military services directly to the government. The sense that this gave the Qin kings of a capacity to do things hitherto impossible was very likely exhilarating, but it probably undermined the First Emperor's awareness that there were still limits. In particular, the maintenance of the several hundreds of thousands of soldiers who were sent against the Xiongnu barbarians to the north and west of the great loop of the Yellow River, at the end of difficult supply lines, imposed a fearful logistical strain. In the end, as the *Han History* said, "although the men toiled at farming, there was not enough grain for rations; and the women could not spin enough yarn for the tents. The common people were ruined."

The Qin epoch, however brief, marked a cultural divide in Chinese history. The destruction of books and the compulsory reform of the script meant that almost all the old writings were imperfectly transmitted to later ages, or lost altogether. On the other hand it also saw the definitive establishment of a blueprint of administration that, however imperfectly realized at times, and however much subject to changes in details of titles and institutions, was to change remarkably little in the next two millennia. Perhaps its most important feature was summed up by the Tang essayist Liu Zongyuan. The First Emperor, he said, was "the man who, for the first time in history, introduced and put into practice an administrative apparatus so just and impartial that all men, if qualified, could participate in it."

The Underground Army

In 1974 a group of people digging a well some 1200 meters east of the outer wall of the mausoleum of the First Emperor of Qin, 64 kilometers from the city of Xi'an in central China, discovered an underground army. The site soon became an ant-hill of activity as hundreds of blue-clad workers pulled away wheelbarrows of earth, uncovering thousands of clay warriors. Heads of infantry emerged from the red earth as if they had been buried alive.

Four separate underground chambers have been discovered, designated pits 1 to 4. Pit 1 is the largest and contains over 6000 figures arranged in military formation. The formation follows military prescriptions in contemporary texts on military strategy. The clay army had been shattered when the roof had caved in and almost all the warriors have had to be pieced together. All the pits had also been plundered for weapons. The looting probably took place in 206 BC when rebel general Xiang Yu is said to have razed the palaces of the Qin capital and destroyed the First Emperor's tomb.

Pit 2 was discovered in 1976 to the northeast of pit 1, and is an L-shaped chamber of smaller dimensions containing over 1400 chariots and cavalrymen. Four basic units have been distinguished: a vanguard of archers with unarmored striding infantrymen; two units of cavalry and chariots; and a further unit of cavalry and chariots subdivided into eight corridors. A third pit to the north of the west end of pit 1 was excavated in 1977 It is a small irregular chamber one-seventh the area of the first pit. Its figures appear to represent an elite command force. A fourth pit was discovered but is empty, suggesting that the work was abandoned before completion, perhaps due to the sudden death of the First Emperor in 210 BC and the downfall of the dynasty.

The ground plan of the mausoleum suggests the lay-out of an ideal imperial city, the inner part representing the emperor's "forbidden city" and the outer part the periphery. The guards of the capital during the Qin dynasty could be divided into the imperial bodyguards who stood guard in the court and the garrison troops who protected the capital. Judging from the positions of the pits, the clay warriors represented the troops stationed outside the city: pit 1 the right-wing infantry division, pit 2 the left-wing cavalry division, pit 4, which is about 4050 square meters, may have been intended for the central force and pit 3 the command unit. The pits themselves resemble army camps.

The terracotta army was not mass produced from molds: each figure was individually modeled. Heads, arms and bodies were modeled separately and then joined with strips of clay. The bodies are hollow and made up of coiled earth and attached to solid legs. A cross-section of a broken warrior showed that a rough model was made first, then a fine clay slip was added, and details such as eyes, mouth, nose and details of dress were carved into

Below An army of over 6000 life-size soldiers and horses sculpted in clay and equipped with bronze weapons was discovered at Lintong county in Shaanxi in 1974. They were created over 200 years ago, as a bodyguard to serve the First Emperor of the Qin dynasty (221–210 BC) in his afterlife.

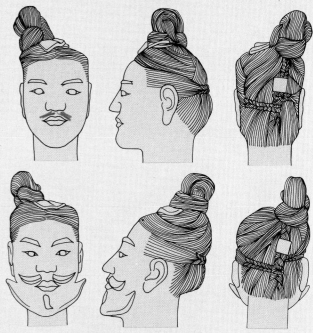

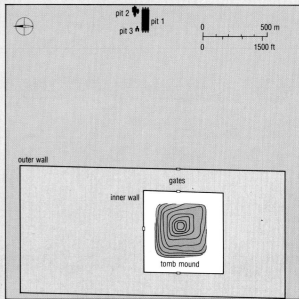

Left This life-size clay warrior comes from pit 2. Almost half of the 252 figures in this pit share a stance reminiscent of a *taijiquan* position, one of the martial arts which can be seen practiced in China today.

Above A plan of the mausoleum of the First Emperor of Qin (as yet unexcavated) showing the pits that housed the Underground Army in relation to the tomb mound.

Right A plan of pit 1, showing a reconstructed arrangement of the underground army guarding the Emperor's tomb.

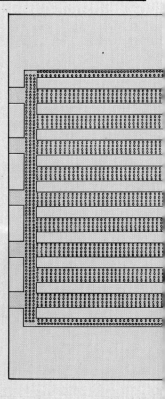

the clay while it was still pliable. Additional pieces such as ears, beard and armor were modeled separately and attached. The whole figure was fired at high temperature, and the pre-fired base attached later. The hair was carved elaborately and shows many distinctive styles and a great variety of topknots. The horses were made in a similar fashion. The large round plugs on each side of the body fill holes that served as vents during the firing. Each horse was equipped with a bronze bridle. Only one of these has been successfully reassembled.

The warriors and horses were originally painted with bright colors, which today have almost disappeared. There were two main color schemes used for the armored warriors. Uniform further distinguishes the role of each figure, and colors may also have indicated different regimental units. The colors on the horses are very poorly preserved, but they seem to be black or brown with white hooves and teeth, and red inside their ears, mouths and nostrils.

War became professional only in the two centuries before China's unification. Before, soldiers had to manage with padded jackets and garments of treated sharkskin and animal hide. The Qin army shows at least seven different styles of armor. Tassels and ribbons represented badges of rank, and officers can be easily distinguished from the ordinary troops by their elaborate armor of small laminated plates with decorations on shoulders, breast and backs, as well as ornate headgear with double folds and ribbons. The unarmored vanguard of pit 1 wear light clothing to facilitate fast movement, and they use long-range bows to avoid close combat. The chariots are guarded by infantry squads wielding long lances to prevent the horses from being killed. Two of the six chariots in pit 1 carry drums and bells which would have sounded orders to advance or retreat. The spearmen were also lightly equipped.

No two faces of the Qin warriors are alike, and anatomical details such as eyes and mouth are surprisingly lifelike. The entire force may have sat for their portraits in lieu of being buried alive. The fact that the warriors show varying physical features of minority nationalities from the far-flung corners of the empire reflects the vast number of conscripts that made up the First Emperor's army.

For all their realistic detail, however, the figures are types rather than portraits. They vibrate with energy and embody the spirit of the powerful Qin army, giving an illusion of reality. There is a saying in China that "too realistic means not realistic." Rather than an exact likeness the figures give us a sense of coiled strength and impending movement which is matched by the alertness of the horses with their dilated nostrils and pricked ears. However it is obvious that the Qin figures were based on reality. By the Zhou dynasty certain bronze articles depicted subjects drawn from real life, such as hunting scenes. The Qin sculptures continue this earlier trend of representational accuracy and combine it with a new monumental scale. This monumental scale, grandiose conception and the sheer numbers of China's underground army testify to the imperial vision and power of the emperor who is said to have led "a million armored soldiers, a thousand chariots and 10 thousand horses to conquer and gloat over the world."

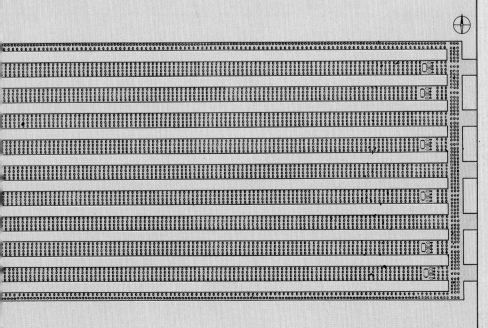

THE IMPERIAL AGE

POLITICS AND POWER

Unity, fragmentation and conquest

The maintenance of the Chinese empire was the most impressive feat of political stamina in ancient, medieval and modern times. The Chinese empire was the equal of the Roman empire, but less far-flung than the caliphate in the days of its suzerainty over the entire Islamic world, and was a mere component part of the Eurasian dominions of the Mongols; its communications were less precariously extended than those of the globe-encircling Spanish empire over the Americas and the Philippines, and its peoples less numerous than those of the British empire in Afro-Asia during its heyday, yet in terms of the subject-years that it ruled imperial China dwarfed them all — possibly even all of them put together.

The record may be summarized as follows, with the help of the accompanying table. For 500 years from 221 BC to 311 AD the core areas of Inner China (namely the northern plain, the valley of the Yangzi and the Sichuan basin) remained a political unit, apart from a brief three-way division towards the end, in the 3rd century AD. Then, from 311 to 589, Inner China was split into two. A series of partly sinicized barbarian dynasties fought each other for supremacy in the north. In the middle and lower Yangzi region a sequence of Han Chinese dynasties preserved and enriched the legacy of their traditional culture, and pioneered the economic development of this still under-populated and backward area. For a further half-millennium, from 589 until 1126, the empire was again reunited, with a 54-year period of fragmentation intervening from 906 to 960. Between 1126 and the late 1270s there was another split between north and south: the Jin dynasty of the Ruzhen people (who may be thought of as the ancestors of the Manchus) ruled to the north of the Huai River valley, while the Chinese dynasty of the Southern Song held sway in the south. The Mongols annihilated the Jin in 1234 and the Southern Song in 1279, so uniting China again, but within the confines of the still larger Mongol empire. Finally, if brief transitional periods are overlooked, it is approximately true to say that Inner China has been under a single political authority since that time. The main exceptions are the period of warlordism that was at its height between 1916 and 1927, and the partial Japanese occupation from 1937 to 1945. It is clear from the table that the political coherence of a Chinese population that grew from about 50 million 2000 years ago to about 1000 million today has been maintained for almost three-quarters of the time that has elapsed since the First Emperor of Qin.

This astonishing achievement raises two distinct but related questions: what were the forces working for and against internal fragmentation, and for and against conquest from outside? Before an attempt is made to answer them in an analytic way, it must be accepted that when these forces were fairly equally balanced there was what is most

Previous page Twenty-four emperors of the Ming and Qing dynasties lived in the "Forbidden City" in Beijing. They seldom left the 250-acre enclosure. There is a wonderful sense of balance between the open spaces and the buildings themselves.

Left A lively Han stone rubbing of horse and carriage dashing with tremendous speed, similar to the mural paintings of a tomb in Liaoyang in northwest China.

Below: Unity and fragmentation of Inner China since 221 BC
A chronological table showing the periods during which Inner China was politically unified, divided into two, or fragmented.

unity	two-way split	fragmentation	dates	population in millions	principal dynasties
			— 200		Qin Former Han
			— 100		
			0 — BC/AD	57	Later Han
			— 100		
			— 200		Three Kingdoms
			— 300		Western Jin
			— 400		Northern and Southern dynasties
			— 500		
			— 600		Sui
			— 700	65	Tang
			— 800		
			— 900		Five Dynasties and Ten Kingdoms
			—1000		Northern Song
			—1100		
			—1200	140	Southern Song/Jin (Ruzhen)
			—1300		Yuan (Mongols)
			—1400	70 (?)	Ming
			—1500		
			—1600		
			—1700		Qing
			—1800	393	
			—1900		Republic/Warlords/Nationalists/People's Republic
			—2000	1 000	

Unity and fragmentation of Inner China since 221 BC

Above This detail of the hanging scroll entitled *Emperor Ming Huang's Journey to Shu* is painted in ink and colors on silk, by an anonymous artist. It is probably a Song dynasty copy of an 8th-century original. The Tang emperor Ming Huang had a famous romance with the consort Yang Guifei, considered to be one of the four most beautiful women in China at the time. Intrigues at court and the An Lushan rebellion (755 AD) caused the emperor to flee to Sichuan. On the way his soldiers mutinied and forced him to have his beloved Yang Guifei strangled as they blamed her for his downfall. The incident became a well-known theme in literature and drama.

with which generals and administrators alike had to contend. The interplay of these factors was intricate, and the first two closely connected with political institutions and state policies. These links need to be spelled out in some detail.

Administration and logistics

It is expensive to govern and defend a large empire. Professional bureaucrats and professional (or at least professionally trained) soldiers have to be paid for out of taxation. This requires both an economy advanced enough to produce the necessary surplus above the subsistence of the workers, and an administration capable of extracting it and using it effectively. If this accessible economic surplus is only barely enough, a fiscal crisis can be caused by an increase in the cost of fighting, perhaps because the enemy has become more skillful, or by an increase in the cost of administering, perhaps because imperial policies are more ambitious or imperial tastes more extravagant. On several occasions in Chinese history a long-term downward spiral was started when peasants tried to avoid the burden of taxes by seeking the protection of powerful local landowners, and so left a heavier burden for the remaining body of taxpaying peasants, who were thus even more inclined than before to look for some means of escape. The position of these local notables was usually ambiguous: as members of the governing class, their interests required an effective and well-financed administration, but as individuals it was to their advantage to exploit their power to offer protection, a favor for which the peasants eventually paid heavily as their tenants and dependants. This was the story of much of the Later Han dynasty which owed its establishment largely to powerful local lords whom it could not thereafter afford to offend. Conversely, if the processes of production in the economy improve in such a way that there is a bigger surplus per worker, this at once eases the strain of paying for the state apparatus and the army. The Grand Canal of the early 7th century underpinned the Sui and Tang reunification by cutting the costs of bringing cheap Yangzi valley grain to the north. The economic revolution that began around the end of the first millennium AD, especially in southern rice farming, helped to pay for the vast standing armies of the Northern Song, which contained at their maximum well over a million men.

The effects of size on a premodern empire, in terms of both population and territory, are hard to evaluate. The cost of communications between the center and the frontiers is obviously proportionate to the distances involved; all the imperial dynasties had to maintain an extensive and expensive courier system using horses, boats and foot runners moving between specially provided relay stations. The map on page 94 shows the Ming courier system, with concentric circles marking the maximum time in weeks permitted to a mounted courier. It seems probable that even a thousand years earlier speeds were not significantly less. It is thus likely that the empires based on Inner China had a communications radius of about five or six weeks. This was of the same order as 18th-century Europe stretching between Lisbon and Moscow with Venice as its imaginary capital.

conveniently described as an element of chance at work. A striking example is the sudden and quite unanticipated seizure of northern China by the Ruzhen Jin in 1126, a time when the Northern Song seemed to be at the height of their confidence and power. (The major Song strategic weaknesses had been present since the start of the dynasty: (1) the lack of an adequate cavalry because of the loss of the best pasture grounds in the northeast to the Qidan and in the northwest to the Xixia; and (2) the retreat, continued from the preceding Five Dynasties period, away from the most natural line of defense in the northeast, which left the capital at Kaifeng on the open plain overexposed to swift attack.) In general, though, the likelihood of both conquest and fragmentation was determined by a shifting balance between three factors. These were: (1) the relative fighting abilities of Chinese and barbarian armies; (2) the capacity of the Chinese imperial government to mobilize human and material resources, and to move these men and supplies over long distances; (3) the nature of the terrain and the difficulty of the communications

Overextension of the empire
The Chinese empire reached its maximum western extension under the Tang emperor Gaozong in the later 7th century. Its protectorates stretched across the Pamirs into Soghdiana and Tukharistan and as far as the frontiers of modern Iran. This far-flung hegemony was impossible to maintain for long. The rise of Islamic power in the west, symbolized by the Arab victory over the Chinese at the Talas River in 751, and the increasing strength of the Tibetans and of the kingdom of Nanzhao in the southwest created strains on resources that were impossible to resist after the internal weakening caused by An Lushan's rebellion in 755. Several decades of Tibetan attacks on the slender Gansu corridor then culminated in a Tibetan victory over the Chinese and their Uighur allies in 791 near Beshbaliq (Beiting), and brought Chinese rule in central Asia to an end for almost a millennium. A few years later, however, Tang counterattacks put a stop to the military expansion of Tibet, and by the middle of the 9th century it was disintegrating as an organized state.

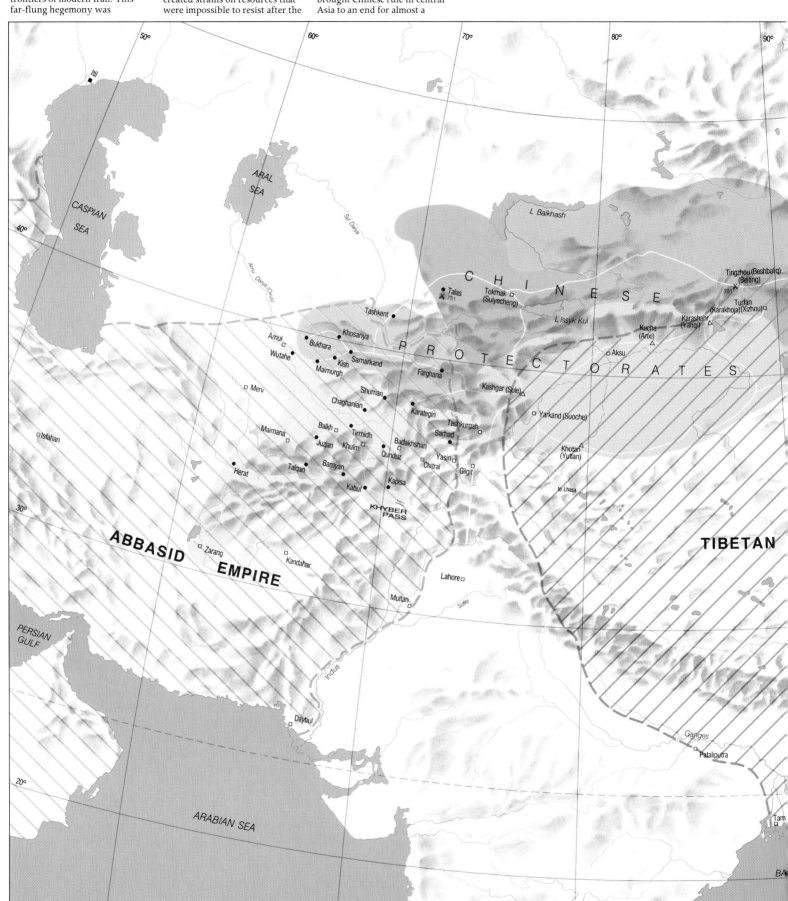

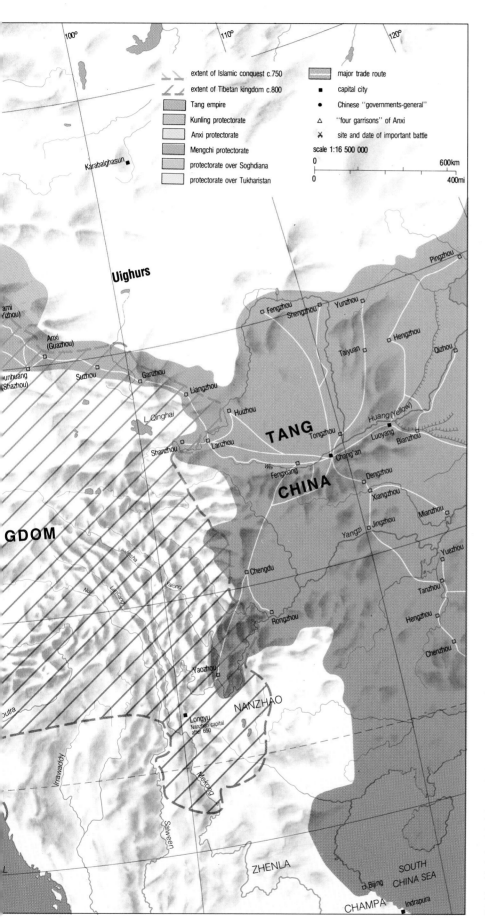

Transportation was a different matter again. If there were no suitable waterways available, the cost of moving supplies for armies marching out from the center could be many times the actual value of these supplies, particularly in the early days. A fairly clear example of the overstretching of China's logistical capacity occurred in the later 7th century under the emperor Gaozong, when Tang political control reached for a short space of time far beyond the Pamirs and in the direction of the Persian Gulf, while virtually touching the frontiers of India. The title of the accompanying map of the Chinese central Asian protectorates describes this as the "over-extension" of the empire, and it is evident how difficult were the Chinese lines of supply through the corridor that ran from Lanzhou to Anxi, flanked by deserts on the north and mountains on the south. In fact this suzerainty could not be sustained for long in the face of local disaffection, and the defeat inflicted by Islamic forces at the battle of the Talas River in 751 AD, one of the decisive engagements of the medieval world, followed by the internal crumbling in China itself caused by the An Lushan rebellion of 755, put an effective stop for ever to Chinese hopes of sustaining this far western extremity of their power. As the map shows, the slightly later expansion of the Tibetan kingdom across the corridor cut off Tang access to Turkestan altogether, an event symbolized by the Tibetan victory in 791 over the Uighurs at Beshbaliq (once Chinese Beiting) on the former northern Chinese frontier.

The logistic problems of empire could also be eased if the troops could to some extent double as farmers and feed, or partly feed, themselves. The soldier-farmer military colony was thus the key to much of Chinese imperial consolidation. Characteristic was the transfer of some 700 000 colonists to the Gansu corridor by the Han emperor Wudi towards the end of the 2nd century BC, and the implantation of self-sufficient garrisons in the semidesert regions further west. The dry climate of this area has permitted the survival of large numbers of the wooden strips on which the administration wrote its records and orders, and so quite a detailed picture is available of the life of these colonists in places such as Juyan (or Etsin-gol). The communities had complex populations of civilian migrants (most of whom had moved at government expense), garrison soldiers, farming soldiers working on regular schedules under supervision, herdsmen, soldiers' families, personal attendants, convicts, slaves, temporary visitors, and barbarians who had submitted. The settlements were guarded by a network of walled cities, fortresses and watch-stations. The Sui and early Tang "divisional militia," which was based on the training of selected peasants as soldiers, was an internal institution with some of the features of the colony concept but not its degree of integrated agro-military organization. The most developed form of the idea was perhaps the Ming institution of "guards and battalions." More than two of the three million men of the armies of conquest were settled in these during the later 14th century, farmers and fighting men being in proportions that varied according to the needs of the locality where they were. It is also interesting to note that as late as the 1870s Zuo Zongtang's reconquest of Eastern Turkestan was based on making his soldiers part-time peasants and on a careful accumulation of supplies before the decisive campaign (see map p. 41).

On the other hand, it would be wrong to overlook possible economies of scale. To the extent that imperial China was eventually able to expand to "natural" frontiers, this diminished the likelihood of swift or easy attack from outside. The eastern seaboard, the southwestern jungles and the western mountain ranges were all to some degree frontiers of this type. Again, when a large population can shelter behind a single well-placed strategic barrier, the cost of the empire's defense per inhabitant may actually fall as the population behind the barrier grows. The Great Wall (which was a complex of defenses including camps and supply roads, rather than a simple linear obstacle) might be seen in such terms. The Song lacked such a wall, using only specially cut waterways and specially planted groves of willow trees to impede the cavalry of their northern enemies, whereas the Ming rebuilt one, completely faced with masonry, and equipped it with the apertures for cannon that can be seen by visitors today. And obviously, but not trivially, greater size means greater resources to draw upon.

"Barbarians" and sinification

A continual source of instability that made every momentary military equilibrium impermanent was the almost continuous improvement in the fighting abilities of the non-Han peoples confronting the Chinese. Thus, in the pre-imperial period, the new nomadic mastery of mounted warfare required the Chinese to expend a great deal of resources and effort to contain the challenge. They developed cavalry of their own, sometimes remarkably well drilled and effective, like that of the early Tang, famous for its controlled maneuvering. But since Inner China is not well suited to the rearing of horses, dynasty after dynasty was obliged to maintain special pasture grounds and to import mounts from beyond the frontiers. Wang Anshi, the would-be institutional reformer who held power for a time in the 11th century, tried having the state give the peasants horses, which could then be used in wartime by the army. The scheme proved impracticable, seemingly because the cost of feeding the animals was too high and it was difficult to keep them healthy. Other arms were used with effect against barbarian mounted archers and shock-troops: crossbows, primitive tanks made by Song dynasty military technologists from wagons covered with rawhide and sometimes linked with iron chains and, from the 14th century on, field artillery. Cavalry technology, for its part, did not stay still either. The stirrup appeared in the Chinese world around the 5th century AD (the date and the area of invention are controversial), and the use of partial iron body-armor for their warhorses by the Xixia Tanguts and the Ruzhen Jin made their charges exceptionally difficult to resist.

A second and equally important source of advances among the non-Han was the diffusion of Chinese skills outwards from the core Chinese area, often carried by Han refugees or adventurers. The growing capacity of the "barbarians" to organize themselves, and eventually in many cases to create states based in part on settled agriculture and cities,

Han dynasty rubbings of figures from battle scenes from the Wu family tombs, Shandong. They show the style of dress and armor of the time.

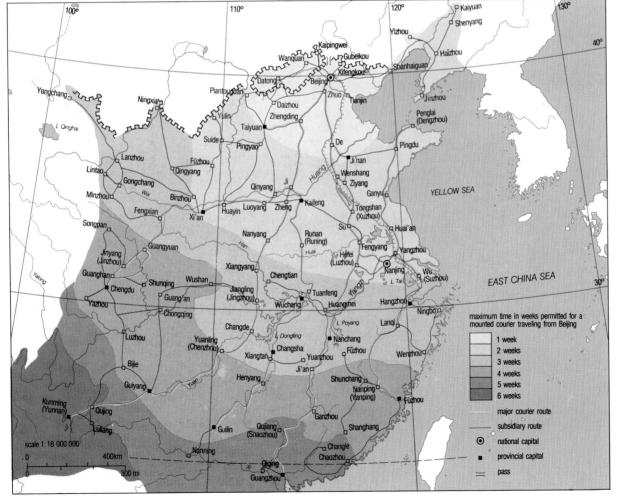

maximum time in weeks permitted for a mounted courier traveling from Beijing	
	1 week
	2 weeks
	3 weeks
	4 weeks
	5 weeks
	6 weeks

— major courier route
— subsidiary route
⊙ national capital
■ provincial capital
= pass

scale 1:18 000 000

Left: The imperial courier service under the Ming dynasty
The courier service was the political nervous system of the empire. The map shows the trunk routes and local routes used under the Ming dynasty, and the cities through which they passed. An idea of the operational size of the late traditional empire may be obtained from the zones laid down a little later by the Qing defining the maximum time permitted for mounted couriers to reach certain destinations from Beijing. Those shown on the map are only defined for the major centers, and minor inaccuracies are probably present as regards cities of secondary importance. As may be seen, in terms of the swiftest premodern communications, the empire was six to seven weeks across.

The Toba Wei state
The Wei dynasty, founded by the Toba (or Tabgatch) late in the 4th century AD, was at first a somewhat brutal regime of conquest based on cavalry power. The huge imperial pasturages shown on the map are a reminder of this reality. As time passed, it became more sinicized, more bureaucratic and increasingly based on revenue derived from agriculture. This shift was dramatized by the removal of the capital in 494 from Pingcheng, in what is now northern Shanxi, to Luoyang in the central Yellow River valley, an event which contributed to the rising of the resentful tribal garrisons in 524 as a result of which the state broke in two.

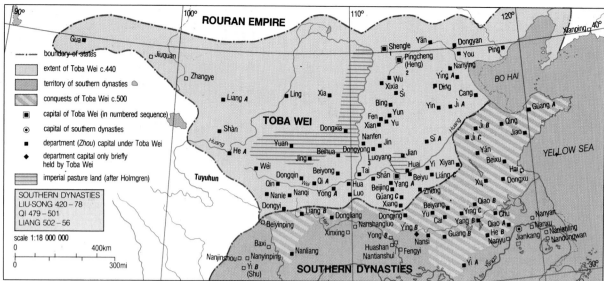

boundary of states
extent of Toba Wei c.440
territory of southern dynasties
conquests of Toba Wei c.500
■ capital of Toba Wei (in numbered sequence)
⊙ capital of southern dynasties
■ department (*Zhou*) capital under Toba Wei
◆ department capital only briefly held by Toba Wei
imperial pasture land (after Holmgren)

SOUTHERN DYNASTIES
LIU-SONG 420–78
QI 479–501
LIANG 502–56

scale 1:18 000 000
0   400km
0   300mi

Alternative names for Toba Wei department capitals

Beihua	Fucheng
Beijing	Yiyang
Beixu	Langya
Beiyang	Beidu
Beiyang	Danyang
Beiyu	Chenggao
Bing	Taiyuan
Cai	Xincai
Chu	Chenliu
Ding	Zhongshan
Dongjing	Huaian
Dongliang	Ankang
Dongqin	Longdong
Dongxia	Biancheng
Dongxu	Xiapi
Dongyan	Changping
Dongyi	Wuxing
Dongyong	Zhengping
Fen	Xihe
Gua	Dunhuang
Guang A	Donglai
Guang B	Beiguang
Guang C	Xiangcheng
He A	Baohan (or Fuhan)
He B	Ruyin/Nanruyin
Hua	Huashan
Huai	Henei
Ji A	Changle
Ji C	Jibei
Jian	Gaodu
Jiao	Dongwu
Jin	Pingyang
Jing	Anding
Liang A	Wuwei
Liang B	Hanzhong
Liang C	Chenliu
Ling	Baoguzizhen
Luo	Shangluo
Nanfen	Dingyang
Nanle	Chouchi
Nanliang	Longzhou
Nanqi	Gudao
Nansi	Yiyang D/Si B
Ping	Liaoxi
Qi A	Pingqin
Qiao A	Xinchang
Qin	Tianshui
Qing	Dongyang
Shan	Hengnong
Shan	Xidu
Si	Jiuyuan
Si A	Weiyin
Tai	Hedong
Wei	Longxi
Wu	Qi B
Xia	Huacheng
Xian	Jianping / Liubicheng
Xiang	Beinanyang
Xixia	Taian
Yan	Guangning
Yang A	Yiyang A
Yang B	Liang/Nanliang
Yin	Nanzhao
Ying A	Zhaodu
Ying B	Helong
Ying C	Ruyin/Yiyang B
Ying C	Yiyang C (Sizhou under Southern dynasties)
Yong A	Chang'an
Yong B	Xiangyang
You	Yan
Yu	Runan
Yuan	Gaoping
Zheng	Yingchuan

meant that the Chinese, if they were to resist effectively, had either to spend more by equipping larger forces of their own or to improve their own technology, whether military, fiscal or diplomatic. A classic illustration of the effects of the transfer of straightforward technical skills is provided by the Mongol conquest of China and Russia. During the 11th century, when the Qidan rulers of the Liao dynasty held sway over what is now Manchuria, they strictly forbade the export of iron to Mongolia. This was the medieval equivalent of a strategic weapons embargo. The Ruzhen Jin, who overthrew them and went on to wrest northern China from the Song early in the 12th century, were not so prudent. The use of imported iron arrowtips, iron spearheads and iron swords, plus the genius of Chinggis Qan, now turned the Mongols from a nuisance into a deadly menace. In 1234 they took the Jin capital at Kaifeng, and at once rounded up all the Chinese blacksmiths they could find so as to equip the expedition that set off a few years later under Batu and destroyed Kievan Russia. In the meantime the massive walled cities of the Southern Song, their stone-throwers and early pyrotechnic weapons, together with the great rivers and the maze of minor waterways in the Yangzi valley, held the Mongols at bay for close to 40 years. Only when the latter had learned the arts of naval warfare and advanced siegecraft, mostly from renegade Chinese, were they able to move south. First Korean and then Chinese naval skills were commandeered to launch the massive Mongol naval expeditions against Japan (in 1274 and again in 1281), and against Java (in 1292–93), all of which were, however, unsuccessful.

Learning Chinese political skills and acquiring some degree of Chinese culture also helped the Koreans and the Vietnamese in particular to free themselves from direct Chinese imperial control. It was just before the end of the 2nd century BC that the armies of Emperor Wudi of Han brought northern Vietnam and most of western Korea into the empire. The millennium that followed saw intermittent fighting in both peninsulas between the Chinese and the various indigenous states that arose in these two areas. Then, after a series of difficult wars, the Tang dynasty unified Korea in 668 AD under its tributary, the state of Silla (or Xianle), destroying the rival kingdoms of Paekche and Koguryo to do so. In 935, however, some decades after the fall of the Tang, a native Korean

dynasty, the Koryo, broke free, annexed Silla and took independent control of the entire peninsula. Shortly afterwards the Koryo introduced Chinese-style examinations for the recruitment of bureaucrats. At the other end of the Chinese world at about the same time, the Vietnamese made themselves independent of the Southern Han who were then in control of Guangdong, and in 1009 the Ly dynasty set up the state of Dayue (or Dai Viet) that lasted until 1225.

During the second millennium AD both Korea and Vietnam had to mix diplomacy and military resistance in order to maintain a de facto independence. They acknowledged, as appropriate, the authority of whoever was ruling in China and sent tribute, but they fought against direct occupation. Thus in 1425 the Vietnamese ejected the forces of the Ming dynasty, which had made them into a province again since 1406; and in 1787 a Qing expedition was likewise defeated. The Vietnamese copied the Chinese civil-service examinations in 1554, but sinification had its limits. As in Korea, there was a tension between underlying indigenous traditions (such as the Vietnamese informal "folk-hero" ideal of kingship) and the Chinese overlay. Racial tensions also surfaced from time to time. In the course of the Vietnamese civil war of 1782, for example, numerous Chinese colonists were massacred. This, then, was another form of limit to the empire: effective borrowing and adaptation of Chinese culture on the part of the enemy.

Besides Korea and Vietnam there were other partly sinified states in and around the Chinese sphere of influence, but they were not so long-lasting. An early example was the Wei dynasty of the Toba (or Tabgatch) people who ruled what is now Inner Mongolia and much of northern China from the late 4th century AD until the early 6th century. Their original capital, founded by Emperor Daowu, who had dissolved their old tribal organization, was at Pingcheng on the frontier between grazing land and arable; but the administration became slowly more and more Chinese in style, and the economic base shifted increasingly to taxing settled agriculture. In 494 the capital was moved further south to the old Chinese metropolis of Luoyang. This precipitated a crisis that in various forms and with various outcomes was to beset all these mixed regimes, namely, cultural conflict between those who favored Chinese ways and those

95

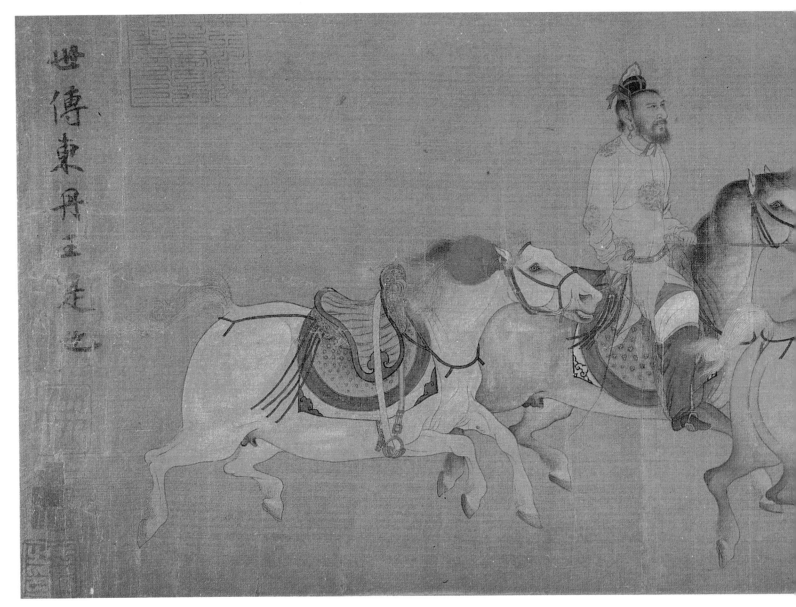

who wished to preserve the values of their non-Han heritage.

Among the more striking differences between most of the northern tribes and the Chinese were the greater freedom and respect given by the former to women, a system of government that stressed consultation among the ruling group and a feeling that (rightly or wrongly) they possessed such military virtues as loyalty and straightforwardness to a much higher degree than the Han. They also feared the softening effect of Chinese habits on their own martial hardihood. One 4th-century Xianbi general declared, ''We ought to install the Chinese in the walled cities, and assign them to agriculture and sericulture, so that they may supply us with the resources that we need for our army and administration. We should ourselves practice the arts of war, so as to be able to kill those who do not submit to us.'' The most extreme view was that taken by the generals of Chinggis Qan almost a thousand years later. They are said to have wanted to raze Chinese cities to the ground, not understanding how any human being worthy of the name could live in such rabbit warrens. Yet the logic of logistics worked remorselessly in the military sphere. It was access to the resources of north and later also of south China that enabled Qubilai Qan (Chengzu of the Yuan dynasty) first to defeat the efforts of his

younger brother to set up a Mongolian steppe regime independent of China, and then to drive off a coalition of rival Mongol leaders who had taken a vow on the banks of the Talas River to retain the nomadic life and customs of their ancestors. These were the sort of cultural tensions, then, that were at work when the Toba Wei were brought down by a revolt of their unsinified and resentful frontier garrisons in 524.

Among the other partly sinified states that deserve mention are: (1) the Liao of the Qidan people, which ruled much of Manchuria from 916 to 1124; (2) the Jin of the Ruzhen people who followed them and conquered north China as well; (3) the Tangut kingdom of Xixia (or ''Western Xia'') with Toba antecedents, that dominated the region west of the loop of the Yellow River from 1032 until their destruction by the Mongols in 1227. Both the Qidan and the Xixia had a dual administrative structure, one half a copy of the Chinese bureaucratic model and the other half derived from their own tribal structure. Both the Xixia and the Ruzhen also had their own distinctive scripts which were inspired by the Chinese. That of the Ruzhen can still be read today, but that of the Xixia has so far defied interpretation. The case of the Xixia state is of particular interest in that it was based on irrigated agriculture in the Ningxia plain, and on an

Above A detail of a handscroll depicting nomads traveling on horseback painted in ink and color on silk in the late Tang dynasty style. The An Lushan rebellion in the mid-8th century AD forced the Tang to withdraw their garrisons from the northwest. Noblemen such as the leader of this group, dressed in a richly embroidered Chinese robe, controlled much of northwest China during the Five Dynasties and Song periods (10th–13th century). After the Tang withdrew they remained on trading terms with their northwestern neighbors who were mainly interested in horse trading, which they carried out on their own exorbitant terms.

international trade with China in wool, camel-hair, materia medica and various mineral products. Its rulers, notably Yuanhao, its founder as an independent polity, relied heavily on Chinese advisers and sponsored Confucian scholars; but they tried at the same time to promote their own literary culture with translations of Chinese and Buddhist scriptures. There is evidence that works in Xixia writing were read in northwest China for some considerable time after the end of its political power. It is surprising that the Xixia state, with a population not much greater than a single Northern Song circuit, was able to sustain armies strong enough to make it impossible to subdue. The reason seems to be that every male of adult years was organized for fighting or directly supporting a man in the army, and that the Xixia armored cavalry was extremely mobile, led by generals who appreciated the value of harassing and delaying tactics when facing an enemy at the end of long supply lines, and was difficult to resist when it did attack.

In later times the most obvious example of the political and cultural sinification of a non-Han people creating a menace for the Chinese was that of the Manchus, the descendants of the Ruzhen, in the early 17th century. The chief architect of the future Manchu (Qing) dynasty in the 1620s and 1630s was Abahai, who managed to attract and make use of numerous Chinese councillors and generals, the latter introducing him to artillery of European design. As in the earlier case of the Xixia, the Manchu rise to power was accompanied by the adoption of a script for their own language. Although derived in this case from the Mongol script, it was perfected by Manchu scholars outstanding for their familiarity with Chinese. The Manchus initially grew in strength by learning farming and ironworking from the Chinese and the Koreans. Their armed forces, based on heavily armored foot soldiers with spears and swords, and backed by archers and a mobile mounted reserve to strike the decisive blow, were however vulnerable to Ming firearms. They cannot, in fact, be said to have "conquered" China. It was conquered for them by Chinese frontier generals (like Wu Sangui) who defected to their side in a time of violent internal unrest in China. Their survival in power for the first 50 years of the dynasty depended critically upon Chinese military leaders. Their sinification, though far from complete, was enough to make them broadly acceptable.

Another important aspect of the relations of the Chinese with the barbarians around them was their use as military auxiliaries and their settlement in large numbers within the confines of the empire. As early as 27 AD the Later Han rulers had found it

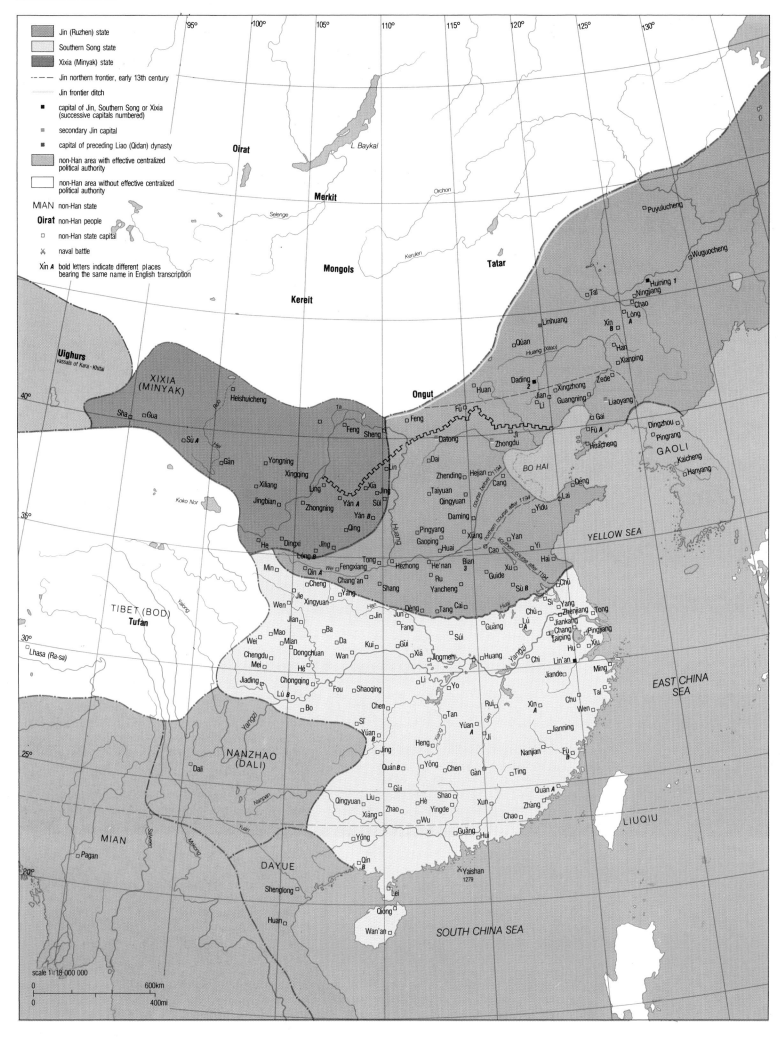

The Liao and Xixia states, and the two-fold political division of China in the Southern Song/Jin period
After the medieval revolution the increased wealth and productivity of the south allowed it for the first time to maintain a military balance with the north as a whole. The surprise capture of the Northern Song capital of Kaifeng by the Jin (Ruzhen) in 1126 did not give the conquerors, as it would have earlier, access to such a preponderance of resources that the conquest of the rest of the empire was only a matter of time. For a century and a half China was divided along the line of the Huai River, approximately the frontier between dry-farming and wet-farming.

The Southern Song set up their capital at Hangzhou, calling it Lin'an, which means "Temporary Tranquillity." It was the only seaport capital in Chinese history, and the Southern Song relied more heavily on taxes on trade, much of it maritime, than any dynasty before or after.

The straightforward two-fold political division of Inner China during this period was complicated by the presence of the Tangut state of Xixia (or Minyak, to use their own term for themselves) in the northwest. Perhaps fortunately for the Chinese the political power of Tibet, *Bod* in the Tibetan language, which had been so formidable an antagonist in the preceding age, was now disintegrating as Tibetan society took on the overwhelmingly religious orientation that it was to keep until modern times. Early in the 13th century the rise of Mongol power under Chinggis Qan cut away the northern domains of the Jin, who moved their capital south to Bian (that is, Kaifeng), but the city fell in 1234 after two long and debilitating sieges.

convenient to bring in barbarian cavalry to crush internal revolts. Later in the same century the greater part of the forces so successfully led against the Xiongnu barbarians by General Du Xian were non-Chinese cavalry. Similarly, many of the crack troops of the statesman-poet Cao Cao, effective founder of the short-lived state of Wei in the 3rd century AD, were barbarian mounted bowmen. Though the question is not a simple one, this apparently dangerous recourse to the enemies of the empire for the empire's defense can be seen as a logical division of labor. Under the Former Han there had been military conscription for two years incumbent on every adult male farmer. Under the Sui and the early Tang there had been a selective mobilization of a semi-elite of peasant-soldiers favored with certain tax advantages. These systems had some good points: a large reserve of trained military manpower that was relatively immune to the blandishments of ambitious military officers intent on coups d'etat, and – in the case of the Tang – largely able to equip themselves. But neither was an efficient way of guarding the frontiers of a large empire. It made more sense for this purpose to use professional soldiers who were not concerned about being away from their homes or missing the busy farming season, and to tax the peasants to pay for them. Some of these professionals were of course Chinese, but many were not. This created a danger, namely a much greater threat of internal instability. The most famous case in which the threat materialized was the rebellion started in 755 AD by An Lushan, a Sogdian general who had made his reputation and whetted his ambition in various frontier commands.

The settlement of large numbers of non-Han inside the empire, mostly in the north and northwest, began in the 3rd century AD. It was linked with the use of these people as soldiers, but it had implications beyond this. When internal disorders occurred, they formed many of the elements of the mosaic of non-Chinese states that took over the north China plain after 311 AD and thus inhibited a swift reunification under Chinese rule.

Regional militarism was equally a major cause of fragmentation. One of the consequences of the An Lushan rebellion was that much of China during the later Tang period was dominated by semi-independent military governors, and the ensuing Five Dynasties were even more afflicted by this tendency. The rulers of the Song house, which came to power in 960 AD, were resolved to prevent its recurrence and emphasized as had never been done to the same degree before in China the supremacy of the civilian side of imperial rule. While the Song maintained a huge professional army, they shifted the geographical postings of the units around as frequently as they could, and strove to keep their generals without any long-lasting personal connections with any particular body of troops. Inevitably this reduced their effectiveness. It might be said that concern with the prevention of fragmentation was one of the reasons why the Northern Song were so vulnerable to conquest.

Conquest and reunification
In Part One it was suggested that the relatively great weight of the north China plain region with respect to the other regions of China considered individually might have played a role in keeping the empire together. Applied without discrimination to all periods of Chinese history, this notion is inadequate, and in one or two instances quite misleading. As evidence in its favor, however, consider the two most impressive reconquests from the north after a period of division. These were the reunification accomplished by Emperor Wen of the Sui between 588 and 589, and that undertaken by Taizu and Taizong of the Song between 960 and 979. They were different in several respects. Emperor Wen, after his coup d'etat, took over a united northern China, including Sichuan. This unity was the legacy of the Northern Zhou dynasty whom he had served and helped to accomplish this feat in 577. He faced only one serious remaining opponent, the state of Chen south of the Yangzi. The subjection of Chen was the result of a massive logistical mobilization, based on extending transportation

Right "Barbarian" warriors on armored horses were brought in to crush internal revolts, as represented by these small clay figures of the 6th century AD.

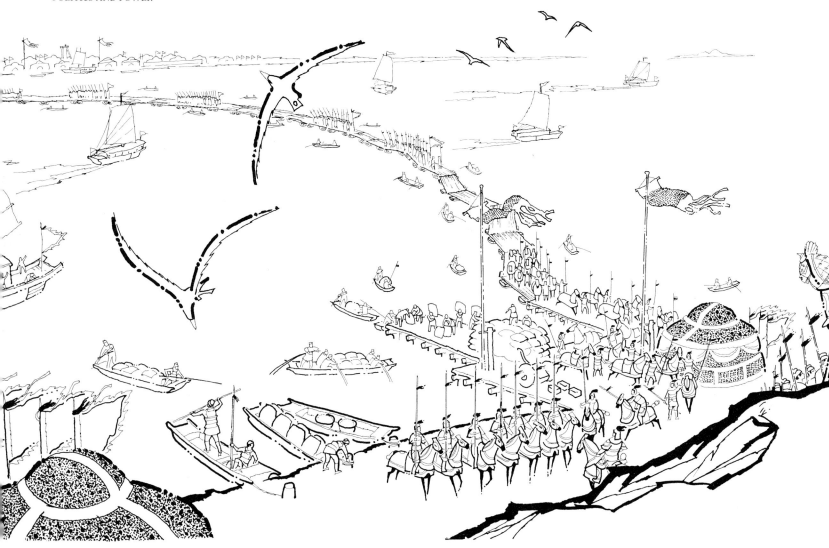

canals, building a granary system, constructing a fleet and then launching over half a million men against the southern state in eight different assault forces. The further south, still only lightly sinicized, was not conquered but won over through the cooperation of an astute aristocratic lady of non-Han race who had come to dominate that region.

Taizu of Song, on the other hand, was faced with seven opposing states, and a south whose economic resources were much more developed than they had been in Emperor Wen's days. He moved, approximately, in sequence from attacking the smallest and weakest to the strongest. The first to fall was Jingnan, which was in the central Yangzi area and contained a mere 16 counties, and then Hunan or Chu to the south of it, which contained 66. Both of these states were already weakened by internal disorders prior to being attacked. Next a two-pronged offensive was launched on Shu, one force descending from the north and the other coming up the Yangzi. A campaign of 44 days took 198 counties, but the Song armies treated the local inhabitants so badly that a revolt was provoked which was put down only with difficulty. Five years were passed in internal consolidation before measures were taken against the Southern Han, a state based on Guangzhou (Canton) and ruled (allegedly) by a spendthrift sadist who depended largely on eunuchs. Here the quality of the Song forces rather than the relative numbers, in which the northerners were probably at a disadvantage, was decisive; a further 240 counties were acquired.

The next victim was the Southern Tang, who had changed their name to the more modest Jiangnan ("South of the Yangzi") in order not to offend Song imperial susceptibilities. The forces sent by Taizu were only a fifth the number sent against Chen by Wen of Sui, and they were again somewhat outnumbered. The resources available to the Song are indicated, however, by their ability to build a bridge of boats across the Yangzi River, the first time this had ever been done. Intrigue and picking off the Jiangnan forces one by one were other important elements in a victory that secured a further 180 counties. The neighboring state of Wu-Yue now felt so pressured that its ruler simply surrendered peacefully to Taizu. This left only the Northern Han, whose capital was at Taiyuan in present-day Shanxi. The campaigns against this city and other Northern Han towns were the hardest, in part because of the help given by the barbarian Qidan to the Northern Han. Ultimate success under Taizu's successor Taizong depended on the defeat of the relieving Qidan armies (see map p. 102).

The most striking feature of the entire Song reunification process is that none of the victims allied with each other. Indeed Wu-Yue foolishly went to war against Jiangnan to help the Song, only to find itself defenseless thereafter. Alliances might well have brought the Song effort to a standstill, as the effectiveness of the intervention of the Qidan in support of the Northern Han indicates. This second process thus shows not so much a northern logistic

Above The reconstructed
drawing depicts the emperor
Song Taizu's campaign against
the Southern Tang. The victory
was due to Fan Ruoshui who
masterminded the building of a
bridge of boats across the Yangzi
River. After failing to pass the
official examinations he spent his
time planning his ambitious
project. For months he rowed in
a small boat trailing a silken
thread backwards and forwards
across the river to determine its
width and the strength of current.
Finally he presented his plan to
the Song emperor, suggesting
that they use several thousand
dragon boats strung together
with bamboo to form a floating
walkway. The emperor decided
to go ahead with the idea and
appointed Fan Ruoshui governor
of Cizhou. In three days the
bridge was constructed and
spanned the river exactly. The
drawing shows General Pan Mei
and Governor Fan Ruoshui
directing forces on the southern
bank of the Yangzi.

superiority and material preponderance, though
Taizu increasingly had both, as the way in which
whoever controlled the central plain could usually
hope to deal with his enemies one by one and in
turn.

The Ming dynasty was exceptional in being the
only dynasty of imperial times to reunite the empire
by moving northwards from a heartland in the
Yangzi valley. This reversal of the common pattern
was made possible by the drastic economic decline
of the north under the rigors of Ruzhen Jin and
Mongol rule during the 12th, 13th and early 14th
centuries, combined with the rise of the south,
mainly through the wider spread and improvement
of rice farming. During the early Ming the northern
plain had virtually to be recolonized.

A classic illustration of the main themes involved
in the effort to prevent fragmentation was the
campaign of the Tang emperor Xianzong to subdue
the independent province of Huaixi in the years 815
to 817. Huaixi was isolated from the other
independent provinces at this time, which were in
the northeast; and it was fairly small, having
perhaps a million inhabitants, but imbued with a
sense of local patriotism. To guard against any
successful loyalist commander from growing too
strong, the central government felt obliged to
assemble a composite force drawn from as many
regions as possible. The soldiers were all professionals, but the commands were subdivided, and
integration was poor. Huaixi was better coordinated, and could draw on its civilian militia as

well. The attacking armies were only slightly more
than twice as numerous as the defenders, but to
have increased the ratio would have meant weakening the frontiers and other strategically important
areas. Given the difficulty of taking well-fortified
towns, and even the lesser field forts used by the
Huaixi commanders to create a defensive zone in
depth, the war was basically one of attrition. Some
of the other independent provinces gave indirect
help to Huaixi by harassing government forces and
positions intermittently from the rear. Huaixi was
unusual in having a supply of its own horses for
cavalry, and adopted a policy of active defense
through constant counterattack, while the state
forces tried to contain their mobility and crush the
province's economy by encircling it with a ring of
forts and posts. Final central success depended
greatly on the presence of the exceptional strategist
Li Su, who was expert in retraining troops, and used
barbarian horsemen, espionage and diplomacy
(based on an appeal to the virtues and benefits of
loyalty) to good effect. The Huaixi population
began to suffer food shortages from the semi-siege
conditions imposed on them; and this would have
led inevitably to some sort of political compromise
in the long run, given that the central government
on its side was finding the extra financial strain
almost too much to bear. As it happened, the
campaign was brought to a decisive end by the
brilliant surprise attack launched by Li Su during a
snowstorm, in which he exploited the Huaixi lack of
manpower to break through to the provincial

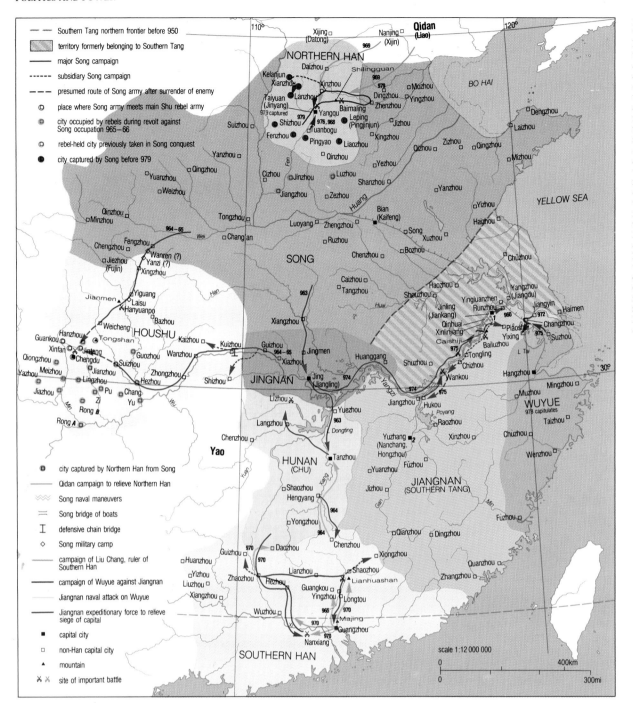

Left: The campaigns of Song Taizu and Taizong
From 963 to 979 AD Song Taizu, the founder of the Song dynasty, and then Taizong, his brother and successor, planned a series of campaigns that brought under their control the states lying around the periphery of the northern plain. The map shows the main lines of military movement, and makes two points clear. 1) The Song were able to attack their enemies one by one, without meeting any coordinated resistance. (Wuyue even collaborated with the Song in the war against Jiangnan, only to find itself relatively so weak thereafter that it gave in without a struggle.) 2) The conquest of an enemy's capital city was usually decisive. Hinterland areas, however large, usually submitted peacefully once their capital had fallen. Only in Shu did the barbaric misbehavior of some of the Song armies provoke something like a general resistance after the capital had surrendered.

capital and take it. While other factors cannot be discounted, the supremacy of logistical factors is the underlying motif of this episode as of many others somewhat like it.

One basic reason why the Ruzhen Jin, who controlled most of north China after 1127, failed to subdue the Southern Song was that the south by this date was sufficiently economically developed to support, for the first time, a sustained military resistance against the north. The importance of this shift in the balance of logistic strength can be seen again following the internal disintegration of Mongol rule after 1355. Out of the various regional warlords and independent states that then emerged, it was Zhu Yuanzhang's state based on Nanjing that eventually proved victorious. As we have seen, the conquest of the north from the south led by this state, the future Ming, was a feat never performed before in Chinese history.

The fragmentation of the Mongol (Yuan) empire just referred to was the result of the combination of two causes. One was the latent social unrest, the roots of which lay in the harsh conditions of the serfs and servile tenants who worked the great landed estates of this age. The moment that political control weakened, this unrest would break out into uprisings, often associated with the White Lotus sect brand of millenarian Buddhism. These occurred in the later 1330s and again in the 1350s. The second factor was the inability of the Mongol regime to put together a stable political system that was acceptable to and yet capable of containing its more influential subjects, whether Mongol, central Asian or Chinese. By 1328 the Confucian-bureaucratic tradition had, in general terms, won out in its battle against the purely Mongol legacy of the steppes, but anti-Chinese racialist suspicions could still poison the polity, as they did under Great Chancellor Bayan. It is equally significant, though, that Bayan was unable to secure the loyalty of many important Mongols and central Asians, whom he felt driven to persecute and purge; and his abolition of the state

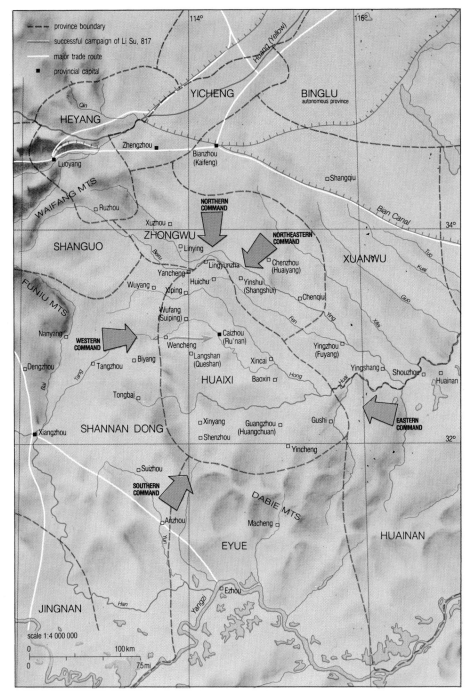

The Tang reconquest of Huaixi
The rebellion of An Lushan in the middle of the 8th century, though eventually defeated, left the edifice of Tang imperial rule in ruins. Power outside the capital lay largely in the hands of powerful provincial governors backed by their own armies. Central control was painstakingly reestablished, except in the northeast and Huaixi. The map shows the campaign ordered by emperor Xianzong against the last-mentioned region, which resisted from 815 to 817. Although it ended in spectacular fashion with Li Su's attack through a snowstorm, the operation was essentially a battle of logistics: superior resources and blockade against internal lines of movement and local patriotism.

dynasties was a major feat of political skill, and one that should not be underestimated simply because of its familiarity.

It is sometimes said that while the Chinese invention of firearms undermined the military social structure of feudal Europe, it had no comparably great effect on China itself. This is only partly true. The use of of field artillery, the famous "supernatural mechanism cannon," was the basis of the Ming success against the Oirat-Mongol cavalry on the steppes in the early 15th century. Fixed cannon defending city walls and, above all, the Great Wall, rebuilt by the Ming emperors over a century and a half, were of great help in resisting invasions from the north. The defeat of Nurhaci, the founder of the Ruzhen-Manchu kingdom, outside the walls of Ningyuan in 1626 shows that this continued to be the case. (The Manchus, it may be recalled, did not, strictly speaking, conquer China. They were let in at a time of internal disorder by disgruntled and ambitious Ming frontier generals.) Firearms thus played a part in preserving the Ming empire from conquest. The other crucial element was the effective Ming system of military supply, based chiefly on the rehabilitated and realigned Grand Canal. The empire's defenses from 1368 to 1644 may be said to have rested on logistics and gunpowder.

Under the Manchus (Qing), Chinese military resources and skills, especially firearms, plus a number of Chinese generals, were combined with Manchu military forces to annex Outer China. Taiwan was taken by Admiral Shi Lang in 1683. In 1696 the empire acquired a vast territory in the northwest with the defeat of Galdan, ruler of Zungharia, gaining most of Eastern Turkestan and Outer Mongolia, though the Zunghar heartland remained for the moment outside its grasp. Rivalry between the Zunghars and Manchus as to who should control Tibet led to the conquest of that country first by the Zunghars and then, in 1720, by the Manchu (Qing). The subjugation of Zungharia and the further parts of Eastern Turkestan was finally accomplished in the 1750s, with considerable brutality. This colossal expansion left the empire without foes worth serious consideration, the only major power with whom it had direct contact being Czarist Russia, still a very tentative presence in the lands beyond the Urals.

In contrast to the part played earlier by artillery in preserving the empire, the spread of handguns through the civilian population in the later 17th and 18th centuries weakened the control of the authorities, and was a factor making for fragmentation. The ban on the private ownership of firearms had to be lifted for Fujian province in 1749, and for the country as a whole in 1760. Not to have done so would have given bandits too great an advantage over law-abiding people. Handguns were much easier technically to master than the bow and most other traditional weapons. The result was to reduce the fighting effectiveness of the professional soldier relative to the civilian. The consequences of this were becoming apparent in the growing internal instability of the early 19th century, just as the empire was about to face a qualitatively quite new military and cultural challenge to its territorial integrity and self-confidence – from the recently industrialized nations of Western Europe.

civil-service examinations in 1335 antagonized not only the Chinese but many non-Chinese who benefited from examination quotas biased in their favor, and who had begun to accept Confucian values, and even to intermarry with the Chinese elite. Under the two periods of office of Chancellor Toghto (1340–44 and 1349–55), the fierceness of factional infighting between those who favored an active government policy (like the chancellor himself) and those who preferred a less interventionist approach destroyed the coherence of the central administration. When local rebellions broke out again, effective action depended on the personal political machine of one man – Toghto – and the dynasty became so frightened of his possible treasonable ambitions at the head of the apparatus of pacification that it dismissed him, and thereby condemned itself to impotence and collapse. These events serve as a reminder that the subsequent maintenance of imperial unity for over two centuries in each case by the Ming and the Qing

Grand Canals

Of all the Grand Canals, that of the Song (*opposite*) carried the greatest volume of government supplies to the capital—more than 6 million *shi* of grain a year (or over a third of a million tons). It was apparently also the only canal to make use of the double-gated or pound lock, which allows the passage of larger boats than a haul-over. With the relocation of the capital on the site of modern Beijing under the Mongol (Yuan) it became necessary to cut a new northern extension across the western spurs of the Shandong hills. The technical problems in keeping this stepped route supplied with water were not fully solved until early Ming times. The Mongols therefore made partial use of sea transportation from the Yangzi delta, including a route via Jiaozhou Bay that required the cutting of a canal across the Shandong peninsula.

Right inset: The earliest transportation canals
The lowlying valleys of the Huai River and its tributaries form a natural area for the building of simple canals. They join the two great river systems, those of the Huang and the Yangzi, and have such gentle gradients that comparatively little engineering skill is needed to keep artificial waterways filled to a suitable level. The first outline of a Grand Canal system linking north and south dates back to the 5th century BC, and was probably constructed for the transportation of military supplies.

Right: The Grand Canal and the transportation of tax rice to Beijing in the 18th century
The imperial capital depended on a limited number of prefectures for the supply of its tax grain, most of them concentrated in the lower Yangzi valley. The map shows the quotas for Qing times and also the official locations of the battalions of soldiers who were responsible for much of the transportation. It is not clear whether or not those outside the areas supplying grain had any operational reality.

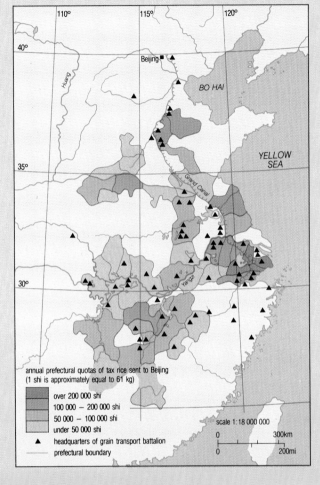

annual prefectural quotas of tax rice sent to Beijing
(1 shi is approximately equal to 61 kg)

- over 200 000 shi
- 100 000 – 200 000 shi
- 50 000 – 100 000 shi
- under 50 000 shi
- ▲ headquarters of grain transport battalion
- — prefectural boundary

scale 1:18 000 000

0   300km
0   200mi

Below Waterborne traffic on the southernmost section of the Grand Canal where it runs through Suzhou, a city famous for its numerous lesser waterways. In the past, hauling, poling and fishtailing over the stern with an oar were the commonest means of propulsion. Engines are the norm now, and long trains of boats behind a tug have become quite a common sight. Many people used to live on board their craft, but apparently they have all been settled on land in recent years.

Right inset: The Sui dynasty canals
The first complex of man-made waterways to be recognized as a "Grand Canal" system by historians was dug much later, in the early years of the 7th century AD, by a great force of conscripted laborers assembled at the orders of the emperor Yangdi. In addition to crossing the Huai valley it had a southern branch tapping the fertile triangle south of the mouth of the Yangzi, and a northeastern extension for the provisioning of frontier armies. The Sanmen gorges, just below the point where the Huang River turns sharply east to enter the plain, prevented a continuous waterborne supply line from the southeast to the Sui capital. In the Tang dynasty that followed, this was to be one factor making it difficult to maintain a capital west of the gorges.

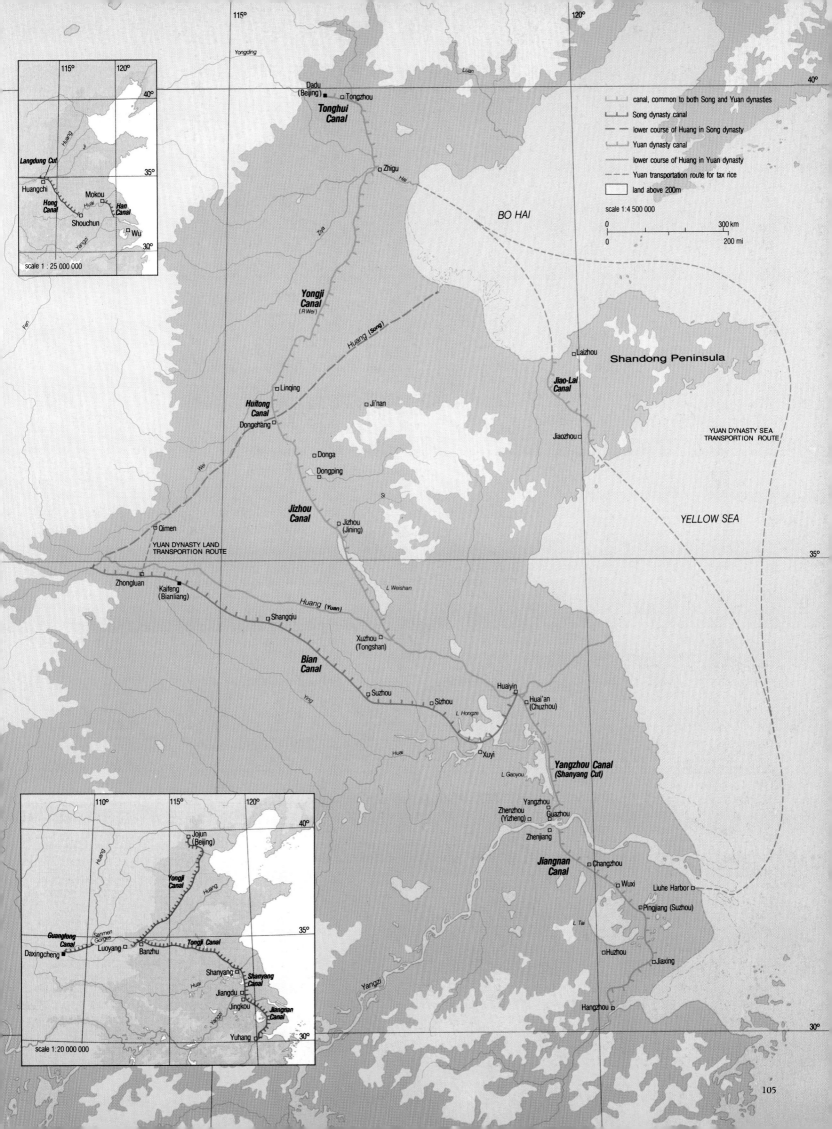

Legend

canal, common to both Song and Yuan dynasties
Song dynasty canal
lower course of Huang in Song dynasty
Yuan dynasty canal
lower course of Huang in Yuan dynasty
Yuan transportation route for tax rice
land above 200m

scale 1:4 500 000

0 ———— 300 km
0 ———— 200 mi

Main map labels

BO HAI

YELLOW SEA

Shandong Peninsula

YUAN DYNASTY SEA
TRANSPORTION ROUTE

Dadu (Beijing)
Tongzhou
Tonghui Canal

Zhigu

Yongji Canal (R Wei)

Huang (Song)

Linqing

Huitong Canal
Dongchang

Ji'nan

Laizhou
Jiao-Lai Canal
Jiaozhou

Donga
Dongping

Si

Jizhou Canal
Jizhou (Jining)

Qimen

YUAN DYNASTY LAND
TRANSPORTATION ROUTE

Zhongluan
Kaifeng (Bianliang)
Shangqiu
Huang (Yuan)
Xuzhou (Tongshan)

L Weishan

Bian Canal

Suzhou
Sizhou
Huaiyin
Huai'an (Chuzhou)

L Hongze

Yang

Huai
Xuyi

L Gaoyou

Yangzhou Canal (Shanyang Cut)

Yangzhou
Zhenzhou (Yizheng)
Guazhou

Zhenjiang

Jiangnan Canal

Changzhou
Wuxi
Liuhe Harbor
Pingjiang (Suzhou)

L Tai

Huzhou
Jiaxing

Hangzhou

Yangzi

Fen
Zhe
Hai
Luan
Yongding
Wei

Top-left inset (scale 1:25 000 000)

Langdung Cut
Huangchi
Hong Canal
Mokou
Han Canal
Shouchun
Wu

Huang
Ji
Huai
Yangzi

115° 120°
40°
35°
30°

scale 1:25 000 000

Bottom-left inset (scale 1:20 000 000)

Jojun (Beijing)
Yongji Canal
Huang
Guangtong Canal
Daxingcheng
Sanmen Gorges
Luoyang
Banzhu
Tongji Canal
Shanyang
Shanyang Canal
Jiangdu
Jingkou
Jiangnan Canal
Yuhang

Huai
Yangzu

110° 115° 120°
40°
35°
30°

scale 1:20 000 000

105

ART OF THE IMPERIAL AGE

Tombs of the Qin and Han

There are few surviving remains of the Qin dynasty apart from the life-sized terracotta army that guards the tomb of the First Emperor. Qin Shihuangdi's tomb remains legendary in its splendor. According to Sima Qian's *Historical Records* the tomb is guarded by crossbows triggered to fire automatically, and contains models of palaces, towers and official buildings, as well as utensils, precious stones and rarities. A map of the world with rivers of mercury covers the floor and heavenly constellations are depicted on the ceiling.

Tombs of the Han dynasty have yielded a great variety of objects from jade, bronze and lacquer to earthenware models of buildings, figures and scenes of farm life. The latter in particular give us an insight into the way of life during the Han period. Some tombs and shrines were decorated with stone slabs engraved with mythological and historical scenes as well as daily scenes of hunting and farming. This mixture of real and imaginary characterizes the art of the early empire.

Much of our knowledge of Han architecture is derived from reliefs and engravings on stone slabs lining the walls of tombs. These models show the post-and-lintel system supporting a heavily tiled roof. The weight is carried by wooden pillars distributed down through a bracketing system. The walls were relatively insubstantial and made of clay screens or bamboo matting. The size of the building was increased by repetition rather than height. Miniature models of earthenware buildings, both painted and glazed, give an indication of the appearance of their larger originals. Watch-towers, farmhouses, granaries and pigsties were modeled in earthenware and from these it is possible to distinguish regional styles of architecture. Figures and farm animals were modeled with lively naturalism from strips of rolled clay; others were mass produced in molds. In areas where the clay was poor, figurines were made of wood or stone.

Han dynasty sculpture is associated with burials and tomb construction. A "Spirit Way" lined with monumental stone animals led to the tomb. Stone pillars sometimes marked the entrance to the "Spirit Way." Few of these survive from the Han period, and it was not until the mid-5th century, when Buddhism was supported by the Northern Wei rulers, that stone sculpture on a large scale was widely produced. The most notable of the tomb animals are the lions and winged felines of the 5th and 6th centuries that guard the imperial tombs of the Qi and Liang dynasties.

Stone shrines and tombs were often decorated with engraved or incised designs. Stone slabs from the Wu family shrines near Jiaxiang in Shandong, dating from 145 to 168 AD, combine scenes of myth and legend with stories from official histories. The figures appear in silhouette like figures in a shadow play. The narrative unfolds in a series of scenes arranged in horizontal bands, one above the other,

which can be read in comic-strip fashion as the figures act out their parts from the base line. There is little indication of foreground or background, and occasionally depth is indicated by lifting the figure from the base line. In contrast to these are the molded clay bricks lining the Later Han tomb at Guanghan in Sichuan, executed in a sketchy manner and showing lively scenes of hunting, harvesting and daily life. Tomb decoration was also carried out with brush and ink. Figures of horses and chariots are depicted in swift spontaneous strokes in the murals from the Later Han tomb at Horinger in Inner Mongolia built between 140 and 177 AD. Scenes of herding sheep and of an acrobatic show are depicted against a plain ground. There is no suggestion of any setting and limitless space is suggested by the blank ground. This sense of space is characteristic of later scroll paintings. The painted tomb tiles of the Later Han, now in the Museum of Fine Arts in Boston, give us an idea of figure painting of the lost murals that once decorated Han palaces. The painted tiles show that individual facial expressions were observed, and the figures are drawn in sweeping calligraphic strokes, omitting unnecessary details.

During the Han period the construction of tombs varied. The family tombs of the marquis of Dai (c.160–150 BC) excavated at Mawangdui near Changsha in Henan illustrate the shaft type. Tomb 1, containing the body of a woman thought to be the wife of the marquis of Dai, is perfectly preserved. It consists of three coffins, one inside the other,

Above left An inscription on this lamp tells us that it once belonged to the Changxin Palace. It came from the tomb of Dou Wan (late 2nd century BC) who was buried in a suit of jade tablets at Mancheng in Hebei. The lamp is knee-high and the cylinder around the wick revolves so its light can be adjusted by a handle on its base. The smoke rises and flows through the arm of the hollow figure so that the room is kept smoke-free.

Above The bronze "flying horse" with one hoof on a swallow was unearthed along the Silk Route in Wuwei county in Gansu. It is approximately 30 centimeters in height and its balance is superbly controlled. It seems to epitomize the Chinese saying "a body as light as a swallow."

Right These parcel-gilt bronze leopards—exquisitely made and inlaid with silver, with eyes of garnets—are two of a set of four. They were used as weights and were found together with the bronze lamp and other precious objects in the tomb of Princess Dou Wan.

107

Left A dog and chicken look on as a Han farmer pounds grain with a tilt-hammer to the left of a stone grain-mill.

Above An archer drawing his composite bow with a tang-pointed arrow aimed at a stag and doe, a detail of a tile over the doorway of a Han dynasty tomb.

Right Guardian figures holding the ancient halberd "dagger-ax" stand guard over the deceased.

Above This knee-high model of a granary in glazed earthenware gives an excellent idea of granary architecture in the 2nd century AD.
Right The interior walls of Han tombs were lined with incised stone tiles or stamped earthenware bricks. This rubbing from a tomb in Sichuan shows lively genre scenes of threshing and harvesting in the late 1st or 2nd century AD.
Below Monumental stone-winged felines guarded the spirit way to tombs during the 3rd and 4th centuries AD. Huge stone animals also guarded the tombs of ancient Mesopotamia, but this beast is thoroughly Chinese.

encased in a large wooden structure fitted with compartments for personal possessions, which was placed in a shaft sunk to a depth of 20 meters. The bottom of the pit was paved with white clay, the coffins were surrounded by a tightly packed layer of charcoal 4·5 to 5·8 meters thick, on top of which was another layer of white clay and then filled in with earth. Among the burial goods, which are now housed in the Changsha museum, is a remarkable silk banner which was placed over the innermost coffin with paintings depicting the heavenly world, the world of man and the underworld. Dragons and fabulous mythological beasts intertwine between the real and imaginary worlds. Other objects from the tomb include lacquer mugs, containers and ladles for everyday use decorated with sweeping scroll and volute designs of red on black. A great quantity of silk including embroidery thread in 20 colors was found in the tomb. Geometric and "cloud" patterns were printed, painted or embroidered on a variety of silks ranging from gauze and damask to brocade. Silk was an important commodity at the time and bolts of silk were used as a medium of exchange. Tombs 2 and 3 brought to light many books written in ink on silk, including two versions of *The Way and Its Power* and a medical treatise recording several thousand prescriptions and the causes of diseases and their symptoms, as well as the earliest Chinese maps ever discovered. The inner coffins on tomb 1 were painted with bright colors; the interiors were painted red, and the exteriors include designs in long swirling scrolls which epitomize the vitality that swept through the arts in the Han empire.

In the north of China two Former Han tombs, cut out of the cliffs at Mancheng in Hebei, illustrate the chamber type. They consist of several linked chambers containing the bodies of Liu Sheng, who died in 113 BC, and his wife Dou Wan, buried in suits of jade. The rear chamber contained the body; the central chamber yielded a variety of articles of bronze, iron, lacquerware, gold and silver as well as many pottery and stone figurines representing servants. The chamber on the north side of the entrance was reserved for foodstuffs and wine, and that on the south side for chariots and horses. In Liu Sheng's tomb the bones of 17 horses were found and from the metalwork that survives six wooden chariots have been reconstructed. Judging from the lacquer that remained, the chariots were originally painted red and decorated with cloud patterns in red, white, green and brown. Finds from Dou Wan's tomb include a gilt bronze lamp in the form of a servant girl, and two miniature parcel-gilt bronze figures of leopards. The technique of parcel-gilding gradually replaced that of bronze inlay. An amalgam of gold and mercury was applied to the bronze filling in the outlined design. The bronze was then heated, the mercury evaporated, leaving the gold pattern. Fewer bronzes and jades have survived from the Later Han dynasty, and lacquer and silk and ceramics generally replaced them in tombs. Glazed earthenware imitated and superseded bronze vessels in tombs and, in general, items of precious metal were replaced by materials of lesser value.

A tomb of the Later Han dynasty dating from around the 2nd century AD has yielded over 200 items, mostly of bronze. It was accidently dis-

covered in 1969 by villagers from Leitai village in Wuwei county in Gansu. An inscription on the chest of one of the miniature bronze horses – ideal versions of the "celestial horses" acquired in China after the Ferghana campaign in the early 2nd century BC – records the name of the owner as General Zhang Yechang. Among the many bronzes was the famous "Flying Horse" balanced with one hoof on swallow, possibly alluding to Flying Swallow, one of a famous team of nine horses belonging to Emperor Wendi (179–157 BC).

The impact of Buddhism

The first Buddhist missionaries came to China along the trade routes in the 1st century AD. Buddhist cave temples and shrines decorated by sculpture and painting can be traced from northwest India following the trade routes to Kizil, Kucha and Bazaklik near Turfan, in modern Xinjiang, to Dunhuang in Gansu. However it was not until the 5th century that Buddhism became widely spread and associated with the branch of the Xianbi who established the Toba Wei dynasty (386–535 AD) and succeeded in gaining control over much of northern China. The early cave temples were cut into the cliff face at Dunhuang in the late 4th century, and by the mid-5th century the first cave temples were hewn out of the rock at Yun'gang ("Cloud Hill") west of the city of Datong in Shanxi.

The early caves at Dunhuang are decorated with mural paintings and painted clay sculptures. At first the caves were small in size, containing a sculpted figure of the Buddha surrounded by rows of tiny Buddhas arranged in tiers covering every available surface of the walls and painted in black, white, red, blue and green against a russet background. The caves became larger in size and scenes on the walls expanded to include Buddha figures, musicians, flying apsaras and Jataka stories illustrating the former lives of the Buddha. The latter were arranged in horizontal bands around the side walls as in cave 257 or on the slanted sections of the ceiling as in cave 428. The style was light and airy, and ribbons floated from the robes of the figures whose bodies were schematically rendered. The main structure of the body was simplified and outlined in broad strokes. The light quality of the caves has been modified in some cases due to a chemical reaction which has caused the white pigment to turn black, so giving them a more somber atmosphere.

At Yun'gang over 53 caves have been carved out of the sandstone cliff, the majority of which were completed by 494 AD when the Wei capital moved to Luoyang. The five earliest caves (numbers 16 to 20) contain huge Buddha figures sculpted in stone. The largest of them is a gigantic seated Buddha almost 13·7 meters high which is exposed to the open air and dominates the site. Folds of drapery are carved in parallel bands over one shoulder of the block-like body, and the features are modeled in a graphic manner. Caves 7 and 8 illustrate a more rounded plastic style. Full-bodied figures with round faces fill small niches that crowd the walls, bordered by decorative bands of floral and geometric designs. This modeled plastic style gives way to a harder, more chiseled and analytic style as seen in caves 5 and 6. Here the walls are subdivided into registers filled with relief figures surrounded by Buddhist images, flying apsaras and musicians, while the lower registers illustrate stories from the life of the Buddha. The reliefs were originally painted in bright colors of red, blue, green and white, and many of them have been repainted over the years, thus retaining their original appearance.

The Wei capital moved to Luoyang in 494, and in the early 490s a new cave site was opened at Longmen ("Dragon Gate") near the city on the banks of the Feng River. The caves on the east side of the river have been mostly destroyed. On the west side over 1000 caves have been cut into a cliff resembling the Yun'gang ridge, but composed of a darker, harder rock. Many of these are small, consisting of a tiny niche cut into the cliff surface. A number of the larger caves carry dated inscriptions and are known by the names of the patrons who dedicated them. The Guyang cave continues the analytic style of caves 5 and 6 at Yun'gang; the figures are elongated and the drapery is executed in flat planes, terminating in "fish-tail" patterns. This style is reflected in small bronze figurines which follow the general trends of the larger works. The variety of styles that led up to the Sui dynasty (581–618) is not easy to follow and forms no logical development. The 5th and 6th centuries mark an experimental stage in Buddhist sculpture which is characterized by sudden changes and sharp contrasts in style.

Elongated forms also characterize tomb figurines in the late Six Dynasties period. Earthenware models of horses are more down-to-earth than the flighty creatures of the Han; their features are slightly exaggerated and elongated. Female figurines of both glazed and unglazed earthenware also display elongated slender forms.

As Buddhism dominated the arts in the north, painting and calligraphy developed in the south during the Six Dynasties. The common use of brush and ink bound together calligraphy and painting from their earliest use. The development and widespread use of paper in the Han dynasty opened new possibilities for calligraphic style. The "cursive script" (cao shu) developed as a quicker written form from the formal angular "clerical script" (li shu) and became an art form in its own right. Wang Xizhi (c. 303–c. 379 AD), one of the earliest of the great calligraphers, developed a flowing "running script" (xing shu), a simplification of the early "standard script" (kai shu) and in part derived from the earlier "clerical script." Little survives from the pre-Tang period to illustrate the painting or calligraphy of the early masters whose names are mentioned in surviving texts. However a painting held to be close in subject and style to the work of the 4th-century painter Gu Kaizhi survives in the British Museum. It is entitled *The Admonitions of the Instructress* and exhibits strength of line and style of painting. The scenes are set against a plain silk background, outlined in ink and filled with a little color, while a calligraphic text describes and separates each scene. The line depicting the figures is even and wirelike, and both calligraphy and painting display a superb control of the brush. Fluid line is expressed in stone incised on the 6th-century coffin now in the Nelson Gallery, Kansas City, depicting stories of filial piety. The figures are set amid rocks and trees which are used to separate the different scenes, as in the narrative Jataka stories depicted on the ceiling of the Buddhist cave temple (number 428) at Dunhuang on the Silk Road.

Above These Tibetan-style Buddhist figures decorate the ceiling of cave 465 of the Mogao Caves at Dunhuang along the Silk Road in Gansu. The cave itself is set apart from the main body of caves, and is probably of 13th-century date.

Buddhism in China from the 1st to the 5th century AD Buddhism began to filter into China during the 1st century AD, though possible indirect influence may be traced back even earlier. The chief route by which it traveled was from northern India and Kashmir via the Buddhist kingdoms of central Asia such as Khotan and Kucha, and the silk roads that came down the Gansu corridor to Chang'an. There were also some contacts via the seaways to southeast Asia.

At first the new faith was mostly a religion of foreigners, but by the end of the 3rd century AD the upper levels of Chinese society had begun to assimilate it in decisive numbers. The map shows mainly the early centers of this elite Buddhism. The more popular variety, which was certainly present, is not well enough documented to trace with similar precision.

Buddhism in China may have been largely confined at first to the cities, but soon the influence of Daoism led monks to found monasteries and hermitages on mountains. Some of these sites became sacred to both faiths.

The coverage of the map stops in the early 5th century, because of the great increase in Buddhist foundations in the following hundred years: from 1768 to over 15 000 early in the 6th century and almost 40 000 by the end of that century.

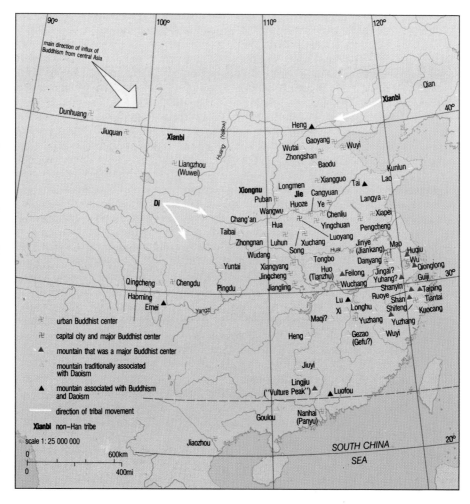

Far left Three of the walls of cave 465 at Dunhuang are divided into three subsections, each containing Tibetan-style Tantric figures in the ultimate state of enlightenment. According to Tantric belief, the male symbolizes compassion or method and the female knowledge or wisdom: when they are wedded the state of nirvana is realized. Lamaism, referred to in the West as Tantrism, was introduced into the Mongol court in the 13th century; on stylistic grounds it is likely that this cave dates from that era.

Left A section of the Chinese Buddhist scriptures consists of codes that regulate the lives of monks and nuns. They dictate the food to be eaten and dress to be worn. In this detail of a mural in the Mogao Caves at Dunhuang nuns are following the procedure of having their heads shaved for ordination.

Top The head of the monk Kasyapa from the Longmen Buddhist caves in Henan, made in the Northern Wei period and probably of the early 6th century. This arhat, or Lohan, is a Buddhist monk who has become a perfected being or saint through the practice of an aloof religious life by himself and, in a sense, for himself. By the late Tang the representation of such figures had become extremely realistic.

Right The intensely realistic image of this seated Lohan of the Liao (Qidan) dynasty that ruled in Manchuria during the 11th century contrasts strongly with the 6th-century Northern Wei head, shown above.

Top right Painted relief carvings illustrating stories of the life of the Buddha decorate the interior of the Buddhist caves at Yun'gang near Datong in Shanxi province. They date from c. 470–80 AD.

Above Sakyamuni Buddha with an attendant Buddha carved from the cliff face in Yun'gang in the late Northern Wei dynasty, c. 470–80 AD.

Above This miniature gilt-bronze is of Prabhutaratna and of Sakyamuni, who has caused the former Buddha to appear in the heavens by the power of his preaching. Sakyamuni ascends and sits beside the former Buddha and continues the rest of his sermon. This exquisitely wrought piece is dated 518 and is in the Musée Guimet in Paris.

c. 460–80

c. 495–530

c. 550–80

c. 580–620

c. 620–750

Above The development of the Buddha image.

Right A crude and powerful image of the Buddha, c. 70 meters high, hewn from the rock at Leshan in Sichuan in the 8th century. The tiny rooftop by the left foot gives an indication of its enormous size.

Tradition and innovation

Chang'an (present-day Xi'an) became the capital of a Tang empire which stretched at its greatest extent from the China Sea to the Caspian. The city had been laid out during the brief Sui dynasty (581–618) and elaborated on during the Tang. It was planned on a grid system with a north–south axis. Very few buildings survive from Tang times as most of them were constructed of wood. One of the earliest surviving brick buildings is the Great Goose pagoda in Xi'an. It was built on the orders of the monk Xuan Zang on his return from his travels to India in the mid-7th century, and was rebuilt on the original plan under Empress Wu in the early 8th century on the lines of a Han timber tower. For temple architecture we must look to Japan, where the Horyuji temple compound at Nara reflects the 7th-century temples of Chang'an. The roofs show a slight curve which was to become more pronounced in the succeeding centuries, and a complex bracketing system holds the weight of the beams supported by wooden pillars.

Outside the ancient city of Chang'an monumental stone figures of warriors and horses line the "Spirit Way" leading to the tomb of Emperor Gaozong (died 684). They stand squarely and solidly and are less animated than the feline creatures and winged lions of the previous age. So too are the six favorite horses of Emperor Taizong, sculpted on monumental stone panels in the mid-7th century.

Monumental Buddhist sculpture displays a new naturalism in the early Tang period at a time when there was religious tolerance that welcomed contacts with the outside world. From 672 to 675 the gigantic Vairocana Buddha was carved at Longmen with a roundness of form very different from the geometric and columnar shapes of the late 6th century. This so-called Indianizing style spread through Buddhist sculpture and murals. By the 8th century an international style emerged combining the Indian feeling for volume with Chinese flowing line, and spread through the arts from Dunhuang on the Silk Road eastward to Korea and across to Japan.

Paintings on silk of *Ladies at a Game of Chess*, from Tang tomb number 187 at Astana near Turfan, are depicted in bright colors filling precise outlines in the *gong bi* (skilled brush) manner. Their bodies and drapery are modeled by means of shading which gives a fullness of form and feeling of the third dimension. The same characteristics are seen in the handscroll entitled *Portraits of the Emperors* of which the latter section is attributed to the court artist Yan Liban (died 673). Like the Astana figures, volume is indicated by shading and modeling of drapery and the figures are outlined in fine wirelike lines. Again fine line and slight shading are seen in the painting, attributed to Han Gan (active 740–60), of *Night White*, one of Emperor Ming Huang's favorite horses.

No original paintings survive of the great 8th-century master Wu Daozi (died 762). An indication of his calligraphic brush may be seen in the murals at Dunhuang in the scene of Vimalakirti's interview with Manjusri in cave 103. Here the line is not of even thickness, but broken, and varies in width as it flows. Murals from the passage wall of Prince Zhang Huai's tomb in the Qian Ling mausoleum of Emperor Gaozong outside Xi'an also illustrate a looser calligraphic style. Here the figures are placed in a rudimentary landscape of rocks and trees and depth is indicated as horses gallop behind these. In the pre-Tang period landscape was used to separate narrative scenes and played a secondary role to figures. In the Tang dynasty murals at Dunhuang landscape still plays a secondary role to figures in the main paradise scenes, but in the small side panels landscapes of mountains and streams receding into the distance are depicted in their own right. The growing interest in nature heralds the rise of the monumental landscape paintings of the 10th century.

The international flavor and exchange of ideas are well reflected in the decorative arts of the Tang dynasty. Persian coins have been found along the Silk Road from the Tang tombs at Astana to a burial cache outside Xi'an, and in turn Chinese pottery shards have been found at Samarra, the early 9th-century residence of the Abbasid caliphs. Silks at Astana are designed with pearl roundel motifs which are typically Sassanian, and metalwork unearthed from the cache near Xi'an is decorated with floral motifs and hunting scenes typical of the Near East and central Asia. In Japan the lavishness of Tang court art can be glimpsed in the collection of Emperor Shomu at the Shosoin treasury dedicated by Empress Kōken in 756 at Nara, where inlaid lacquerware, metalware and textiles are decorated with intricate designs of Near Eastern and Chinese origin.

Foreign forms are vividly expressed in the three-colored glazed funerary figurines, not least by the figures themselves. Camels carry figures of "big-nose" foreigners. Glazed and unglazed earthenware horses standing nearly a meter high are modeled in a strikingly realistic manner, while the features of monster guardian figures are exploited in the manner of caricature. A very beautiful stoneware with splashed polychrome glaze applied in a painterly style was produced at the Huangdao kilns at Jiaxian in Henan; and, in the southeast, foundations were laid for the supplanting of stoneware by porcelain, which was invented during the Tang period. It was made of extremely fine kaolin-type clay, which crystallized when fired at a high temperature, so increasing the hardness of the

Above One of the six famous horses of Tang Taizong sculpted in relief after designs by the court artist Li Yanben (died 673) on monumental limestone slabs which were placed in his tomb. Four of these are now housed in the museum in Xi'an; the other two can be seen in the Pennsylvania University Museum, Philadelphia.

Right Three-color pottery of yellow, green and brown flourished in the Tang period and was made mainly for funerary use. The blue glaze on this figure puts it in the rare group known as "three colors plus blue" ware.

Below Glazed and unglazed earthenware figures of dancing girls, musicians, camels and bearded foreigners were placed in tombs during the Tang dynasty reflecting the lively cosmopolitan character of the time. By the late 10th century the practice of furnishing tombs had declined and from then onwards tombs were decorated with less lively and sophisticated items.

clay. This plasticity and hardness allowed it to be fashioned into extremely thin-walled wares.

After the persecution of Buddhism in the 9th century monumental Buddhist stone sculpture declined. However wooden sculpture and mural painting continued throughout the Song and in the Liao and Jin dynasties in north China. Lohan figures of three-colored lead glazed earthenware are disturbingly life-like and illustrate the secular trend in Buddhist sculpture. They contrast with the heavily decorated wooden sculptures of Guanyin (goddess of mercy) with high head-dress and swirling drapery. The wooden figures either stand, with their bodies slightly swaying, or sit with one knee bent and an arm resting on it in

a nonchalant manner, in a posture of "royal ease."

Emphasis on brushwork and the dissolution of form were the main characteristics of the Chan (or Zen) Buddhist artists active in the monasteries of south China in the 13th century. Mu Chi's *Six Persimmons* and Liang Kai's painting of the poet Li Bo are typical examples of their swift brushwork and magical variation of ink.

There was a revival of Buddhist sculpture under the patronage of the Mongol emperors. Tantric Buddhist sects were imported from Tibet and their influence can be seen in the reliefs on the interior of the monumental gate Juyong Guan north of Beijing, and in the mural painting of cave 465 at Dunhuang illustrated on page 111.

Landscape painting

The hanging scroll *Traveling amid Mountains* and *Streams* by Fan Kuan (active c.990–1030) epitomizes the monumental style of landscape painting of the Northern Song. A sheer cliff rises from a misty middle ground, while the details of the foreground are picked out with minute brush strokes. *Cun* (texture strokes) fill the massive form of the mountain which dominates the scene. Every detail is carefully studied. The Neo-Confucian philosophy of the time found a means of expression in landscape painting as it stressed the importance of nature and the study of this world in order to gain an understanding of the whole.

In his painting *Early Spring* (dated 1072) Guo Xi depicts the dry northern country and uses mists to create distance. The effects created are summed up in his doctrine on the "three distances": high distance, looking from the mountain foot up to the peak; deep distance, facing the mountain and seeing the land stretch far away behind it; and level distance, looking from a nearby mountain towards a remote mountain. These terms define points of view of a beholder standing in the imaginary space within the picture. According to Guo Xi, a painting should make one feel as if one were bodily there, and the aspect of the landscape should change from every angle as many times as the point of view. This shifting perspective gives a many-sided view of a mountain, which in Chinese landscape painting is seldom a particular mountain but a distillation of many.

Guo Xi inherited the monumental style of Li Cheng who painted in the Five Dynasties period. The paintings attributed to Dong Yuan and Ju Ran of the same period were said to have created a new style with pale ink and light mists; those attributed to Dong Yuan show touches of wet ink without the use of hard outline. Mi Fei (1051–1107) took the play of ink a stage further. Paintings attributed to him show blunt uniform dabs expressing the personal impression of the artist. Mi Fei's paintings were very different from the "skilled brush" style favored by Emperor Huizong, which was painstakingly accurate and decorative. Figure painting continued in the tradition of the Tang, and flower-and-bird paintings were particularly favored by Emperor Huizong who founded an imperial academy and imposed his own taste. In 1125 the Northern Song was overthrown and the court moved to Hangzhou where the emperor set up a formal academy at Wulin. The main exponents of the Southern Song landscape painting were Ma Yuan and Xia Gui. Ma Yuan (active 1190–1225) painted in an angular manner, using wash and fine line, and pushed his landscape to one side of the hanging scroll or album leaf; this won him the nickname of "One-Corner Ma." Xia Gui (active 1180–1230) painted in a more dynamic manner, using ink only and no color. He made heavy use of the "ax-cut" texture stroke as did Li Tang whose paintings in the early 12th century can be seen to link the monumental style of Fan Kuan and the Ma/Xia school of the Southern Song.

The Yuan masters of landscape

Painting in the Yuan period was both backward looking and forward moving. Qian Xuan (c.1235–c.1300) looked back to the Tang masters

Right   Early Spring by Guo Xi (c. 1020–80) is painted in ink and slight color on silk and bears a date equivalent to 1072. Guo Xi painted in China's mountainous northern regions whereas the great 10th-century masters had painted the gentler contours of the Jiangnan region near Hangzhou. In the great landscape paintings of the Northern Song dynasty human figures were reduced to a minute scale (as in the foreground). Guo Xi uses mist to veil the sudden jumps in distance and create the monumental proportions of his landscape. Detail.

Far right These cypresses were painted in ink on paper by Wen Zhengming (1470–1559), one of the leading painters of the Wu school. Like the earlier Yuan masters Wen Zhengming painted for a small circle of friends with literary and artistic interests.

Below A detail of a handscroll by Xia Gui (active 1180–1230), one of the foremost court painters of the Southern Song Academy. The handscroll was unrolled slowly so that sections could be viewed at leisure. By nature the handscroll was more intimate, but in general landscape paintings in the Southern Song did not attempt to create vast scenes of the 11th century but rather more intimate ones.

Bottom This detail of *Dwelling in the Fuchun Mountains* by Huang Gongwang shows the build-up of individual brush strokes used to create landscape in the mid-14th century.

*Far left Returning Home at
Evening* by Dai Jin (1388–1452), a
member of the Zhe school named
for Zhejiang province. This
shows the influence of the 13th-
century Southern Song masters
with the use of ink washes to
create mist.

Left Detail of a landscape by
Wang Hui (1632–1717) in the
style of Huang Gongwang (1269–
1354). Like other members of the
Orthodox school of the Qing
dynasty Wang Hui based his
paintings on creative
reinterpretations of earlier
landscape masters.

and his landscapes are painted in a deliberately archaic manner, yet they incorporate brushstrokes which are not typical of the early period. This can be more readily seen in the work of Zhao Mengfu (1254–1322), as in his handscroll *Autumn Colors on the Qiao and Hua Mountains*, which is archaic in spirit but inventive in light texture brushstrokes. In his bamboo, tree and rock paintings he uses a rapid ''flying white'' stroke over the surface of the paper which leaves some areas white. He was also a great calligrapher. Like scholar-painters of the 11th century, he held that painting was a means of expressing the inner feelings of the artist and emphasized the close relationship of painting and calligraphy; but above all he stressed the spirit of antiquity.

Zhao Mengfu looked back to the Tang and Northern Song masters for a feeling of their work which he combined with a calligraphic freedom of brush, a development which was to be taken further by the Four Masters of the Yuan: Huang Gong-wang, Ni Zan, Wu Zhen and Wang Meng.

Dwelling in the Fuchun Mountains by Huang Gongwang (1269–1354) is one of the masterpieces of Chinese painting, catching the essence of the landscape with variation of brush and ink in perfectly balanced strokes. His inscription on the painting tells us that he painted it for a friend, and took over three years between starting and inscribing it in 1350. In his landscape paintings Wu Zhen (1280–1354) combines brushwork in the manner of Dong Yuan and Ju Ran of the Northern Song with a daring use of open space, yet he avoids the misty romanticism of the Ma/Xia school. Ni Zan (1301–74) shunned court life and public service under the alien Mongol rulers who denied the scholar class the prestige it had formerly enjoyed; like many artists and poets of the time, he withdrew to live the life of a hermit. ''With a flat boat and my bamboo rain-hat I went to and fro around the lakes.'' His paintings were mainly of sparse landscapes and he showed a masterly restraint in his use of ink. Of his bamboo paintings he says, ''I did them simply to express my overflowing heart.'' Ni Zan is said to have painted bamboo by candlelight and when he got up next morning and looked at it, it bore no resemblance to bamboo. He laughed and said, ''Ah, but a total lack of resemblance is not an easy thing to achieve!'' The weightlessness of his paintings reflects the spirit of the man. His *Rongxi Studio* is executed in deft horizontal strokes, with the vertical lines of trees balanced in perfect harmony. Wang Meng (1308–85) wielded his brush in a more closely spun network of strokes. He built the landscape with dense texture strokes, using a dry brush to build up foliage, so giving the painting a restless, vibrant movement. He used wash for distant foliage and ''burned'' ink for the texture of bark and his landscapes snaked up the full height of the scroll. These Four Masters set the mood for the scholar-painters of the Ming period.

Ceramics of the imperial age are described and illustrated on pages 200–01 below.

Detail of *The North Sea*, a handscroll by Zhou Chen (c. 1455–c. 1536).

THE EVOLUTION OF SOCIETY

Chinese society was continually changing during the two thousand years or so that the empire lasted, but it is not easy to find satisfactory categories with which to describe these changes simply. In particular, different criteria produce different lines of division, as will become apparent.

The most fundamental distinction to be made is clearly that between the periods before and after what may be called the "medieval economic revolution." This took place approximately halfway through the imperial age, in the centuries on either side of 1000 AD. In broad terms, Chinese society after this watershed was much more productive, commercialized, monetized, urbanized, literate and numerate than it had been before. It was also much larger in numbers. The population rose from a maximum in the times of the greatest prosperity of perhaps 60 to 70 million to possibly 140 million at the height of the Song, and then, after a decline in the 14th century, to an eventual premodern maximum of 430 million by 1850. There are no generally accepted terms that summarize this overall social transition. Provisionally, it may be suggested that the before and after stages may be called respectively "pre-economic society" and "economic society." The word "economic" points

not only to the virtually universal involvement of people in trade and money transactions in Song and post-Song times, it also suggests the emergence of an empire-wide *system* of the circulation of goods, people and ideas. There was a trend towards the functionally rational structuring of society at this time, a symptom of which was the generalization of the use of competitive examinations to select civil servants.

The term "pre-economic society" should not be taken to imply that there was not considerable commercial activity in the earlier age. There was, but it was almost entirely related to meeting the needs of the upper classes rather than, to some extent at least, of everybody. It might also be more appropriate to designate the already quite complex social life of the time immediately before the Song as "proto-economic." Likewise, the more exact phrase "pre-scientific economic society" can be used to mark off the later imperial age from early modern times, when Western technology and ideas had begun to make an impact on China. The terms "pre-industrial" or "pre-capitalist" will not do. Already under the Northern Song it is possible to find standardized mass production (most notably in the state armaments industry, which produced 16·5

A brief section of the panoramic scroll by Zhang Zeduan entitled *Going on the River at the Qingming Festival*. Scholars generally agree that it shows the Northern Song capital of Kaifeng around the turn of the 11th and 12th centuries AD. The structure of the picture is a triumph of quietly dramatic design. Far to the right of the scene shown here the viewer begins his imaginary walk in the countryside among the spring willow trees and herds of cattle. He makes his way leftwards through a growing suburban bustle like that in the section below, on a pictorial progress that culminates – out of sight again – with his entry through one of the city's stone gates set in the great wall of rammed earth.

million arrowheads a year) and very sizable concentrations of mercantile capital.

The details of the medieval revolution in farming are presented in the section on Chinese agriculture (pp. 208–13). It had four main features: better preparation of soil and methods of soil conservation, including rotations; much-improved strains of seed, either through importation or selective breeding, with the result that double-cropping and staggered maturing seasons were much more easily attained; better techniques of water control and an extension of irrigation; and more local specialization because of the growth of trade and transportation. Most of the new techniques were pioneered in the lower Yangzi valley, from where they spread around the rest of the country through the circulation of the official elite, the migration of farmers and the study of books on farming (printed by woodblocks).

Land transportation was improved by the surfacing of many inter-city routes with stone slabs or bricks. It was, however, inland water transportation that became the foundation of the new commercial economy. The network of routes was linked up into an integrated whole by means of all sorts of improvements, such as institutionalized transshipment of goods around dangerous places and innovations like the hauling-way for pulling junks up the Yangzi gorges, the double or pound locks on part of the Grand Canal and paddle-wheel tugs (worked by manpower) in harbors. Chinese oceangoing vessels were now built with iron nails waterproofed with the oil of the *tong* tree, steered with axial rudders rather than steering-oars, and equipped with watertight bulkheads, bamboo fenders, outrigger and lee-board devices and magnetic compasses for navigation. They quickly gained the upper hand over ships from southeast Asia and the Persian and Arab worlds. So great was the expansion of ship-building that southern Chinese forests were seriously depleted as a result.

Trade and industry

The huge growth in the money supply between the Tang and the Song was both a symptom of and a contributing factor to the economic revolution. The desperate search for more currency in the 10th century makes both amusing and somewhat sad reading. There were bans, at times, on making cooking pots out of copper, and Buddhist statues were melted down to provide cash. In the northeast, clay money was even used for a time, such was the shortage of metal. At its height the Northern Song annual output of copper cash was about 20 times the Tang maximum. But the growth in money supply was even greater than this ratio would suggest. There was an immense increase in the use of all sorts of bills, tallies, tickets and primitive forms of fiduciary money; in 1024 AD in Sichuan the world's first true paper money was printed. Before long China also experienced its first printing-press inflation, caused by the difficulties of financing the war against the Xixia. The use of money spread through the peasant economy to such an extent that when travelers found barter still being used in an out-of-the-way place it was an occasion for comment. Credit mechanisms were routinely inserted into the organization of production, storage and distribution; written commercial contracts

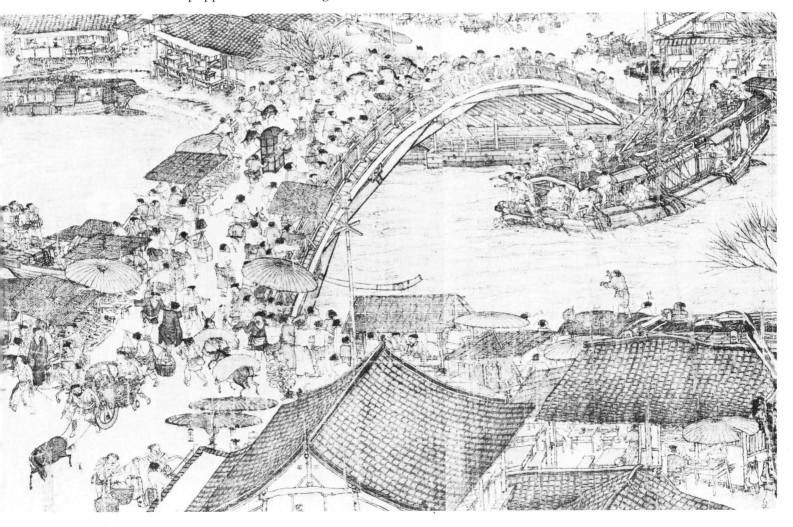

became commonplace.

In proto-economic times, the only items of general use that were traded on a large scale were salt and iron tools. Otherwise, as has been indicated, most production for the market was limited to supplying the needs of the better-off. Tax revenues, in the form of government orders and official salaries, were probably one of the most important sources of demand for the commercialized sector of the economy, rather than the spending-power of the private consumer. With such a concentration of demand in the administrative centers, it is understandable how it was possible for legal trading to have been limited to specified market areas in, or just outside, the larger cities. Shops and stalls in the same line of business were placed together and put under government supervision. Weights and measures were subject to state control; often these markets were confined within walls. By the 8th century, however, there was a flourishing network of unofficial markets in the countryside, usually held periodically, while within the cities merchants began to set up shops and stalls wherever they pleased. The old system collapsed in the 9th century, and was replaced by a high degree of commercial freedom. Taxing was now performed by customs-houses along the main trade routes, and, under the Southern Song especially, trade provided a large proportion of state revenue.

Increased contact with the market made the Chinese peasantry into a class of rational, adaptable, profit-orientated petty entrepreneurs. A wide range of new occupations opened up for them in the countryside: timber-growing, oil-pressing, sugar-refining, fish-rearing, paper-making, weaving textiles of hemp, ramie, and – from the 13th century on – of cotton, and making lacquer and iron goods. When villagers lacked raw materials, they often imported them.

The local markets were the foundation of a hierarchy of higher-level markets that linked together almost the entire Chinese economy. There were three main economic regions: north China, centered on the Northern Song capital at Kaifeng; eastern central China, centered on the complex of cities around the Tai Lake; and Sichuan, centered on the cities of the Chengdu plain. Within these regions there was an extensive trade in the staples of everyday life, especially grains and clothing fabrics. Trade between the regions was, however, limited to the more valuable commodities, such as silks, porcelain and medicines. There was, in addition, a flourishing international trade with Japan and southeast Asia and even further afield. The fruit production of Fujian became partly linked to overseas demand, and Fujian lychees sometimes ended up as far away as Persia.

The commercial system advanced to the stage where its larger operations revolved around brokers who coordinated the operations of traveling merchants and retailers. This points to flexible rather than to routinely stabilized patterns of long-distance exchange. These latter seem only to have become the rule in the later 17th century. Some of the entrepreneurs of the pre-scientific economic age employed large workforces. That of the ironmaster Wang Ge, for instance, in the Southern Song, may have reached several thousand.

More productive agriculture and cheaper trans-portation made possible larger cities, though the possibility should not be overlooked that the growth of the cities may have often been the stimulus for these improvements in the first place. In case after case, the old cities spilled out from within their original walls, and grew until the original nucleus was all but lost in the surrounding conurbation. A rough estimate, based on extrapolating from the limited figures at our disposal, suggests that between 6 and 7·5 per cent of the population were living in cities of 100 000 or more at this time. China was therefore almost certainly the most urbanized society of the high Middle Ages.

Considerable progress was also made in science and technology, though "revolution" would be too strong a word to use here. The basic patterns of thought did not change sufficiently radically to justify such a description. There were, however, both new inventions and a much wider use of methods and machines inherited from the preceding age. In mathematics a general technique was found for the solution of numerical equations containing any power of a single unknown. In astronomy a new level of observational accuracy was achieved with the casting of much larger instruments, and the perfecting of hydraulic clockwork for turning celestial globes. In medicine a start was made on systematic anatomy with the revival of the dissection of corpses, and more precision was attained in the description of diseases, including some of the so-called crowd diseases and occupational disorders. In metalworking coal certainly (and coke possibly) was used for the extraction of iron from iron ore, by a crucible method. In warfare gunpowder was developed from a material for fireworks into a true explosive; flame-throwers, poison gas, fragment-ation bombs and – finally – the gun were invented. Much of the new knowledge was spread by woodblock printing, which had probably been invented in the 9th century AD by Buddhist missionaries as a part of their effort to propagate their faith. The state published numerous compil-ations ranging from the Confucian scriptures to herbals (which were also pharmacopoeias), while private enterprise produced books like Yang Hui's *Mathematics for Daily Use*, printed in 1262.

The most interesting and tantalizing of the Chinese inventions of the medieval economic revolution was mechanized spinning. Some time during the Northern Song dynasty a method had been perfected for the mechanical reeling of silk. Worked by a treadle, the reeling-machine drew a number of filaments simultaneously from a tub of boiling water in which the silkworm cocoons had been immersed. The filaments passed through eyelets, then hooks, and then on to a ramping-arm that laid them down back and forth in broad bands on a rotating open-work reeling-frame. In the 13th century the basic idea embodied in this reeling-machine was adapted for the spinning of hemp thread. A line of spindles carrying hemp roving (a loosely twisted thick strand of the fibers) was put in the place of the somewhat similarly shaped but of course much smaller cocoons. Hollow bobbin-rollers, not unlike the rings of later ring-spinning, and twirling to impart a twist, were put in the place of the eyelets. The device could be powered by men, animals or a waterwheel, the transmission coming through a driving-belt. This machine is described

The Three Kingdoms period and Northern Song marketing regions
After the breakdown of the Later Han dynasty towards the end of the 2nd century AD, China split into three kingdoms. These were Wei in the north, Wu in the east and south, and Shu in the Sichuan basin. It was a militarily unstable configuration and Inner China was reunited from the north in AD 265 by the Western Jin dynasty, the successors of Wei.

In economic terms, however, this tripartite division reflected a reality that long endured. It is still possible to think of the Nothern Song empire, 700 years after the Three Kingdoms, as having been composed of three great regional markets corresponding to the vanished realms of Wei, Wu and Shu. (The status of the northwest was slightly ambivalent, as it had links with both the northern region and Sichuan.) These geographical divisions are underscored by the fact that the main communications routes between the three economic regions were all man-made: the Grand Canal linking north and south, the hauling-way through the gorges of the Yangzi linking the south with Sichuan and the Gallery Road joining Sichuan with the northwest.

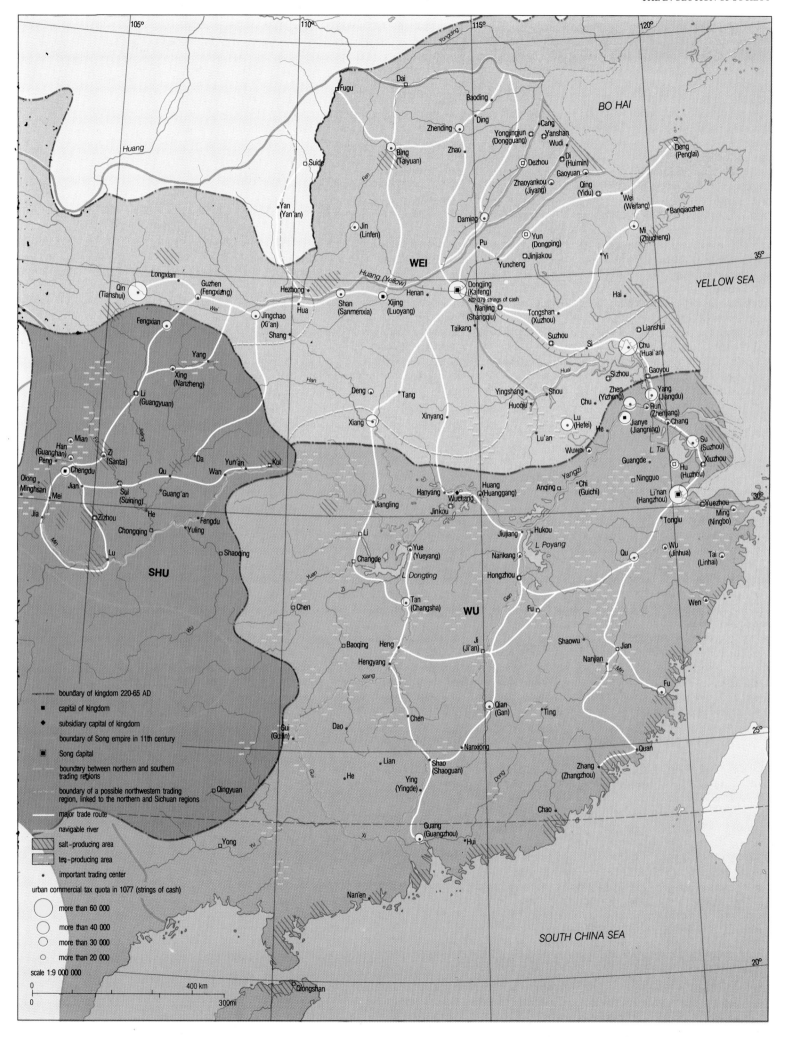

BO HAI

YELLOW SEA

Fugu
Dai
Baoding
Zhending Ding
Zhao Cang
Yongjingjun Yanshan
(Dongguang) Wudi
Suide Bing Zhao Dezhou Di Deng
(Taiyuan) Zhaoyankou (Huimin) (Penglai)
Yan (Jiyang) Gaoyuan
(Yan'an) Daming Qing
Jin (Yidu) Wei
(Linfen) Pu (Weifang)
Yun Banqiaozhen
(Dongping) Mi
Longxian Yuncheng Jinjiakou (Zhucheng)
Qin Guzhen Yi
(Tianshui) (Fengxiang) Hezhong Huang (Yellow)
Hua Shan Xijing Henan WEI
(Sanmenxia) (Luoyang) Dongjing Hai
Fengxian Jingchao (Kaifeng)
(Xi'an) Shang 402 379 strings of cash
Yang Nanjing Tongshan
(Shangqiu) (Xuzhou) Lianshui
Xing Taikang Suzhou Chu
(Nanzheng) Si (Huai'an)
Li Han Gaoyou
(Guangyuan) Deng Tang Sizhou Yang
Mian Yingshang Zhen (Jiangdu)
Han Zi Da Shou Chu (Yizheng) Run
(Guanghan) (Santai) Yun'an Kui Lu (Zhenjiang)
Peng Chengdu Xiang Xinyang He (Hefei) Su Chang
Qiong Jian Qu Guang'an Lu'an Wuwei Jianye (Suzhou)
Minghshan Sui Fengdu Guangde (Jiangning) Xiuzhou
Mei (Suining) Huang Hu
Jia Zizhou He Yuling (Huanggang) Anqing Chi (Huzhou)
Chongqing Hanyang (Guichi) Ningguo
Lu Jiangling Wuchang Yangzi Li'nan
Shaoqing Jinkou (Hangzhou)
Li Tonglu Yuezhou
SHU Changde Yue Huang Ming
(Yueyang) Jiujiang Hukou (Ningbo)
Chen Tan L Dongting Nankang Qu Wu
(Changsha) L Poyang (Jihua)
WU Hongzhou Tai
Baoqing Heng (Linhai)
Hengyang Ji Fu Shaowu Wen
(Ji'an) Jian
Chen Nanjian
Dao Qian Ting Fu
(Gan)
Gui Chao
(Guilin)
Lian Nanxiong Zhang
He Shao (Zhangzhou)
Ying (Shaoguan) Quan
(Yingde)
Chao
Qingyuan Guang
(Guangzhou) Hui
Yong
Nan'en

BO HAI

SOUTH CHINA SEA

boundary of kingdom 220–65 AD
■ capital of kingdom
◆ subsidiary capital of kingdom
boundary of Song empire in 11th century
☐ Song capital
boundary between northern and southern
trading regions
boundary of a possible northwestern trading
region, linked to the northern and Sichuan regions
major trade route
navigable river
salt-producing area
tea-producing area
• important trading center

urban commercial tax quota in 1077 (strings of cash)
○ more than 60 000
○ more than 40 000
○ more than 30 000
○ more than 20 000

scale 1:9 000 000
0   400 km
0   300 mi

by Wang Zhen in his *Treatise on Agriculture* of 1313, where he says that its 32 spindles could spin about 60 kilograms of thread in a full day's work. The device was never, so far as is known, adapted for cotton; and this would have been difficult to do without extensive modification, given the shortness of cotton fibers, especially Chinese varieties. Interestingly, though, the key to Arkwright's spinning frame half a millennium later, the use of pairs of rollers for drawing out the fiber while it was being spun, was known to the Chinese at this time in the form of the cotton gin, which squeezed the seeds out of raw cotton rather the way an old-fashioned mangle squeezes water out of wet clothes. It is evident from this machine that the Chinese had already come by 1300 to the brink of the ideas and practices that underlay the early industrial revolution in Western Europe.

The chronological clarity of this divide between "pre-economic" and "economic" society is a little impaired by the depression into which the Chinese economy fell during the 14th and 15th centuries. North China was severely afflicted both by the Ruzhen Jin occupation and then by the Mongol conquest and Ming campaign of repossession. The Huai valley too was badly depopulated, being the scene of much destructive fighting between the Southern Song and its northern enemies, the Ruzhen and the Mongols.

The Jin occupation was founded on groups of locally stationed tribal garrison households, who were given large quantities of the better farmland. They owed taxes in proportion to the fields, oxen and horses, serfs and slaves that they owned or had been allocated by the government. They often tried to reduce this tax obligation by selling off their servile subordinates, and then induced or coerced Chinese peasants to become their tenants. They had little personal understanding of agriculture, and the general effect of this unstable system was to disrupt the northern farming economy. Under the Mongols, who followed the Jin, great tracts of arable land were also turned into pastures.

The Chinese economy was unable to recover quickly from this depression. In part this was because of the filling up, during the preceding period, of the most productive parts of the south by a population that had become so large that the dynamic impulses, which had once flowed into the economy from the exploitation of new resources along a frontier of settlement, had all but died away. The medieval economic revolution had owed much to the swift extension of wet-field rice farming in the south. Now only marginal land was left untilled, the former surplus was being absorbed by population growth, and the earlier effects of increased per-person demand had vanished.

So much was probably unavoidable. The same could not be said of the policies of the Ming government. In the areas of overseas trade, coastal shipping and currency, disastrous damage was unnecessarily inflicted on the economy during the later 14th century and the early 15th century. Previously, the Southern Song had permitted virtually unrestricted foreign trade, subject to the issue of licenses. The Mongols, in fits and starts, had then imposed an officially controlled system. The founder of the Ming dynasty converted this into a purely tributary trade, based on diplomatic mis-sions from those foreign nations that acknowledged China's suzerainty. In 1371 Chinese were forbidden to go overseas. Early in the next century even coastal shipping was fobidden. This "Maritime Interdict" lasted until 1567, when it was partially lifted. It temporarily ruined much of the economy of the southeast coast, and deprived China of the stimulus of new ideas and techniques from abroad, just at the time when the great maritime expansion of the West was beginning. The Ming government's basic motive seems to have been political security: to avoid the creation of centrifugal coastal centers of power that would be hard to control.

The imposition of an inconvertible paper currency by the early Ming was also to some extent the outcome of the dynasty's pursuit of economic self-sufficiency and its political isolationism. There was also an inadequate domestic supply of copper and other metals, which was itself partly the result of the flight of silver into western Asia in response to the reckless issue of inconvertible notes by the last Mongol rulers. In the same way that the maritime interdict had set the state at war with powerful coastal interests that had been tempted to turn to smuggling, the currency policy set the state at war with its own merchant class. The official insistence on the use of paper money gradually collapsed during the middle third of the 15th century, and the liquidity situation was to some extent saved by the illegal and semilegal import of silver from abroad. From the end of the 16th century, of course, silver imported from the New World through Manila in the Philippines allowed China to go over to a silver-based currency system for all major commercial transactions.

Even in the depression, though, there is no evidence that the economy became so decommercialized or demonetized that one can speak of a return to a "pre-economic" condition. But there was one casualty of importance. The Chinese largely (though not entirely) lost the art of inventing. Why this should have been so, among a people hitherto among the most technically creative in the world, is still something of a mystery. We shall return to this question later when we consider why China failed to have a self-generated industrial revolution.

Administrators and landowners

The fundamental two-fold division of China's economic and social history just described had certain political and even intellectual counterparts. With some reservations it is possible to describe the upper-level political leaders of the first period as "aristocratic" in the sense that they came from well-known, long-established and influential lineages, usually with some sort of localized powerbase. This was not altogether true for the Former Han, and there were of course always newcomers breaking into the charmed circle, but it is a workable approximation. In contrast, the upper-level political leaders from the Song onwards cannot be described as aristocrats, with the possible exception of some non-Chinese under the Mongol and Manchu dynasties. They were "bureaucrats" or "meritocrats." Very few lineages now remained important at the national (as opposed to the local) political level for more than one or at most two generations. The social reservoir from which the elite was drawn deepened from Tang to Song to Ming, though it may

後周武帝宇文邑在
位二十八年五帝共廿五年
毀滅佛法

Above The Emperor Wu of the Northern Zhou is portrayed in the Tang courtly style by the artist Yan Liban (fl. 640–70)–although part of the handscroll is thought to be a Song dynasty copy. He portrays 13 emperors from Han to Sui in ink and color on silk. The painting shows the less important figures smaller in scale.

Left Detail from a Ming dynasty handscroll in ink and color on paper showing a victim of famine.

called the "system-state" and "organic society." Time and again, from the Qin dynasty onwards, reforming rulers tried forcibly to impose various blueprints of organization on society; time and again society, following a different logic, distorted and subverted these imposed schemes. The actual forms of social life at any one place and moment reflected some particular compromise between these two forces. The schemes were never merely paper; the reality was virtually never as it was statutorily meant to be.

Under the early empire the chief threat to the collection of revenue and the conscription of soldiers was the growth of huge estates owned by officials or merchants and worked by slaves or tenants. These estates were in practice able to resist most of the demands placed on them by local government authorities. There was also, under the early Former Han, a regional aristocracy, that sprang from collateral members of the imperial house and ran what amounted to almost independent domains in a good portion of the country. In the later part of the 2nd century BC Emperor Wu of the Han dynasty broke their power by declaring 127 out of the 197 princes and marquises to be guilty of some crime or without a proper heir. Their lands were confiscated on such a scale that the state itself became the largest single landowner. New taxes were imposed on business, and used, directly or indirectly through accusations of non-compliance, to ruin most of the larger merchants. Government monopolies on the sale of salt, iron and wine were introduced, partly to block some of the main avenues to big business fortunes.

The most uncompromising attempt to destroy the power of the large landowners was made by Wang Mang, a high official who had usurped the throne in 9 AD. His blueprint was derived from the *Rituals of the Zhou*, a highly idealized account of the institutions of antiquity, in which people were shown as living in semi-communal groups of eight families. Wang tried to redistribute farmland, and he forbade the buying and selling of fields and the traffic in slaves. He was, however, quite unable to have these measures enforced.

After the Later Han restoration a system of quasi-feudalism emerged in which local strongmen drew most of the social and economic power into their own hands. Their lands were worked by slaves or dependent tenants, and their military retainers provided them with private armies. They were also often substantial traders. Many of them built fortified camps and castles in the interior. Peasant uprisings became more common, and culminated in 184 AD with that of the Yellow Turbans, religious sectaries who organized themselves on communal lines and looked forward in messianic hope to the coming of an age of "Great Well-Being." The Han empire fell apart as a functioning institution in the ensuing chaotic civil wars.

The next social blueprint of importance was devised by Cao Cao, the soldier and poet who was the effective founder of the state of Wei. In contrast to Wang Mang's, it was entirely pragmatic. The financial underpinning of the government was provided by rent (or taxes) from state colony lands worked by state tenants, an idea partly derived from the Han frontier colony. The core of the Wei army consisted of hereditary military families,

have thereafter stayed about constant in relative size. Importantly in the long run, the new top-level administrators were increasingly "mandarins"; that is to say, they were officially recognized on the basis of their degrees as masters of the Neo-Confucian orthodoxy defined in the 12th century by the philosopher Zhu Xi, and hence, in some respects, as a sort of political priesthood possessing special ideological qualifications entitling them to rule. The Northern Song conducted civil-service examinations in a number of practical topics, including mathematics, but by Ming times only ideological and literary accomplishments were tested. The mandarin ideal spread slowly downwards through society over the centuries, eventually ideologizing nearly everyone with any claim to literacy and learning, until respected status and thorough indoctrination in Neo-Confucianism were almost inseparably linked.

The history of Chinese society in the imperial age can be more finely subdivided in a number of ways. One of the most revealing is in terms of the changing pattern taken by the struggle between what may be originally Cao Cao's personal retainers. These two classes amounted to almost half the population of the new state. Cao Cao also broke up the bodies of dependent tenants and private military retainers assembled by other great lords, turning the dependants into free peasants with grants of land and incorporating the soldiers into the state's armed forces.

The Wei state colonies were vulnerable to the ambitions of the agricultural officials who administered them. Often they turned the colonists into what amounted to their own dependants. The system was dismantled by the Western Jin dynasty in 280 AD, and superseded by another blueprint that was both more practical and more complex. This was the land regime known as "allocation and possession" (*kezhan*). Previous colony land was allocated to the ex-colonists in standardized amounts and taxed at a relatively high level. A maximum limit was also placed on the quantity of land that might be owned in private possession by a household of commoner status, and this type of land was taxed at a more lenient rate. Larger estates were only permitted in the form of service-tenure fiefs held by officials in accordance with a scale determined by their rank. This was a compromise with the realities: the state asserted the principle of its control, but local power in the form of large landowners with official rank was in practice permitted to exist.

When Western Jin rule collapsed in northern China early in the 4th century AD, under the blows of barbarian attacks, some of the better-run islands of independent Chinese power that survived there showed in a particularly clear form how what we have called "organic society" functioned at this time. Once bureaucratic government had vanished, the leading men would swear an oath of obedience to the most respected of their number. A carefully defined hierarchy of rank and age would be established in the communities under their control, based on popularly esteemed natural leaders. A strong pervading sense of moral unity would be fostered, and concern would be shown to ensure that the burdens of defense and taxes were allocated as equitably as possible. Of course the less well-run enclaves were little more than dens of robber-barons.

The next blueprint worthy of the name was promulgated in the years 484 to 486 AD in the Xianbi state of the Toba (or Tabgatch) Wei in the north of China. It was devised by a coterie of Chinese statesmen around the empress-dowager, and must be seen against a social background in which great local landowners were also hereditary officials, depending on their own rents to pay for their administration. Officials who were not local residents had to manage on forced levies, commerce and money-lending. The basis for the registration of the population, and hence taxation, was now changed

This picture of a polo player is seen on the wall of the passage leading to the tomb chamber of Prince Zhang Huai (654–84) who was buried at Qianling, the imperial mausoleum of his father the emperor Gaozong at Liangshan in Shaanxi province. The murals there also depict the pomp of a Tang royal hunt as a large procession of huntsmen with bows and quivers, some carrying falcons, gallop through wooded hills suggested by sketchy brushstrokes. Polo was introduced to China from Persia in the 7th century and became a popular sport of Tang dynasty emperors and princes. When still a prince, the Tang emperor Xuanzong played in an international match together with three other royal relatives and claimed victory over the Tibetan team.

from the household to the married couple, in order to bypass the practice whereby large clans under a single powerful head were enrolled as a single family for tax purposes. The nuclear families were then formed into a hierarchy of deliberately artificial units called "neighborhoods," "cantons" and "groups." Farmland was allotted to commoners for their lifetimes, with extra acres for those with their own oxen and slaves. Skepticism is warranted about how universally this land distribution was enforced, but in the 6th century it was certainly put into effect in some parts of the successor states that followed the Toba Wei. As under the allocation and possession system of the Western Jin, provision was made for officials to have larger estates, their size graded by rank. One difference was that they were meant to be allocated to the officials out of the public land in the areas in which they were serving. This, in summary, was the famous system of "equitable fields" (*juntian*). One of its consequences, arising out of the need to conciliate local magnates, seems to have been a proliferation of low-level administrative units – to provide the required official posts for large landowners. Once again, under the superficial appearance of rigid state prescriptions, it was in practice a compromise.

In the state of Western Wei during the middle of the 6th century a new military institution was also devised in order to extend central control over the personally led levies of locally important people. To begin with, these local leaders were simply given official ranks and commissions and brought within a unified command structure. Then a more elaborate form was developed in which every six of the better-off farming households had to support and equip a militiaman. He was trained in the off-season under the local prefect, and was personally exempted from taxation. Local loyalties were little by little eroded by shifting the upper-level officers around between different postings. This was the famous "divisional militia" (*fubing*), a geographically dispersed semi-elite of farmer-soldiers remarkably resistant to subversion or rebellion.

The equitable fields system and the divisional militia were inherited and further elaborated by the reunited empire of the Sui and early Tang. Yet within little more than a century they had both decayed to the point of virtual collapse. There were some important technical reasons for this. Part-time militia were not well suited to guarding distant frontiers, and the periodic redistribution of land was inappropriate in wet-field farming regions, because it took away from those who had made it the fruits of the enormous investment of labor needed for irrigated agriculture. The equitable field system was never effectively extended to the Yangzi valley, probably for this reason, and the south was at this time becoming more and more important in the imperial economy. The heart of the matter, however, was that the state had tried to use both institutions to exert such a degree of control over society that it came into serious conflict with a number of social realities.

The basic objective of the 7th-century imperial government was to make service in the divisional militia and the state bureaucracy the general aspiration of the well-to-do and the talented, and to this end it tried to make such service the only acceptable avenue to landed wealth or reputation.

The state did not, however, dispose of sufficient resources to pay in full measure the rewards that meritorious military service earned. Enthusiasm to participate understandably waned as a result. More seriously still, when Emperor Wen of the Sui tried to strengthen the power of the central government by decreeing that prefectural and county officials were to move once every three years, and did away with the previous grants of extra land to those with slaves, he caused the land laws to come into opposition with the interests of a large number of landowners. Unlike the officials of the Toba Wei and its immediate successor states, those of the Sui and Tang were not usually local magnates decked out with the titles of office, and with some measure of hereditary right to their offices and hence their larger holdings of land, but genuine bureaucratic appointees. Faced with losing their public estates when they moved or retired, officials struggled to put together private estates and to hold on to them. By the later 8th century Chinese society was again dominated by large private latifundia worked by dependent tenants, in conditions that were soon to become semi-servile.

After the middle of the Tang, the Chinese imperial state was never again able to determine the shape of society directly. There were partial interventions. Thus the Southern Song tried in its final years to reduce the size of large landholdings; and the founder of the Ming dynasty confiscated numerous private estates in the lower Yangzi valley, and turned the peasants there into state tenants. The Mongols for their part instituted a system of four ethnic classes: (1) Mongols; (2) central Asians; (3) northern Chinese plus sinicized Ruzhen, Qidan and Koreans; (4) southern Chinese. The chief purpose of this system was to perpetuate the hold of the first two categories on the bureaucratic apparatus. With about 3 per cent of the registered population, they came to occupy about 30 per cent of the posts in the regular civil service. There were also some differences in legal status. The most notable of these was the ruling of the Mongol Chancellor Bayan in the mid-1330s that no Chinese might carry weapons or retaliate if struck by a Mongol or central Asian. The founder of the Ming dynasty imposed hereditary status on a limited but not insignificant number of artisans and soldiers. None of these measures can be compared to the earlier efforts to impose general social blueprints, and the more complex society that had developed in the course of the medieval economic revolution was one of the basic reasons for this change.

In designing the lowest level of its local government the Song dynasty came directly to terms with the realities of rural society. It developed to a quite new level of importance the institution of what may be called "conscripted administrators." (These had their historical roots in the "rural officials" of Qin and Han times, such as the commune chiefs and hamlet chiefs, but the element of coercion was recent.) The wealthiest people in each group of registered households, apart from the very small number (perhaps of the order of 20 000) containing a member of the regular imperial bureaucracy, were obliged to shoulder in rotation, and without pay, the basic tasks of village government. They were responsible for collecting taxes, maintaining order, settling minor judicial disputes, distributing famine relief, organizing the mending of the roads, transmitting documents and providing various services to regular officials. The precise nature of the system varied from time to time and from place to place. In general the most important of these village officers were the so-called superior grand leaders (*dubao-zheng*) and the household chiefs (*hu-zhang*). They bore such heavy obligations – for instance, making good from their own pockets any of the local tax quota that they had failed to collect – that those liable for duty would sometimes flee rather than perform it. They could also suffer from the demands of the professional clerks in the prefectural and sub-prefectural offices. Over those below them, however, they clearly wielded great power. Not only were legal matters and control of the militia in their hands, but also the allocation of tax obligations among the individual households.

These members of the rural elite, and the holders of bureaucratic office, lived mostly off estates worked by semi-servile laborers who may be loosely described as "tenant-serfs." They were bound to the soil in practice, though the state occasionally tried to ease the conditions of this bondage. Thus it was decreed, though to little effect, that they might leave after a year's harvest was in or if the land changed owners. A good general picture of rural servitude is provided by a passage in a letter written by the scholar Hu Hong about his native Hunan in the middle of the 12th century:

> There is a chain of obedience stretching down from masters to tenants. It is by means of this that the state is supplied. It cannot be dispensed with for a single day. Since this is so, how can tenants be allowed to do as they please? This would result in their masters being unable to control them! Tenants depend on their masters for their livelihood; and so they have to provide them with services and submit to their discipline. Officials should inflict a vigorous punishment on tenants, and forbid them to act in accordance with their own pleasure, in the event that a master lays a plaint on any of the following grounds: (1) that his tenants are behaving perversely, and refusing to recognize the distinction between superior and inferior; (2) that they are practicing commerce, and not working hard at sericulture and farming; (3) that they are drinking or gambling without restraint, and are unamenable to discipline; (4) that, being unmarried, they are enticing away other men's wives; or (5) that, having many adult males in their families, and more than enough food and clothing, they have been able to buy half an acre or an acre of farmland and a house, have set up a tax-paying household of their own and wish to leave their master.

Right Under the Mongol (Yuan) regime (1279–1368) access to official careers was more difficult for Chinese men of letters than before (partly because of examination quotas set on a racial basis), and many turned to art and drama. The drawing illustrates a *zaju* ("variety") play taking place. Banners advertise local wine and pawn shops, and a dagoba constructed by the Mongols is seen in the background. The ruling Mongol class, in native costume, ride by as the local Han population watch the play. To avoid being criticized by the Mongol regime, a contemporary play would be staged in Song dynasty costume.

As in all rural societies, actual conditions varied greatly from place to place. In some areas, like the Chengdu plain in Sichuan, there were huge unified estates worked by serfs under the lash of the overseer's whip. In others the estates were divided into a central domain cultivated under supervision by tenant-serfs, with outlying fields farmed by tenants merely owing rent. There were "official manors" set up in areas like northern Jiangsu (to give it its present-day name) that needed to be rehabilitated after years of warfare. In some places, like the southern, mountainous part of modern Zhejiang, a free peasantry was the nearly universal rule and servile tenure virtually unknown. In all other areas, though, there seems to have been a constant battle between the wealthy, who tried to enserf peasants in one way or another, and their servile tenants, who strove to find some way to set up on their own and become independent.

There is no way of making a meaningful estimate of the proportion of the peasantry subjected to serf status, especially since the degrees of subordination were so various. What is certain is that in most areas there were also large numbers, maybe sometimes a majority, of formally free, tax-paying farming households. What seems likely is that the larger landowners, who dominated rural society through their officially backed positions as superior general leaders and household chiefs and controlled much of the farm economy through their leadership of water-control projects, had as their social base the exploitation of unfree labor. To this extent it is appropriate to speak of a "manorial society," but it is important not to be misled by this term into imagining that the Chinese type of manor was anything like universal, or that every Song peasant was a serf. The link between substantial estates based on servile tenancy and the system of conscript administration, based on well-to-do landowners (or their paid substitutes and agents), was however fundamental, in that one made the other possible. When the servile estate finally disappeared in the later 17th century, what were by then the remnants of conscript administration perforce vanished with it.

The reforms of Wang Anshi

The last premodern attempt to use government power to alter directly the functioning of society as a whole occurred in the years between 1069 and 1074. These were the mostly short-lived reforms of the remarkable chief minister of the Song emperor Shenzong, First Privy Councillor Wang Anshi. Wang began his career as a provincial official, but he was also a theoretical philosopher of some ability and a competent poet. The background to his political thought was the semi-mystical Confucian idea that by making one's person tranquil and so accumulating charismatic virtue – the mental art of grasping the inner structure of the universe and so "entering into the spiritual domain" – one could acquire the power to act effectively and at the decisive moment. As had been the case with Wang Mang, his institutional inspiration was the idealized society of the *Rituals of the Zhou* in which, he said, "the honorable and the humble had their proper places, and the younger and older their proper precedence." In one of his poems he referred with nostalgic romanticism to the golden age of the Three

Dynasties of the Xia, Shang and Zhou when the rulers "treated the common people like their children, and there was no distinction between public and private property .... Taxes were given of people's spontaneous free-will; and accumulating and engrossing were abhorred as depravity." But he was well aware that times had changed, and that the old formulas could not be applied mechanically.

His view of human nature was that it was, like the ultimate principle of the universe, neither good nor bad in itself. This led him to attach the greatest importance to the effects of habit, conditioning and education. Although he believed that the true art of moral instruction was so subtle that the recipients themselves were unaware of their own transformation, his intolerant emphasis at court on a uniformity of views may have played some part in the later development in China of the "indoctrination state."

There were also strands of the legalist or realist tradition in his thinking. "From time immemorial, in the management of affairs, power has been the only way to lead the masses and cause ruler and ruled to be as one." "If one only wishes the condition of the people to be as their desires would have it, why should there be any need to establish a ruler?" In one of his poems, written after his fall from office, he observed, possibly a little ruefully, that the men of his own day had no right to criticize Lord Shang of the state of Qin since "whatever he commanded he was able to have done." Other poems show Wang to have been imbued with the Buddhist feeling that the world about us is only an illusion, and something of the Mahayana ideal of compassion and service to humanity. His personal psychology and his view of the world were both complex and typical of an age more complex than any that had preceded it.

The numerous "New Laws" for which Wang successfully sought Emperor Shenzong's approval were, however, precisely formulated and practical in their basic conception. The core of his ideas was to rationalize the bureaucratic apparatus and to use it in part as a sort of national economic development bank. He believed in an expanded budget, balanced by encouraging the economy to grow and yield more revenue, rather than by cheese-paring economies. At the upper level, he had the topics covered by the civil-service examinations shifted away from literature and towards more practical matters, including law. Lower down, he had salaries introduced for the clerks who ran the sub-bureaucracy, removing from them the right to meet their expenses by farming such minor state revenues as the taxes on markets and official liquor factories. At the same time he opened up for them the right of entry into the regular bureaucracy, on certain conditions including the passing of a test. Some of the conscript administrators were replaced by hired personnel. His finance planning commission, which was for a short time the power-center of the administration, undertook an economic survey of the empire and its prospects. He initiated several large-scale hydraulic works, and had a resurvey made of the arable land, the registration of which for tax purposes was grossly inadequate. Various tax burdens were simplified or made more reasonable. The most critical and

Portrait of the philosopher Zhu Xi (1130–1200) who believed that moral action involved the investigation of various principles of nature, all of which were aspects of the one great universal principle and set forth in the Confucian scriptures. His interpretation of the Confucian scriptures was officially recognized as orthodox in assessing the examination papers of civil service candidates.

ambitious schemes, though, were those to provide state credit at what was then the low interest rate of 20 per cent to all farmers unable to finance themselves across the difficult period preceding the main harvest, and to all small merchants who, pressed by time and a lack of resources, would otherwise have had to sell their goods at unreasonably low prices to well-financed brokers. These schemes ran into two insurmountable obstacles. To begin with, they struck at one of the foundations of the propertied classes, namely usury, and so provoked a storm of political protest dressed up in respectable Confucian garb. The state, it was argued in orthodox tones, should not compete with "the people" for profit. The second problem was that the clerks who had to administer the schemes, and such crucial undertakings as the land survey, were too corrupt to be entrusted with responsibilities that would have tested even the best of modern bureaucracies with temptations. Abuses soon gave criticisms of Wang's measures some real force, but they survived until Shenzong's death in 1085.

The only one of Wang's innovations that had real staying-power was the ward and tithing militia (*baojia*). This was based on groups of 10, 50 and 500 families providing ward soldiers for neighborhood patrols and guaranteeing each other's good behavior. It had been Wang's intention to develop these forces into a citizen-soldiery resembling the Tang divisional militia and to use them in place of the cripplingly expensive professional armies maintained by the Song. This did not occur, but the *baojia* merged with the conscript administrator system to serve as the basic local-level institution for preserving internal security.

Civil-service examinations and the scholar-gentry

Thus it came about that after the middle of the Tang dynasty the Chinese state proved to be incapable of imposing an institutional blueprint on society. Instead, it gradually found its way towards imposing a psychological blueprint on the minds of its more influential and ambitious subjects. This process began in the Southern Song dynasty, but it cannot be said to have been reasonably complete until the middle of the Ming, around 1500. It is arguable that its full social consequences were not apparent until even later, perhaps a little after 1700. This new development was based on systematically linking almost all honorable status in society, almost all access to political power, virtually all privileges pertaining to exemptions from duties such as conscript administration, and gentler treatment when accused of a crime, to the possession of a degree won in the civil-service examinations. The only exceptions of importance, outside the non-Chinese border areas and such special institutions as the imperial clan and the palace eunuchs, were military examination degrees and some low-level degrees and official titles that could be purchased.

Study for these examinations was prolonged, and done entirely at the expense of the candidate's family. The percentage who passed out of those who studied seriously is unlikely to have been over one per cent. In this way the energies and aspirations of the ablest men were nearly totally absorbed into a continual scholastic competition, the more so since passing a regular repeat examination was required

for the retention of the lowest-level degree.

The curriculum was altered so that it concentrated almost completely on the Neo-Confucian orthodoxy defined by the Southern Song philosopher Zhu Xi, and on refined literary skills. The candidates' minds were thus molded, of their own volition, into a unified and rigid pattern. No external inquisition could ever have imposed such effective mental fetters. Effective, too, because Neo-Confucian orthodoxy was not a simple-minded catechism of dogmas, but a powerful synthesis that drew on the collective efforts of centuries of thinkers since the later 8th century AD. As Wu Zhifang, mentor of the Mongol Chancellor Toghto, observed in the middle of the 14th century, "When the examination system is in operation, not everyone will be assured of an official post and salary. But, even so, it is by means of this that families will have students; and, when everyone studies, naturally no one will dare to do wrong things. This has an important bearing on the process of orderly rule."

It may be noted in passing that to find the explanation of why China did not develop some sort of modern science out of her own rich medieval empirical and speculative traditions we do not have to go much further than the massive obstacle to free thought outlined in the preceding paragraph. Western Europe was oddly lucky in that historical accident opened up a significant separation between state and church. In the social and intellectual space made possible by this separation new thought of all kinds was able to flourish in a way that was impossible in later imperial China, where ideological orthodoxy and secular power at all levels were not just associated but effectively identified.

Under the Tang and earlier dynasties only a most restricted use had been made of the examination system. New bureaucrats were chosen through various forms of recommendation and sponsorship by existing bureaucrats, and through the limited right of hereditary entry for one son of a higher official, known as the "shadow" privilege. Under the Song the examinations were virtually the sole way into the civil service. The result, once the curriculum became thoroughly ideologized, was a new class, the "mandarins," that is to say, bureaucrats with a priest-like ideological qualification to rule. At first, entry under the new system remained relatively restricted to well-established and well-to-do families, and those from the families of merchants, artisans and certain base occupations, were banned from competing. The Ming lifted the ban on merchants and artisans, and the social group from which the mandarins were drawn expanded greatly. The examinations became a true "career open to talent," and a major ladder of upward social mobility. The availability of cheap, woodblock-printed books reduced the cost of study, and teachers – drawn from the ranks of the less successful degree-holders and candidates – were fairly inexpensive too. Lineages would often invest in the education of a promising young member, and merchants, bearing in mind the high potential rewards of office, often backed a gifted son as an examinee rather than putting the funds needed for this into trade or industry.

The first examination degree of *shengyuan*, or "raw official," did not entitle the holder to be considered for a bureaucratic post. For that, one of the higher degrees was required. Moreover, the number of higher-degree holders was soon much in excess of the number of substantive bureaucratic jobs available at any one moment. The consequence was the creation of a class of scholar-gentry, including former officials not currently in office, that was outside the serving mandarinate and living at home. This class had several names, of which the commonest was probably *shenshi*, literally "scholars wearing belts with hanging ends." They were exempt from conscript administration (known in the Ming as *lijia* or the system of "cantons and tithings"), and this made it particularly profitable for them to acquire large estates. Other people also often "entrusted" land to them so as to avoid conscript administrative duties. This scholar-gentry became the new local elite. They had effective access to county officials, on terms of relative social equality. They stuck together in defending their interests through links formed with their examiners and educational officials. It was thus imprudent to offend them. In the 15th century it was still possible for those of social prestige and wealth, like the "tax-captains" of the lower Yangzi valley, to disdain the examination system. A hundred years later the scholar-gentry had come so totally to dominate local society that anyone who wanted to be anybody had to study his way into joining them – or, at the least, buy himself a degree.

The appearance and rise of the scholar-gentry combined with several other developments to transform the nature of Chinese rural society in the course of the 17th century. Because of the exemption enjoyed by the scholar-gentry landlords from the conscript administration that looked after tax collection, the maintenance of local order and water-control projects, a heavier burden was thrown on landowners of moderate means, who were less able to bear it. Again, the growing number of landowners who now lived in cities and often owned land in scattered fragments, which made them unavailable for local administrative duties, worsened this situation. The result was that it became more and more difficult to keep the cantons and tithings system going. This had some serious consequences. In the lower Yangzi, for example, the state had to become more directly involved in some water conservancy that would not have otherwise been carried out. In the course of the 17th century the old system collapsed, though at different times in different parts of the country. It left some of its nomenclature confusingly attached to bailiffs and other similar low-status personnel with police-type functions.

The same age saw the waning of the managed estates worked by servile or semi-servile labor. In some areas, like the lower Yangzi, which was the economic heart of the Ming realm, the spread of rural handicrafts, interlinked with a dense network of rural markets, reduced the dependence of the peasants on farmland and those who owned it. It is also likely that it was discovered that as farming grew more and more intensive, the independent family unit was the most productive system of operation, whether under non-servile tenancy or ownership. The trend towards a purely monetary tenancy was further reinforced by the move of many landlords to the towns, from where they

could no longer exert day-to-day control. The new upsurge in the commercial economy that began in the 16th century, together with a growing tendency on the part of the tenants to resist the payment of their rents, redirected the flow of new investment away from farmland and into pawnbroking, trade and urban real estate, all of which were subject to less tax and more profitable. Without the reassembling of large estates in each generation, the Chinese system of partible inheritance soon broke every patrimony into fragments.

The slow crumbling of the servile status order may be seen in Ming dynasty manuals telling owners how to handle their serfs. They show a marked fear that the master's authority may be lost through improper treatment. The masters' position was also weakened by the fact that it was technically illegal under the Ming for a commoner family to own serfs; they had to be disguised as "adopted sons," which ran the danger of giving rise to some eventual assumption of a true kinship link. The movement away from servile tenancy culminated in the great serf uprisings in the Yangzi valley in the middle of the 17th century. Some of the leaders took the name of "leveling kings" and declared that they "were leveling the distinction between masters and serfs, titled and mean, rich and poor." In one county in Jiangxi the local gazetteer recorded that "Thousands joined together, burning houses and seizing bonds [of servitude]. The sky was covered with smoke. The serfs occupied [the houses of the rich] as squatters and their masters offered them food. If the latter showed the least sign of reluctance, they flogged them on the spot. It was an uprising such as has not been seen for a millennium." With only a small number of exceptions, such as the serf lineages in parts of Guangdong, imperial China after 1700 was a society

of free men, and so much closer in this respect at least to Western Europe than to either Eastern Europe or Czarist Russia.

In the later 17th and 18th centuries the scholar-gentry moved in to fill much of the void left by the disappearance of the conscript administrators. But these managerial gentry who directed water control and other projects, administered charities, supervised markets and sometimes (improperly) contracted to collect taxes, operated in a different fashion from their conscripted predecessors. Their service was honorable and voluntary, and it was based on status rather than the ownership of land. It was also, we may assume, reasonably rewarded. One striking illustration of the changed circumstances may be seen on the county-wide assemblies of scholar-gentry that were now occasionally convoked by magistrates to ask advice about and help with such matters as water control.

From the point of view of the imperial government, the scholar-gentry provided a cheap system of indirect rule. Direct state administration, with some marginal exceptions such as the yellow posters put up in the villages, stopped at the county magistrate's office. In Qing times, this had a staff of about a thousand: the magistrate himself (bound by law to be an outsider and changing every few years), his personal advisers, the permanent clerks and the lictors and runners. They had to deal with a population in an average county of from a fifth to a quarter of a million. This was too many for effective control, even with the services of a network of local bailiffs (men who bought or inherited their jobs) to call on. In practice the county government relied on the scholar-gentry, with their local knowledge and their network of social relations through which they could get things done and disputes settled. Central control was confined to the selection of this local elite, and their ideological conditioning, through the examination system.

The (so-called) Communist government of the People's Republic today has inherited both the older impulse to impose a precise institutional blueprint on society, and the more recent but still centuries-old practice of governing through an ideologically qualified elite, both locally and nationally. The regimentation of rural society under the commune and brigade system has had its own distinctive features, and pattern of evolution, but it is still in part the product of a historically conditioned set of concepts about how the state may or should treat social institutions – in essence, comprehensive prescription rather than piecemeal adaptation. (That this way of thinking remained potent in late imperial times may be seen from the land regulations promulgated by the Taiping rebels in 1853, even though they were an ideal that remained unimplemented. They defined a strictly disciplined, ideologically indoctrinated, communitarian society derived in many respects from the *Rituals of the Zhou*, even as regards much of their terminology.) The Chinese Communist Party differs from the Qing scholar-gentry both in its doctrine and in its internal structure, besides representing about 4 per cent of the population rather than 0.25 to 0.5 per cent. But for its popular acceptance, and for the general understanding of its place in society, it draws substantially on the traditions of the older political culture.

ART OF THE LATE EMPIRE

Decoration, creation and stagnation

The Forbidden City is a moated imperial palace within the inner city of Beijing. What we see today was mainly constructed during the Ming and Qing periods, based on the Yuan dynasty plan. The outer city south of the imperial city was built in the early Qing, and its splendor lies in the symmetry and logical placing of the buildings along the central north–south axis, flanked by the temple of agriculture to the west and the temple of heaven to the east. From the Yongding gate the axis runs almost eight kilometers due north to the bell tower near the north wall of the inner city, punctuated by gates, avenues and the halls of the Forbidden City which today lies north of Chairman Mao's mausoleum in Tiananmen Square, the central area of the city. The buildings of the Forbidden City are constructed in the traditional style using the wooden post-and-lintel system on stone platforms supporting the golden-yellow tiled roofs with elaborately painted brackets.

What we see of the Great Wall today was also built during the Ming dynasty. Reconstruction began under the first Ming emperor, who set up court in Nanjing. The third emperor moved the main capital back to Beijing where he and succeeding Ming emperors were buried. An avenue of lions, mythical animals, camels, elephants, horses, guardians and officials carved from single blocks of marble stand guard along the "Spirit Way." Thirteen tombs there are roofed with brilliant yellow, green and red tiles. The ridge of each roof carries figurines and mythical animals. The curve of the roof is more restrained than the sweeping curves and more intricate decoration typical of the southeast. Under the eaves the crowded brick imitation of bracket arms is merely an ornamental feature. Even on the wooden buildings of the Forbidden City, the eaves have become so heavily laden with decorative carpentry that an additional colonnade supports the weight under the outer edge, reducing the bracket system to mere decoration.

With the support of court patronage the decorative arts flourished. The imperial kilns were at Jingdezhen in Jiangxi, where wares from the Late Tang period onwards had included proto-celadon and Xingzhou-type whiteware. Under the Song they also featured Qingbai ware, which falls between celadon and pure white porcelain. During the Yuan dynasty technical experiments resulted in a decorative method of applying molded motifs to Qingbai ware and in underglaze blue decoration. The establishment of official kilns at Jingdezhen at the end of the 14th century in the Yongle era led to improvement in all wares. During the rest of the Ming dynasty blue-and-white ware was further developed, with more refined drawing and greater control over color. Towards the late Ming difficulties in obtaining pure cobalt from the west led to the use of local pigment which produced a paler hue. The Jingdezhen kilns supplied most of the

Beijing did not assume national importance until the Qubilai Qan chose it as his seat of government in 1260. The city was established as the main capital by the Ming emperors in the early 15th century and what we see today was built in the succeeding centuries. The outer city was added during the Qing dynasty. The plan (*right*) remained unchanged until 1949, since when the city walls and gates have been demolished.

Below Plan of the Forbidden City.

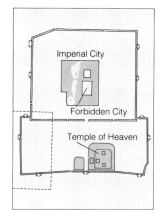

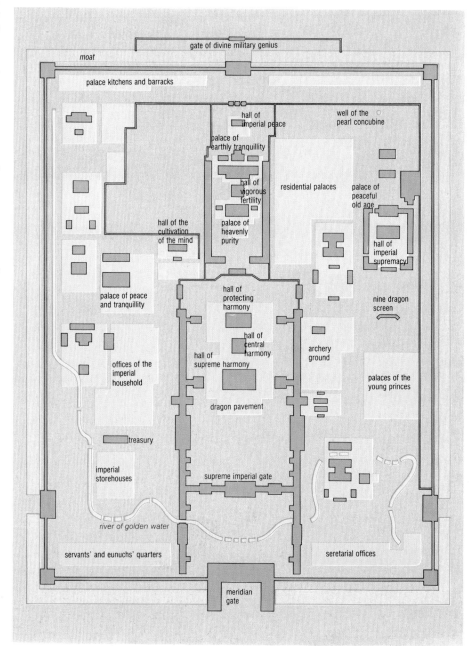

Above This spectacular view of the Beijing skyline, seen looking towards the Western Hills, is taken from the top of a newly constructed building in the Central Academy of Fine Art.

Far left Formerly the northeast corner of the Forbidden City was the residential area for the imperial family. A nine-dragon tiled screen on the southern wall protected the entrance to the Palace of Peaceful Old Age and the Hall of Imperial Supremacy. Today it guards the collection of paintings housed there.

Center left Ferocious hybrid beasts watch the entrance to palaces in the Forbidden City.

Center right The Temple of Heaven, situated in the southeast corner of Beijing, was built during the early 15th century. This hall was rebuilt on the original plans after a fire in 1889 for which 32 officials and guardians were beheaded.

Left Looking southwards over Beijing's Forbidden City. This photograph was taken in 1901 from Coal Hill. Today Beijing's skyline is rapidly changing. The same view shows a series of multistory buildings in the background although the foreground remains the same.

decorated porcelain of the Ming and Qing dynasties, and styles changed gradually from more formal to natural floral motifs; the 16th century saw an increase in the use of pictorial polychrome decoration in three or five colors. Porcelain in overglaze yellow and red added to the increasing brightness of Ming wares. Enamel was fired on metalware in lavish and rich colors, and lacquer was carved with rich pictorial designs in a vigorous and slightly rounded style, often depicting dragons similar to those on porcelain.

Printing from woodblocks had long been practiced in China, and the earliest dated illustration is the *Diamond Sutra* of 868 AD from Dunhuang. Many fine editions, some with illustrations, were pro-

duced during the Song, including the first painting book on plum blossoms. In the late Ming, the method of color printing from separate blocks was perfected. Erotica and other illustrated books were produced, culminating in the works of the Ten Bamboo Studio. Later the influential *Manual of Painting from the Mustard-Seed Garden* was produced (1679–1701). Qing book production seldom achieved these high standards but single-sheet prints of great excellence were produced in Suzhou and other centers.

The love of color was also seen in the Ming and Qing official costumes using the *kesi* (silk-cut) tapestry weave to produce pictorial effects. From the 14th century the claws on the "dragon robe"

Above Colossal figures of officials, warriors and animals guard the "Spirit Way" to the Ming tombs outside Beijing where 13 Ming emperors are buried. If you throw a stone on to the back of a stone animal and it lodges there, your wish is said to come true. The padded collar harness seen on these animals was a Chinese invention in use in the 5th century AD. This harness development took about 500 years to reach the West where the throat-and-girth persisted to choke the horses and limit the loads they could pull.

Dai Jin (1388–1462) painted at the Ming court until he offended the emperor by painting a fisherman in a red jacket (red was reserved for courtiers dressed for audience with the emperor). Expelled from court, Dai Jin returned to his native Hangzhou and his name continued to be linked with a group of professional and court painters who painted in the romantic style of the Southern Song academy. They were known as the Zhe school.

Dai Jin's painting *Returning Home at Evening*, shows obvious Southern Song elements such as the asymmetrical composition, the angular branches of trees and the misty voids. However the brushwork is looser than the early Ma/Xia style, and the *dian* (dot) strokes and texture of foliage are more apparent. Wu Wei (1459–1508) of the Zhe school painted genre scenes of fishing villages, and Bian Wenqin (c. 1400–40) produced flower-and-bird paintings in the Southern Song academic style with precise line and bright color. Academic "court" paintings such as these were spurned by the scholar-artists of the rival Wu school for their "prettiness."

These scholar-painters of the early Ming continued painting landscapes in the manner of the Four Masters of Yuan, forming a school around their founder Shen Zhou (1427–1507) who came from Suzhou or Wu in the Jiangnan area. Shen Zhou himself painted in the style of Ni Zan, Wu Zhen and Huang Gongwang but added a boldness of composition and more obvious *dian* brushstrokes to punctuate the landscape and vary the ink. He also used finely graded washes in the background and added touches of color which differentiate his work from the early Yuan masters.

It was in Suzhou in the 16th and 17th centuries that many gentlemen scholars who lived in comfortable town houses transformed their garden courtyards into landscape paintings in the round. Rocks and trees were placed to be viewed from various positions from wooden balconies and through lattice windows. One could wander through a miniature landscape of rocks as if in the mountains, in the same way as wandering in spirit through a landscape painting.

The painters Tang Yin (1479–1523) and Qiu Ying (c. 1494–c. 1552) cannot be labeled as belonging to either Zhe or Wu groups. Tang Yin painted in a conservative manner looking back to the Northern Song monumental style, whereas Qiu Ying was a great copyist and looked back even further, to the archaic "green-and-blue" manner of the Tang.

At the end of the 16th century the scholar-painter Dong Qichang (1555–1636) exerted tremendous influence on the succeeding generations of artists and art critics. He divided painting into "northern" and "southern" schools, the "northern" school representing the court and professional academic artists who painted in a decorative and colorful manner, and the "southern" school representing the amateur literati (*wen ren*) artists who were concerned with poetic insight and the use of landscape as a means of expression. To the "northern" school he assigned all academic and court painters including Ma Yuan and Xia Gui of the Southern Song back to the "green-and-blue" masters of the Tang. Dong Qichang maintained that through painting the scholar could express his understanding of nature, and hence of man. This was the result of his knowledge of the classics which gave him an

were numbered to indicate rank. Five claws were strictly reserved for the emperor and his family; four claws were allotted to officials and nobles. Rank was also indicated by decorative "mandarin squares" embroidered on the front of the robe.

The first Ming emperor established a painting academy at Nanjing, but when the main court moved north to Beijing in the early 15th century the artistic center of gravity remained in the south in the Jiangnan area of southern Jiangsu and northern Zhejiang provinces. The cities of Suzhou, Wuxi, Nanjing and Yangzhou were rich centers of commerce; painters, scholars and collectors of private means chose to live there rather than follow a government career.

understanding of things, combined with a nobility of taste, which the professional painters could not hope to achieve, being bound by conventions of the academy. He believed that in the play of brush and ink the amateur scholar-painter had the freedom and the means to convey ideas and feelings.

Dong Qichang's own paintings are strongly structured. He talks of the *shi* (the gravity or trend) of the mountains as the force which causes them to rise and fall. He uses slanting planes and stylized units to build up his landscape with a clarity of structural parts.

The painters known as the Four Wangs carried on the literati tradition of Dong Qichang and represent the conservative scholar-painters of the early Qing. Their works are based on a combination of Yuan versions of Northern Song landscape. Wang Shimin (1592–1680) was a pupil of Dong Qichang and master of the other three Wangs: Wang Qian (1598–1677), Wang Hui (1632–1717) and Wang Yuanqi (1642–1715), the most talented of the four.

Individuality of composition began to replace individuality of brushwork in the landscape paintings of the 17th century. The different responses of scholar-artists at the beginning of the Qing to the alien Manchu rule can be seen in the paintings of Gong Xian (1620–89), whose dark foreboding landscapes carry a feeling of impending doom, whereas the airy landscapes of Hong Ren (1610–64) seem to transcend it. The unorthodox artists of this period are termed "Individualists" and two of the greatest of these were Zhu Da (c. 1626–1705) and Dao Ji (1641–c. 1710). Zhu Da (also known as Bada Shanren) was descended from the Ming imperial house. He became a Buddhist monk and spent his life wandering. He painted in several styles, one after Dong Qichang but with a wetter brush, and the other in the manner of Chan Buddhist painters, combining a rapid and unrestrained use of ink with a play of wet and dry brush to give balance and harmony. He is said to have painted in a frenzy and often when drunk. Dao Ji (also known as Shi Tau) was descended, like Zhu Da, from the Ming imperial line. He also entered a monastery and spent his life traveling before finally settling in Yangzhou, where he spent his time "piling up stones"—in other words, designing gardens. His paintings show creativity in composition in which he homes in on details and brings out the characteristics of the rocks in an exaggerated manner. He also uses color in wet *dian* strokes and ink with great freedom.

The exaggerated tendencies of Dao Ji were taken up by the Eight Eccentrics of Yangzhou, a group recognized as major painters of the 18th century. Forms were distorted and deliberately nonconformist. Gao Qipei (c. 1672–1734) abandoned the brush and painted with his fingernails. Jin Nong (1687–1764) and Lo Bing (1733–99) playfully distorted the forms of ancient models. By the 19th century patronage had declined, and the individualism of scholar-artists faded. The followers of the conservative branch led by the Four Wangs offered little that was new. Amateur scholar-artists were obliged to earn a living.

During the Qing dynasty there were many competent court artists painting in the decorative "court" style. Castiglione, an Italian Jesuit missionary who arrived in Beijing in 1715, introduced a Western style of painting to the court. He created a synthesis of Eastern and Western art by exploiting the technique of the East with the modeled forms and use of light and shade of the West. His paintings were popular at the time but had little far-reaching effect.

The decorative arts of the early Qing with their intricate designs and bright colors appealed to the Manchu taste. Jade carving was of high quality and rivaled the jades of the Warring States period in terms of skill, but the designs were decorative and lacked the restraint and simplicity of the early work. Enamels, textiles, jade, ivory, carved lacquer and porcelain shared many motifs and were made in the workshops set up in the palace by Emperor Kangxi in 1680. Lacquer was carved in the south, and the Jingdezhen kilns in Jiangxi, which had declined in the early 17th century, were revived. Additional colors were added to the five overglaze colors of the Ming to produce what is known in Europe as *famille verte*.

Left A beautiful example of Ming decorative arts, a 16th-century tripod of copper covered with cloisonné enamels in red, white, blue, green, yellow and aubergine on a light blue ground.

Below Beihai Park in Beijing, set among pavilions and lakes. It was a retreat within the city for the scholar-official. Being in a Chinese garden is like walking through a three-dimensional traditional landscape painting.

Above Detail of a 19th-century mandarin's silk robe. The bats are symbols wishing the wearer good luck. Various forms of characters were incorporated into the designs of special garments, for example *xi* ("joy"), *ji* ("luck") and *shou* ("longevity"), of which four versions are given here (*right*).

THE
MODERN
AGE

PROSPECT AND RETROSPECT

By the end of the 18th century the Chinese economy, the Chinese political structure, Chinese thought and Chinese art had reached a magnificent dead end. It is necessary to insist on both the magnificence – the wealth, the power and the sophistication – and on the deadness, the incapacity any longer to generate new ways of thinking, seeing, feeling and doing from within the old Chinese tradition. Through state policy, the empire was almost a closed world again, as it had been in the early and middle Ming. It was forbidden to travelers, except for a favored few who came on tributary delegations, or took the risks of illegal entry like some Catholic missionaries, and – in the 1830s – Robert Fortune, the botanical spy who stole tea plants for the Indian tea industry. Legal trade with European nations was limited to two frontier cities, Kiakhta for the Russians (after 1737) and Canton for Westerners (after 1757), and the activities of the merchants were strictly controlled. Even the minute trickle of foreign influence that had come in since the late Ming through the Jesuits – Western hydraulics, astronomy and mathematics, perspective drawing, the improved casting of cannon, the great *Atlas* of 1717 and even a musical notation using characters – had dried up. The practice of Christianity had been banned in the Sacred Edict of 1723. While it was not that severely enforced, the only Catholic priests who were sanctioned were a handful of Jesuits kept on at court to perform useful technical functions, like correcting the calendar.

On the surface, however, the late imperial economy presented an appearance of astonishing vitality. The population was close to 400 million, and intensely hard working and competitive. One of the French missionary authors of the *Reports on the Chinese*, published in the 18th century, speaks of how the Chinese people "puts merit ceaselessly in competition with merit, diligence with diligence and work with work in a manner that prevents great fortunes." The intensive rice agriculture of the central and southern parts of the country had pushed yields per hectare close to the limit of what premodern technology would allow (see pp. 209–10). There was an ever denser network of periodic rural markets and market towns, and the volume of trade astonished observers. One British ship that lay off the coast near Shanghai in the 1830s estimated the size of its sea-borne trade to be about the same as that of the city of London's. When Father Huc traveled through the Yangzi valley in the middle of the 19th century, he observed, "There are in all the great towns important commercial establishments, into which, as into reservoirs, the merchandise of all the provinces discharges itself. To these vast storehouses people flock from all parts of the Empire, and there is a constant bustle of going on about them – a feverish activity that would scarcely be seen in the most important cities of Europe." And he goes on to talk of "the thirst of

gain, and the desire of traffic by which this people is incessantly tormented." "The whole country," he asserts, "is like a perpetual fair," and "Volumes might be written on the frauds, more or less ingenious and audacious, of the Chinese merchants; and the habit of trickery is so general, the fashion so universal, that no one is offended at it; it is simply a mode of showing that you are clever and wide awake . . . . It is only just to observe, however, that this want of probity and good faith is chiefly found among the petty traders; the great commercial houses are . . . remarkable for the uprightness and integrity of their dealings." The impression of economic energy that comes across from the Chinese sources is equally impressive. Here is one description of the great porcelain-making center of Jingdezhen in Jiangxi province: "Tens of thousands of pestles shake the ground with their noise. The heavens are alight with the glare from the fires, so that one cannot sleep at night. The place has been called in jest 'The Town of Year-Round Thunder-and-Lightning.'" The countryside was full of machines worked by water power (or oxen) for husking rice, crushing sugarcane, pulping fibers for paper and other purposes.

But the old flair for invention had vanished. The number of new techniques of any importance created in China since Ming times can almost be counted on the fingers of two hands: the Chinese type of windmill (luffing sails set on the rim of a merry-go-round turntable); multicolor printing with woodblocks; improvements in artificial incubators for poultry eggs and in the cotton-gin; the methods of killing and preserving silk moths by packing them in salt and by heat-drying, which joined the older techniques (notably steaming); the art of extracting pure zinc; new oilseed and green fertilizers; and air-blowers for ventilating mines. A few enthusiasts experimented with neglected agricultural and hydraulic techniques mentioned in old books or with Western devices like the Archimedean water-screw. Early in the 19th century Qi Yanhuai wrote these wry lines on the water-screw he had had built:

Eight bands that spiral round a central post,
A revolving streambed, winding back and forth,
A bottomless bucket, with both ends open!
Its narrowed waist held in a waist-ring's grip,
Thousands of feet straight down the water drops,
– Quite unaware of being lifted up!

But there was also a certain self-conscious dislike of innovation. Cheng Tingzuo, writing in the middle of the 18th century, observed: "Far-off Europe! . . . Its people are known for their many-sided cleverness, excelling particularly at mathematics. Apart from this, everything else they do is *excessive ingenuity*, enough to amaze those of little knowledge. So often to play around with things is to bring a myriad burdens on oneself. They have investigated to the

Above Jesuit priests were accepted by the Chinese as literati from abroad and admired for their learning. They wore Chinese robes in an effort to convert the Chinese and made some notable converts such as Xu Guangqi, president of the Ministry of Rites. On the whole, though, there was a less enthusiastic response to their Christian teaching than to their knowledge of astronomy, geography and physics.

Right The Qing emperor Kangxi (1654–1722) supported the Jesuit Ferdinand Verbiest who supervised the refitting of the observatory with the latest instruments in the 17th century. The observatory, built in 1296, is situated on the southeast side of Beijing. The instruments have recently been removed by the present regime and the surrounding area cleared to make room for highways and hotels.

utmost such cruel things as firearms.'' Though farmers and artisans eagerly adopted any small improvements that came their way, men of education lacked the exuberant European inventive imagination, sometimes absurd but often fruitful. They remained untouched by the romance of machinery, so evident in the European treatises of the later 16th and the 17th centuries known by such titles as *Theaters of Machines and Instruments*. Nor did their minds have the new European capacity to see the geometrical ghosts in machines, and to analyze abstractly what they were doing, even with the stimulus before their eyes of Chinese craftsmen intuitively adapting their creations to the varying needs of local conditions.

The gradually decreasing intellectual vitality of late imperial China as compared with early modern Europe may also have been connected with the absence of any universities or specialized educational institutions for such subjects as medicine or law. Would-be students learned from a master on a personal basis. The so-called academies had become almost exclusively cramming schools for the higher-level civil-service examinations. In the 16th century, under the influence of the philosopher Wang Yangming, they had showed a spurt of independent intellectual life, and in 1579 this had led to the partial closure of private foundations at the instigation of the practically minded and intolerant statesman Zhang Jucheng. He feared their threat to state orthodoxy and their involvement in factional politics. The attack was renewed with a new ban in 1625. In China during these last centuries of the empire it seems that institutions more and more served either strictly particularist ends, such as the use of education as a means to personal advancement, or the purposes of the state, notably the indoctrination of the elite – or both at once. Apart perhaps from a few of the monasteries, they never seemed to have served universal ends, such as piety or good learning, not tightly linked to the state's requirements.

Modern scholarship has delighted in unearthing Chinese thinkers from the last few centuries of the empire whose heretical views, scientific originality or practical concerns have accorded with modern tastes. Among the most interesting are some of the heretical philosophers of the southeastern coast, with their ideals of universal brotherhood and their vitriolic dislike for the Confucian apostles of ''sensitive concern for others'' who, in the words of Li Zhi, ''used virtue and rituals to govern men's minds, and institutions and justice to bind men's bodies.'' He Xinyin devalued hierarchical relationships, such as that between father and son, in favor of the equality of mutual friendship, and declared that man should ''have no ruler but the entire universe''; he wanted to abolish personal property and replace it with collective lineage property. Li Zhi, author of *Letters to be Burned*, published in 1590, was a restless, skeptical opponent of the Confucian scriptures. He believed that morality lay in the unconditional recognition of the dignity of other people, and that ''whoever has lost the spirit of childhood has lost the true spirit.'' Like He Xinyin before him, he was put in prison for spreading pernicious ideas, and committed suicide there at the age of 76.

Tantalizing hints of a possible homegrown Chinese science haunt the history of the later 16th century and the first half of the 17th. The traditional genre of the herbal reached its culmination in the *Pharmacological Catalog* of Li Shizhen (1578), much of it based on personal investigation. Wu Youxing used systematic reasoning and observation to suggest what amounted to a micro-organism theory of disease in his book *On Epidemics* (1642). Song Yingxing produced a magistral survey of economic technology in his *Commodities Developed by Nature and the Artificer* (1637), and his essay ''On Matter-Energy'' went far beyond its initial inspiration in the basic ideas of the Northern Song philosopher Zhang Zai. He was also far more systematic than the earlier brilliant polymath Shen Gua, who represented much of the best in Song science, though perhaps lacking some of Shen's flair for quantification and the building of models. Song Yingxing's section on acoustics, for example, speaks of sound as the matter-energy (qi) of the air set into motion by a stimulus, demonstrates the difficulty of accounting for its creation and propagation on other hypotheses and explicitly compares its behavior to the pattern of waves set up by a stone tossed into water. Though Song Yingxing remained firmly in the grip of the traditional Chinese organic-musical model of the cosmos, there are several embryonic concepts that – with hindsight – it is hard not to think of as having had a promising but unfulfilled potential for growth. An example, from the foregoing essay, is the idea of "the position-power of matter-energy" (*qi shi*), applied to water falling from a high mountain.

Fang Yizhi's *Brief Record of the Principles of Things* (1664) is mostly a typical piece of traditional encyclopedism, quoting items on the sciences culled from previous writers. But it also contains accounts of some topics, such as optics, in which he and his son had a keen personal interest, probably did some experimenting and tried to define relevant general principles, such as the refraction of light. Fang Yizhi was probably also the first Chinese writer to draw a clear distinction between moral and natural laws. The Neo-Confucians of the Song dynasty, he said, "had concerned themselves only with normative principles. As regards the general principles of the objects of existence, and the order of periods of time, they did not reach the truth." He added that normative principles had their place in matters concerned with government and doctrine, but "when one is speaking exclusively of reaching the germinal elements of causation then what is at issue are the ultimate general principles that make the objects of existence what they are." But, for Fang, even a purely intellectual illumination could not be reached by induction from what he called "substantive research." It required an intuitive leap of the spirit to put itself in touch with the all-pervading spiritual power that moved the world. He remained bound by his faith in the validity of the ancient patterns revealed in the *Scripture of the Changes.*

The important point, historically, is that these apparent beginnings led nowhere. The works of Li Zhi and Song Yingxing virtually disappeared during the Qing dynasty and were recovered with some difficulty in the 20th century. Important parts of Wu Youxing's text became garbled, and he had no continuators. Apart from Li Shizhen, who was writing fully within a tradition, these men were all but forgotten by their fellow countrymen. So far from being a proof of the vitality of late traditional culture, they show the opposite: its capacity to suppress and blot out lines of thought that did not accord with its already established predispositions.

The growth of science in late imperial China was held back by an epistemological subtlety that doubted whether empirical inquiry could ever reveal the thing-in-itself. Fang Yizhi spoke for a common (though not universal) view in Ming and early Qing when he stated that, "Since it is only the mind that knows and perceives, everything is shadows and echoes." Thus, "the laws of the objects of existence . . . are simply another way of referring to the laws of the mind." Cheng Tingzuo, for his part, represented a humanist instinct that intuitively feared the moral and social consequences of the Promethean quest for knowledge. Neither of these viewpoints was without insight, or crudely mistaken.

Art and literature

The Chinese visual arts were also caught in a sophisticated impasse. There was a link in Europe between the art of the Renaissance and early science. This connection can be most clearly seen in the Western painters' exploration of the projections of three-dimensional space, the exactness of their observations of anatomy and natural phenomena (as in Leonardo's studies of water and storms) and their treatment of colors and light almost as entities in themselves. Except in some woodcuts of scenes of everyday life, Chinese artists did not avail themselves of vanishing-point perspective. Their interests did not lie in *trompe-l'oeil* representation. In the *Discourses on Painting* of Shi Tau, published in 1728 and one of the world's great books of aesthetic philosophy, the author emphasizes that what matters is to achieve, through painting, a certain state of exaltation, and then to transmit this back through the depicted landscape, which thereby becomes a vehicle for it. "From the moment that one has grasped the unique principle, the multitude of particular principles may be deduced of themselves." The painter is able "to participate in the metamorphoses of the universe." "Mountains and rivers," said Shi Tau, "have charged me to speak for them. They are born in me, and I in them."

At the same time that Shi Tau was expressing this magnificent vision, Chinese painting was for the most part sinking into a stereotyping of perception that was lifeless beyond the worst Western academicism. This world of accepted forms found its ultimate crystallization in the *Manual of Painting from the Mustard-Seed Garden*, compiled by Wang Gai and his brothers between 1679 and 1701. It is a complete how-to-paint-it handbook, of remarkable delicacy, showing the brushstrokes and arrangement of elements required to portray, in the manner of the great masters, everything from grasshoppers and donkeys to rocks, pines, orchids and chrysanthemums. It was precisely because this synthesis was so nuanced, all-embracing and satisfying that the Chinese became imprisoned in it. There were eccentrics who did not conform with all its conventions. One such was the mid-19th-century Cantonese painter Su Renshan, with his curiously wiry and yet solid modeling. But there was no breaking of the conceptual mold.

The one domain in which a strong creativity remained alive was prose fiction. The Ming and the Qing were the great age of the Chinese novel. The structure of these stories was originally episodic or at most polyphonic, with characters abruptly appearing and disappearing rather as they do in real life. This was a legacy of the market storytellers, from whose art they sprang. Their subject-matter ranged across legend, history and contemporary society. Gradually the ability emerged to fashion an overall structure, and this culminated in *The Story of the Stone* (or *Dream of the Red Mansions*), published in 1792. This book, written by Cao Xueqin and an unknown continuator, and revised and edited by Gao E, is one of the handful of the greatest novels of all time. Haunted by a sense of the unreality of the "real world," and the ever-presence of change and decay in the midst of splendors and success, it describes the slow moral and financial ruin of a great family. Its most remarkable characteristics are the author's exquisitely differentiated depiction of the varieties of feminine psychology, and his exploration of such deeply repressed themes as the fear, alienation, resentment and competition hidden

Above The 17th-century Chinese artist was perfectly capable of foreshortening and using vanishing-point perspective as seen in this woodblock illustration. In painting he deliberately avoided scientific perspective since it included only that which could be seen from a fixed point. Chinese painting with its multi-point perspective allows you the freedom to view the whole from many sides.

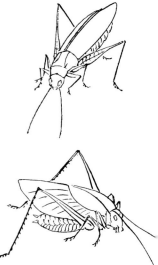

Above Chinese painters for the past 300 years have learned from handbooks of style and technique. The *Manual of Painting from the Mustard Seed Garden* gives descriptions and step-by-step methods of how to paint. Examples of insects illustrated in the manual for use in paintings of grasses and herbaceous plants include crickets, beetles, the praying mantis and this grasshopper. Such books have had a stultifying effect on the capacity of the Chinese to see nature for themselves.

under the obligatory obedience of a son to his father. This vitality in late traditional imaginative prose is significant, for of all the arts of China it was the only one that had little intrinsic difficulty in coming to terms with the challenge and inspiration of the modern West.

Economic stagnation

The cultural immobility of Qing China (with the qualification just made) was complemented by an even more intractable difficulty of an economic nature. This was the so-called "high-level equilibrium trap," the lingering effects of which still hold back the economic growth of those parts of the Chinese world not closely linked to the international market. The essential features of the trap are easily stated; but, since the situation to which they refer had no familiar historical parallels in the West, it is not so easy to convey their implications. In brief, Chinese technological progress in farming and in water transportation during late traditional times was arrested by discontinuities that only a measure of modern scientific knowledge, and modern industry, could have overcome. The effects of this arrest were to inhibit change in sectors of the economy other than farming and water transportation by reducing the ease with which customer demand and the supply of essential materials could be enlarged.

Put in other terms, the high level of premodern Chinese technology in farming and water transportation meant that there were no remaining simple ways to increase productivity, either per worker or per hectare in the case of agriculture. Therefore it was exceptionally hard to bring into being compact but rapidly growing markets that offered new opportunities to entrepreneurs.

Further, the exploitation of virtually all the arable land that was economically exploitable under the given technology (with the exception of Manchuria) meant that the supply of materials like cotton could not have been expanded to meet the needs of an industrial revolution in the textile industry. Labor too was cheap in an economy that, though highly commercialized, lived quite close to subsistence. There was an absence of caste, political and cultural barriers to both social and geographical mobility, but labor remained cheap because there was by now almost no option for peasants to move to a more productive frontier region. The last premodern example of such a possibility was Yunnan, where the population rose from 3·1 to 6·3 million between 1775 and 1825 in response to opportunities in farming, mining and trade. On the whole, the ease of internal migration probably restricted the emergence of regional centers of wealth and high per-person demand. Generally, therefore, employers were less interested in economizing on labor than on other factors of production, such as materials. Finally, the sheer size of the commercially integrated Chinese economy – the largest in the 18th-century world – made it difficult for a local or an external rise in demand to create a shortage of labor and so prompt a search for mechanized methods. Similarly, the sheer scale of the Chinese economy meant that shortfalls in supply were difficult to meet by imports.

It is important to emphasize that there was quite adequate mercantile capital in late imperial China to finance the beginnings of an industrial revolution. For example, the great salt merchants and the members of the foreign trade monopoly guild had working capitals of several million ounces of silver each. What was crucial was that there were no profitable opportunities for them to invest it in such a way that it would have helped to induce a revolution in the means of production. Some of the markets for particular goods were also huge. Cotton cloth made in Shanghai was sold in places 1300 kilometers apart. The greatest Suzhou cotton cloth wholesalers handled more than a million bolts of 40 Chinese feet each every year. Similar comments could be made about ironware from Foshan and porcelain from Jingdezhen. Had the wholly rational short-term pursuit of profit been capable of leading to an industrial revolution under Chinese conditions, it would have occurred. Neither Marx, nor Weber, nor Nurkse nor other development theorists, have explanations to offer that satisfactorily account for the Chinese failure to generate internally an industrial capitalism.

A critic looking at the foregoing compact summary of a complex theory might reasonably raise certain questions. The exact definition of "premodern" and "modern" technology in farming is not easy. The absence or presence of inputs based on mechanized industry and/or experimental and quantitative science is, however, a rough but usable criterion. In specific terms, characteristic "modern" inputs are chemical fertilizers, scientifically selected seeds, concrete, metal and plastic piping and the internal combustion engine used for pumping or traction. The accuracy of our general impression of high Chinese seed-to-yield ratios is also empirically hard to validate. Scrappy evidence suggests that for wheat it may have been two to three times as high as the 18th-century European average of about 1:5. The universality of the use of the best techniques has likewise been questioned. In some of the cases mentioned by critics it turns out that the explanation is the depletion of resources by arable farming and a dense population. Thus a shortage of pasturage often led to an under-use of animal manures. The falling number of good opportunities for agricultural investment, though also hard to prove, is hinted at by the declining number of new water-control projects in the Qing dynasty and the numerous failures to create permanent new arable because of erosion and salinization due to the clearing of unsuitable land.

This is the background against which we have to evaluate the forcible opening of China by the West during the second half of the 19th century. It set in motion what was – in the broad social sense – a devastating process of cultural erosion, cultural degradation and cultural impoverishment that only accelerated later under the Nationalists and especially under the Communists. At the same time it offered a way out of the impasse: the technology for further economic growth, and access to the markets, ideas and arts of the rest of the world. This situation, sometimes painful, sometimes exhilarating, almost always confused and interspersed with the humiliation of intermittent defeats and invasions, has given rise to a historiography full of myths and propaganda, both Chinese and Western. We shall try to consider it with a steady, though not necessarily a dispassionate, regard.

Below A charming woodcut of Baochai ("precious clasp"), one of the many female characters delicately and distinctively outlined in *The Story of the Stone*. A sensible and perceptive girl, she is chosen by family agreement to become the wife of the hero Baoyu ("precious jade"), although – sadly for her – his deepest affections had long been given to another.

THE FILM OF EVENTS

In our effort to understand what has been happening to China in modern times, it is useful to begin with a swift survey of the main events of the last 150 years. They can be seen as falling into ten periods, some of which overlap.

1 The opening of China

During the 1840s and 1850s Great Britain and France used a limited application of force to open China to unrestricted foreign trade through a number of specially designated ports. They compelled it to conduct international relationships on the European model of equality between nations, and not on the basis of the tributary system which regarded China as universal suzerain and other nations as vassals. Later propaganda has (with an exquisite audacity) turned the treaties establishing this international equality into "the unequal treaties." The grounds for the use of this term are the secondary, but not unimportant, aspects of the settlement reached: the Western powers obliged China to permit Christian missionaries to live and make converts in the interior of the country, to allow foreigners accused of crimes in China to be tried in courts run by their fellow countrymen and to limit the import duty it levied to 5 per cent. Of these impositions, only extra-territorial legal jurisdiction can be seen as morally reasonable, given the assumption that Chinese and Westerners were going to have any contact with each other at all. Chinese lawsuits at this time involved the routine torture of the accused and witnesses (except for holders of state degrees), and the convention that required *someone* to be executed in expiation of every homicide led to the judicial murder of innocent people.

The reason that the Chinese imperial government did not put up a prolonged resistance to British and French demands was that it fairly soon realized that the foreign powers were not aiming at territorial conquest. It was therefore safer to give in and to try to ensure that these powerful outsiders had an interest in maintaining stability.

Another set of myths has grown up around opium. The wars of 1839–42 and 1856–60 are often termed the "Opium Wars." A better name would be the "Wars of Diplomatic Recognition." It is widely believed that the British somehow forced the Chinese (from outside!) to consume opium, and that these wars were fought to ensure the continuation of this trade. This is almost complete nonsense, as a quick recapitulation of the history of opium in China will show.

As of about 1600 the Chinese did not use opium as a narcotic. It was taken as a painkiller, as it was in Victorian Britain until the end of the 19th century when it was replaced by aspirin, with which of course you can also kill yourself. Addiction to opium began to spread through China during the 17th century, as the habit of lacing tobacco with the drug became commonplace. The first decree against

Above Opium smokers relaxing in Shanghai at the turn of the century. Opium smoking has been banned both by the Nationalists and by the Communist Party.

growing or trading opium dates from 1729, long before it was imported. In the second half of the 18th century, Westerners began to form offshore connections with the Chinese drug-trading network to sell high-quality Indian opium to the upper end of the market. A little later Chinese merchants can also be found (illegally) running Indian opium to the Dutch East Indies. Imports into China were first explicitly banned in 1800; but it is clear from the imperial decrees against the traffic that even in the 1830s, the height of the anti-opium-import campaign, that the Chinese state was always more concerned with getting rid of domestic production, which seems to have been on a larger scale than imports at all times.

Two other myths concerning opium are that it was draining large amounts of silver out of the Chinese economy to pay for it and that it was seriously deleterious to the nation's health. Westerners valued opium highly as a product to sell to China (though they could not deal in it openly or legally) because Chinese demand for other Western goods was frustratingly low. Some silver undoubtedly ended in India, but most of it was clearly recycled straight back into the purchases of Chinese goods for export. The impression of a silver drain, reversing the flow of New World silver into China since the later 16th century, was probably due to the worsening internal exchange rate of copper coins against silver. This has now been shown to have been a by-product of the government's adulteration and depreciation of the copper currency at this time.

Finally, it must be said that straight opium, unlike its deadly concentrates, is not more than moderately bad for the health, one of its worst effects being constipation. Many addicts (such as some high officials) functioned effectively into late old age; Chinese railway workers in the United

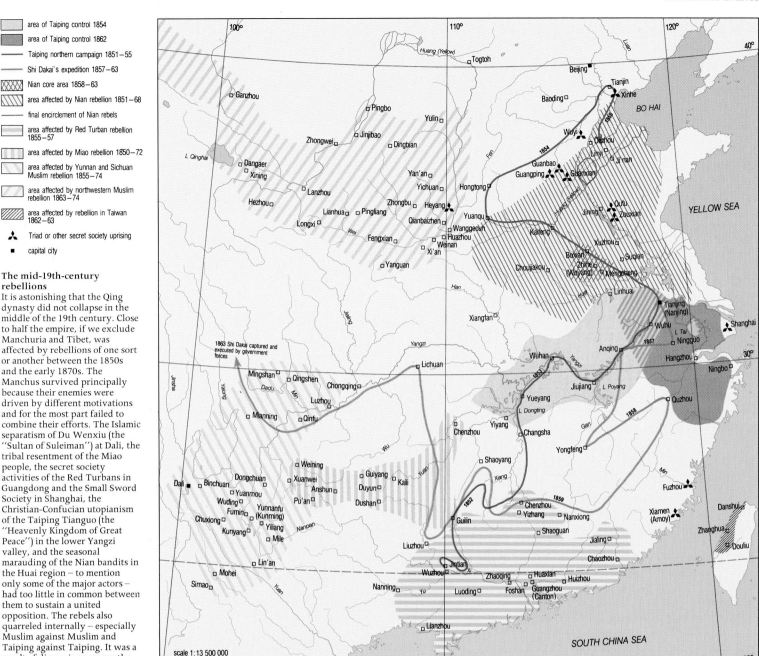

area of Taiping control 1854
area of Taiping control 1862
Taiping northern campaign 1851–55
Shi Dakai's expedition 1857–63
Nian core area 1858–63
area affected by Nian rebellion 1851–68
final encirclement of Nian rebels
area affected by Red Turban rebellion 1855–57
area affected by Miao rebellion 1850–72
area affected by Yunnan and Sichuan Muslim rebellion 1855–74
area affected by northwestern Muslim rebellion 1863–74
area affected by rebellion in Taiwan 1862–63
Triad or other secret society uprising
capital city

The mid-19th-century rebellions

It is astonishing that the Qing dynasty did not collapse in the middle of the 19th century. Close to half the empire, if we exclude Manchuria and Tibet, was affected by rebellions of one sort or another between the 1850s and the early 1870s. The Manchus survived principally because their enemies were driven by different motivations and for the most part failed to combine their efforts. The Islamic separatism of Du Wenxiu (the "Sultan of Suleiman") at Dali, the tribal resentment of the Miao people, the secret society activities of the Red Turbans in Guangdong and the Small Sword Society in Shanghai, the Christian-Confucian utopianism of the Taiping Tianguo (the "Heavenly Kingdom of Great Peace") in the lower Yangzi valley, and the seasonal marauding of the Nian bandits in the Huai region – to mention only some of the major actors – had too little in common between them to sustain a united opposition. The rebels also quarreled internally – especially Muslim against Muslim and Taiping against Taiping. It was a result of dissensions among the Taiping leadership that Shi Dakai, one of the Taiping "kings" set off on a western expedition that foreshadowed the Long March of the Chinese Communists, but – unlike its later counterpart – it ended in disaster.

States, who took it, competed more than adequately against Irish emigrants addicted to whiskey. Its chief damage was probably to the family budgets of those not able to afford it. In brief, opium was an irritant in Sino-foreign relations, not a basic cause of war, and its historical significance has been exaggerated.

2   The mid-century rebellions

From the early 1850s until the middle of the 1870s the empire was afflicted by a number of largely unconnected rebellions. Most of them were eventually subdued by regional armies fighting on behalf of the central government, but only loosely under its control. A critical factor in their victories was that they used firearms either imported from the West or made in imitation of Western models, and their opponents did not.

The most menacing of these uprisings was the Heavenly Kingdom of Great Peace, or Taiping Tianguo, led by Hong Xiuquan. At the height of its power, from 1853 to 1864, it occupied most of the lower Yangzi valley, which it ruled from the "Heavenly Capital" of Tianjing (present-day Nanjing). The Taiping movement prefigured the Chinese Communist movement in several important ways. Its leaders preached a new ideology, which they claimed had been divinely revealed to them, and which promised both a personal salvation to believers and a better social order. This ideology was a blend of the utopian Confucianism of the *Rituals of the Zhou* and the Old Testament Christianity picked up by Hong Xiuquan from a missionary tract. Its social ideal, which was preached but probably never put into practice, was a theocratic collectivism built around small rural communities, each with its church and common storehouses and under religious leadership. Its most surprising, and significant, obsession was with the extermination of what it called "demons," that is to say, with the destruction of the traditional Chinese folk religion.

The life of every Chinese community before

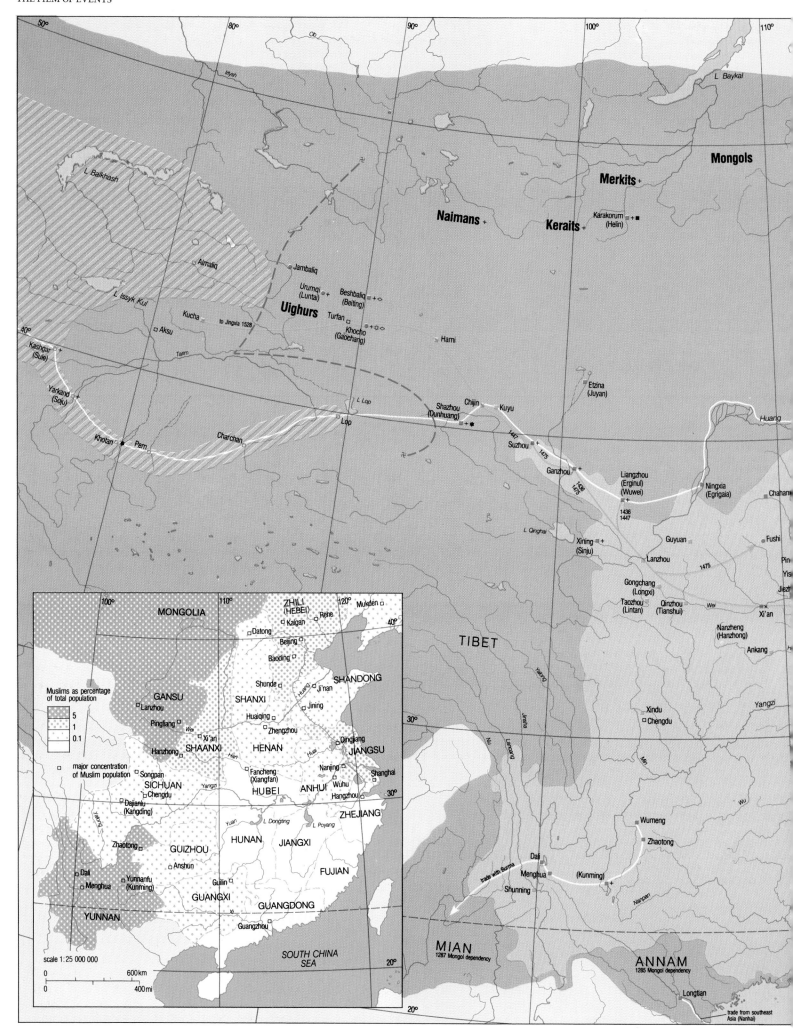

50°   80°   90°   100°   110°

L. Baykal

Mongols

Merkits +

Naimans +   **Keraits** +   Karakorum ■ +
(Helin)
                                                                    +

L. Balkhash

Almaliq   Jambaliq

Urumqi   Beshbaliq
(Luntai)   (Beiting) ■ + ◇
Uighurs   Turfan
Kucha   to Jingxia 1528   Khocho   + ◇
L. Issyk Kul   (Gaochang)
Aksu   Hami

40°
Kashgar □ +   Tarim
(Sule)   Etzina
                                                                               (Juyan)
Yarkand +   Huang
(Soju)   L. Lop   Shazhou   Chijin   Kuyu
                                    Lop   (Dunhuang)
Khotan ★ Pem   Charchan   + ✱   1447   Liangzhou   Ningxia
                                                  Suzhou   +   (Erginul)   (Egrigaia)
                                                          1475   (Wuwei)
                                                  Ganzhou   1436   Chahar
                                                            1475   1436
                                                                           1447   Fushi
                                                                 L. Qinghai   Pin
                                                                 Xining +   Guyuan
                                                                 (Sinju)   Yisi
                                                                         Lanzhou   1475   Jiezt
                                    TIBET   Gongchang
                                                                 (Longxi)
                                                                 Taozhou   Qinzhou   Wei
                                                                 (Lintan) (Tianshui)   Xi'an ×
                                                                                       Nanzheng
                                                                                       (Hanzhong)
                                                                                                  Ankang

Inset map:

100°   110°   ZHILI   120° Mukden
MONGOLIA   (HEBEI) Kalgan Rehe   40°
                          Datong   Beijing
                                              Baoding
                          GANSU Shunde   **SHANDONG**
                          Lanzhou   **SHANXI** Huang Ji'nan
                          Pingliang   Jining
                          We   Huaiqing
                                       Xi'an   Zhengzhou
                          Hanzhong **SHAANXI** **HENAN** Huai **JIANGSU**
                                                 Han   Qingjiang
Muslims as percentage   Fancheng   Nanjing
of total population   (Xiangfan)   Shanghai
  5   **SICHUAN** Yangzi **HUBEI** **ANHUI** Wuhu
  1   Chengdu   Hangzhou   30°
  0.1   Dajianlu
                        (Kangding)   **ZHEJIANG**
□ major concentration   Yuan L. Dongting L. Poyang
  of Muslim population Songpan
                        Zhaotong **GUIZHOU** **HUNAN** **JIANGXI**
                        Anshun   **FUJIAN**
                        Dali   Guilin
                        Menghua Yunnanfu
                                 (Kunming)   **GUANGXI**
                        YUNNAN   **GUANGDONG**
                                              Xi
scale 1:25 000 000   Guangzhou
                                                    SOUTH CHINA
0   600 km   **SEA**   20°
0   400 mi

30°   Xindu
           □ Chengdu

Yangzi

                                                    Wumeng ■

                                                    Zhaotong ■
                              Nu

                                    Dali ■
                         trade with Burma Menghua
                                    Shunning   (Kunming)
                                                              +

20°
MIAN
1287 Mongol dependency   **ANNAM**
                                          1285 Mongol dependency

                                                        Longtian
                                                        trade from southeast
                                                        Asia (Nanhai)

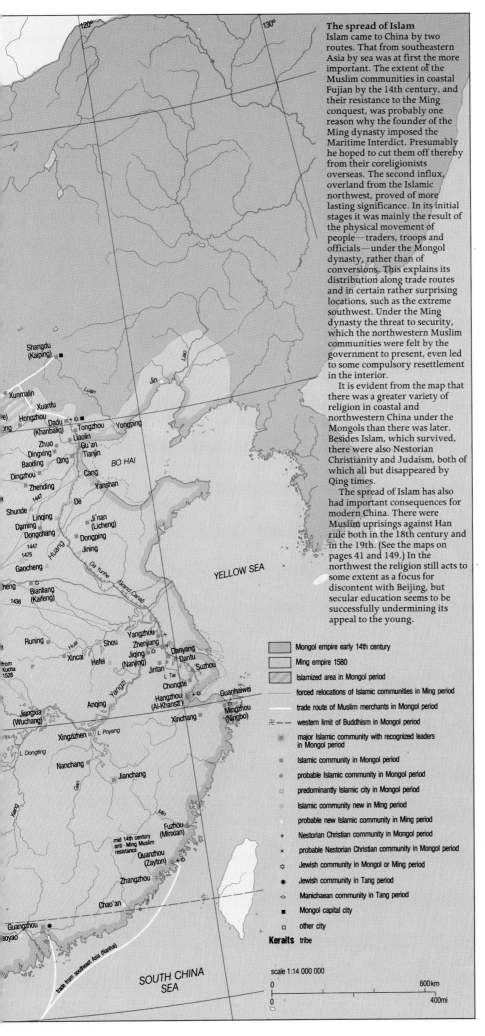

The spread of Islam
Islam came to China by two routes. That from southeastern Asia by sea was at first the more important. The extent of the Muslim communities in coastal Fujian by the 14th century, and their resistance to the Ming conquest, was probably one reason why the founder of the Ming dynasty imposed the Maritime Interdict. Presumably he hoped to cut them off thereby from their coreligionists overseas. The second influx, overland from the Islamic northwest, proved of more lasting significance. In its initial stages it was mainly the result of the physical movement of people—traders, troops and officials—under the Mongol dynasty, rather than of conversions. This explains its distribution along trade routes and in certain rather surprising locations, such as the extreme southwest. Under the Ming dynasty the threat to security, which the northwestern Muslim communities were felt by the government to present, even led to some compulsory resettlement in the interior.

It is evident from the map that there was a greater variety of religion in coastal and northwestern China under the Mongols than there was later. Besides Islam, which survived, there were also Nestorian Christianity and Judaism, both of which all but disappeared by Qing times.

The spread of Islam has also had important consequences for modern China. There were Muslim uprisings against Han rule both in the 18th century and in the 19th. (See the maps on pages 41 and 149.) In the northwest the religion still acts to some extent as a focus for discontent with Beijing, but secular education seems to be successfully undermining its appeal to the young.

Mongol empire early 14th century
Ming empire 1580
Islamized area in Mongol period
forced relocations of Islamic communities in Ming period
trade route of Muslim merchants in Mongol period
western limit of Buddhism in Mongol period
major Islamic community with recognized leaders in Mongol period
Islamic community in Mongol period
probable Islamic community in Mongol period
predominantly Islamic city in Mongol period
Islamic community new in Ming period
probable new Islamic community in Ming period
Nestorian Christian community in Mongol period
probable Nestorian Christian community in Mongol period
Jewish community in Mongol or Ming period
Jewish community in Tang period
Manichaean community in Tang period
Mongol capital city
other city
Keraits tribe

scale 1:14 000 000
0   600km
0   400mi

modern times was interwoven with a complex of rituals that regulated its relations with a labyrinthine other world of gods and spirits. Small groups of families were bound together by the shared burning of incense, larger groups by festivals of celebration, offering and purification. Social time throughout the year was structured by its occasions, and its lucky and unlucky days. The imagery of its liturgy, its tales, ballads and theater full of the gods who were in a sense the servants of the community, and of the immortals, who had achieved freedom beyond the constraints of human morality and society, dominated the popular mind. The centers of social life in villages and city quarters were the often magnificent temples, with their red pillars, gleaming tiled roofs, painted and sculptured beams and statues of the divinities that were periodically taken out and carried in procession around their domains of spiritual jurisdiction. It was a religion without a congregation, since it embraced the entire community, and without a clergy in the Western sense, though it had spirit-mediums and their manipulators (who answered the questions of inquirers), and Daoist masters of ritual who conducted the grander ceremonies.

The first public acts of Hong Xiuquan were to attack this traditional religion and to preach a monotheism heavily colored by Confucian morality. His earliest writings emphasize filial obedience, social harmony and a total opposition to such vices as theatrical performances, gambling and prostitution. His followers (understandably) lived in a state of conflict with their neighbors. They were virtually forced into rebellion as the pressures and suspicions of the authorities grew more severe. Once in partial power, they tore down many temples and monasteries in areas where they ruled — a cultural devastation that might be likened to the destruction of churches and cathedrals in Europe. The Taipings were also revolutionary in the greater social freedom that they accorded to women, and the at least theoretical equality they gave them in many respects, such for example as the right to hold land.

After 1859, the Taiping prime minister, Hong Ren'gan, drew up an elaborate program for economic modernization based on what he had learned from Westerners in Hong Kong. His proposals, which remained as far from realization as the scheme for holding lands in common, included banks, railroads, newspapers, post offices, voting by ballot, patents for inventions, the prohibition of alcohol, a ban on geomancy, because it tended to prevent the profitable mining of minerals, and the creation of a secret police.

The defeat of the Taiping rebellion and the other mid-century uprisings was managed only with the greatest difficulty. The narrow margin by which the established order escaped destruction was probably responsible for the extremely wary attitude taken by the Court in the 1870s and 1880s towards even the most limited economic, social or political innovations. There was, however, some discussion of technical modernization. Li Hongzhang, one of the architects of the destruction of the Taipings, told the throne in 1865, "Western machinery can produce farming, weaving, printing and pottery-making equipment for the daily use of the people. It is not solely for the purpose of making weapons.

What is wondrous is that it uses the power of water and fire to save labor and material resources." He was however opposed by the conservatives, who argued like Woren that "the basic policy of the state is to cultivate men's minds and not techniques."

3 Agitation for institutional reform

The French conquest of Annam in the 1880s, and Japan's swift defeat of China in the war of 1894–95, which led to the loss of Taiwan until 1945, prompted an increasing flow of proposals for institutional reforms. The objective underlying most of these suggestions was a greater degree of intercommunication (*tong*), and hence of mutual support and sympathy between rulers and ruled. They were first put forward by Chinese who had lived among Westerners, like Dr He Kai, and by relative outsiders to the political scene, but they were swiftly taken up by some of the younger officials. Representative of this group was Chen Zhi whose reform proposals, under the deliberately disarming title *The Book on the Unchanging Element in Human Affairs*, were studied by the emperor himself. The main demands of the reformers were for a codified law, elected local officials and consultative assemblies, a national parliament, and newspapers under state control, for "there is nothing better than uniting numberless people to be of one mind."

It was during the 1890s that the complex amalgam of modern Chinese nationalism began to take shape. The oldest stratum was a premodern culturalist universalism. Its ambiguities are represented by the double sense of the Chinese term "All Under Heaven" (*tianxia*), which can mean both "the Chinese Empire" and "the Whole World." It was a pervasive feeling that China was, in a sense, humanity, certainly civilized humanity at its best. Hence the destiny of humanity was almost synonymous with the destiny of Chinese culture or even (which is not quite the same thing) of the Chinese race. Initially this was an obstacle to change. Alcock, the British minister to Beijing in the later 1860s, remarked on the Chinese "pride of race and what they conceive to be a real superiority in civilization to all outside nations."

In the 1890s this stratum was overlaid by a growing concern with the international struggle for survival, an idea borrowed from the then fashionable Social Darwinism. At its center was an awareness that China was a nation-state among many others, and engaged in what was, in some sense, a life-and-death struggle with these rivals. Its characteristic formulation was given in 1900 by Yan Fu, the translator of Huxley, Adam Smith and John Stuart Mill:

> In overcoming ignorance, we must exert our utmost efforts to seek out knowledge. We have no time to ask whether this knowledge is Chinese or Western, or whether it is old or new. If one course leads to ignorance and thus to poverty and weakness, even if it originates with our ancestors, or is based on the authority of our rulers and teachers ... we must cast it aside. If another course is effective in overcoming ignorance, and thus leads to the cure of our poverty and weakness, we must imitate it, even if it proceeds from barbarians and wild beasts.

The origins of the Boxers 1898–1900
The anti-Christian and anti-foreign Boxer movement of 1898–1900 resulted from the fusion of two geographically distinct components. One of these—the proto-Boxer local militia forces—was active north of the Huang River. The other—the Great Sword Society—originated south of it. They met and merged by moving respectively eastward and northward.

The map shows the close linkage of the Boxer movement with the Grand Canal, and its rather poor geographical correlation with the areas of greatest Christian presence (around missions) and foreign presence (in treaty ports). It also emphasizes its spatial separation from other, approximately contemporary, movements against Christians and foreigners in the province.

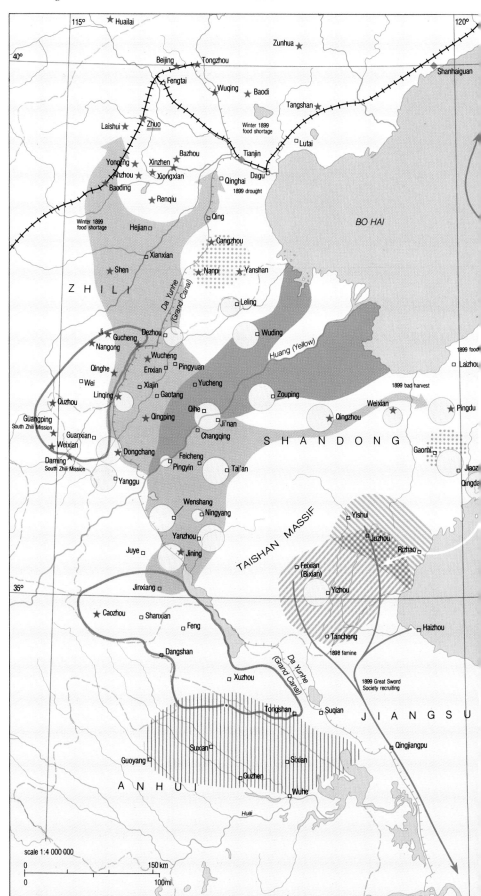

Right The Empress Cixi with ladies of the court and the chief eunuch.

proto-Boxer heartland

Great Sword Society, 1896—97

area flooded, 1892—98

anti-Christian propaganda, 1898

refugee movements, 1898—1900

non-Boxer rebellion, Jan—May 1899

Yizhou anti-Christian movement, Jan—June 1899

Jimo anti-Christian movement, Apr 1899

German military expedition, May—June 1899

Rizhao anti-foreign movements, 1899

Gaomi anti-railroad movements, 1899

Boxer activity, Aug 1899—Feb 1900

★ center of Boxer activity, Mar—July 1900

Xinzhen Boxer headquarters, Mar 1900

Zhuo Boxer headquarters, early July 1900

Christian community in Shandong:

2000—6000 people

400—2000

fewer than 400

treaty port or foreign leased area

The first effective expression of this new sense of nationalism as a struggle for survival was probably the manifesto composed by Kang Youwei, then a junior official, in the wake of the 1894—95 defeat by Japan, when examination candidates staged a mass protest in Beijing. With biting rhetoric he observed that "there is no conservative country in the world that is not like a shattered tile." He described British India as a land where "the teeming natives are kept like cattle or horses." Together with Wen Tingshi, tutor to the emperor's concubines, he started the Society for Studying How to Grow Strong, and this soon led to the widespread creation of "study societies," the forerunners of modern political parties.

In 1898 Kang was made in effect the emperor's special adviser, and he embarked with the overhasty speed of an inexperienced enthusiast on numerous reforms. The more important of these included the modernization of the civil-service examination system, the rationalization of the administrative structure on functional lines, the updating of the educational curriculum and an initial measure of democratization. The justification for this "democracy" was not the belief that the people had rights, but that it conferred national strength through an organic unity. In the words of Chen Zhi, "When something is proposed, there is no extravagant talking, and no neglect in its execution. It is like the body controlling the arm, and the arm controlling the fingers, with one heart and one mode of behavior, uniting every ambition so as to form a mighty rampart." After slightly more than three months, however, Kang Youwei and his associates were driven from power by a conservative coup d'etat led by Empress-Dowager Cixi, her confidant Ronglu and the eminent official Yuan Shikai who controlled an army near the capital.

4 Ultra-conservatism

The third element in modern Chinese nationalism is a xenophobic allergy to everything not Chinese. If we keep to our geological metaphor, it can be thought of as hot emotional lava that periodically forces its way up through the other strata, spilling out with a shortlived but violently destructive effect, before cooling into dikes and sills that remain behind like scars upon the surface. It found its classic expression in the Boxer Uprising of 1899 and 1900.

The popular roots of the uprising were in the fusion of two anti-Christian movements, whose chief victims were in fact Chinese Christians and those alleged to be believers. They practiced martial arts enveloped in the theatrical aura of the traditional religion, including spirit-possession and claims to invulnerability, and drew the greater number of their recruits from teenagers. The rising was restricted to a fairly limited area, mainly the more northern reaches of the Grand Canal, which was then in severe economic recession and full of displaced and *déclassé* persons. It was to some degree promoted by a handful of local officials, ultra-conservatives who had never approved of the policy of compromising with foreigners. The most important of these were Li Bingheng, governor of Shandong province in the mid-1890s, and Yuxian, governor in 1898 and 1899. Once the movement was under way, however, they had virtually no control over it, and it took on aspects of a political saturnalia in which officials were ignored, abused, maltreated and even murdered.

The Boxer movement was a pogrom in that it tried to kill those whom it saw as a source of ill-fortune. A poster put up in Beijing conveys the attitudes at work:

The supernaturally assisted Boxers ... have only arisen because devils [that is to say, Christians and foreigners] have plagued the North China plain. They have urged people to believe in Christianity, which is to usurp Heaven. They do not respect the gods or Buddhas, and are forgetful of their ancestors. These men have no principles in their human relationships .... The rain does not fall. The ground has dried up. All this has happened because the Christian churches have put a stop to [the workings of] Heaven. The gods are angry, and the immortals vexed .... If you want to drive away the devils, it will not take much effort. Pull up the railway lines! Smash the great steamships! ... Once all the devils have been slaughtered, the great Qing dynasty will enjoy a peaceful ascendancy.

A rendering of a contemporary drawing of a Boxer practicing swordplay. There was a great deal of theater about Boxer martial arts, and adepts believed that their magic made them invulnerable to blades and bullets alike. Masters often induced a state of hypnotic trance in their disciples before they performed their military exercises, and sometimes claimed themselves to be possessed by deities such as Guandi, god of war.

These and other fears, such as that of universally present spies, were offset by a belief in an instantaneous, magical regeneration and prosperity if the "devils" were wiped out and Boxer rituals followed.

Most conservative officials at this time supported a program of strictly limited westernization, especially in military matters, as a way of avoiding having to make more far-reaching changes later. Boxer anti-foreignism appealed to a small number of ultra-conservatives, mostly officials at court with little experience of practical administration, who thought that even this degree of westernization was unnecessary. They believed that the will-power of the mobilized masses, under suitable control, and a heightened ideological consciousness, could be used to drive out the foreigners altogether and to get rid of the treaty ports and Christianity. Yuxian declared, "Our country is continually declining because the will of the people is not being developed." Tanji, tutor to the heir apparent, was of the view that "the spirit of righteous anger is sufficient to repress insults." The throne spoke of "the will of the masses" as like a rampart. Some tried to rationalize the superstitious aspects. Others, like Prince Duan, were more cynical. "It is only a matter of using their feelings," he said. "Why do you talk about their magic?" The first attempt at mass mobilization in Chinese history was thus the work of reactionaries.

The ultras won the debate at court and embarked on a campaign to exterminate Chinese Christians (or reform them through so-called self-renewal offices) and to get rid of foreigners. The more realistic provincial authorities in central and south China courageously refused to follow imperial orders, and thus avoided a general war with the foreign powers in which China might well have been dismembered. As it was, the northeast was pacified by a composite foreign expeditionary force, and the Chinese government was obliged to punish many of the officials allegedly responsible for the movement and to pay a large indemnity.

The Boxer Uprising revealed with exceptional clarity aspects of Chinese political behavior that were to surface again from time to time, notably in the Cultural Revolution of the 1960s. Hatred was the basis of mass mobilization. Scapegoats for suffering were invented and then murdered. It was believed that all would be miraculously well once these evildoers had been destroyed. Superior technology was regarded as of little importance as compared to having faith, and many ordinary people believed in the promise that, with the correct ideology, they could accomplish superhuman feats. The activists were obsessed with a symbolic purification of words, dress and objects, striving to abolish everything (except foreign firearms) that was tainted with an outside origin. Theatrical devices were used to arouse the emotions, and drama and real life tended to become confused. The enthusiastic young were the most numerous recruits to the cause, and those who died for it in greatest numbers. The mass movement swelled as the result of encouragement from part of the state apparatus, but the civil and military bureaucracies became split into two factions, one for and one against it. Deadly feuds arose from this antagonism. Though overtly loyal to the throne, the movement was in fact out of

Percentage Distribution of Domestic Product in China in 1914–1918 and 1931–36, ranked by sectors in order of rate of growth.					
	Output (billions of 1933 *yuan*)		Percentage of Gross Domestic Product		Index (1914–18 = 100)
	1914–18	1931–36	1914–18	1931–36	
Modern					
Industry	0.33	1.21	1.4	4.2	367
Transportation	0.25	0.50	1.0	1.7	200
Construction	0.26	0.48	1.1	1.6	185
Finance	0.17	0.28	0.7	1.0	165
Traditional					
Trade	2.23	2.71	9.2	9.3	122
Government	0.76	0.91	3.1	3.1	120
Personal services	0.30	0.35	1.2	1.2	117
Agriculture	16.00	18.32	66.0	62.9	115
Residential rent	0.91	1.04	3.8	3.6	114
Handicrafts	1.93	2.18	8.0	7.5	113
Transportation	1.10	1.15	4.5	3.9	105
GDP	24.26	29.13	100.0	100.0	120

Note: Subtotals are rounded.
"Transportation" covers communications.

Output per Person in Agriculture and Industry in the Four Economic Systems of China, 1952–1953, in 1952 Yuan.					
	Population (1953) (millions)	Output (1952) (million *yuan*)		Output per Person (*yuan* per person)	
		Agriculture	Industry	Agriculture	Industry
Hinterland	507	38 158	16 932	75	33
Former treaty ports	8.9	—	8 346	—	938
Resource-rich frontiers	46.9	5 063	7 514	108	160
Outer China	12.7	1 835	404	144	32

Above The construction of a network of railroads was started in the last years of the 19th century This photograph shows a crowded station platform at the port of Tianjin taken in 1908.

Left: Economic growth
Table 1. Percentage distribution of domestic product in China in 1914–18 and 1931–36, ranked by sectors in order of rate of growth

The first two columns of figures show the value of the output of the Chinese economy (including Manchuria) by different sectors, divided into the two rough categories of "modern" and "traditional," at the time of World War I and in the early 1930s. The overwhelming preponderance of the traditional sectors, especially agriculture with over 60 percent, is evident from the third and fourth columns, which express each sector's share as a percentage of the total. The last column shows the proportional growth of each sector between the two periods, taking the value of its output in 1914–18 as equivalent to 100. The much swifter expansion of the modern sector, especially industry (which grew more than 3½ times) is equally evident.

Table 2. Output per person in agriculture and industry in the four economic systems of China, 1952–53, in 1952 *yuan*

control, set up its own rival administration in some places and was used by the criminal underworld as a cover for malpractice. Popular credulity was easily aroused, but shallow. Support collapsed as common sense observed that the promises made were not fulfilled.

5 Democracy

By about 1903 almost all educated Chinese opinion had become convinced that some sort of general political and social reform was essential if China was to survive. The emerging consensus was summed up in the influential *Theory of a New Citizenry*, published in 1902 by Liang Qichao, a former disciple of Kang Youwei, and perhaps the most influential publicist in Chinese history. China, he said, needed a new society and a new psychology that included liberty, equality, independence, self-respect, self-government and a sense of public morality. With his emphasis on popular sovereignty, he changed the focus of the old concept of "loyalty" (*zhong*) from an individual ruler or dynasty to the nation as a whole. Thus the concept of "the people" (*min*) came to replace that of Heaven (*tian*) as the ultimate legitimating principle. A careful study of world history later convinced Liang that organic development was essential, and that a republican form of government would be too sharp a break with Chinese tradition to be practicable. He carried opinion with him on this until the later part of 1910. There was also a more extreme group in Tokyo, the Revolutionary Alliance led by Sun Yixian (Sun Yat-sen) and Hu Hanmin. In their journal, the *People's Paper*, they advocated not only the abolition of the monarchy, but also a measure of economic collectivism. As of 1905 and 1906, however, their views had relatively little influence.

At the same time, several gradual technical and institutional changes had altered the nature of the political arena. The spread of the electric telegraph, which had begun in the 1880s, was now complete enough to link almost all the county capitals into a national, and international, network. The size of the empire, in terms of communications, had shrunk by about two orders of magnitude (weeks to hours) in a couple of decades. Events began to move much faster, and intermediate levels of government, such as prefectures, lost their relevance as information was exchanged directly between localities and the center. People and goods were also traveling more quickly between major cities because of the steamship lines and the expanding rail network. The proliferation of newspapers likewise created an authentic public opinion for the first time, at least in the cities. For all these reasons, national self-awareness was more sharply defined than it had been even a decade before.

But there was a problem. These advances were concentrated in the great urban centers, particularly the leading treaty ports like Shanghai and Tianjin. Profound differences were opening up between different parts of China, as a result of differing degrees of exposure to outside influences. Their full significance did not appear until a few years later, and therefore, in order to make what was happening comprehensible, it is convenient to step aside for a moment from a strictly chronological treatment and look at economic growth in the modern sector during the next period, which is the

first for which there are reasonable figures. The right-hand column of the first table shows the comparative rates of growth for the modern and traditional sectors between 1914 and 1936. It is clear that the modern side of the Chinese economy, though a small part of the total, was highly successful. The percentage rates for modern industrial growth in China, including Manchuria, in fact averaged 5·6 per cent a year from 1912 to 1949. The rate was 13·4 per cent a year from 1912 to 1920, when World War I removed much European competition. Between 1928 and 1936, a time of comparative peace and unity under the Nationalist government, it was 8·4 per cent.

The crucial social factor was that the geographical distribution of this growth was grotesquely skewed. In the second table, which shows the situation shortly after the takeover by the Communists in 1949, China is divided into a crude approximation of the four main systems: hinterland China, the former treaty ports, the resource-rich frontiers (here Manchuria, but in which Taiwan could also be included), and Outer China. It is evident from the last two columns, which give the output per person in each system, that we are dealing with four different economic worlds.

It is clear from the above that the assertion that Western "economic imperialism," which was largely concentrated in the treaty ports (and, after 1932, Manchuria), oppressed the modern part of the Chinese economy is one of the most spectacular falsehoods of recent propaganda. The historian's problem here is not explaining failure, but success. The short answer is that the treaty ports opened by the foreigners were linked with the world trading system (like the more recent success stories of Hong Kong and Taiwan), and this link freed them from the restraints on demand and supply, inherited from the high-level equilibrium trap, that continued to hold back the growth of the hinterland.

Once localized development had started, there were the usual positive feedbacks leading to the continuing locational concentration of modern enterprise. Foreign trade opened up treaty-port markets for new goods through the demonstration effect. Would-be Chinese entrepreneurs were attracted by the facilities available to them: telegraphs, telephones, newspapers, steamships, rail terminals. Capital was available through Chinese banks funded by Western banks. Technical knowhow, special services and products, skilled managers and workmen, were all on the doorstep. It has been estimated that by 1933 the share of the modern sector owned by the Chinese produced an output worth more than three times that of the share owned by foreigners.

Shanghai provided one of the most striking cases of the effective transfer of technology anywhere in the world. Chinese industrialists had in front of them, in the foreign factories, what amounted to a permanent exhibition of machinery from different countries all over the globe, and the means to progress step by step from repair, assembly and part-manufacture to cut-price imitation and the creation of their own designs. Chinese-made machine tools were first exported overseas from Shanghai during World War I.

These diverging trends were well under way by the first decade of the present century, and help to

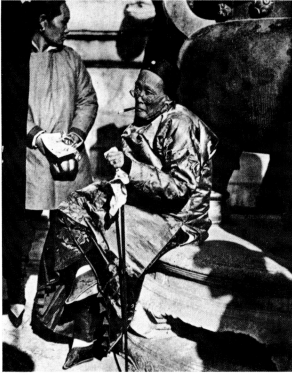

explain why the institutional reforms of this time, which began so promisingly, ended eventually in confusion and failure. They really flourished only in the already more than half modernized world of a few cities, while most of the countryside and towns were left behind, incapable of adapting.

In the first few years of the present century, the central government, still under the adaptable empress-dowager until her death in 1908, dismantled much of the old social and political order with astonishing speed. They abolished the civil-service examinations, speeded up the creation of a modernized and educated army officer-corps, introduced chambers of commerce, and set up elected local councils and assemblies for self-government at municipal and rural district levels. They provided for elected provincial assemblies, and finally, in 1910, for a proto-parliament, half indirectly elected and half appointed. The more advanced local self-government bodies, such as those that ran the Chinese parts of Shanghai and Tianjin, were effective improvers. They built roads and bridges, expanded primary education, took over public sanitation and sometimes the police, pioneered means to control traffic, inspect factories and limit fire and health hazards, and promoted tramways and supplies of clean water.

Under this surge of reforms, a change took place in the nature of political power. The millennial link between education and access to office had been cut. This probably reduced social mobility. It certainly created a new class of intellectuals, no longer firmly committed to the established order. The new Western-style education now needed to enter the elite was also more expensive than the traditional sort, often requiring study in Japan or the West to finish it off. This opened up a gap in values between a semi-westernized ruling group and the rest of Chinese society. At the local and provincial level, the scholar-gentry and the merchants with whom they were associated in places like Shanghai, were now given in formal fashion the power to run their own localities, which they had previously only had informally. In those areas where self-government flourished, the imperially appointed local officials soon found themselves playing a much reduced role, both to their annoyance and the impoverishment of their subordinates.

Finally, this extraordinary first decade of the century saw the start of several new movements that were to be of great importance later. Among them were first true trade unions, mass boycotts of foreign goods used as a weapon of political protest, the spread of education for women and the attempt to create a "national language" spoken by all Chinese if only as a secondary lingua franca.

6 The republican revolution of 1911

Late in 1910 the regent Zaifeng, who held the reins of power in the Manchu court, turned abruptly against the widely supported movement for the immediate introduction of a properly elected national parliament and a responsible cabinet. Although the government's constitutional program called eventually for the first, and the question was therefore mainly one of timing and not of principle, this obduracy brought into being an anti-Manchu sentiment among numerous influential citizens with

a place in the established order. These included scholar-gentry and merchant leaders of local self-government councils and provincial assemblies, as well as officers in the modernized armed forces. Little by little these groups became aligned with the small number of professional revolutionaries in the Revolutionary Alliance, the Return of the Light Association and other less important undercover movements.

Anti-Manchuism had been kept alive since the 17th century in the ritualistic Ming revivalism of secret societies such as the Triads. It was revived by the Taipings, who referred to the emperor as "this Tatar fiend ... the perpetual enemy of our Chinese race." Sun Yixian gave it a further lease of life in the 1890s. One of his associates in his unsuccessful rising of 1895 declared, before being tortured to death by the authorities, that the "Manchu-Qing, the robbers of Manchuria, conquered our country, stole our land, killed our ancestors, seized our sons and daughters," and that "if we do not now exterminate the Manchus, it will be impossible to restore the Chinese race." This line of simplistic but persuasive propaganda, blaming all of China's ills on the Manchus, culminated in a genocidal pamphlet called *The Revolutionary Army* written by Zou Rong, and published in 1903. More moderate revolutionaries did not call for a mass slaughter, but only argued, like Hu Hanmin, that once their political power had been broken, the Manchus "will become assimilated to us, and disappear."

The significance of anti-Manchuism was that it served as a cement to hold together for a few months a complex of improvised alliances between socially disparate elements that otherwise had little in common. Contrary to another quite common historical myth, the revolution of 1911 was not organized by Sun Yixian (who was in Denver, Colorado, when it broke out, much to his surprise). There was no concerted plan. What happened was that a revolutionary group in the army at Wuhan rose in a hurry in October to prevent a pre-emptive strike against them by the authorities. As the news of their initial success spread, there was a series of responses in other cities in the central Yangzi valley and in western China. A month later, these were followed by responses in the lower Yangzi delta and south China. As may be seen from the map, the 1911 revolution was almost entirely an urban phenomenon, that leapt across the intervening countryside thanks to the electric telegraph. Only in the Guangzhou delta was there a clearly rural component to the revolution, in the so-called People's Armies that marched upon Guangzhou. In each city the alliance that carried out the seizure of power was a different mixture of the following elements: army officers, self-government councils, merchants with their merchant militias, students and teachers, secret societies and — in Shanghai — part of the criminal underworld, actors, peasants' militias (in Guangdong) and of course the professional revolutionaries. It is not really surprising that, once the theory putting the blame for everything wrong on the Manchus had showed itself to be the nonsense it was, these alliances fell apart.

Imperial power had collapsed almost overnight in three-quarters of China, in some places with virtually no bloodshed. But not in the northeast and the capital. To prevent a situation developing in

Above Shanghai merchants enjoyed considerable power in the first decade of the 20th century and participated in their own local self-government. This photograph shows two prime examples of the opulent merchant class.

Above center A well-to-do woman takes a rest while her servant holds her brass hand-warmer filled with charcoal embers.

Above left This young girl sitting on a Western-style chair poses for her photograph as formally as her equivalent in Victorian England. Already her feet have been bound.

Left Eating, drinking, fortune telling, haircutting and many other activities took place in the open air.

which internal conflict offered opportunities for foreign intervention, the revolutionaries negotiated a settlement with Yuan Shikai, the former high official whom the court had called out of retirement to help them in their difficulties. It was agreed that Yuan would jettison the Manchus, and that a republic would be set up of which he would be the first president.

Once in power, Yuan deliberately sabotaged the new democratic institutions, using decrees, terror, murder and military force against his opponents. By early 1914 almost nothing substantial was left of the creations of the preceding decade. Foolishly, he tried to make himself emperor, but could get support neither from the progressives, who hated him as the destroyer of democracy, nor from the

traditionalists, who loathed him as a traitor, disloyal to the dynasty he had served. He relinquished his imperial claims, but an insurrection led by army officers from the southwest was moving against him when he died in 1916.

The revolution of 1911 was perhaps the greatest tragedy of modern China, not because it caused the most immediate suffering – in fact, it caused remarkably little – but because it wiped out for several generations China's peaceful and organic progress towards a modern and democratic future. It was led by many brave and idealistic men, far better than their imperial opponents, as well as the usual proportion of scoundrels, but it brought about a collapse of political authority, hence an internal chaos, for which there was no remedy

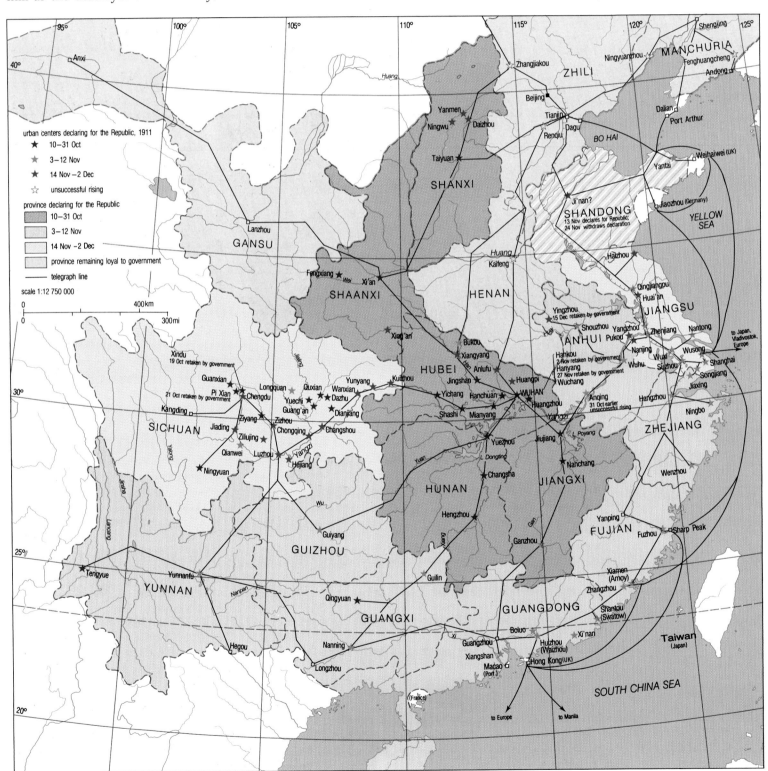

Left: The 1911 revolution
Every insurrection in Chinese history before 1911 involved the movement of rebel forces across the country; 1911 was different. It was prepared mostly in cities far apart from each other, through the new force of urban public opinion given expression in newspapers. After the initial outbreak at Wuhan, it spread from city to city in a non-continuous fashion, bypassing most of the intervening countryside, by means of the electric telegraph. In the years since the early 1880s the telegraphic revolution had collapsed the communications size of the empire by about two orders of magnitude, and had greatly accelerated the working of political processes. The novel spatial pattern taken by the 1911 uprisings and depicted here was in great measure the result of that technical revolution, though it was also conditioned for each specific locality by other factors specific to that locality, such as nearness to armed forces still loyal to the Manchus.

except strong-arm methods. The legitimacy of the old order, based on Confucian ideology and the mandarinate, had been broken. The legitimacy of the emerging new order, based on popular sovereignty and elections, had not yet had time to establish adequate roots. Most tragic of all was that the collapse could have been easily avoided by any statesman able to read the signs of the times. This is not hindsight. Zaifeng was warned by many conservative voices late in 1910 about the fatal consequences of trying to slow down the movement for a constitution that almost every politically aware Chinese regarded as vital for the nation's welfare.

7 Warlords, parties, mass movements

When President Yuan passed from the scene, power at the center fell into the hands of two of his military subordinates, Feng Guozhang and Duan Qirui. The cliques of army officers led by these two fought each other for the next four years. Feng's Zhili clique emerged the winner, but now under the leadership of Wu Peifu. In 1924 Wu's power was broken by Zhang Zuolin, the ex-bandit military boss of Manchuria, who now disputed the hegemony of north China with Feng Yuxiang, known as the "Christian General." In 1927 Nationalist forces under Jiang Jieshi (Chiang Kai-shek) reunited the greater part of Inner China in the course of the so-called Northern Expedition from Guangzhou.

During the years 1916 to 1928, and in some places long after that, the provinces not near the capital were ruled by numerous other warlords. These militarists controlled what amounted to regional armies of occupation, allocating the tax revenues from particular areas to specific subordinate officers in a semi-feudal fashion. These officers sometimes

collected the levies directly, but more often they relied on local gentry and militia to perform the task for them. Each warlord domain also usually had its own currency. The economic burden on the peasants of supporting this swollen military establishment was far heavier than the burden of rents (where these were paid) and the ordinary taxes of the previous period.

Warlords differed considerably in character. Several of them were improvers or reformers in one way or another, if only to the extent of promoting compulsory swimming or other pet projects. One of them, the durable Yan Xishan of Shanxi, achieved a limited measure of industrialization in the 1930s. (It was his experts who invented the famous Chinese wood-burning engine for trucks.) His methods of social control (such as "Heart-Washing Societies" and the obligatory study of his writings) were partly inspired by the Communists and partly anticipated them.

The enthusiasm ignited in China by the October Revolution of 1917 in Russia led in 1924 to the reorganization of the Nationalist Party (or Guomindang). This was a movement that had been created by Sun Yixian as a successor to the old Revolutionary Alliance. The restructuring was done on broadly Bolshevik lines, with the help of Soviet Russian advisers such as Borodin. The same enthusiasm also led to the founding of a Chinese Communist Party by Chen Duxiu and Li Dazhao. Its official year of birth was 1921, though scattered groups had been in existence before this time. The two parties soon entered into an alliance, the far less numerous Communists joining the Nationalist Party as individuals and quickly coming to dominate many key positions.

The allied parties both exploited, and in some measure helped to create, the great movements of the 1920s: among factory labor, women and peasants. As the first successes of these movements raised in increasingly acute form the problem of whether there was, or was not, going to be a thoroughgoing social revolution, the right and the center of the Nationalists under Jiang Jieshi turned against their left wing and against the Communists. As the Northern Expedition advanced toward victory, Jiang became hostile to the mass movements, and then broke with the Communists, murdering as many of them as he could, and driving the residue of the party underground, reduced to about a tenth of its former size.

There was only a small industrial working class in the China of the 1920s, perhaps two million in all, of whom quite a large proportion were women and children. The majority were probably not hired directly by their employers, but through labor contractors. One of the objectives of the new trade unions was to remove these contractors and take over their function. Discipline was harsh in factories. Corporal punishment and the withholding of part of the wages were common. The early 1920s saw the first large-scale strikes based on permanent organizations, and demands that went beyond higher wages to be concerned with the improvement of general conditions of hiring and work.

The usual conflict developed between revolutionary labor organizations, under Communist influence, and those of a reformist or welfare orientation, some of which were inspired or dominated by the employers. The secret *Brief History of the Communist Party*, prepared in 1926, is quite frank about the workers' fear of being exploited for political ends: "The laboring masses regarded the party's actions as dangerous and radical. They believed that the labor movement should stay within legal limits .... On witnessing the fiery actions of the Communists, the laborers suspected them of being spies for the capitalists or propagandists for Sun Yixian. In short, the workers feared being utilized by others as instruments of violent struggle." The radicalization of much of the labor movement came about through the association of trade-union activity with protests against the presence of foreign interests in China. The climax of this trend was the sequence of events running from the May Thirtieth Movement in 1925 in Shanghai, a huge protest against the killing of a worker in a Japanese factory during a bout of machinery smashing and the subsequent shooting of demonstrators by the British police of the International Settlement, to the Guangzhou and Hong Kong strike of 1925–26. The latter was aimed at a complete transformation of labor conditions in the colony, including an eight-hour day and an end to the labor-contractor system. When demonstrators were killed by foreigners in Guangzhou, Hong Kong was economically boycotted for over a year. The most significant development, though, was the way in which the strike committee in Canton turned into a miniature government, with its own courts, armed force, schools and so forth.

The most ambitious effort at this time to set up a workers' government was that made in Shanghai during the first few months of 1927 by the General Labor Union, a body under Communist control. The

first attempt was meant to be a response to the approaching troops of the Northern Expedition, but it was crushed by the local warlord, Sun Chuanfang. According to an American newspaperman, "After the heads of the victims were severed by swordsmen, they were displayed on the tops of poles or placed upon platters and carried through the streets. This sight in a parade through crowded thoroughfares had the effect of creating a veritable reign of terror." The second attempt, led by Zhou Enlai among others, set up a provisional municipal government that lasted almost three weeks. It collapsed because its leaders, as members of the Communist International, obeyed Stalin's instructions not to fight against Jiang Jieshi. They therefore refused the offer of one of his leading military commanders to defect to the Communist side, with his troops. Jiang then disguised his soldiers as workers and, in collaboration with a local secret society called the Green Gang, massacred the revolutionaries.

The women's movement drew on a variety of late traditional antecedents. Unconventional philosophers like Li Zhi, novelists like Cao Xueqin, poets like Yuan Mei (who encouraged and published women writers) and satirists like Li Ruzhen (author of *Flowers in the Mirror* showing women playing the roles of men) had all pointed to the waste of talent caused by the underestimation and mistreatment of

Above Discipline was harsh and corporal punishment common in the early 1920s. Punishments such as this one had been used in China for centuries. Small bronze figures of the 1st century BC on the top of a drum unearthed in southern China show men with their heads in stocks.

Right This powerful woodcut image entitled "Roar" by Li Hua captures the anger, frustration and restlessness of the Chinese peasant in the 1930s.

women. Taiping women soldiers and the "Red Lanterns," the young female counterparts of the Boxers who were so active in Tianjin in 1900, offered models of military and political activism. The pioneer of female emancipation in China, Qiu Jin, who was born in 1875, was influenced by these antecedents, and by the old stories of female knights errant, most of them fictional. She rode horseback, used a sword, drank heavily and wrote verses, but also engaged in revolutionary activities, practiced making bombs, taught girls military drill and started the *Chinese Women's Journal*.

The Suffrage Alliance of 1912 had stormed the Nanjing parliament in an unsuccessful attempt to secure equal political and social rights for women, but it was only in the early 1920s that the movement acquired a mass basis. It was split between a social revolutionary wing and a more strictly feminist wing. Xiang Jingyu, the foremost woman Communist of the decade, complained that most educated women only wanted westernized families, participation in business and personal liberty. She kept her harshest strictures for the "romantics," girls who believed in free love and individual happiness.

There was a conflict between feminist mobilization and revolutionary mobilization that was never resolved. In the countryside, peasants, who had often paid large sums for their wives, were alienated from the revolutionary peasant movement when the women's associations began to grant divorces. But, if the women were not given divorces, they would not back the peasant movement. There was also an inter-generational conflict. Mothers-in-law, who in fact exercised the day-to-day control over their sons' wives, rarely welcomed the loss of the services of their daughters-in-law.

The movement with the greatest impact on the future was that among the peasants. It started in 1922 in Haifeng and Lufeng, two scenically spectacular counties in eastern Guangdong not far from Hong Kong. It was here, over the next six years, that most of the characteristic forms of the Chinese revolution were to crystallize.

Like much of the far south, Haifeng and Lufeng were an area of large lineages. These owned perhaps half the arable land as collective property. They also had their own armed forces, and government control over them was never strong. There was an exceptionally high rate of tenancy (around 70 per cent), though about two-fifths of the tenants had rights of permanent tenure. The people were of a remarkable ferocity, many of them being members of the Red or Black Flags, semi-secret organizations of 19th-century origin that periodically engaged each other in savage fighting. It was a common ritual practice to eat parts of slaughtered enemies.

Recent developments had opened a political space for a peasant movement. An increase in economic differences between the richer and poorer members of same lineage, and the exploitation of the humbler members by the lineage managers, had weakened peasant faith in the bonds of kinship and led them to join bodies like the Flags. The traditional local leaders were losing the trust of those below them, especially as they conducted their own affairs more and more on the basis of pursuing their own wealth and power, rather than of social obligation. A symptom of this trend was a new form of rural

armed force, the gentry militia, recruited for the defense of the privileges of the local notables. Security of permanent tenure was crumbling, and traditional taxes were augmented with new levies to pay both for the increased number of troops and for new projects, such as modern education, from which the peasants benefited little.

But peasant resentment was never class resentment. (That was a notion imported from outside by the intellectuals.) It was outrage at the absence of equity and fairness within the accepted framework of social relationships. The motive of their actions was to restore equity, achieve social respectability and assure economic security. Their method was equally traditional: to find a protector — whether lineage or secret society leader, warlord or Communist cadre — a man of destiny in whom they could believe, and who would give them what they wanted. There was thus at all times a divergence of interests between the peasants, struggling against economic exploitation, and the professional revolutionaries, who strove to exploit them politically, so as to seize power on the basis of their discontent, and then transform society.

Eastern Guangdong was the domain of one of the most "progressive" warlords, Chen Jiongming. A native of Haifeng, a supporter of Sun Yixian for several years and an adherent in theory of many of the anarchist-socialist ideas then fashionable, Chen allowed an unusual measure of freedom to early peasant movement propaganda.

In 1921 there stepped into this restless and complex milieu a young man called Peng Pai. He was destined to show the Chinese Communist Party how to arouse the countryside. Scion of a powerful local lineage, educated partly in Japan, he held the view that "The world belongs to all, and must be shared equally by all." Finding that agitation among the students was getting him nowhere, he started a Peasants' Union in 1922. He burned the title deeds to his own lands, and made an enormous effort to remold his own personality, so that he himself became like a peasant. He was soon to wield an immense authority, but he always saw himself as the servant of those whom he led, taking his orders from the people; and this was a new attitude in China.

The Union was a protection and welfare organization that spread rapidly by absorbing the remnants of the old Flag networks. Besides resisting landlord extortions, it pioneered innovations such as practical schooling of use to peasant children. Its success soon led it to take over government functions, such as settling disputes. As its ideas and practices spread into other areas, Peng was drawn into the provincial arena. He joined the Communists in 1923 and was the chief force behind the Peasant Movement Training Institute in Guangzhou, set up in 1924 with Nationalist backing. It was there that he also began to create the first rudiments of a peasant revolutionary army. Mao Zedong taught for a time at the Institute and drew his ideas and inspiration for peasant revolution largely from Peng.

As the opposition of the rural gentry, and their allies in the military, grew more resolute, the Peasant Union moved away from limited welfare objectives towards a class struggle, a shift more welcome to its leaders than to the rank and file. A

complex civil war raged in and around Haifeng during the next four years, in which conflicts at the national, provincial and local levels were interwoven. As one side, then the other, gained the upper hand, both began to practice terror. Quite early on, Peng had announced that "mercilessly killing landlords, interested only in money, is right." By 1926 trials and executions of landowners were common. The next year the Guangdong Communist Party committee decreed that "the killing of landlords should continue until not one is left." Finally the order was given to kill all those "in any way officially serving the old authorities," or even giving help and comfort to such persons. Many fled, in spite of efforts to make their families responsible for their return. One legacy of peasant-style revenge was the holding of mass meetings for disfiguring and torturing captives before killing them. The forces of reaction replied in kind.

In the periods between 1924 and 1926 when Haifeng was ruled by the Union or its successor the Peasant Association, and during 1927–28 under the Hai-Lu-feng Soviet, many practices appeared that were to be of continuing significance later. Peasants were politically mobilized to support the regular troops through transport, spying and sabotage. Traditional religion and Christianity were attacked. Pagodas were destroyed, monasteries cleared out and temples taken over, sometimes to the displeasure of the peasants who tried to save their idols by daubing them in red to show their progressive political sympathies. Children were indoctrinated to the extent that some denounced their mothers as counterrevolutionaries. Moves were made to stop brothels, concubinage, the buying and selling of

people, opium-smoking and gambling. Late in 1927 Peng Pai announced "the destruction of the system of private property." Land was to be distributed in accordance with numbers in a family and labor power; but the policy was too unpopular with peasants to be widely put into effect. Factories were likewise meant to be given to their workers. Economic equality of all was the key objective. There was a secret police. The order was given to burn all books in libraries and private collections "since they breed counterrevolutionaries." All in all, the new revolutionary world was a mixture of elemental morality and elemental barbarism, part modern and part medieval. In spite of its heroic resistance, Nationalist forces with much superior weapons wiped out the Soviet in 1928.

Much of the tragedy inherent in the Chinese revolution may be seen in the personal transformation of Peng Pai. His selflessness and sincerity impressed even his adversaries, and his humanitarian idealism of 1921 and 1922 was given a direct and practical expression. But, by 1927 and 1928, having had most of his friends killed around him, he had become an enthusiastic practitioner of mass murder, to the extent of showing youngsters in person at a mass meeting how to cut off the head of an enemy captive with a knife. Haifeng was the cradle of peasant revolution in east Asia, but it was a peculiar place, not typical even of much of China. It seems likely that some of its special characteristics — the importance attached to landlordism (which was not of great significance in north China) and the conviction that blood-letting was an indispensable part of social transformation — left their imprint on subsequent events.

Chinese Nationalist soldiers march along the Great Wall during the war against Japan (1937–45).

Below Civil War between the Chinese Communist Party and the Guomindang (Nationalist Party) was fought in China from mid-1946 until the victory of the Communist Party in 1949. This oil painting by Tang Muli depicts Mao Zedong and Zhou Enlai leading the Communist forces and is an example of the Soviet-style realism that dominated the arts in the succeeding decades.

Li Hua's woodcut "Flood of Wrath" shows the anger of the Chinese peasants unleashed against the Japanese at the time when Communist and Nationalist forces had formed a united front against the invaders. In fact resistance was generally more cautious than this picture suggests.

8 The Nationalist government

Like Yuan Shikai before him, Jiang Jieshi neutralized or destroyed the social and political forces that had brought him to power. He disbanded or broke up the mass movements in so far as he was able. He neglected the Nationalist Party. The Nanjing government over which he presided from 1928 to 1937 was based on a statist approach to ruling; most of the institutions and personnel in the warlord domains absorbed by his regime were kept on with minimal changes. He maintained himself at the top as the indispensable arbiter between rival factions. In order to overcome the corruption and immobilism of the administration he created the "Blue Shirts." These were a sort of fascist-communist elite group who were meant to promote a selfless, nationalist morality, militaristic values and a cult of Jiang himself as "China's Hitler or China's Stalin." This organization had to be disbanded in 1938 as part of the United Front against the Japanese agreed on with the Communists.

Prior to this later renewal of a formal alliance in the face of an external threat, the Communist Party was almost driven out of the cities, and its principal rural bases in Jiangxi were destroyed in 1934. The Communist forces, split by internal feuds, survived as an archipelago of tiny rural enclaves of which the most important was at Yan'an in Shaanxi. As most of the remaining warlords capitulated, Nanjing ended by controlling about two-thirds of the total population by 1937.

The Nanjing regime helped economic growth by bringing internal peace, removing internal customs barriers and establishing a uniform currency. This new money, introduced in 1935, was not convertible. The aim had been to get around the difficulties caused by the outflow of silver to America, but it led to an inflation and so unintentionally served as a sort of Keynesian policy that helped to pull China out of the depression of the 1930s. There was also a major expansion in primary and in university education. Major modernization by the government was prevented by the fact that servicing foreign debts took 30 per cent of the budget and military expenditures over 40 per cent, while the provinces were able to prevent the central authorities recovering control of the land tax.

Jiang's regime was military-bureaucratic. It was not (as another myth has it) the representative of the big commercial and industrial interests. It treated these interests as a source of revenue, even using kidnapping to exert the required pressure. Though it protected the general welfare of the rural ruling class, it was also in conflict with it over revenues and the control of police and military powers. As is suggested by its nationalization of 70 per cent of China's domestic banking resources in 1934, and the setting up of state bureaus for the production of steel and machinery, the long-term thrust of its policies was towards a form of state capitalism.

In 1931 the Japanese had moved into Manchuria, where they built up industry and new cities with astonishing speed. This was based on a massive inflow of Japanese capital and skilled personnel. If 1944 is compared with 1927, the output of iron ore had quadrupled, steel production had risen from nothing to almost half a million tons a year, coal output had rather less than quadrupled, cement production had decupled and electric power generated had gone up more than 13 times. These crude but eloquent figures show that by the end of World War II, Japanese imperialism had put Manchuria into a different economic class from the hinterland of the rest of Inner China. This transformation took place in what was a broadly planned mixed economy. Key sectors were directly managed by the Japanese authorities, while private undertakings were permitted in other sectors under a system of licenses. Russian economic looting in 1945 later destroyed about half the immediate productive capacity in Manchuria's modern sector, though infrastructure and skills largely survived.

Jiang Jieshi put the forging of internal unity before resistance to the Japanese in Manchuria. In 1937, however, partly because they feared that he was beginning to succeed in this, they invaded the north China plain.

9 The war of resistance and the rise of Communist power

Jiang Jieshi withdrew the central government to Chongqing, "trading space for time" in much the same way as the Russians had resisted Napoleon. The Japanese occupied the main cities and communications routes in the eastern two-thirds of the country. This occupation, and popular insistence on a measure of cooperation against the Japanese by the Nationalists and Communists in a new United Front, took much of the pressure off the beleaguered Communist headquarters in Yan'an. Removal of central government power also left vast areas behind the Japanese lines into which the Communists could infiltrate and take over many of the scattered local military forces of resistance, banditry and community self-defense. They did this with particular effectiveness in the last phase of World War II, as Japan began to weaken in her conflict with the United States; and they showed great skill in deepening their control with a judicious mix of relatively mild political and economic reforms. By 1945 the Red Army had grown from about 40 000 men to about half a million; the Party had grown even faster; and the Communists exercised some sort of jurisdiction (often partial and fragmentary) over a claimed 90

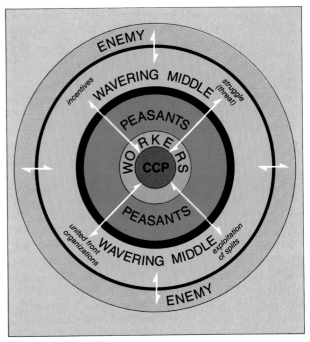

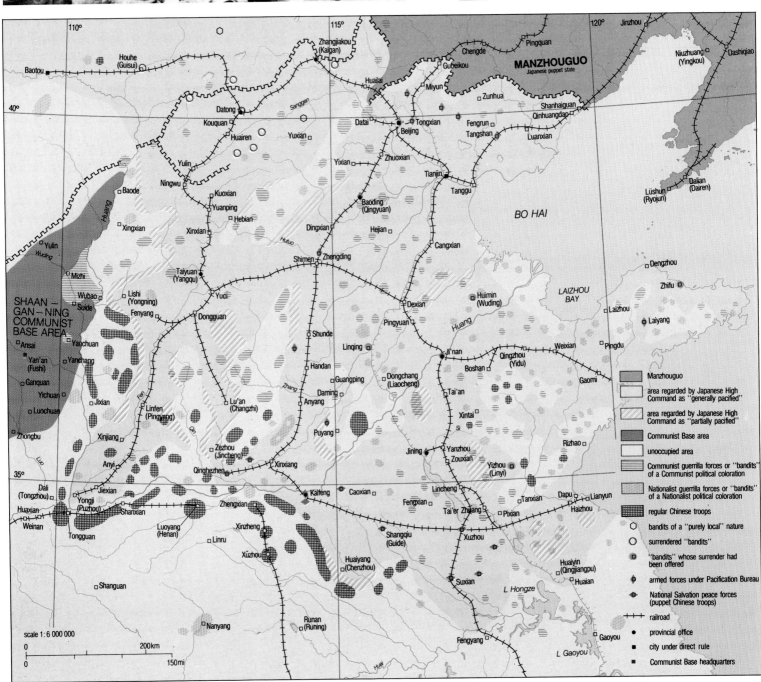

SHAAN–GAN–NING COMMUNIST BASE AREA

MANZHOUGUO
Japanese puppet state

BO HAI

LAIZHOU BAY

L Hongze

L Gaoyou

scale 1:6 000 000

0   200km
0   150mi

	Manzhouguo
	area regarded by Japanese High Command as "generally pacified"
	area regarded by Japanese High Command as "partially pacified"
	Communist Base area
	unoccupied area
	Communist guerrilla forces or "bandits" of a Communist political coloration
	Nationalist guerrilla forces or "bandits" of a Nationalist political coloration
	regular Chinese troops
O	bandits of a "purely local" nature
O	surrendered "bandits"
	"bandits" whose surrender had been offered
	armed forces under Pacification Bureau
	National Salvation peace forces (puppet Chinese troops)
+++	railroad
•	provincial office
■	city under direct rule
■	Communist Base headquarters

million people in 16 separate base areas. When the American atom bomb destroyed Japanese military power, the internal balance of forces had changed in China. The Communists had become serious contenders.

Communist success was not due to mobilizing a peasant nationalism activated by the horrors of occupation. Their best organized bases were in remote areas that were hardly touched at all by the Japanese attack. In regions under more effective Japanese control, guerrilla groups normally did not inflict even the limited damage on the enemy of which they were capable, for fear of savage reprisals against the villagers who sheltered them and the loss of popular support in consequence. Their basic concern was with surviving, and staying strong for the eventual showdown with the Nationalists, far more than with fighting. (It is another myth that Communist Party resistance played a major part in defeating the Japanese.) The crucial factor in the Party's success was its organizational vitality, its greatly improved political technology since the crudities of Hai-Lu-feng days and the dedication of its members that made it into what can only be termed a political religious order.

This transformation can be seen in the Party documents of the late 1930s and early 1940s. Liu Shaoqi declared of the Party member that "he 'bears the sorrow of the world now for the sake of its later happiness' .... He has a stature that 'riches cannot corrupt, poverty cannot change and terror cannot surmount.'" In 1960 the *People's Daily* was to go so far as to say that "a man without the correct political thinking is a man without a soul." The joyous subordination of the individual in the collective redemptive enterprise comes out clearly in Chen Yun's "How to Be a Communist Party Member" of 1939:

> The Communist Party is a party fighting for the complete liberation of mankind. ... A Communist Party member who is willing to dedicate himself to the Communist cause must ... formulate a revolutionary view of life that will lead him to fight relentlessly for the realization of Communism ... and have a firm faith in the inevitable realization of a Communist society in the future.... The interests of the nation, and the people, and the Party are identical. ... The interests of the Party member are identical with those of the nation, the people, and the Party.... Every Party member should sacrifice unhesitatingly his individual interests, and bow to the overall interests of the revolution and the Party ... in every concrete act of daily life.

Although the Party stopped short of demanding the "blind obedience" prescribed for Jesuits, Liu Shaoqi stated that, "in order to uphold their own opinions on principles, comrades definitely cannot stand in opposition to the Party on the organizational level, disobey the majority or superiors, or have freedom of action." In 1960 the *People's Daily* went slightly further, declaring that "to be a docile tool of the Party is a noble quality peculiar to the proletariat." Party members lived in a perpetual climate of the fear of sin, of the "deviation" in thinking, and hence in action, that arose from

personal moral shortcomings and could imperil the success of the collective crusade. Hence there was a constant round of criticism, self-criticism and more forcible correction, interwoven of course with the cynical calculations of factional struggle. The alternating "distress" and "comfort" of which St Ignatius spoke, the ice of despair and the warmth of exaltation, can be found here too. Perhaps the clearest statement of this was made a little later, in 1959: "As far as an individual is concerned, participation in political campaigns, the unfolding of ideological struggles and the review of one's mistakes will bring mental agony." But, "provided he goes through the ideological struggle to enhance his consciousness, he will be able to realize his mistakes, and is bound to acquire another state of mind. He will feel that while the bitter sea had no bounds yesterday, the shore is near at hand today, and there is a bright future for him."

This soul-control was often corrupted into a weapon for the exercise of power. According to Liu Shaoqi, "'Struggle meetings' are frequently held ... arranged beforehand ... to attack certain men, not to struggle primarily against 'things' but against individuals . ... The 'struggle meetings' are essentially courts of justice set up by Party members ... with the object of suppressing those comrades who dare to hold views of their own ... or those comrades who get in the way." At best,

> They intentionally select an 'opponent' (a Party member) as a representative of opportunism, ... sacrificing this single comrade so that cadres and Party members will work zealously. ... They formalistically and unsystematically extract those of his statements and activities that are not quite proper, isolate them, and consider them a complete picture. ... They even fabricate, rely on subjective suspicions and completely unreliable rumors, and recklessly lodge all types of accusation against this comrade. Inevitably he becomes dizzy.... If he says a word in his own defense, they go on to say that he is intentionally defending his error, and that his confession is not complete.... As a means of escaping attack, nothing can equal a full confession.

Thus initiative, creativity and good faith were eaten away and destroyed.

Wang Shiwei, who criticized the material privileges enjoyed by the higher cadres at Yan'an, and tried to uphold a more humanist Marxism, described the psychology of the Communist elect as follows: "[The Communist] makes himself different from the ordinary in every respect. As to the comrades under him, he does not care a bit how they are, whether they are sick or not, dead or alive. ... [Communists] talk nicely – friendly love and what not. But they have no sympathy man to man. They seem to be all smiles when you meet them. But these smiles are skin deep. At the slightest provocation they will blow up, assert themselves and tell you off." He was imprisoned and later shot for making this sort of remark.

The essence of the Party's strategy at this time towards those who were not members is summed up in the diagram devised by Van Slyke to represent the United Front. The Party was seen as the core of a worker/peasant alliance. This alliance was surrounded by a large intermediate group, perhaps half of the population, who were of indeterminate loyalty. Beyond that lay the enemy, never more than 5 per cent or 10 per cent of the total. Party policies at any particular time were adjusted in such a way that, as far as was possible, the pattern of political sympathies matched that in the diagram. It was vital never to take on too large an enemy.

The construction of policy required the use of the so-called "mass line." This was explained in the 1943 resolutions of the Party on "Methods of Leadership":

> The ideas of the masses [that is to say, those who are not members of the Party], which are scattered and unsystematized, are concentrated through the process of research and transformed into concentrated and systematized ideas, after which they are propagandized to the masses and explained, and transformed into the masses' ideas, so that the masses grasp them firmly and manifest them in their actions; and we can discover them in actions of the masses whether or not these ideas are correct.

This was not leadership on the basis of a continual public opinion poll, but a way of finding and consolidating a temporary community of interests between the Party and a majority in order to further the growth of Party power.

To work a strategy of this sort required secrecy at the center and the deception of the majority of temporary allies as to the Party's true long-term aims. Non-Party front organizations had to be created or supported to mobilize the widest possible popular support against the enemy 5 per cent, in accordance with the Party's line of the moment. These bodies had to be infiltrated and controlled by undercover Party members.

A further objective was "winning over representative political and economic figures from all strata in each locality." To this end, elaborate dossiers were built up on targeted individuals, and undercover Party members were told:

> Plans must be made for the regular seeking out of subjects with whom to build friendships. . . . We must use all possible social connections (relatives and family, fellow-townsmen, classmates, colleagues, etc.) and customs (such as sending presents, celebrating festivals, sharing adversities, mutual aid, etc.), not only to form political friendships with the subjects, but also to become personal friends with them, so that they will become completely frank and open with us.

Thus emotive and affective life was drained of any reality that was not political. Intelligence documents from Nationalist archives sometimes reflect a grudging admiration for the skill of Communist duplicity. One description of the infiltration of part of the army of the Shanxi warlord Yan Xishan describes how "at first they were full of sweet words, flattery and obsequious distortions." They worked so hard and with such apparent loyalty that

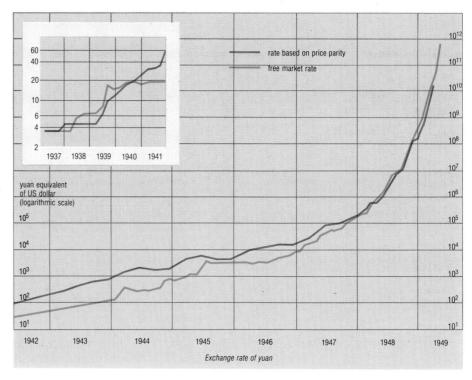

Exchange rate of yuan

Above: The Chinese hyperinflation
The diagram shows the exchange rate of the Chinese dollar from 1942 to 1949 relative to the United States dollar. The hyperinflation of these years has made it necessary to use a logarithmic scale running from 10 to 1000 (American) billion.

(The pages of more than 160 million copies of the present Atlas would be needed to carry a scale measured in equal half-inch steps per dollar.)

Below After "Liberation" the government faced the problems of redistributing land and restoring the war-wrecked economy. In spite of the killing that accompanied the campaigns against landlords and counter-revolutionaries, and the violence of campaigns against many businessmen, bureaucrats and scholars, the years immediately following the Communist victory in 1949 were relatively happy ones for the majority of people.

Above The control of hyperinflation was another problem facing the Communist government in 1949. This photograph shows a "gold rush" in Shanghai in 1948/49. As people pushed to change their paper money into gold many were trampled to death in the crowd.

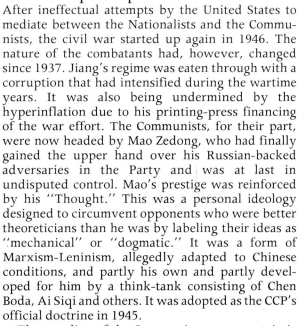

"any lord would have been delighted to have had such slaves." But once they had established themselves "they turned at once and bit, acting with no hesitation." The report concludes with the observation: "The more respectful and obedient they are in the beginning, the more terrible they will be later on."

10   The People's Republic

After ineffectual attempts by the United States to mediate between the Nationalists and the Communists, the civil war started up again in 1946. The nature of the combatants had, however, changed since 1937. Jiang's regime was eaten through with a corruption that had intensified during the wartime years. It was also being undermined by the hyperinflation due to his printing-press financing of the war effort. The Communists, for their part, were now headed by Mao Zedong, who had finally gained the upper hand over his Russian-backed adversaries in the Party and was at last in undisputed control. Mao's prestige was reinforced by his "Thought." This was a personal ideology designed to circumvent opponents who were better theoreticians than he was by labeling their ideas as "mechanical" or "dogmatic." It was a form of Marxism-Leninism, allegedly adapted to Chinese conditions, and partly his own and partly developed for him by a think-tank consisting of Chen Boda, Ai Siqi and others. It was adopted as the CCP's official doctrine in 1945.

The standing of the Communists among patriotic intellectuals and other makers of opinion, was also rising. Even Zhang Dongsun, modern China's most perceptive philosopher and a socialist and democrat who was well aware both of Russian Communist atrocities and of the uncompromising insistence of the CCP on its own brand of Marxism, had come to feel that the Communists were China's only practical way out. He merely hoped that, once in power, they would be more tolerant and moderate. The mood of the country was swinging away from the Nationalists.

In spite of this swing, Jiang Jieshi only lost with

the speed that he did because of straightforward military errors. Starting with about three times as many troops as the Communists, he uselessly sacrificed his best forces by sending them first (in defiance of much expert advice) to attempt the reconquest of Manchuria. Here their overextended and vulnerable supply-lines proved a fatal weakness. In general, the Nationalist strategy was one of the static defense of fixed points, which did not take into account that they could be picked off one by one. They also failed, with few exceptions, to use their well-trained airforce against concentrations of enemy troops on the ground. Jiang tried to retain commanders of proven political loyalty rather than promote those with a military capacity. Even so, there were defections by his leading officers at critical moments. A huge and decisive battle, masterminded by Zhu De, the Communist commander-in-chief, was fought around Xuzhou at the end of 1948 and during the first days of 1949. It was lost by the Nationalists because their superior equipment was quite inadequate to compensate for their poor strategy, poor coordination, poor supplies and collapsing morale. No real effort was then made to hold the line of the Yangzi, and not long afterwards Jiang fled to the island of Taiwan. Guangzhou was taken by the Communists in October. The average speed of the last part of their advance through south China was 10 kilometers a day, a feat possibly without parallel in military history. But it was a conquest by force of arms, not a revolution.

The rulers of the People's Republic established in October 1949 set out to destroy every existing social institution, with the partial exception of the nuclear family. Their intention was to eliminate every source of power, prestige, influence, information and creativity that was not under Communist Party control. To this end they ran a series of mass campaigns, carefully orchestrated movements involving propaganda, political drama in the form of meetings of accusation and struggle, selective terror, torture and executions, touching every sector of society. "Land Reform" broke residual landlord power and involved the peasants in a shared blood-guilt. An average of perhaps two people were killed in every village in the country. The drive against "counterrevolutionaries" eliminated those who had been in some way connected with the Nationalists. The "Three and Five Antis" tamed civil servants and well-to-do businessmen. "Thought Reform" humiliated and "remolded" prominent intellectuals. Persuasion was backed by a public security apparatus several million strong, created by Luo Ruiqing, and a network of forced labor camps peopled in effective permanence by a new stratum of slaves.

What emerged was fundamentally a two-class society: members of the apparatus (known as "cadres" or *ganbu*) and the masses. (Both classes of course had numerous subdivisions.) Great efforts were made to keep the conflict between the two classes concealed. Propaganda asserted that their interests were identical; a public appearance of austerity and frugality was cultivated by the new powerholders as the politically indispensable homage paid by vice to virtue; public opinion was confused and distracted by the fury of concocted battles against largely manufactured enemies —

"reactionaries," "rightists," "capitalist-roaders" and the like. Human, intellectual and artistic isolation from the contamination of the non-Communist world, screened with a facade of internationalism and the puppet-play of sympathetic visiting delegations, was another essential component in the stunting of independent imagination and independent action.

The feasibility of the entire operation remains incomprehensible if we forget the volcanic emotional force of Chinese Communism at this time, and the deep reserves of patriotic commitment and public goodwill on which the fires of political action could feed. The rhetoric of selfless service to the common good touched feelings that were honorable and admirable. It seemed to give to the squalor and chaos of life a new direction and meaning, free of the pettiness and exploitation of the old order. The enhanced international power and reputation of China after a century of humiliations were also – simply – intoxicating. As in many revolutions, exaltation and crime went hand in hand, the first making the second tolerable, even in some subterranean sense desirable, as a proof of commitment and authenticity.

It only sank in slowly – especially through the economic disasters in the years that followed the Great Leap Forward of 1958, and through the vicious internal faction-fighting of the Great Proletarian Cultural Revolution of the later 1960s – that the rhetoric was a betrayal. To some extent, too, the lesson had to be relearned by each generation as it passed through the deintoxification effects of experience: the true purpose of the ideals held before it was to serve as the tools of those in power, and fervor was no substitute for understanding in the pursuit of growth or a better society. Today the emotional drive has weakened almost to the point of disappearance, and what is left is a system too strong to be broken, too rigid to develop rapidly and adaptable only to the extent that survival requires a certain adequacy of performance.

It is possible today to see clearly the central contradiction in Chinese Communism: that between social vitality and political control. It is not possible, over the long run, to maintain a tight political hold over people's personal lives, their economic activities, their overtly expressed thinking and their creative activities and, at the same time, produce open and honest individuals, enterprising entrepreneurs or radically inventive scientists, scholars and artists. Without social vitality, progress and modernization remain at best unnatural growths, forced along by inputs of political will and dependent on imitating what has been done elsewhere. When those at the top in China have become aware of the problem, they have reacted in one of two ways. Sometimes they have tried to produce spontaneity and creativity to order, so giving rise to a frenzy of activity that is only a simulacrum of the real thing. (The "Million Poem Movement" is a small but eloquent example.) Or else they have attempted a partial relaxation, and found – as from the "Hundred Flowers" period of 1956–57 onwards – that they cannot go very far. Each resurgence of social or cultural vitality, once it begins to gather strength, is inevitably hostile to the interlinked orthodoxy of institutions and ideas. It has, therefore, to be repressed again. "Isn't it too

much," pleaded the journalist Zhu Anping in 1957, "that within the scope of the nation there must be a Party man as leader in every unit, big or small, section or sub-section; and that nothing, big or small, can be done without a nod from the Party man?" "It must be understood," came the answer next year, "that all policies of the Party can be carried out only through the organization of the Party." As Mao had said, "It is the Party that exercises its direction in everything."

This is another of the tragedies of the Chinese revolution. Creativity was coming alive once more between the 1890s and the 1940s. On the mainland, the Communist government almost totally sterilized this renaissance after 1949. But, were any relaxation today to go more than a little way, it is quite likely that the country would fall apart in new disorders, a bitter paradox for a nation so richly endowed with talent as the Chinese.

The Party and the people

In broad outline, the Chinese Communist system works through two parallel hierarchies, which control not only government in the narrow sense but most of the economy as well. These are (1) the administrative hierarchy, and (2) the Communist Party hierarchy. The second exercises a general supervision over the first, in which Party members occupy the majority of important positions. A similar dualism is also found in the People's Liberation Army in the double command structure of regular military officers and political work officers (or "commissars").

The polity is not democratic, though decorated with both state and party congresses, since delegates are not chosen through contested elections. Participation in politics is, however, a duty for citizens. It involves a continual round of study sessions, guided meetings and discussions (where at times loyalty must be proved by attacking others) and demonstrations and parades. Order is maintained by a system of discipline and arbitration, similar to that used in a Western school or army. There is no law in the European or American sense, no concepts of rights and of clearly defined rules above political expediency and to which all are subject without exception.

The economy is not "planned" like that of the Soviet Union, where there is a precise pre-arranged quantitative control of inputs and outputs for every sector. The Chinese do not have the statistical service for this, nor a sufficient number of skilled personnel. Neither do they have an equivalent of the Soviet Union's agency for directing the supply of materials (Gossnab). Enterprises, which are under political control, work on the basis of politically negotiated plans for output and investment. Performance is evaluated in terms of profits (which are partly determined by state-set prices for many items), and by other criteria which have varied from time to time. Economic activities are monitored by the People's Bank, through which all funds are meant to move. Procuring supplies and making sales remain the major area of what amount to being market relationships between enterprises.

Political direction of the economy has led to cellularization. Wherever possible, economic relations have been kept within provincial, or even smaller, boundaries. There has been some loss of

Top Students brandish posters of Chairman Mao and his *Little Red Book* of sayings during the "Great Proletarian Cultural Revolution" of 1966–76. During this period schools often ceased to function properly, and atrocities were committed by the Red Guards until they were brought under control by the army. Today the Cultural Revolution is a convenient excuse for anything that has gone wrong in China.

Right The crushing of the "Gang of Four." Mao's wife (Jiang Qing) and her three radical associates Wang Hongwen, Zhang Chunqiao and Yao Wenyuan were toppled from power in 1976. The power of this image suggests the working of divine resolution. Popular reaction was more mundane. On the day of their arrest every wine shop in Beijing was, allegedly, sold out of alcohol.

Above Large propaganda posters were painted on walls throughout the country advertising Mao's works. Since Mao's death in 1976 political posters have been replaced by advertisements for tape recorders and hair sprays.

and prevents a drift to the cities (where under-employment and even unemployment have long been problems). On the other hand, collective farming undermines enthusiasm for work and removes small-scale initiative. It also wastes scarce skilled manpower in administration and complex book-keeping. The limited revival of family farming in the last few years has brought gains, though it is doubtful if there is enough "slack" for the improvements to continue for more than a few years.

The general economic philosophy of the Chinese Communists has been to stress willpower and effort rather than efficiency, and the extensive mobiliz-ation of resources rather than the best use of resources. This reflects the CCP's early experience in backward base areas, like Yan'an, where technology was simple. Mobilization is also the Party's speciality, what it is good at. After a short and not very satisfactory attempt to copy the Soviet model in the middle 1950s, this approach came to a climax in Mao's Great Leap Forward of 1958. It was believed that the economy could be abruptly lifted to an altogether different level by a burst of all-out effort, in which surplus labor on its own, unbacked by capital or by prior skills, could create new productive capacity just by trying. The failure of the Leap showed the inadequacy of the Maoist conception of economics, and led to a political crisis in 1959 in which the Party chairman only just survived, and after which his power was sharply reduced.

About the same time a quarrel had developed with Russia. The dispute began with Krushchev's efforts to use the bait of access to military nuclear technology to gain the sort of control over China's defense system that he already had over those of the Warsaw Pact powers. China's insistence on her independence of action led to the withdrawal of the Russian technicians who had been helping to develop modern industry in China, a blow severely felt at the time. Ever since, China has been wary of close relations with the Soviet Union, fearing Russian capacity to interfere with her internal affairs.

The 1959 crisis created or exacerbated the factional tensions and policy differences that in due course led to the Cultural Revolution in 1966 as Mao made his comeback. The chairman had used his last remaining power-base – the political work officer system in the army – to build up a semi-magical cult of his own personality. Now he extended this, appealing particularly to the frustrated idealism and ambitions of teenagers. He created in the Red Guards a Communist counterpart to the young Boxers, and they tore apart the Party bureaucracy headed by his opponents State President Liu Shaoqi and Party Secretary Deng Xiaoping. Claiming to be rooting out the evils of the old society and scotching the re-emergence of a bourgeoisie, the youngsters also attacked intellectuals, who were humiliated, tortured and sent off to labor in the countryside. They assaulted universities (which had to close for a time) and scientific institutes (where they did enormous damage, as by destroying the plants used by botanists to breed new varieties of agricultural crops). The publishing of new books and the life of the mind virtually stopped. People were sometimes killed merely for having links with overseas Chinese

wealth through the drastic restriction of the great web of interdependent markets that covered late traditional and early modern China. The labor force, in marked contrast to pre-Communist times, is almost immobile. Young adults are assigned to work-units and often stay there for the rest of their lives. The unit (*danwei*) becomes one of the major forces shaping personal lives, helping with prob-lems such as finding housing and deciding in which year a woman may have her baby.

Agriculture has gone through many changes in its organization. During the early 1950s the Land Reform removed the element of tenancy from the family-farm system. In the middle of the decade, small-scale collectivization was introduced, and in 1958, with the communes, extended to much larger units of some tens of thousands of persons. In the early 1960s, in the face of severe food shortage and some regional famines (notably in Anhui), the scale of day-to-day management was reduced again and more scope allowed for private plots. At the very end of the 1970s, family-farm operation was partially reintroduced under the so-called "re-sponsibility system," a complex of differing arrangements, but which might be described as renting from the collective as a landlord.

These shifts have been responses to a number of partly conflicting policy goals. Collectivization provides a means of controlling the peasants, and making sure of the flow of taxes on which the state financial system rests. Cadres decide who does what task, worth how many work-points; and at times points have even been awarded for progressive political attitudes. The collective likewise offers a framework for investments of the type that cannot easily be split up between individual farmers, such as water-control installations and large machinery. Off-season surplus labor can also be easily mobil-ized through a commune or its subordinate brigades. The collective binds farmers to the soil or foreigners. Large numbers of old temples and monuments were smashed or vandalized. In the end the disorder was so bad that the army was called in to repress the Red Guards and other factions, which they did, sometimes with considerable bloodshed. Officers (who were also of course Party members) continued thereafter to run much of the non-military administration, usually as the dominant members of the revolutionary committees set up at provincial and lower levels.

The next eight years of faction-fighting at the top saw the death of many old comrades (such as General He Long) in conditions of great cruelty. The first to dominate the scene was the minister of defense, Lin Biao, designated by Mao as his successor. He died under mysterious circumstances in 1969, allegedly after the failure of a coup d'etat. After Lin's fall, Mao's third wife, Jiang Qing, a gifted propagandist who preached the all-conquering power of revolutionary moral fervor, was pitted against the more pragmatic prime minister, Zhou Enlai. Zhou died in 1975, and the leadership of the moderates was taken over by Deng Xiaoping. Mao's own death the next year broke his wife's hold on power, and, after an interlude in which Hua Guofeng (a little-known figure from the public security apparatus) was chairman, Deng re-emerged as the dominant political force in Beijing.

Although Deng's policies of moderation, modernization and pragmatism have brought a welcome stability back to China, there is evidence that the excesses of the last decade and a half have morally bankrupted the regime. There is extensive corruption in Party and government, and much popular cynicism and disillusionment. As the *People's Daily* itself observed: "The hearts of the youth are cold."

Taiwan, under the Nationalists, has been a different story. Beginning as a relatively repressive regime, concerned to maintain the grip of the 1949 migrants from the mainland over the Taiwanese, the government of Jiang Jieshi and his son and successor Jiang Jingguo has moved steadily in the direction of allowing considerable personal freedom and a substantial, though still incomplete, measure of democracy. Unfettered by local political obligations, they carried out a successful land reform, and set in motion a process of modern economic growth even faster than Japan's. The per-person income today in Taiwan is five times that in the People's Republic. This economic take-off was helped by a limited quantity of American civil aid (about US $100 per person), small size and close links with the international market. But aid ceased in the middle 1960s, and progress since then has been even more remarkable. Equally surprisingly, the distribution of income has grown more equal during the process of modernization. It has often, and rightly, been said that had the Nationalists governed China as they have governed Taiwan, they would never have had to leave the mainland.

No one can visit Taiwan, a country that is thoroughly modern and thoroughly Chinese, and take an honest pleasure in the sight of people well fed and prosperous, who have to endure some (relatively modest) intellectual and political restrictions, but who are personally free to leave if they so wish, without wondering in what sense the entire terrifying drama of the Chinese revolution can be said ever to have been necessary.

Above The gap between urban and rural life has been widening since the beginning of modern times. The lure of the city persists today, with its greater possibilities for education, entertainment, employment and welfare services. This photograph of the old city in Shanghai has much of the feeling of the past.

Right During the "Great Proletarian Cultural Revolution" (1966–76) all women either had their hair trimmed so that it did not fall much lower than the ear lobe, or, if long, tied back and plaited. Long hair worn loose was considered "bourgeois" and "reactionary." Today a looser style prevails and shoulder-length hair is permitted. This photograph shows the naturally straight hair of a Chinese girl being painstakingly permed.

Right Before the 20th century formal education for women was not sanctioned by Chinese society, and advanced literacy which meant knowledge of the Confucian scriptures was mastered only by a small number of males who studied for the civil service examinations. In the 1920s and 1930s mass education movements were launched by the YMCA and others, and after 1949 the Communist movement aimed to make basic education available to all. Political conditioning started in the kindergarten and it was taken to excess during the educational chaos of the "Cultural Revolution" when for some years many schools were closed. Since 1976 schoolchildren have had a more subject-oriented curriculum.

Above Since ''Liberation'' the Chinese state has encouraged strictly disciplined mass exercises. Modern gymnastics have little in common with traditional *taijiquan* (shadow boxing) which involves the correct flow and distribution of *qi* (energy).

Left Chairman Mao said: ''Women hold up half the sky,'' but their position in Chinese society today is far from being equal to men's. Women face the additional load of the major responsibility for running the household and, in the countryside, receiving unequal pay for farmwork. This girl is punting on the Gui River.

ART OF THE MODERN AGE

Below To avoid the heat of summer the Qing court would leave the Imperial Palace and stay in the Summer Palace northwest of Beijing by the Kunming Lake, landscaped to resemble the West Lake at Hangzhou. This print shows the layout of the Summer Palace with the western hills in the background.

Bottom The view across the Kunming Lake to the Hill of Longevity and the Pavilion of Buddha's Fragrant Incense, a four-storied tower which dominates the lake. Since the

The Qing court of the 19th century provided little patronage and there was a general tendency towards repetition and elaboration in the arts. At the end of the 19th century there was a brief revival of the arts under the influence of Empress-Dowager Cixi, who rebuilt the present Summer Palace, which became her residence. The buildings and their decoration are representative of the ornate style of late Qing architecture. They were built with funds appropriated by the empress-dowager which had been allocated for the modernization of the navy. The beams supporting the roof of the covered way along the lake side that leads to the Marble Barge are decorated with legendary scenes and landscapes. These were whitewashed over during the Cultural Revolution (1966–76) and those too damaged to be restored have been replaced by landscapes in a stiff academic style.

From the late Qing period onwards a synthesis of Chinese- and Western-style buildings arose in the major industrial ports and cities. The Capital Hospital in Peking combines a green-tiled roof in the Chinese style with a Western-style brick facade. This hybrid style combining Western and Chinese architecture elements touched little outside the major industrial cities of the newly founded republic.

The decorative arts of the late 19th and early 20th centuries were based on the ornate style of the Qianlong era in the late 18th century, although they lack the finesse of the earlier works. Much of the decorative porcelain, jade and lacquerware which can be seen in Europe belongs to this period. Porcelain, painted for the export market at the turn of the century, combines meticulously copied Western drawings with decorative borders in the traditional Chinese style; this was very popular in Europe at the time. Polychrome overglazed porcelain was decorated in bright colors and heavily outlined in black. Lacquer screens and black-lacquered cabinets decorated in gold displayed a synthesis of native and alien styles and were exported worldwide. Painting on glass was introduced into China from Europe and the backs of mirrors were painted with decorative genre scenes. The decorative arts of the late Qing court and those for export displayed marked Western influence, whereas folk art and handicraft which catered for popular taste in China remained essentially traditional.

Art of the 20th century falls into two periods: before 1949 and after 1949. In the 1920s and 1930s painting displayed a conflict between new alien styles and entrenched traditional ones. Art schools opened in Shanghai, Beijing, Nanjing and Hangzhou, where students carried out experiments in oil painting and life drawing. Apart from stylized portraits, the tradition had not taught artists to draw figures from life; students learned to draw from casts, and drawing from nude models caused a public scandal in Shanghai in the 1920s. Chinese

lake of the Summer Palace is man-made it is very shallow and freezes easily, making it an excellent skating rink in winter. It is now a public park and summer days can be spent boating on the lake.

Below A covered walk-way leads around the lake to a marble barge. There is a popular belief that by the time a courting couple reach the barge they will be engaged. The empress-dowager Cixi rebuilt the Summer Palace in 1888 with funds intended for modernizing the navy.

Bottom The view from the Pavilion of Buddha's Fragrant Incense onto the golden-tiled roofs of the hall below.

People's Republic, drawn from Soviet blueprints. The honeymoon with Russia was soon over. The Great Hall of the People, completed in 11 months in 1959 and situated on the west side of Tiananmen Square, is in an international style which shows no obvious national characteristics apart from its massive scale. Multistoried buildings in the so-called modern international style started to spring up in Beijing from this time onwards. Until recently Beijing was a sprawling city of single-storied buildings with gray-tiled roofs, crisscrossed by narrow lanes with high walls concealing inner courtyards.

With the revolution of 1949 political criteria became the most important factor in art. Works of art in the National Historical Museum were interpreted as showing "the skill of the laboring masses" and the "greed of the feudal oppressors." Art bowed to politics and crude realism was the order of the day. This can be seen in the sculpture of the *Rent Collection Courtyard* which consisted of life-sized clay figures enacting scenes in a former landlord's mansion. Landlords were portrayed as degenerates with sly expressions, while peasants strained every muscle in their struggle to assert themselves and veins of fury are shown in their taut faces. Giant block-like figures of Chairman Mao were dotted around the country.

There was a ban on abstract expressionism, and revolutionary romanticism reigned. Painting in both traditional and oil mediums depicted life on people's communes, smiling factory workers and steel plants; very few paintings showed landscape without pylons and electricity wires. Political study was rigorous in schools. Artists were told what they could and could not paint, and art was limited and conformist. The country plunged into the Great Leap Forward (1958–59), which was followed by an attack on "rightists" from 1963 to 1965, during which period many artists suffered, and paintings of peasants, soldiers and workers were promoted. The Cultural Revolution began in 1966 and the arts plummeted, powerless against the onslaught of violence and destruction. Art schools were closed and artists disbanded. Many were imprisoned and others were sent to the countryside to work on farms, and painted only in their spare time if at all. Publication of art journals was suspended from 1966 for the following six years. Cultural oppression continued until the fall of the Gang of Four in 1976 marked the end of the Cultural Revolution.

The decorative arts flourished particularly after the Cultural Revolution with the increase of foreign trade, and a growing tourist industry which resulted in a vigorous revival of jade and ivory carving, basket weaving and textile manufacture. New dyes had been introduced at the turn of the century and synthetic materials began to replace cotton for everyday use. The level of craftsmanship remained extremely high but in general technique, aided by mechanization, triumphed over art. Traditional subjects were rendered permissible by infusing them with revolutionary symbolism and in this way popular themes and even legendary figures could toe the Party line.

The nude, forbidden in 1965, one year before the Cultural Revolution, was again studied in art schools in 1978; it was considered the "scientific" base of the human body and thus an aid to realism.

students studied in Europe and Japan but Western-style paintings found little response in China apart from the small cosmopolitan set of artists and writers in Shanghai. Xu Beihong (1864–1955) returned from Europe wearing a floppy hat and bow tie, and experimented in a semi-Western style. Qi Baishi (1863–1957) remained in China and painted in a highly individual traditional manner, whereas Fu Baoshi (1904–65), having studied in Japan, drew from a wide range of traditional styles. In general the emphasis moved from landscape to figure painting.

In the 1920s the writer Lu Xun launched a woodcut movement which drew heavily on German prints, in particular on the works of Käthe Kollwitz, who showed the stark poverty of postwar Germany. The woodcuts of Li Hua (born 1907) depicted the fury of the Chinese peasants against the Japanese invaders in 1937, but as China sank into the chaos and confusion of the 1940s there was little energy left for the arts.

After 1949 the arts were centrally controlled by the state, and were profoundly affected as they were subjugated to politics. The art of woodblock cutting and printing flourished since it could be most easily used as a tool for political propaganda. After "Liberation" many artists were sent to the Soviet Union to study, and Soviet-style socialist realism exerted a considerable influence on the arts of the 1950s. Soviet influence was also apparent in the construction of buildings, and unimaginative institutional blocks appeared throughout the

Contemporary Painting

One of the main preoccupations of Chinese artists today is working out how to adapt and absorb foreign influences within their own traditions. The works illustrated here cannot cover the many different styles and experiments in technique current in China today, but they reflect the state of flux there has been since the Cultural Revolution.

The artists whose works are shown here have been influenced by both international trends and by Chinese traditional painting. The works of Fang Zhaoling have been exhibited recently in both Beijing and London. Although she herself has lived outside China since 1947 her works show a strong traditional influence, yet are entirely modern. Yuan Yunsheng's creative paintings are a synthesis of both Chinese and Western traditions and pave the way for future developments. Chen Dehong trained as a sculptor and is now concentrating on painting. The inspiration for his works is deeply rooted in the traditional past but his experiments with form and structure show the influence of Western art, whereas Wang Jia'nan's painting displays the creative reworking of the Chinese tradition. Tang Muli taught himself oil painting during the Cultural Revolution when art education ceased. He is an extremely versatile artist who works in a wide range of styles. The variety of subject matter, styles and techniques are typical of the experimental state of art in China today.

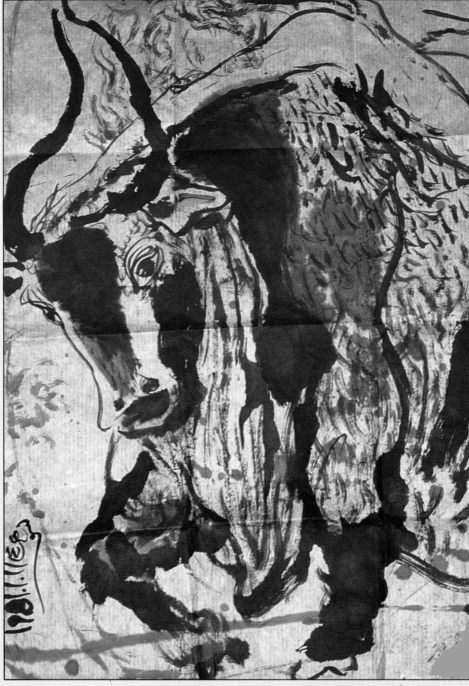

Left This detail of a large mural painting by Yuan Yunsheng (1937–) entitled *Water Splashing Festival, Song of Life* in the ''foreigners'' canteen at Beijing international airport caused considerable controversy since it depicted nudes in a public building.

Above This buffalo by Yuan Yunsheng is depicted in ink on paper. This spirited painting perfectly captures the character of the animal. Although Yuan uses traditional techniques his style breaks away from traditional depiction of the subject.

Right The strength and power of the brushstroke is seen in this painting entitled *Drift* by Yuan Yunsheng. His work may be considered avant-garde for its attempt to break free from the bonds of realism.

Above Here Chen Dehong takes traditional Chinese painting in a new direction in his depiction of two Chinese characters, *song* ("pine") and *yun* ("cloud"). He extends their calligraphic shapes with landscape elements to create an abstract composition.

Left The words of the Tang dynasty poet Li Bo, "Water from the Yellow River comes from the sky" are here brought to life by Chen Dehong. It combines innovation with tradition in an exciting new way.

Below This painting, *Beauty on the Perilous Peaks*, is by Fang Zhaoling (1914–) who left China in 1947. She can be seen as a pioneer of the 20th-century modern movement in Chinese art.

Left An illustration for the *Cradle Song* by William Blake by Tang Muli (1947–), one of the first artists to be sent by the Chinese government to study abroad (at the Royal College of Art in London). His work shows a blending of Eastern and Western techniques with a lyrical quality that is unmistakably Chinese.

Right This lively mythological scene of a warrior and his wife casting swords by Wang Jia'nan (1956–) is distinctly Chinese in character and illustrates the traditional *gongbi* ("skilled brush") technique of line and color. A strong influence of ancient Buddhist wall paintings permeates the entire composition.

Abstraction was not encouraged in art schools, and figure drawing and painting ranged from intense realism to a slight distortion that stopped a long way from abstraction. Art students were preoccupied by discussions on Chinese traditional art combined with Western art, Western abstraction in art and the nude. Marxist aesthetics, Mao's literature on art, socialist realism and the Huxian peasant paintings were not discussed. There was a hunger for ''modern'' art and an ignorance of it, as China had remained culturally isolated from the outside world since 1949, apart from a brief interlude of contact with the Soviet Union in the 1950s. Teachers who had studied in Russia produced their copies of French Impressionists for their students to copy secondhand.

At the art college in Beijing, oil painting, figure painting, traditional landscape and flower-and-bird painting, sculpture, mural painting and graphic art were taught in separate departments. Classes were well disciplined and the students were told what to paint, which resulted in a uniform style. Within working hours students had little chance to paint outside the dictates and limits laid down by their teachers. If they strayed outside what was considered permissible they were criticized. Conformity was the rule. The individual dared not differ, or did so at his peril. However there were exciting experiments carried out within the acceptable limits. Liu Hong, a former research student in the mural painting department, found inspiration in ancient bronze patterns, and experimented with mosaics.

Han Xin, a talented young artist now living in America, also experimented in different media and his oil painting entitled *The Violin* is a masterpiece of precision. Chen Danqing, another young artist from Shanghai painting in oils, spent some time in Tibet in the late 1970s and his paintings of Tibetan people are depicted in a highly realistic manner which shows a penetrating insight and sensitivity. An equally talented graphic artist, Wang Jia'nan from Harbin, combines Western and traditional styles in engraving and woodblock prints. He expresses landscape with fluid lines, attaining a balance between inked and uninked areas.

In contrast to the realistic styles of oil painting, Yuan Yunsheng, one of the most talented artists in China today, tested the limits of artistic freedom by depicting two nudes in his mural painting in Peking's International Airport. A raging controversy followed on whether or not a nude should be depicted on a public building. His composition entitled *Water Splashing Festival, Song of Life* depicted a legend of the Dai nationality of southern Yunnan. The artist's intention was to depict the legend and not the actual annual festival. He was accused of ''distorting the figures'' and causing ''shame to the Dai people'' by including the nudes, and a panel has been fixed across the section of the wall to cover them. Figures are depicted in graceful movement and flowing rhythm. The artist worked with two assistants and covered the wall with canvas. He then made a sketch of the composition and transferred it to the canvas and painted with acrylic colors imported from Hong Kong. Yuan Yunsheng also paints in brush and ink on paper. His work is highly individual, and his semi-abstract drawings with brightly colored felt pens show the stroke of genius.

Since the Cultural Revolution ''foreign'' students were admitted to the art colleges in Beijing and Hangzhou, and artists of the younger generation are now studying abroad. Some Chinese artists of the older generation, such as Wu Zuoren who studied in Paris in the 1930s, have reverted to traditional painting. The scholar-artist Zhang Anzhi also studied abroad before 1949. His landscape paintings of Mount Huang epitomize the spirit of the scholar-artist expressed through brush and ink.

Exhibitions of ''foreign'' art have attracted great attention in the major cities in China since the Cultural Revolution, and exhibitions of Chinese works of art have traveled to the West. A large exhibition of contemporary Chinese paintings was held in Paris in the spring of 1982, illustrating a cross-section of works including many in the revolutionary romantic style, and others in the traditional *gongbi* (skilled brush) style of the Dunhuang murals, executed by Pan Jie'zi. The exhibition also included a work of Zhang Lichen painted in monochrome ink with the fingers, and a fine sculpture by Zhang Dehua of a woman's head emerging from a rough block of wood. In Beijing the talented sculptor Wang Keping's work shows a bold and expressive manner. Exciting experiments are being carried out by small groups of artists and individuals in remote regions throughout the People's Republic. The variety and contrast of styles and techniques reflect an experimental stage following the Cultural Revolution when the arts and artists are cautiously moving into a more tolerant and healthier phase. When asked if art must still serve the people, the minister of culture, Huang Zhen, is said to have commented, ''I think you can produce anything.'' Artists are better off today than at any time since 1949, and in the words of a contemporary Chinese artist, ''everybody has the right to see for themselves.''

Chairman Mao died on 9 September 1976 and his mausoleum was built in the center of Tiananmen Square by a workforce of almost a million volunteers. The architecture has very little that is recognizably Chinese.

PART THREE
SYMBOLS AND SOCIETY

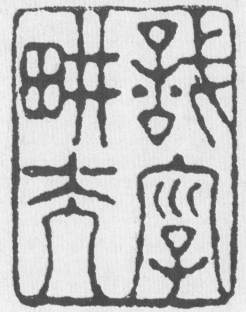

Language, Writing and Calligraphy

Language

The Chinese language is in some ways one of the simplest in the world, but also one of the most elusive. What follows is an attempt to give something of its feeling and flavor. As a description it makes no claim to being either rigorous or complete.

The central peculiarity of Chinese is that the basic units of meaning retain an unaltered form at virtually all times. This has several implications. Most simply, compound words do not fuse as thoroughly as they do in European languages. Thus the Chinese for "heliotropism" is *xiàng-rì-xìng*, or, literally, "towards sun nature." The construction is similar to that of the English word (which, however, uses Greek rather than English roots), but each component bit keeps its own identity. It is apparent, in passing, how easy it is in this way to create new scientific terms in Chinese. However, they keep their basic meanings more in the forefront of the listener's mind than do most of our terms; compare "laser" with the Chinese "stimulate-light-tube."

Because the basic units of meaning have this relatively more independent existence, it is common for the Chinese to split them. Thus *zǒu-lù* means "to walk" (literally "walk-road"), but "to walk three miles" is *zǒu sān-lǐ-de lù* (literally, "walk three miles of road"). As a consequence, words do not have such a clearcut existence in Chinese as they do in English.

The traditional Chinese writing system is based on these unchanging units of meaning. Each graph or "character" normally represents one such unit. This requires a stock of 5000 to 6000 graphs for normal use. In contrast, our alphabet system, which has in principle a distinct graph for each distinctive unit of sound, needs only 26 or thereabouts. The only English "characters" in common use are the numerals 1, 2, 3 etc.

The Chinese writing system is not well suited to a language with inflected forms. Suppose we wanted to write "at sixes and sevens" with such a system. We should have to create modified graphs like "6s" and "7s", which would be clumsy. When the Japanese took over the Chinese script in the 7th and 8th centuries AD, they had to do something much like this, as Japanese is an inflected language. The result was a hybrid, using Chinese graphs for the basic meanings and Japanese syllabic script for the endings.

The oldest forms of Chinese did modify roots to indicate a change in sense. The residues of this can still be seen in pairs of works with related meanings that differ only in tone or in their initial consonant. Examples are *hǎo* ("good") and *hào* ("to think good, to love") and *jiàn* ("to see") and *xiàn* ("to be seen, appear"). But for more than 2000 years now these basic units have not been subjected to such modifications.

Not having inflections, Chinese grammar necessarily depends on words with special functions and on word order. For nouns there are no formally specified numbers (singular, dual or plural), and no specified cases (nominative, vocative, accusative and so on). For verbs there are no formally specified tenses (past, present, or future), no formally specified moods (indicative, subjunctive, imperative, optative), no formally specified voices (active, reflexive, passive), and no aspects (perfective, imperfective) built into the verb itself. For this reason Chinese often appears to the Westerner to have a generality and timelessness that is disconcerting. Context plays a large part in determining specific sense. Most further clarification is done by such devices as stating time (e.g. "yesterday") or number (e.g. "all," "three," "some") or by the addition of auxiliary words like *bèi* ("to suffer"), which shows a passive sense, and *yǐ* or *yǐ-jīng* ("already"), which show a past sense.

Chinese word order has much in common with that of English, but there are traps for the unwary analyst. With only a few exceptions, words cannot be defined out of context as definitely being certain parts of speech, such as "nouns" or "verbs." Most words have a predisposition to function as one or the other, but position determines function. Thus *zǒu* means "go, walk," but it is permissible to say *zǒu hǎo* ("to go is good" or "going is good").

Second, Chinese sentences do not have a subject-predicate structure. They have a topic-comment structure. The first part of the sentence as it were asks, "what about X?"; the second part replies, "Such-and-such." The importance of this distinction can be shown from the sentence "*shū mǎi-le*," literally "book buy-finish." Formally it is the same as *wǒ mǎi-le* ("I buy-finish" or, in proper English, "I bought it"). But the first sentence will usually mean "the book has been bought." We have therefore to interpret it as "[As for the] book, [someone] has bought [it]."

At the level of the phrase, words that qualify other words precede them, as in "a very early spring morning." However at the sentence level, Chinese has a predilection for going from the general to the particular. Sentences often begin with contexts of time and space, and with topical contexts having the underlying sense that "given that such and such is the case, then ...," before the topic and the comment. The comment can be followed by further specifications as to purpose and direction. This, in a certain sense, reverses the phrase-level ordering, and so helps to keep phrases and sentences distinct.

We could parody our conclusions up to this point, at the cost of misusing terminology, by saying that Chinese is a language without words, grammar or subjects. A little more exactly, we could say that it is morpheme-oriented, without inflections and based on a topic-comment structure.

So far we have talked about Chinese as if it were a single language, and implied that its nature was much the same at all times, all places and all contexts of use. For the general features that we have been discussing, this is not far from the truth. Let us conclude, however, with a quick look at some of the changes that have taken place in the last 2500 years.

Early Chinese was much richer both in vowels and in consonants than modern Chinese. Many words that were once distinct in sound have now converged and become identical. This phonetic impoverishment had three main consequences. First, in speech, tones were increasingly used to distinguish words that would otherwise have

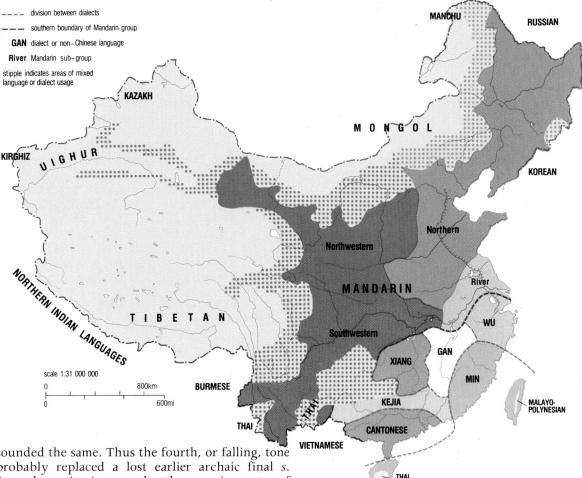

division between dialects

southern boundary of Mandarin group

GAN dialect or non-Chinese language

River Mandarin sub-group

stipple indicates areas of mixed
language or dialect usage

Dialects of Chinese
Chinese is in one sense a single
language since, generally, any
two places speaking two
different dialects of it can be
linked by a chain of adjacent
intermediate places all of which
understand their immediate
neighbors without difficulty.
Looked at very close to,
however, it is a baffling mosaic of
subdialects in which, for
example, the speech of Baoding is
markedly different from that of
Beijing less than a hundred miles
away. Any sharply defined
scheme of division into dialects
thus does less than justice both
to the underlying unity and to
the local diversity. The present
map follows the work of Paul
Kratochvil, a Czech scholar who
studied the problem in China
during the 1950s.

sounded the same. Thus the fourth, or falling, tone
probably replaced a lost earlier archaic final *s*.
Second, again in speech, the requirements of
intelligibility led to the doubling-up of units of
meaning with much the same sense to form new
words (e.g. *kan-jian* = "look-see" = "see").
Modern Chinese cannot sensibly be described as a
"monosyllabic" language, though archaic Chinese
came close to it. Third, the written and the spoken
languages diverged to an extent that has few
parallels elsewhere. Since each of the words in the
list above continued to be written with a distinctive
graph, the older and terser form of the language
remained perfectly clear *when written down*. This
literary style remained the commonest medium for
writing until the 1920s. As a result, for over a
thousand years, administrative documents, history,
philosophy, most poetry and a great deal of prose-
fiction were partly or wholly unintelligible if read
aloud.

Over a very long period of differentiating from a
common source, the dialects of Chinese have grown
into what are almost different languages (see map).
The north China plain, with its constant circulation
of people, is the most nearly homogeneous. The
southeast coast, with its mountain enclaves, is the
most varied. Within each major dialect area there
also developed a high degree of subdialect variation.

Linguistic unity was maintained in the empire
through the traditional written language, which
was understood by all educated people. In the
administration, the higher officials spoke a form of
Beijing dialect called "official speech" by them and
"Mandarin" by Westerners. Since, by law, the
higher officials governed areas of which they were
not natives, this meant that more often than not
they could not easily converse with those over
whom they ruled.

Early in this century a movement started to create
a "national language," based on "official speech."
The aim was that this should be spoken by
everyone, if only as a second language. First under
the Nationalists, and now under the present government, this rather artificial language has become
widespread. The basic motivation for this unification of the spoken language was and remains
political. But there is a further potential advantage:
once everyone's pronunciation is much the same, it
will be possible to replace the old characters with an
alphabetic system, without impairing national intercommunication. The time when this will be
possible is some time off. If ever decided upon, it
would constitute a dramatic cultural rupture with
the past.

There was a second movement that proceeded in
parallel: that to abolish the use of the traditional
literary language and use either a much simplified
version or the new national spoken language for
writing. In the People's Republic, the simplified
literary style is no longer used. In Taiwan and
among overseas Chinese it is still found, most
obviously in government documents and in
newspapers.

The greatest damage done by the two language
movements has been to kill the possibility of a
flourishing imaginative literature written in
regional vernaculars. For most writers the new
language is almost as artificial as the old, and is not
rooted in the texture and flavor of a particular
community and its life. This is sad and ironic,
because several of the pioneers of linguistic reform
knew the regional languages of China well and
cherished them.

Writing

Writing has long been held in especial esteem in China. The term for "civilization" (*wén*) is the same as that for "pattern" or "script." In traditional times paper with writing on it was sacred, and it was improper to put it to any profane use. Old men used to collect scrap paper bearing characters for ritual disposal, usually by burning in special pagodas.

The earliest system of writing in China used pictures to represent objects. This can still be seen in a number of simple graphs, such as those for "mouth," "forest" (two trees) and "dawn" (the sun rising above the horizon).

Since not every word has an obvious pictorial representation, this system was soon extended by phonetic loans. Words that could not easily be drawn were represented by pictographs of words that sounded the same or nearly so. Thus *wàn* ("ten thousand") was written with the graph for *wàn* ("scorpion"). Related words were often written with the same character. Thus *shēng*, a picture of an ox's horns and meaning "a living creature, a sacrificial animal" and hence "life, give birth to," and *xìng* meaning "natural disposition, what one is born with," were once written with the same graph.

Confusion could arise from such substitutions once people were writing long, continuous texts. To avoid this, special graphic elements showing to which general category a word belonged were added. Thus a "cattle" element was added to *shēng* in the sense of a sacrificial animal, and a "heart" element to *xìng* meaning nature. There were just over 200 of these category-markers, which are usually known as "radicals." The vast majority of Chinese characters today are made up of a phonetic element plus a category-marker. Thus *yáng* ("sea") has the phonetic *yáng* ("sheep"), and the category-marker "water" on its lefthand side.

Near the end of the 3rd century BC the Chinese script was drastically altered. Acting on the advice of his prime minister Li Si, the First Emperor of Qin had about half of the old characters abolished, and many of those remaining restructured. One major consequence of this was the distortion of texts of all pre-Qin literature transmitted by copying. Except of course for inscriptions, all such texts we have today are not written in their original form. Substitutions must have been made for abolished characters, and altered graphs must have given rise to errors in copying. It is also striking how often the original pictorial quality was destroyed. An example is the word for "white" (*bái*) which probably originally showed an egg. In the reformed graph it is impossible to see this unless perhaps one already knows the earlier form.

The formal versions of the Chinese characters were structurally stable from the Qin reform until the present century. But cursive and abbreviated shapes were invented for informal use. These destroyed most of the vestiges of pictorial representation, and obscured the structural origins of the graphs. Between the later 1950s and the 1970s the government of the people's Republic made the use of increasing numbers of these abbreviated characters obligatory. Further simplified forms have also been created. In consequence the Chinese writing system has been split into two. In Taiwan and among overseas Chinese generally, the traditional characters are still used. In the People's Republic, the simpler forms are mandatory, and people find the earlier literature not easy to understand unless it has been reprinted with the new characters.

The design and the aesthetic qualities of the characters have been affected by the tools with which they have been scribed, and the materials on which they have been written. The stylus imposes a uniform thickness of line, and requires a relatively low speed of execution, but in return permits subtle curvilinear forms. Strokes are cut in groups according to their orientation on the surface. Mirror-reversal of graphs is quite common, sometimes together with reversal of the usual right-to-left ordering of the vertical columns of characters. By contrast, casting in bronze allows lines of variable thickness. Individual piece-molds for characters, the first form of printing, imposed spatial discipline. For ease of assembly each graph has to fill an identical square space. Narrow wooden strips also oblige a restricted and fairly standard width. The brush requires swift execution without retouching or second thoughts, as ink spreads on absorbent paper if the brush lingers too long. Approximately rectilinear strokes are easiest with a brush, with a slight curvature. Stroke order is from top to bottom, and left to right. There are new aesthetic dimensions in the easily varied width of strokes and the variable density of ink.

Woodblock printing was a somewhat cruder version of brush calligraphy in that the characters would first be drawn on a sheet of thin paper, which was then pasted face down on a block, so that the carver could cut out a mirror-image of the text. Copies were taken by inking the block, covering it with paper, and rubbing the paper with a stiff, dry brush. With the introduction of spectacles for short sight in the 17th century, it also became possible to move to much smaller type.

Cast metal type, typewriters and computer graphics compel further standardization in that each character can be drawn in only one way, which was not the case for woodblock printing.

The development of the character *wàn* (scorpion): from left to right, archaic Shang, oracle Shang and modern.

The development of the character *yáng* (sheep): from left to right, archaic, small seal, modern script, modern written form.

The character *bái* (white): on the left the original egg-like form, on the right the form used after the alteration of script near the end of the 3rd century BC.

Piece-mold characters used for printing in the 6th or 5th century BC.

Calligraphy

Above "By order of the emperor," a character written by the Song dynasty emperor Hui Zong (reigned 1101–35).

Calligraphy has long been regarded as an art in its own right in China. Traditional aesthetic theory has evaluated individual brush strokes according to four qualities, which should be perfectly balanced in faultless writing:

1. **Bone:** Such a feeling of strength in the strokes that it appears impossible to break them, yet without brittleness.
2. **Flesh:** A well-nourished quality in the strokes, without however self-indulgence or fatness.
3. **Muscle:** The appearance of one stroke being joined to the next by invisible ligaments, and also one character to the next.
4. **Blood:** A full texture in the ink, which should resemble neither water nor sludge.

Above all, writing has to feel "alive." The composition of the characters has to give a sensation of balanced movement, as if a dancer had been swaying and gliding, walking and leaping across the page. The ultimate inspiration of Chinese calligraphy, which may be thought of as the world's earliest abstract art, is nature. The form of the strokes has something of the organic quality of leaves, creepers, stems, clouds, rocks, flames, waterdrops and ripples. The standardized regularity of modern typography is the antithesis of this aesthetic.

There have been four broadly defined styles of writing in the last 3000 years:

1. **Seal scripts:** These may be thought of as in

some sense "drawn," curvilinear, and with little variation in line thickness. They range from Oracle Bone writing to the Small Seal style officially adopted by the Qin.

2. **Regular brush scripts**: These may be thought of as composed out of a set repertoire of types of brush stroke, each of which remains distinct. They range from the "official script" first used informally under the Qin and then formally under the Han to the "regular style" that is the basis of today's printed characters.

3. **Running script**: A looser, cursive version of the foregoing, in which the strokes flow into each other.

4. **"Grass" script**: A shorthand scrawl, whose highly abbreviated characters cannot be recognized without special study. It has a loose, swiftly flowing elegance of its own.

Right This cursive style of calligraphy by Wen Zhengming (1470–1559) has been called "the dance of the brush." It is used as a means of artistic expression: the character itself is less important than its expressive quality.

Below The character *yong* meaning "eternity" combines the eight basic strokes used in Chinese calligraphy. Although there are many more than these basic strokes, the excellence of a piece of calligraphy is largely determined by the individual brush strokes. A more refined classification specifies at least 30 to 40.

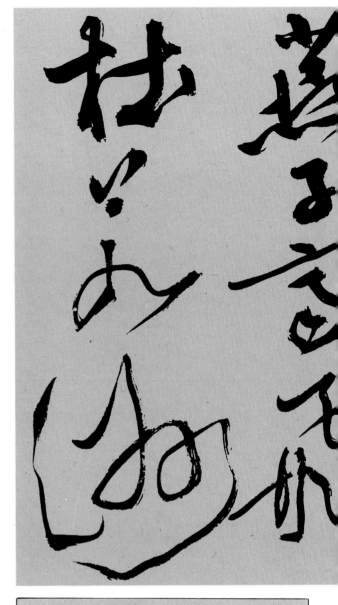

Below left This example of Seal script was used on a Zhou dynasty bronze vessel.

Below center An example of *caoshu* (Grass script). This rubbing is taken from an engraving of the work of Wang Xizhi (4th century AD), one of China's most famous calligraphers, with whom this style is associated. Strokes could be joined together and several characters written with one continuous flow of the brush,

which often makes it difficult to read.

Below right Kaishu (Standard or Regular script) derived from *lishu* (official or clerical script) and was developed in the 1st century AD. The strokes must each be clearly defined and possessed of tensile strength or "bone."

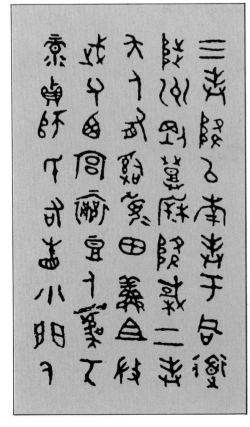

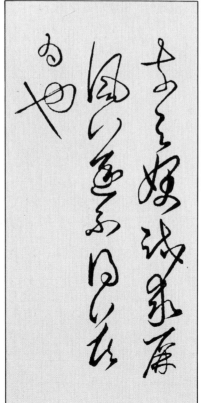

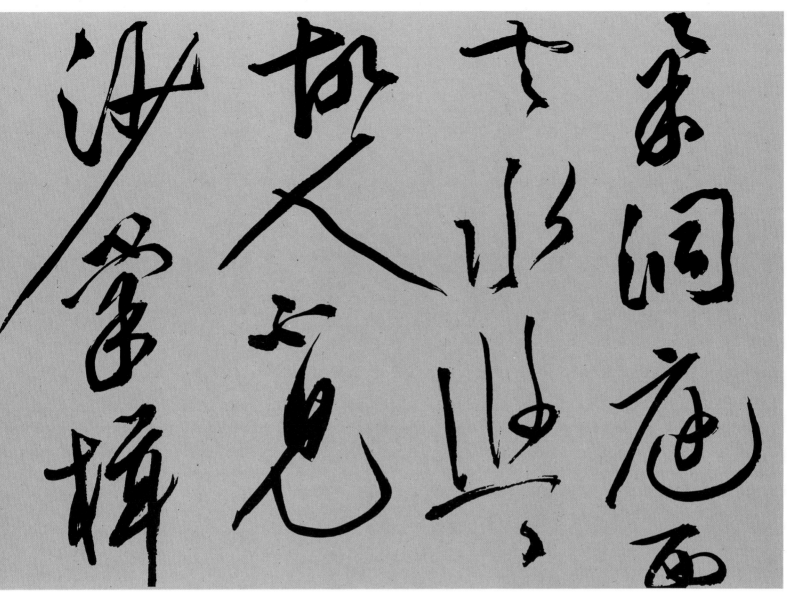

Above Three kinds of archaic graphs: *top* complex single-element graphs whose modern parallels are direct descendants of archaic forms; *center* simple multiple-element graphs lacking modern equivalents; *below* complex multi-element graphs with either modern descendants or equivalents.

The archaic characters on tortoise shells and oracle bones were presumably originally derived from pictographs, but in many cases formalization has already made many of them difficult or impossible to interpret in a pictorial sense.

Right Unlike Arabic calligraphers, the Chinese have rarely combined characters to form images. This Tang dynasty stele in Xi'an Museum, on which running script characters join in the shape of a man, is an unusual and vital creation.

Voices in Poetry

There is a window through which we can still see something of the emotions that stirred people in ancient and medieval China. This is their poetry. With the passing of the centuries, the accumulation of styles from different regions and periods produced an extraordinarily complex poetic tradition, and offered poets a wide range of modes and conventions of expression from which, eventually, they could choose as a matter of more-or-less deliberate taste. Instead of attempting to describe these intricacies, we shall approach the art by suggesting that there were perhaps four main "voices" in which a Chinese poet could speak, and describe each of them briefly, with examples.

The first voice might be termed "bardic" in that the poet speaks for the feelings of society as a whole, whether his theme is collective or individual emotion. This voice is associated with the earliest of the anthologies, the *Scripture of Poetry*, songs composed in the northern states between the 9th and 7th centuries BC. They are rhymed, with a ballad-like terseness, and always controlled and rational in mood. All of them were set to tunes – love songs, laments, satires, encomia, work chanteys, and odes for feasting, worship and hunting – and often performed at the royal and princely courts.

The second voice may be called the "possessional," though only in the loose and suggestive sense that those who speak the lines are felt to be in rapport with the spirit world. This voice is characteristic of the Chu poets who composed the late archaic *Songs of the South*. The lines are long and rhapsodic, the sensual and the religious are closely mingled, and the imagination, inspired by the trance journeys of shamans, sweeps across time and space with a freedom unknown to the northerners. Within this voice we may also, with only apparent paradox, place most self-consciously self-oriented poetry.

The third voice is that of "depersonalized absorption," and is characteristic of poetry describing nature in which the poet remains only as an intangible interpretative presence. During the first half of the first millennium AD this voice developed from the cold magnificence of the panoramic surveys of themes such as the sea found in the prose poems of the Later Han to the delicate expression of the "delighting heart" spoken by Xie Lingyun at the beginning of the 5th century, a sensibility capable of looking beneath manifold phenomena to sense the inner logic or inner structure of the universe.

The last voice, typical of the mature and sophisticated middle empire under the Tang, is harder to sum up in a single phrase. It might be said to be one of "humanism and resonance." The world of men and the world of nature are held in a new balance, but with human concerns ultimately preponderant; and the poet is at a greater psychological distance from his subject matter, subtly and consciously stage-managing structures, references and allusions. The topics thought acceptable for poetry were increased in number, especially by Du Fu, who wrote as easily on the subtle psychology of intimate family scenes or haggling over a few pounds of rice during a natural disaster, as on the more conventional grander matters.

What might be thought of as a fifth voice was that of "everyday life." With its unsentimental compassion for the miseries and duties of life it deserves rescue from the neglect into which it has fallen.

Man of the people, how you kept me laughing,
Hemp-cloth in your arms, come to barter for silk.
But skeins of silk were not what you were after,
You were there with schemes to make me come with you.

And so – I went with you, across the Qi river,
To the Mounds of Dun we went together.
Don't say that it was I put off our day of marriage –
You'd found us no-one to serve as a go-between.
So, when I urged you to put away your anger,
We fixed the date for a day in autumn.

I climbed the crumbling wall.
I watched the toll-barrier for you to come back to me,
I watched the toll-barrier, but could not see you.
My tears fell and fell.

Once I had seen you return to the barrier,
We laughed, then we talked.
You burnt cracks in tortoise-shell, cast stalks of milfoil,
No word of ill-luck.

Before leaves fall from the mulberry tree
They are glossy and green.
Doves, don't eat of the mulberry fruits!
Girls, don't pleasure with gentlemen!
If a man takes his pleasure, he'll still be excused.
If a girl takes hers, she's no excuse.

When the leaves drop off from the mulberry tree,

They lie brown and discolored.
In three years with you,
I have eaten poor food.

Qi's waters swell and flood,
Our carriage hangings are wet.
Nothing I've done has not been straight,
Nothing of yours but bent.
You set no limits to what you did,
– Man of too many inner selves.

Three years a wife!
Effort no effort,
Getting up early, late to bed,
No day for myself.
– It is finished now,
My brothers ignore me
With biting laughter.
I think in silence,
Sad for myself.

I came to you – to grow old with you.
We grew older. You made me resent you.
Qi at least has its shore-line, marshes their edges.
– When my hair was still up, as a girl's is,
How we talked, how we laughed our contentment,
Vowed good faith so intently,
Not thinking it all might be altered,
The change that was not to be thought of,
This change that has happened.

1

"First light, and I am ready, coming from the East,
Shining rays on my threshold, the Tree of Suns.
Gentle with my horses, I drive them forth slowly,
Night-time dissolving, it's already day.

I yoke dragons for my shafts, I ride on the thunders,
Bearing banners of cloud-wrack, shaking and streaming.
I sigh, I sigh deeply, as I start the path upwards.
My heart is reluctant. I look back with longing.
For so sweet are the sounds, and the sights so enchanting,
That who sees is at ease. He forgets to return."

Tune-up the zither-strings! Sound the answering phrases!
Chime the bells together! Set the bell-frames rocking!
Pipe on the cross-flutes! Resound the reed-organ!
Those possessed by the spirits are illumined and lovely,
They fly this way and that, like kingfishers darting,
The flow of their song in accord with their dancing!
How perfect their pitch! How in time is their rhythm!
The God is descending! Shield your eyes from the Sun!

"O my robe of blue clouds, and skirts of white rainbows!
I have shot forth a sunbeam, pierced the Wolf of the Sky.
I take hold of the Bow, and soar through the heavens.
I lift up the North Dipper and pour cinnamon wine.
Drawing back on the reins now, I sink to my home-coming.
I plunge deep into darkness. I go back to the East."

2

What, then, is the nature of this, the Great Mountain?
Beneath, on Qi and Lu, lies endless green,
Up here, demonic beauties gathered by Creation,
Where Dark Force and Bright Force split shade and sun.

In my overfull heart the layered cloudbanks form,
Into sight strained with searching come birds winging home.
Some time, when I have trod on that uttermost summit,
Under one wide gaze – shrunk the mountains below.

4

Leaning on my staff, I come to see the recluse.
An overgrown path blocks past and present off.
No mortised roof-beams in the mountain cave,
But somewhere in the hills a zither's song.

There is still white snow on the dark north slopes,
In the sunlit forests red buds gleam,
The rock-spring washes over precious stones,
Slender fish come up to the surface or submerge.

No need for silken string or flute of bamboo.
An unsullied music is in the streams and hills.
Who would wait for human singing when the clustered trees
Murmur in their sadness for themselves?

3

When crows are at roost on Gusu's tower,
Xishi drinks in the Wu King's hall,
Wu songs and Chu dances not the height of their pleasure,
The sun half-swallowed behind the green hill.

The silver pointer sinking in the golden basin,
Water through the water-clock drips apace.
They rise, see the autumn moon falling towards the waves. . . .
When that slow sun climbs the East, what pleasures shall they take?

5

Above Mount Huang in Anhui province.

Left The finest piece in the *Scripture of Poetry* (though one of the least "bardic" in tone) was written by a woman and tells the story of her unhappy marriage after a premarital affair. (Doves, it should be explained with respect to the allusion made to them, were thought to grow as intoxicated from eating mulberry leaves as girls from making love before they marry.)

Right below For virtuosity, vivid imagination and dramatic irony Du Fu's contemporary Li Bo had no equals, His theme in the "Song of the Roosting Crows," indicated only by the allusion to time running out, is the last night spent by the king of Wu with his lovely consort Xishi, unaware of what the reader already knows: that tomorrow he will be destroyed by the state of Yue. The effect is that of Hérédia's sonnet on Antony gazing into Cleopatra's eyes and seeing there the prefiguration of their ruin: "a vast sea all about and galleys fleeing."

Top "The Lord of the East" gives a glimpse of the religion of the Chu, of the ecstatic union of priestesses and deity. It is easy to imagine the dramatic performance that would have accompanied these words.

Above Du Fu, who lived in the 8th century, was a master of the last-minute shift of visual and emotional perspective. Here, in an early poem on Taishan, he ends by suddenly widening the reader's horizon.

Left These lines were written by Zuo Si in the last years of the 3rd century AD. They touch on what was at this time the controversial theme of the hermit, who deserted society to seek the secrets of immortality or enlightenment in the mountains.

From Confucius to Confucianism

Between the late 6th century BC and the early 3rd century BC Chinese thinkers became aware of the intellectual problems posed by morality and truth. The preceding age had hoped above all to find the secret of successful action – action in harmony with the will of Heaven and the wishes of the spirits. Experience and reflection had now bred a measure of skepticism and prompted men to look more deeply into the justification of their beliefs.

Four basic ways of thought emerged. The relatively agnostic and secular conservative humanism of Kongzi (Confucius), Mengzi and Xunzi stressed the cultivation of the organic social links between individuals, and the power of personal virtue working in appropriate fashion within this nexus. Mozi preached a different form of moralism, one that was utilitarian, meritocratic and authoritarian; and he was confident that heaven invariably rewarded good and punished bad behavior. In contrast, Zhuangzi was inspired by the vision of an amoral absorption of the self into the all-embracing cosmic-natural process (*dao* or "way"); and he thought the distinctions made by logical and ethical argument to be impediments to understanding. Lastly, the statecraft realists such as Shang Yang (or, rather, the book attributed to him but written later) and Hanfeizi expounded an immoralism, partly collectivist, partly Machiavellian, that maintained that the state as a whole required standards and values diametrically opposed to those customarily regarded as admirable in individuals. The Daoist statecraft of the 3rd-century BC *Scripture of the Way and Its Power* shared the realists' view of the ruler as a total manipulator untouched by human feeling, but saw the world as too paradoxical and elusive to be controlled by legal direction; and it opposed to the model of state power and economic development the vision of a return to a pristine ecological simplicity that the Sage guided by a kind of magical self-denial.

Kongzi (late 6th century BC) claimed to be no more than the transmitter of the (once golden) past, but in fact his views were a decisive break with it. In place of the old combination of religion and government, and the inherited socio-political roles of Zhou feudalism, he advocated rule by a moral elite. For him the supreme virtue was *ren*, hardly mentioned before his time. Often translated "goodness," it basically means "a sensitive concern for other individuals." Mengzi (later 4th century BC), faced with the rather stoic hedonism of Yang Zhu who posited an irreconcilable opposition between human nature and the demands of society, whose institutions were a form of torture, held that on the contrary a man's heart (*xin*) was innately good, and evil only arose because it had been corrupted. He stressed the need in consequence to revive and nourish one's "moral vitality" (*qi*). The less optimistic Xunzi (early 3rd century BC) desacralized Heaven, making it synonymous with "Nature." Human propensities he regarded as essentially neutral, becoming in each case what they were through cultural conditioning. Morals were explained socio-biologically. Men only survived in a harsh environment because of social organizations, and this depended on the complementary functioning of a differentiation of roles and a sentiment of solidarity. This was assured by the respective psychological effects of "ritual" (*li*$_a$) and "music" (*yue*).

The saddest philosophical casualty of the late archaic age was the complex logic elaborated by the followers of Mozi and also found to some extent in the paradoxes of sophists such as Gongsun Long. ("A white horse is not a horse," "An orphan colt has never had a mother," and so on.) Amid the grim practical problems of the Warring States, this kind of thinking appeared at best useless and at worst socially mischievous. Zhuangzi also attacked it from a mystic's standpoint, arguing that the division of experience by words into distinct categories was a falsification from the start, and that there was no way of relating formal constructs to reality. Xunzi likewise asserted that words had no intrinsic reality, being conventionally agreed means of grouping similar objects into categories. Paradoxes arose from tampering with these conventions. For these reasons, and perhaps others, the strictly logical mode of discourse vanished.

By the beginning of the Early Empire, Confucianism, Daoism, theories of the Five Phases of matter, numerology and other elements had fused into a syncretistic metaphysics that was to be the substrate of most later Chinese philosophy. Its classical expression was the *Scripture of Changes*, a palimpsest of explanations and commentaries overlaid on an ancient Zhou dynasty divination manual. The *Changes* is built around 64 hexagrams that are the total possible permutations of six lines that may be either complete or broken in the middle. They represent respectively the "hard" and the "soft," or the Bright Force (*yang*) and the Dark Force (*yin*). As each of these reaches fullness it turns into its opposite. Each hexagram is the image (*xiang*) of an archetypal situation and formed of a net of hidden correspondences that link particular worlds of experience. Divining, which is done by sorting milfoil stalks or tossing coins, was thought to work because a mutual resonance echoed between the archetype controlling the prevailing situation and its symbolic form in the book.

The full metaphysical system was a multidimensional dualism based on almost countless pairs of contrasting opposites: female and male, warm and cold, form and energy and so on. Such a way of thinking was organic rather than mechanistic, and the cycles of the 64 archetypes reflected the eternal return of vegetable life rather than linear progress. The power that ruled the world was immanent within it, not transcendental and outside it as in the Western tradition. While the overall trends in any situation were effectively given, the

This rubbing is of a stone engraving thought to reproduce an original painting by the Tang dynasty artist Wu Daozi, active c. 720–60, and known for his mastery of line. Confucius is shown here as a court official concerned with the realities of everyday life. The top inscription says: "Picture of Confucius, foremost of teachers, putting doctrine into practice." The vertical couplets in the top right say: "Virtue equal to heaven and earth, his way supreme in past and present, he edited and transmitted the six scriptures, handing down a model for countless generations."

next, was to suffer from the illusion "created by the artist in one's own mind." The subtlest thinkers, such as Fazang (later 7th century), stressed the complete interfusion and interpenetration of all phenomena. In this view no being (in so far as one can talk of any "being") can be untouched by suffering or evil in others, or be unbenefited by others' goodness and enlightenment. The final release from illusion and desire is not possible for one until it is possible for all. This is the point underlying the Mahayana school's cult of the Boddhisattva – the potential Buddha who remains behind in the world to help others – as opposed to the less universalistic Theravada emphasis on the Lohan (arhat), a passionless individual dead to the world even when still in it.

The general dislike felt by many Chinese for the Buddhist devaluation of Confucian familial values and political obedience, as well as its streak of moral nihilism, grew in the early second millennium AD into a rationalist-secularist philosophical reaction based on the old syncretism, Mengzi's faith in innate human goodness, and many elements of Buddhist thought in transformed guise. This reaction is commonly called "Neo-Confucianism" since its leaders placed themselves in the old tradition and expressed many of their ideas in the form of glosses on the Confucian scriptures.

Zhang Zai (11th century) developed the concept of qi – "vital force" or "pneuma" – into "matter-energy," the substrate of potentiality (xu, literally "emptiness") out of which phenomena arise in accordance with "pattern-principle" (li_b). The idea of ren he expanded into "a sensitive awareness of all other beings," so that, as his younger contemporary Cheng Mingdao put it, "nothing is not oneself." The tension between the Confucian demand for hierarchy and the Buddhist instinct for equality remained unresolved.

Cheng Yichuan, Mingdao's younger brother, then made "pattern-principle" *both* natural *and* normative, both descriptive and prescriptive. This finessed the (insoluble) problem of linking "is" and "ought" since if an entity has to have a property (say, compassion) to be a proper something (say, a father), then if it does not have this property it is simply not that something. But the implication that nature (all of it) was inherently good left Neo-Confucians unable to explain where evil came from. The great synthesizer Zhu Xi (12th century) was driven to posit a virtual dualism between pattern-principle (always good) and matter-energy (sometimes good, sometimes bad), but this left the basic strategy in ruins.

The last efforts to evade this dilemma were made by Lu Xiangshan (12th century) and Wang Yangming (late 15th–early 16th century). Accepting that morality could not be deduced from anything outside the individual, they claimed that it could be intuited directly by the heart/mind (xin). Arbitrariness was avoided by positing a pervading universal mind, of which the individual's mind was – or should be – a part. If immoral action arose, this was because intuitive moral knowledge had been contaminated by selfishness. The theoretical debate was abandoned at this point, and when it was taken up again in the 20th century by Zhang Dongsun and others the conceptual background was no longer purely or even predominantly Chinese.

ordinary individual had the freedom within these limitations to act wisely or foolishly, effectively or impotently'. The Sage, who could use the wisdom in the *Changes* to touch developments at their germinal sprouting, could achieve correspondingly more. Through Han times, and the following age of imperial fragmentation, this belief inspired the search for the all-controlling principle that underlay phenomena. It was called "the science of mysterious things."

In the middle of the first millennium AD the syncretistic metaphysics was challenged by Buddhism as the Chinese came gradually to grasp the radical implications of the imported religion. The Buddhist doctrine of "emptiness" (*kong*) held that, while there was an endless flux of causes and effects, both material and moral, to believe that any specific entity (such as a table or a soul) had any enduring existence, even from one moment to the

Religion

There is no generally accepted name for the religion of traditional China considered as a whole. Whatever exactly it was, it was a fusion of elements and accepted as such. The popular dictum held with respect to Confucianism, Daoism and Buddhism that "the Three Faiths are One." Folk wisdom also had it that one took the first as a guide to daily living, had recourse to Daoist practitioners for ritual purifications and exorcisms, and employed Buddhist priests for funerals. But this neat division of labor cloaks the complex reality in which so many seemingly contradictory beliefs coexisted.

There was a usually invisible world of spirits (*shen*) of all natures and degrees of power. This otherworld was intimately interwoven with the fabric of the visible everyday world, which it resembled in many ways. The Jade Emperor at the head of the celestial hierarchy, and Yanluo (Yama) ruler of the infernal regions, were counterparts of the sovereign in Beijing. The city-god found in every county capital was likewise its spiritual magistrate. Quite apart from ancestors and ghosts, many spirits (or gods, as the more important may be called) began their careers as human beings. Guan Yu, God of War under the Qing dynasty, was a great soldier of the 3rd century AD. Li Madou, the God of Clocks, was once – such are the ironies of fate – Father Matteo Ricci, the Jesuit missionary.

Gods could be promoted or demoted according to the service they gave, or at the urgings of imperial whim. The Chinese communicated with these spiritual beings in dreams, or consulted them through spirit-mediums in a state of divine possession.

Below left In preparing for a funeral this animist priest has arranged on his altar of fortune various items including rough rice, dried roots and cigarettes. After the burial he will present each mourner with several grains of rice – a symbol of fecundity – to plant in memory of the deceased.

Below Since 1959, when Tibet was made an "Autonomous Region" of the People's Republic, over 2000 Lamaist monastic communities have been disbanded and most of their buildings razed to the ground. Belief remains strongly alive, however, and pilgrims continue their devotions at the shrines.

Center Incense sticks are burned in the Buddhist monastery of the Qiong Bamboo (a variety of bamboo from Sichuan) northwest of Kunming, in the Hall of the Five Hundred Lohans. The arrival of Buddhism in China during the first few centuries of the present era is shown in the map on page 110. A Lohan (arhat) is an enlightened monk in the Theravada tradition, which stresses individual deliverance, in contrast to the Mahayana teaching, commoner in China, which promises eventual deliverance to all beings.

Top right Ancestor worship is founded on belief in the reciprocal care of the living and the dead. If the spirit of an ancestor is neglected it may become a "hungry ghost" and return to haunt the living. In contrast, geomancy (in its aspect of the selection of permanent burial sites for forebears in such a way as to bring good fortune to specific descendants) is manipulative rather than respectful, and often associated with quarrels between brothers who have conflicting interests. Under the People's Republic these ideas and practices have declined but they continue, as here in Yunnan.

Below center The first Muslim settlers in China were Arab and Persian merchants who came by sea and land during the Tang dynasty. The later influx is shown in the map on page 150. In this mosque in Kunming the minbar is topped by a typically Chinese-style roof.

Above During the Cultural Revolution (1966–76) Christian churches in China were criticized as unpatriotic and imperialist relics. Many were closed and some destroyed. Since then a number have reopened, though the emphasis is on a "post-denominational Christianity" free of foreign links and the freedom of worship is subject to some restrictions.

Left An overseas Chinese lady consults a spirit-medium in Singapore.

Temple and Palace Architecture

In China there is no architectural difference between a Confucian temple, a Daoist temple and a Buddhist temple, and they are all built with the same ground plan and construction as secular buildings. Traditional Chinese buildings from the Song dynasty onwards stand on a raised platform and the weight of the heavy tiled roof is carried to the ground through an elaborate construction of brackets and wooden columns which rest on stone bases on the platform. The walls bear little weight and are made of light material. The most important buildings face south with openings on the southern side. There are no openings on the other sides. All parts of the brackets are dovetailed into each other and are seen as an important decorative element of the building. Wood was painted for protective and decorative reasons and the columns, if not carved, were usually red, the platform white, the walls red, the brackets green and blue, and the tiles of the roof yellow or green. The Imperial Palace in the Forbidden City in Beijing shares its palace-style architecture and decorative features with the temple of Confucius in Qufu, both built in the Ming dynasty, and with the Song dynasty temple of Jinci near Taiyuan.

The pagoda originated in India. It was introduced to China with Buddhism and was used to house sacred objects. Buddhists also used cave temples. Other religious buildings in China follow a precept found in Zhou dynasty texts, viz. that a ritual building should be round above and square below, symbolizing the relationship between heaven and earth. An example of this type is found at Gyantse in Tibet. The Qing dynasty temple of Heaven in the Forbidden City in Beijing is circular and placed within a square courtyard. The mosques in Xi'an and Kunming are buildings in Chinese traditional style whereas the mosque in Turfan imported the Muslim style of the Middle East.

Left This Christian church off Wangfujing on the east side of Beijing was founded in 1666. It has been rebuilt several times and is now a school.

Below The mosque in Turfan, built in 1776.

Above The 14th-century Daoist temple of Yonglegong in southern Shanxi is in the classic palace style of architecture. It houses some of the most magnificent mural paintings in central China.

Below left The temple of Confucius in Qufu in present-day Shandong province, where Confucius was born in the 6th century BC, dates from the Qing dynasty. The main sanctuary shown here was built in 1724 and dedicated to Confucius. The temple houses a collection of musical instruments of which some are only used in Confucian temples.

Below This tiered architectural structure at Dunhuang in Gansu province is built against a cliff into which over 400 Buddhist cave temples have been hewn.

Above The 17th-century Potala Palace in Lhasa was the winter residence of the Dalai Lama who lived in the upper stories of its Red Palace.

Far left This hall of the Buddhist temple of Jinci near Taiyuan in Shanxi province was built in the 12th century. Note the elaborate brackets.

Left Palkhorchorten, known as the Great Stupa of Gyantse, Tibet, was built in the 15th century. It was a center of the ''Yellow Hat'' Buddhist sect, a branch of the Mahayana tradition. Its plan is that of a mandala—a circle within a square. Inside are remarkable frescoes of 15th-century date. The rings on the spire are the 13 levels one must reach before attaining Buddhahood. The eyes of the Buddha on every side of the stupa look in all directions, showing the Buddha's concern for all mankind.

Medicine and Geomancy

The Chinese have long been one of the most health-conscious peoples in the world. Confucian tradition held that as one had received one's body as a gift from one's parents, it was part of filial respect neither to hazard it nor to injure it. The only exception to this was the practice resorted to by unusually devoted sons and daughters of cutting off a piece of their arms, thighs or even livers to make a magical medicinal soup with which to cure a sick father or mother. Scholars often took up medicine in order to care for their parents, and it was perhaps the one profession in which it was respectable for an orthodox man of letters to engage.

The Daoists conceived of the body as an "internal country," a world peopled by a variety of spirits, some benign and some malevolently disposed towards the self whose body it was. Daoist alchemy was in great measure the search for an elixir of physical immortality, to which the manufacture of gold was secondary, its interest being simply in the fact that gold was the least changeable of metals, not in a quest for lucre. Ironically, many of the elixirs were deadly poisons, containing compounds of mercury and arsenic, but there were also hermits who followed macrobiotic diets of vegetarian nature that were presumably more wholesome.

The dispassionate scientific approach to human anatomy had a fitful life in China. The dissection of cadavers began around the start of the first millennium AD, using the bodies of criminals, but was discontinued only to reappear for a while under the Song, after which it largely vanished again until modern times. Subsequent attitudes may be described as a mixture of prudishness and pornographic delectation.

Traditional Chinese medicine was based on two encyclopedic accumulations of empirical knowledge: herb-lore and the effects of stimulating particular sensitive spots on the body. The first came to be embodied in a series of illustrated herbals, first printed in the Song and culminating in the systematic *Pharmacopoeic Catalog* of Li Shizhen in the late Ming. In modern times a few of the traditional herbs have yielded valuable drugs. The elaborate medieval theories developed to explain the mutual interaction of herbal medicines and diseases, based on humors, "ethers" (*qi*) and flavors now seem unlikely to have any permanent value. The second body of practical information related to the therapies of acupuncture and moxibustion, which work primarily on the nervous system. It has proved possible to validate a substantial part of this inheritance in modern times, and to extend it further. The old theory of the circulation of vital energy along primary and transverse meridians, linking sensitive points, is however regarded with skepticism even by most acupuncture specialists today, although it would be premature to say that it has been definitively discarded.

Left A 17th-century carved and painted anatomical figure marked with acupuncture points.

Below This woodcut from the late Ming *Sancai* encyclopedia shows *shehan*, a potentilla whose dried root was used to treat snakebites and the stings of insects.

Bottom Traditional Chinese herbals, published in printed form since the late 10th century, list drugs for their curative properties and also explain preparation techniques. In China today both such herbs and Western drugs are sold in medicine shops.

Right In the earliest times acupuncture and moxibustion may have been employed to expel evil illness-causing demons from the body. Whether or not the traditional energy-theory has any validity these practices are used today both as therapy and to relieve pain as seen in this photograph of a woman being treated for a shoulder complaint.

Right An 18th-century watercolor version of a traditional diagram showing acupuncture points on the pericardium channel.

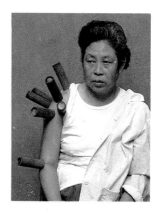

Right above The upper drawing shows the six pulses (three positions, two levels) that can be felt on each wrist (making 12 in all. Diagnosis in traditional Chinese medicine is based on the patient's facial appearance, voice, diet and – above all – his pulse. Each pulse-position corresponds to the "meridian" associated with a specific organ and the strength and quality of the beat are thought to reveal the proper or improper functioning of this part of the system. *Below*, a traditional version.

Right center The geomantic compass is used to divine the most auspicious spot for a burial site. The pseudo-science of geomancy (earth magic) detects the flows of occult forces in the landscape which are in some ways comparable to the flows of vital energies along meridians in the body posited by traditional medicine. Buildings and graves are thought to affect these flows, which allegedly bring good and evil fortune, somewhat in the manner the acupuncturist's needles affect the human organism.

Right below These coffins line the hillside waiting for an auspicious time and place for second and permanent burial as determined by a consultant in geomancy.

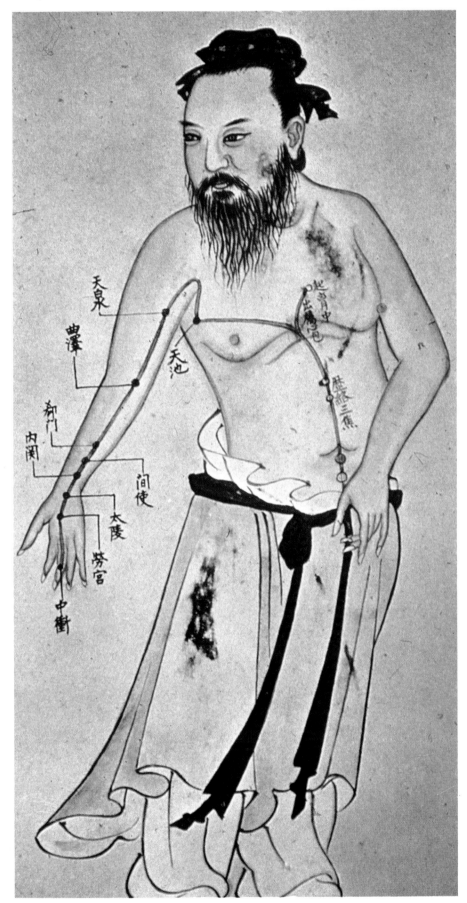

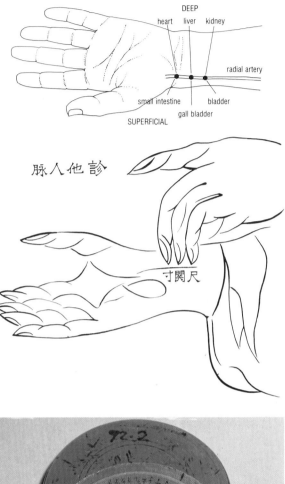

193

Principles of Mathematics

The earliest Chinese mathematics of which we know much comes from the time of the late Warring States and the early Han. It is mostly practical in its concerns, dealing with matters like surveying, engineering and the collection of taxes. Interesting first attempts were made by the followers of the philosopher Mozi in the direction of formulating axioms and giving proofs in the form of step-by-step deduction, but these ideas were never developed. Chinese geometry in particular, which was rudimentary at this date, makes a sharp contrast with that of Greece. A good example of the difference in style is the Chinese proof of Pythagoras's theorem that the square on the hypotenuse of a right-angled triangle equals the sum of the squares on the other two sides. In its earliest form it was little more than a numerical demonstration based on the special case of the 3, 4, 5 triangle, as shown in Figure I. By the 3rd century BC this had been generalized into an algebraic proof (also found in India) which is simpler than Euclid's but without its deductive rigor.

Figure I. The Chinese Proof of Pythagoras

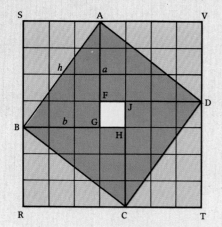

Numerical demonstration Let AG, BH, CJ, and DF be 4 units long, and AF, BG, CH, and DJ be 3 units long. Then the diagonals AB, BC, CD, and DA are 5 units long. This follows from noting that, in terms of area,

square SRTV− triangles ASB, BRC, CTD, and DVA = square ABCD and ∴ square ABCD = $(7 \times 7) - (4 \times 6) = 25 = 5^2$.

Algebraic proof Let h be the length of the four hypotenuses, and a and b the lengths of the other two sides of the right-angled triangles. Since

ABCD = FGHJ + ABG + BCH + CDJ + DAF

it follows that

$$h^2 = (a - b)^2 + 4 \cdot \left(\frac{ab}{2}\right) = a^2 + b^2.$$

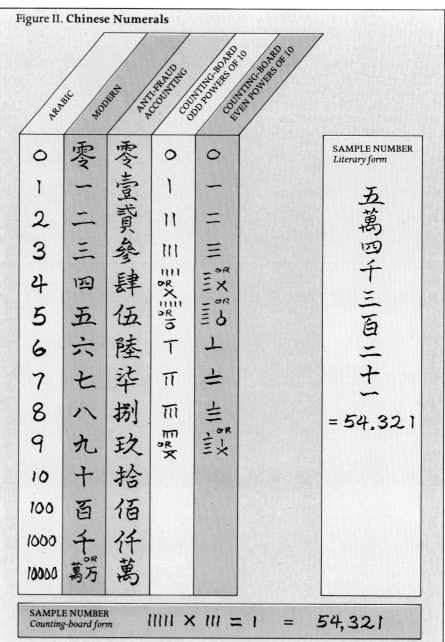

Figure II. Chinese Numerals

ARABIC	MODERN	ANTI-FRAUD ACCOUNTING	COUNTING-BOARD ODD POWERS OF 10	COUNTING-BOARD EVEN POWERS OF 10
0	零	零	0	0
1	一	壹		一
2	二	貳		二
3	三	參		三
4	四	肆		
5	五	伍		
6	六	陸		
7	七	柒		
8	八	捌		
9	九	玖		
10	十	拾		
100	百	佰		
1000	千 OR	仟		
10000	萬 OR 万	萬		

SAMPLE NUMBER *Literary form*

五萬四千三百二十一

= 54,321

SAMPLE NUMBER *Counting-board form*   ‖‖‖ ╳ ‖‖ ≡ ┃   = 54,321

A basic characteristic of Chinese mathematics, as it developed in the course of the first millennium AD, was its use of the counting board for calculations. Since the earliest times the Chinese had used a decimal system of numerals. Special terms (namely, "ten," "hundred," "thousand," "ten thousand," and so on) were placed after the digits to indicate the respective powers of ten. This system lent itself with ease to computing on a matrix of rows and columns where horizontal place value (from right to left) alone determined the power of ten. Counting rods were laid in the appropriate cells in patterns designed to show both the digit and, for extra clarity, whether the power of ten was even or odd. These special numerals are shown in Figure II, with samples of numbers in both literary and counting-board form.

Right above The Chinese rod-and-bead abacus was not in widespread use until about the 14th century. The frame is read from left to right, the columns representing powers of 10. The beads in the upper panel count for five each, the beads in the lower panel for one. Only beads moved towards the central spine are counted, and the illustration thus shows the number 123456789, for a decimal point that can be placed as required. The topmost bead was used only in long division.

Far right "Master and pupils discuss difficulties," a woodcut of 1593 by Cheng Dawei.

At first zeros were represented by blanks in the appropriate columns; but by about the beginning of the second millennium AD an open circle was also used. Around the same time black rods were introduced to represent negative numbers, in contrast to the red ones used for positive numbers.

The counting board resembled a crude, hand-operated computer. Its rows may be thought of as stores of "addresses" containing values constantly being changed by the actions of the operator as he worked through his "program." A peculiarity of the counting board was that quite complicated problems could be tackled without any symbolic notation for operators, for relationships such as " = ", or even for x, y and z in their function as markers for distinct unknown quantities.

Figure III shows multiplication by a method described by Yang Hui, who lived in the 13th century. Though similar to the common Western system, it has three features characteristic of the counting board in contrast to pen-and-ink techniques. (1) The digits of the multiplicand are removed in succession once they have been finished with. (2) The multiplier is successively shifted to the right. (3) Working for which there is no more use is regularly cleared away. As with our method, it presupposes a knowledge of the multiplication table up to 9×9. In reading this and later examples it should be remembered that the line labels shown here did not appear on the Chinese board, but only numbers, and that (like the comments) they have been added here for clarity.

Long division was regarded as a fearsome operation in medieval Europe, but not in China. Figure IV shows how it was done. The operator has to make a guess once in each cycle of calculations; but in the majority of cases knowing the multiplication table

Figure III. Multiplying 247 by 736

							Comments
Multiplicand				2	4	7	
Multiplier		7	3	6			
	1	4					7×2
			6				3×2
		1	2				6×2
Multiplicand					4	7	2 removed
Multiplier			7	3	6		736 shifted 1 place R
Running total	1	4	7	2			Previous subtotals added
		2	8				7×4
			1	2			3×4
			2	4			6×4
Multiplicand						7	4 removed
Multiplier				7	3	6	736 shifted 1 place R
Running total	1	7	6	6	4		Previous subtotals added
			4	9			7×7
			2	1			3×7
				4	2		6×7
Total	1	8	1	7	9	2	

Figure IV. Dividing 256842 by 751

							Comments
Answer Line				3			By inspection
Dividend	2	5	6	8	4	2	
Divisor		7	5	1			$751 > 256$. Align 1 column to R
Removed	2	2	5	3			3×751
Remainder		3	1	5			Dividend − Removed
Answer Line				3	4		By inspection
Dividend		3	1	5	4	2	Remainder + rest of Dividend
Divisor			7	5	1		Shift 1 column R
Removed		3	0	0	4		4×751
Remainder			1	5	0		Dividend − Removed
Answer Line				3	4	2	By inspection
Dividend			1	5	0	2	Remainder + rest of Dividend
Divisor				7	5	1	Shift 1 column R
Removed			1	5	0	2	2×751
Remainder			0	0	0	0	No Remainder. End calculation

and inspecting the first two digits of the dividend and the first digit of the divisor is all that is needed. It is quite likely that this technique, which appeared in China not later than the 3rd or 4th century AD, was transmitted to Europe and lies at the basis of our own schoolroom method.

The Chinese method of extracting a square root introduces two further features: (1) geometrical diagrams were often used to devise procedures; (2) particular rows were reserved on the board to store distinct quantities. It was this second feature that made it possible to do algebra without x's and y's. Figure V shows the counting-board solution of $x^2 = 1300$ (which requires an approximation of a non-integral square root) and its geometrical derivation. Figure VI shows the same sort of approach to solve a quadratic equation.

The tabulations in the Figures make the Chinese method seem more cumbersome than it was. Reading through them is like looking at a moving-picture sequence as stills. On the other hand, different types of equations needed slightly different procedures. Chinese mathematical text-books therefore contained more "programs" than would have been necessary had a more generalized technique been available. Even more serious, as the equations grew harder than the elementary examples shown here, the number of special terms required (like "Flank" and "Follower") proliferated. Conceptual control became more and more evasive. The medieval Chinese solved numerical equations with powers of the unknown as high as the tenth, using methods like those shown; but there was an inbuilt limitation on how far they could go without an explicit formal symbolism. Lack of such a symbolism also inhibited the exploration of the less "realistic"

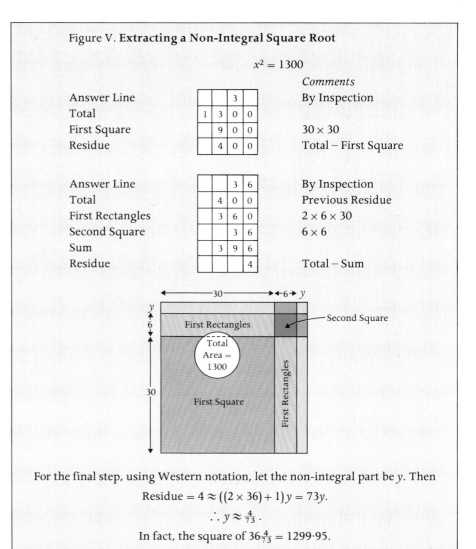

Figure V. Extracting a Non-Integral Square Root

$$x^2 = 1300$$

					Comments
Answer Line			3		By Inspection
Total	1	3	0	0	
First Square		9	0	0	30×30
Residue		4	0	0	Total − First Square

				Comments
Answer Line		3	6	By Inspection
Total	4	0	0	Previous Residue
First Rectangles	3	6	0	$2 \times 6 \times 30$
Second Square		3	6	6×6
Sum	3	9	6	
Residue			4	Total − Sum

For the final step, using Western notation, let the non-integral part be y. Then

$$\text{Residue} = 4 \approx ((2 \times 36) + 1)\, y = 73y.$$

$$\therefore y \approx \tfrac{4}{73}.$$

In fact, the square of $36\tfrac{4}{73} = 1299{\cdot}95$.

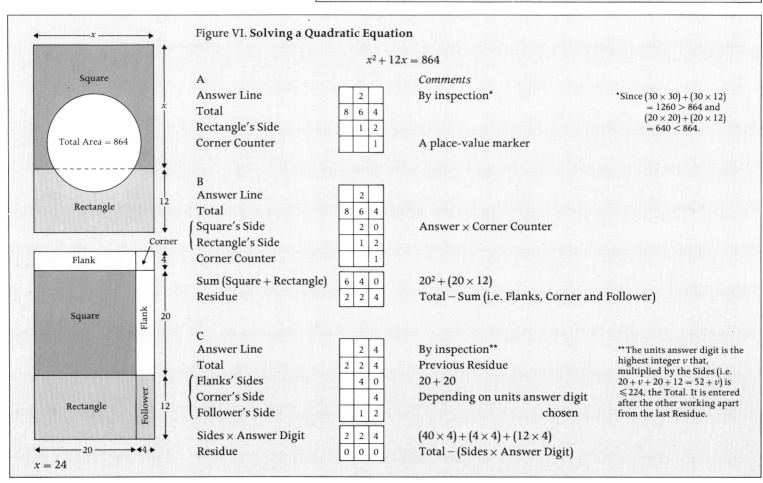

Figure VI. Solving a Quadratic Equation

$$x^2 + 12x = 864$$

A

				Comments
Answer Line		2		By inspection*
Total	8	6	4	
Rectangle's Side		1	2	
Corner Counter			1	A place-value marker

*Since $(30 \times 30) + (30 \times 12) = 1260 > 864$ and $(20 \times 20) + (20 \times 12) = 640 < 864$.

B

				Comments
Answer Line		2		
Total	8	6	4	
Square's Side		2	0	Answer × Corner Counter
Rectangle's Side		1	2	
Corner Counter			1	
Sum (Square + Rectangle)	6	4	0	$20^2 + (20 \times 12)$
Residue	2	2	4	Total − Sum (i.e. Flanks, Corner and Follower)

C

				Comments
Answer Line		2	4	By inspection**
Total	2	2	4	Previous Residue
Flanks' Sides		4	0	$20 + 20$
Corner's Side			4	Depending on units answer digit
Follower's Side		1	2	chosen
Sides × Answer Digit	2	2	4	$(40 \times 4) + (4 \times 4) + (12 \times 4)$
Residue	0	0	0	Total − (Sides × Answer Digit)

**The units answer digit is the highest integer v that, multiplied by the Sides (i.e. $20 + v + 20 + 12 = 52 + v$) is $\leqslant 224$, the Total. It is entered after the other working apart from the last Residue.

$x = 24$

Figure VII

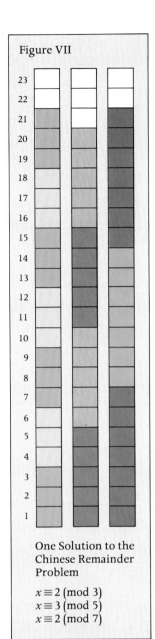

One Solution to the Chinese Remainder Problem

$x \equiv 2 \pmod 3$
$x \equiv 3 \pmod 5$
$x \equiv 2 \pmod 7$

Figure VIII. A Sketch of Qin Jiushao's Solution of the General Remainder Problem

In modern notation the problem is to find the lowest positive value for N when

$$N \equiv r_1 \pmod{m_1} \equiv r_2 \pmod{m_2} \ldots \equiv r_n \pmod{m_n}$$

where the r's are the remainders left after N has been divided by the corresponding m's (the "moduli").* Assume no two m's have a common factor greater than 1. The method used both by Qin and by modern mathematicians may be outlined, in general terms and using the example given in Figure VII as an illustration, as follows:

$$\text{Let } M = m_1 \times m_2 \times \ldots \times m_n$$
$$\text{Then } M = 3 \times 5 \times 7 = 105.$$

For each m_i find a number k_i such that
$$\frac{M}{m_i} k_i \equiv 1 \pmod{m_i} \equiv 0 \pmod{m_{j \neq i}},$$

as in $\frac{105}{3} \cdot 2 = 70 \equiv 1 \pmod 3$ and
$$\equiv 0 \pmod{5 \text{ and } 7},$$

$$\frac{105}{5} \cdot 1 = 21 \equiv 1 \pmod 5 \text{ and}$$
$$\equiv 0 \pmod{3 \text{ and } 7}, \text{ and}$$

$$\frac{105}{7} \cdot 1 = 15 \equiv 1 \pmod 7 \text{ and}$$
$$\equiv 0 \pmod{3 \text{ and } 5}.$$

(A k can always be found since $\frac{M}{m_i}$ is an exact multiple of every m except m_i.)
From the definition of k_i given above it follows, by multiplying both sides by r_i, that
$$\frac{M}{m_i} r_i k_i \equiv r_i \pmod{m_i}.$$

Each term of this sort is an exact multiple of each m except for m_i. Hence summing them gives one solution:

$$N = \sum_{i=1}^{n} \frac{M}{m_i} r_i k_i,$$
as in $N = (70 \times 2) + (21 \times 3) + (15 \times 2) = 233.$

Repeated subtractions of M give the lowest value. Thus $233 - (105 \times 2) = 23.$

*"$\equiv$" should be read as "is congruent to", "mod" as "to the modulus".

Qin made the m's relatively prime in pairs by dividing out any common factor from the terms of one of the congruences. (Thus for m's 25 and 10 the factor 5 can be taken from the 10 and the relationship re-expressed in terms of $m = 2$, which is relatively prime to 25.) To find the k_i he used a method akin to modern continued fractions. To solve $65k \equiv 1 \pmod{83}$ we break down the ratio of the coefficient to the modulus by repeated applications of the relation

$$\frac{a}{b} = \frac{1}{a/b}.$$

Thus 65/83 becomes $\frac{1}{83/65}$ which gives

$$\frac{1}{1 + 18/65} \quad = \frac{1}{65/18}$$

$$= \frac{1}{3 + 11/18} \quad = \frac{1}{18/11}$$

$$= \frac{1}{1 + 7/11} \ldots \ldots \quad \frac{1}{1 + 1/3} = \frac{1}{3}.$$

Such sequences can be compactly expressed in terms of their integer denominators, d_i, in this case $(1,3,1,1,1,3)$. Qin found the k from the last-but-one of these denominators by the following formula:

$$\text{Let } f_0 = 1 \text{ and } f_i = (d_i f_{i-1}) + f_{i-2} \text{ for } i > 0.$$

Then $f_{n-1} = k$, as shown in the tabulation below:

d		f		"The Celestial Unit"
		1		
1		1		$(1 \times 1) + [0]$
3		4		$(3 \times 1) + 1$
1		5		$(1 \times 4) + 1$
1		9		$(1 \times 5) + 4$
1		14		$(1 \times 9) + 5$
1		23		$(1 \times 14) + 9$
3		83		$(3 \times 23) + 14.$

So $f_{n-1} = 23$. That this is k may be verified by noting that $65k = 65 \times 23 = 1495$, which is one more than 83×18.

Figure IX. Qin Jiushao's Use of Determinants

If we use 8 rolls of cotton for 6 men, we have a shortage of 160 rolls. If we use 9 rolls for 7 men, we have a surplus of 560 rolls. How many rolls of cotton are there, and how many men?

Using Western notation, let x be the number of rolls and y the number of men. Then

$$x = y \cdot \frac{8}{6} - 160, \quad \text{and} \quad x = y \cdot \frac{9}{7} + 560.$$

Qin Jiushao's rule for simultaneous equations of the form

$$x = y \cdot \frac{b}{a} - c \quad (1) \quad , \quad x = y \cdot \frac{b'}{a'} + c' \quad (2)$$

was in effect to replace y in (2) by its value in (1) to give, after rearranging,

$$x = \frac{ab'c + a'bc'}{a'b - ab'} \quad (3).$$

This yields the answer 20 000 rolls of cotton and 15 120 men. More interestingly, it is the same expression as that resulting from applying the modern Cramer's rule for finding x_i in a system of n simultaneous equations by evaluating the ratio of two determinants. According to this method the column of values to the right of the "$=$" sign is substituted for the ith column of coefficients, and the determinant of the resulting matrix is divided by the determinant of the original matrix of coefficients. Thus Qin's equations rewritten

$$a x_1 - b x_2 = -a c \quad (1')$$
$$a' x_1 - b' x_2 = a' c' \quad (2')$$

is solved for x_1 (the original "x") by evaluating

$$x_1 = \frac{\det \begin{array}{cc} -a c & -b \\ a' c' & -b' \end{array}}{\det \begin{array}{cc} a & -b \\ a' & -b' \end{array}} = \frac{ab'c + a'bc'}{-ab' + a'b} \quad (3').$$

aspects of equations such as solutions requiring negative and imaginary numbers.

Pre-modern Chinese mathematics further achieved outstanding results in indeterminate analysis. The so-called "Chinese Remainder Problem" appeared as early as the 4th century AD: "We have things of which we do not know the number. If we count them by threes, the remainder is two. If we count them by fives, the remainder is three. If we count them by sevens, the remainder is two. How many things are there?" (See Figure VII.) The explicit statement of a method that would solve any problem of this type had, however, to wait for Qin Jiushao in the 13th century. Figure VIII sketches the main lines of his approach.

The matrix-like nature of the counting board also prompted the consideration of arrays of coefficients; and it is not surprising that by the 13th century Qin Jiushao was using what amounted to the simplest form of determinants to solve simultaneous equations. Figure IX gives an illustration.

As this summary makes evident, Chinese mathematics in the high Middle Ages was the most advanced in the world. Its subsequent stagnation, and indeed decline, is one of the riddles of intellectual history.

Chinese Ingenuity

Below Water-powered bellows, which use an eccentric lug (imperfectly shown in this early 14th-century picture) to produce reciprocating motion.
Below right This treadle-operated pallet-and-trough pump was known to the Chinese as "the dragon's bones pump" because its linked pallets looked like giant vertebrae. Used in areas where currents were not swift enough to power automatic pumps, its virtue was its ergonomic efficiency, making use of the heavy muscles of the thighs in much the way a bicycle does.
Below center A high-lift pot-pump used for irrigated agriculture.

Read a printed book, spend a note, drink tea from a porcelain cup, sit an examination, pull the trigger of a rifle or enjoy fireworks, watch a boat with a rudder going through a pound lock or a horse with a padded collar plowing a field, put on a pair of sunglasses . . . in every case you have the Chinese to thank, or perhaps sometimes blame, for what you are doing. Paper and paper money, printing, gunpowder and the rest are all Chinese inventions, mostly from early medieval times, which made their way to Europe. The list could be almost indefinitely extended, from the watertight bulkhead in ships to (astonishingly) the equal-tempered scale based on the twelfth roots of two.

The Chinese have long had a flair for achieving results with an astonishing economy of effort. Consider the ergonomic efficiency of the traditional trough-and-pallet pump worked by pedals using the heavy muscles of the leg and the operator's weight, just as a bicycle does, or the balanced Chinese wheelbarrow with its central wheel, needing no more than a touch to keep it upright and send it on its way, in contrast to ours where the arms bear half the weight. This gift for economy can be seen even in the humble carrying-pole, balanced on the shoulders, with its subtle flexible resonance matching the walker's movements, in the fishtail oar lazily twisting back and forth over the back of a sampan, or in the "cangue," a broad-rimmed wooden collar preventing self-feeding or proper rest, one of the most unpleasantly cost-effective punishments ever devised. Or indeed in the old method of execution whereby a couple of boards were used to suspend the

victim on tiptoe by his neck until the strain proved too much for his spine.

Chinese ingenuity historically has been such that it is surprising that they did not have an industrial revolution before the West. They could, for example, cast iron long before the Europeans, thanks in part perhaps to a skill with high temperatures learned from ceramics and to the distinctive Chinese continuous-blast double-acting box-bellows. They had water-powered machines for twisting thread by the late 13th century. There was, however, a long and not easily explained hiatus in Chinese inventiveness from the middle of the 14th century to the middle of the 19th, exactly the time when Europe was surging ahead. Only recently has the old flair begun hesitatingly to reemerge.

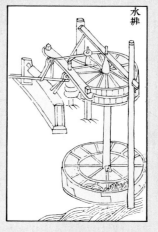

Left This "fierce burning-oil projector" (i.e. piston-and-valve flamethrower), depicted here in a military encyclopedia of the 11th century, was probably used to repel attackers from city walls. The mechanism, as shown in the accompanying reconstruction, made use of a double piston, valves and partial vacuums. It is curious that these techniques were not applied to either water or steam.

Right below Invented early in the first millennium AD, the Chinese wheelbarrow requires less effort to use than the Western kind as it distributes the load evenly around the wheel rather than between the wheel and the handles.

Left Machines like this treadle-operated silk-reeling machine date from at least the Northern Song and are notable for the way a single power-source provides two different types of motion: the rotation of the reeling-frame, which draws the filaments off the cocoons immersed in the tub of boiling water, and the reciprocal alternation of the ramping arm, shifting the eyelets through which the fibers pass so as to lay down a broad band on the frame.

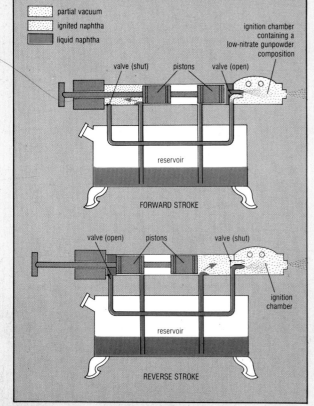

partial vacuum
ignited naphtha
liquid naphtha

ignition chamber containing a low-nitrate gunpowder composition

valve (shut) pistons valve (open)

reservoir

FORWARD STROKE

valve (open) pistons valve (shut)

ignition chamber

reservoir

REVERSE STROKE

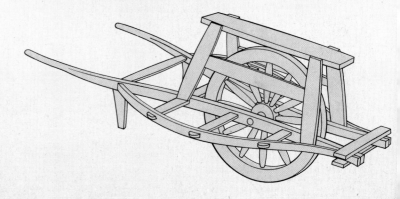

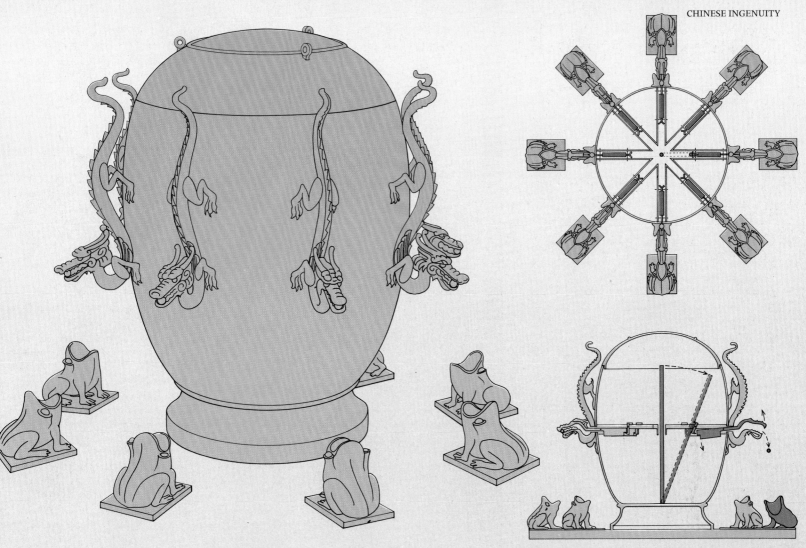

Above The first machine to register earthquakes in China was invented in the 1st century AD (Han dynasty) whereas the first modern seismograph was not set up in Europe until the 18th century. The mechanism illustrated here is one of three possible reconstructions of the original. Eight dragon heads surround a domed cover with a toad sitting under each dragon, each of which has a ball in its mouth. When the machine is shaken by earth tremors a central pendulum swings (or, alternatively, falls) in such a way that one of the balls drops into the open mouth of the toad sitting beneath it, so – at least in principle – indicting the direction of the disturbance. The pendulum falls into a slot so that it cannot activate the other balls until reset (or, alternatively, they are held in place by internal levers). There is doubt, though, as to whether any mechanism of this sort would have distinguished *pressure* waves from *shear* waves at right angles to them and whether it would have distinguished direction as opposed to alignment.

Below This picture shows a reconstruction of the hydraulic clockwork built in the 11th century AD under the direction of Su Song to turn not only jackwork but also a celestial globe (first floor) and an armillary sphere (on the roof, for determining the angles needed for sighting stars) at a speed that matched the apparent rotation of the heavens. The "clockwork" was based on a vertical waterwheel whose rotation was restrained by a tripping mechanism that lifted briefly to permit it to turn through a small angle every time one of the containers on its periphery, fed from a tank kept at constant pressure, filled to the level necessary to activate the trip-lever by outweighing a counterweight.

Left Various experiments with reusable movable types (unlike the piece-molds used earlier for casting characters in bronze, see page 180) were made in China from the 11th century onwards, though woodblock printing remained the commonest way of producing books. The picture shows a rotating typecase in which sticks of type could be stored according to which group of rhyming words they belonged.

Above Paper had by the 4th century AD displaced the wooden strips previously used for most writing. Numerous raw materials were used in its manufacture – paper-mulberry bark, scraps of hemp and bamboo shoots. These were pulped and macerated in a trough and a screen was then used to lift out fine layers of deposit that when dried became sheets. The pictures show various stages in the production process.

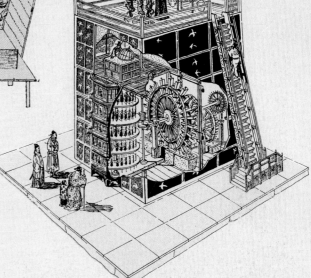

Ceramics

The history of Chinese ceramics may be traced back several thousand years, to the impressed or painted pottery of the early Neolithic. The potter's wheel was in use at least by the time of the black wares of the Longshan culture. The production of the intricate molds for the decorated bronzes of the Shang and Zhou dynasties provided a further exacting test of the Chinese potter's knowledge of the properties of clays.

Glazes were evolved from the high-fired alkaline varieties of the Bronze Age to the low-fired lead green and brown glazes of Han times. Polychrome lead glazing was popular under the Tang, notably in the bright "three-color" wares used both for burials and for domestic purposes. During the Song a true porcelain was developed, translucent and resonant; and by the 14th century had, with stoneware, to a great extent replaced the earlier earthenware.

Just as Chinese calligraphy became the world's earliest consciously abstract drawing, so Chinese medieval ceramics was perhaps its earliest abstract sculpture, based on the intrinsic satisfactions of pure form and color. This section illustrates ceramic decoration from the 12th century AD onwards.

Above This Cizhou-type 14th-century jar with painted design takes its name from Cizhou, modern Cixian, in Hebei province. The design is painted in brown on a whitish slip covered by a thin transparent glaze.

Left A Qingbai "clear white" vase of the 11th or 12th century. The blue tinge is characteristic of porcelain produced in Jiangxi in southern China at that time. Not until the 18th century was absolute whiteness achieved.

Top right A Guan "official ware" vase with delicate pale gray-blue glaze of the 13th century. This glaze is widely crackled, i.e. a network of cracks has been deliberately produced by slightly changing the coefficient of expansion between body and glaze.

Center right A Ju ware bowl with a metal band of the early 12th century. The glaze of these high-fired wares is nearly always crazed. The fine network of cracks was not created deliberately but results from an imbalance in the glaze mixture or simply from age.

Bottom right A Ding dish with incised and carved decoration produced in Hebei in northern China in the early 12th century. This porcelaneous white ware is characterized by its transparent ivory-toned glaze.

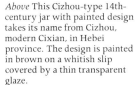

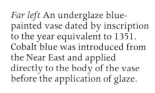

Far left An underglaze blue-painted vase dated by inscription to the year equivalent to 1351. Cobalt blue was introduced from the Near East and applied directly to the body of the vase before the application of glaze.

Left A Longquan or southern celadon vessel of the 13th century imitating the archaic bronze *gui* form. By the 14th century celadon wares were more elaborately decorated with carved designs.

Above A blue-and-white dish of the Xuande period (1426–35). The dragon shows great control of line and skill in the balancing of the design in proportion to the surface area.

Above left A copper-red glazed bowl of the early 15th century. In 14th-century examples the base is not glazed.

Left A Doucai "dove-tailed colors" polychrome jar of the Chenghua period (1465–87). The jar shows a combination of underglaze blue painting with overglaze enameling.

Above A white porcelain flask in overglaze *famille rose* enamels of the Yongzheng period (1723–35). Enamels were applied delicately to the high-fired porcelain dish.

Left A Ming wine ewer from the Jiajing period (1522–66). A significant feature of 16th-century blue-and-white ware is a change from formal designs to lively popular scenes, probably based on woodblock illustrations.

Music in Society

In the running of the state the Confucian school laid particular emphasis upon ceremonial and the rites, and music was a component part. So music held a place in the cosmology as a vehicle for ancestor worship and a link between heaven and earth. It was thus an important educative force.

The ritual music was that of the state from the time Confucianism became the official ideology/religion under the Han emperor Wudi (140–87 BC) until the fall of the Qing dynasty in 1911. Another form of court music was played specially during banquets. Already well developed by the Han period, it reached its apogee in the Tang dynasty (618–907 AD). Banquet music underwent foreign influence as early as the Han, and the "ten kinds of music" of the Tang are especially famous. These were Indian and Korean musics, varieties from five cities of central Asia, Chinese popular songs and dance music combining foreign and Chinese elements. Throughout the imperial period banquet music at the court remained much more cosmopolitan than that for formal rituals.

Court music classified instruments under eight categories according to the sound-producing elements. One was metal, including bells; another, stone, among which were stone chimes. Bamboo comprised a variety of straight or end-blown flutes. Among the silk instruments was the *qin*, a seven-stringed long zither without frets.

A very ancient instrument with a history of over 3000 years, the seven-stringed zither was regularly used not only in the court and other ritual ensembles but also as a solo instrument. It was closely associated with the educated elite, and scholars were expected to be able to play it. Generally lower in pitch than most Chinese musical instruments, it also made extensive use of a quiet ringing form of harmonics.

The seven-stringed zither gave rise to the most highly developed system of notation known in traditional China. This showed pitch, the manner in which the string was played, and tempo, although not the rhythm. Chinese scholars have written many treatises about the instrument. One of the oldest is the *Drills for the Qin* (*Qincao*), probably by Cai Yong (133–92 AD). In it he gives the titles of nearly 50 items popular in his time either for zither solo or accompanying the voice.

One instrument used in banquet music and introduced to China from central Asia by the time of the Wei dynasty (386–534 AD) was the *pipa*. This is a four-stringed pear-shaped lute which the player places upright on his thigh. Until the Tang dynasty a large plectrum was used, but not since then. The four-stringed lute is used both solo and in ensembles. Among the latter are the accompanying orchestras of theater and story-telling forms.

The non-ritual court music of the Qing dynasty (1644–1911) included operas of the aristocratic type called *Kunqu*, which originated in Kunshan, Jiangsu province, in the 16th century. The main accom-

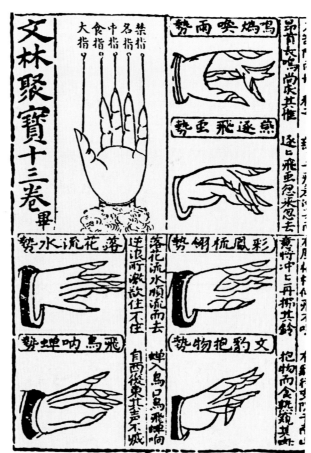

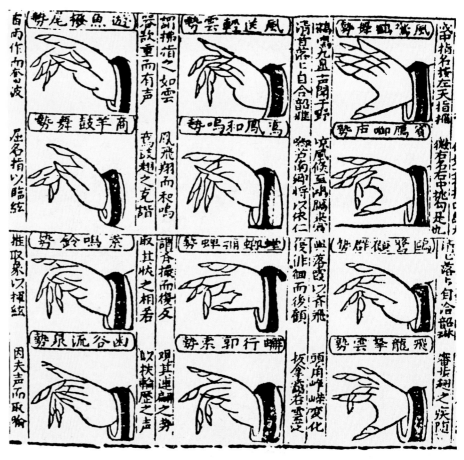

panying instrument was the end-blown flute but the four-stringed lute was among the others. The rhythm was a regular 4/4. The scholar-gentry considered *Kunqu* music the acme of elegance. However, the vast majority of theatrical music forms were popular and hence despised by the educated elite. On the eve of the Cultural Revolution there were some 300 styles of local theater, each of which differed from the others in the dialect it used and in the music.

There were several systems of local drama. One was called the "tunes of Yiyang," after the place where it arose – Yiyang in Jiangxi province. Wandering companies then took it from one place to another where it would undergo variation under the influence of local folksongs or musical instruments. A common characteristic of the styles developed from the tunes of Yiyang was explanatory passages or comment added by a singer or singers among the orchestra, not unlike the chorus of Greek drama. In the earliest of these styles there are only percussion instruments, and no strings or wind. Another system of popular theater is the clapper opera, so called because of the datewood clapper struck with a stick which all of its styles use. Clapper opera flourishes especially in Shanxi and other provinces of northern and northwestern China.

The best known of the systems is called *pihuang* after the two tunes *erhuang* and *xipi* which in

Top Ladies of the court play non-ritual court music on various instruments, including the flute and harp.

Above A figure striking two bronze bells, after a rubbing from a tomb engraving of the 3rd century AD found at Yi'nan in present-day Shandong province.

Left Two examples of finger exercises for the *qin* (zither), originally five-stringed, later seven-stringed and the most refined musical instrument in China.

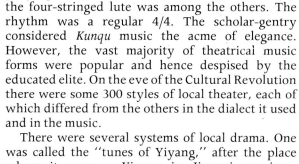

Right This drawing, after designs on a Zhou dynasty bronze vessel, shows bells and chimes and other instruments which would have been played during ceremonial festivals and sacrifices.

Far left Two scholars sitting under banana trees, one playing a four-stringed lute. A painting of the mid-16th century.

Centre left The *sheng* (Chinese mouth organ) consists of 13 bamboo pipes of different lengths fitted to a wind chest with the lower ends each covered by a free reed of bronze. Near each reed is a hole through which air escapes when the pipe's note is not required. When the hole is stopped, however, the air is forced to make the reed sound.

Left A drummer of Dai nationality in Kunming dances to the beat of his drum.

combination and endless variation form its central focus. The major style in this system is the Beijing opera which arose late in the 18th century. Beijing opera music is mainly in simple time, although a fast and completely free rhythm also exists. A clapper beats out the time. This is not the datewood of the clapper opera, but one made of redwood in three pieces, two of them tied together. The player holds the clapper in his left hand and a flick of the wrist produces a high-pitched clicking sound.

The most characteristic instruments of the Beijing opera, and indeed the clapper operas too, are the bowed stringed instruments known generically as *huqin* (Chinese fiddles). Like the four-stringed lute they are held upright on the thigh. There are two strings only, the bow fitting between them, so that the player sounds one string by pushing, the other by pulling, the bow. The origins of the Chinese fiddle are obscure, but the syllable *hu*, which means ''barbarian,'' suggests foreign derivation, probably from the Turco-Mongolian culture. It had been introduced into China, approximately in its present form, by the 13th century.

When the Chinese Communist Party came to power in 1949 it paid particular attention to the music of the local theater because this was the art that the masses loved. Although the Cultural Revolution resulted in the suppression of the traditional opera from 1966 for about a decade, it is currently flourishing. The seven-stringed zither has been reformed and its silk strings replaced by steel for added strength. It is still played, even though the scholar-gentry class that once patronized it has now disappeared. The ancient ritual and banquet court music has died out in mainland China, but remnants survive in Taiwan and South Korea.

Sonic pattern design

Unlike classical Western music, traditional Chinese music did not make a structural use of harmonic sequences. It was built instead on melodic variation, refrains and subtle contrasts of tone-color and of register, both between sections and between individual phrases and notes. As an illustration of this different type of sonic pattern design, a transcription is given below of a section of *Three Variations on ''Plum Blossom''*. This is a famous piece for the *qin*, or seven-stringed zither, based on a tune for the flute which is reputed to be from the 4th century AD. The present version probably dates from the 15th century, and is given as played by Pu Xuezhai. There are 10 parts, each of which has a programmatic title. The Chinese musical graphs below the Western notation show both the string on which each note is to be played, and the manner in which it is to be produced. Traditional Chinese sensitivity to timbre was far in advance of the Western until, at most, the last 150 years.

Far left below The *erhu* or two-stringed instrument of the *huqin* (''barbarian fiddle'') family is held upright on the thigh and played as shown here. In beijing opera the orchestra sits in the wings and is only partially seen. The *huqin* player usually sits in front and is well worth watching for his hand movements.

Right ''Evening moon over the mountains,'' a transcription of the first part of *Three Variations on ''Plum Blossom''*, from R. Cogan and P. Escot, *Sonic Design*, 1976.

Theater

Chinese theater is a composite entertainment. Western theatrical arts are, in contrast, specialized and distinct: plays, opera, mime, ballet, circus and reviews have their own separate lives.

If we speak of the main tradition that existed from the late Song down to the present century, and which still keeps a precarious hold on life both on the mainland and in Taiwan, as well as in the fringes of overseas China, and if we further ignore the wealth of regional and class variations, it is possible to offer the following very general description of the Chinese drama. At its core is a story taken either from the histories or from the Buddhist or Daoist scriptures, or else a traditional tale, and invariably well known to the audience. This is presented in a straightforward chronological fashion by actors in costume and make-up on a stage, sometimes with a few props, but without scenery. Time and place are evoked, in Shakespearean fashion, by the comments of the performers. The symbolic representation of movement from one place to another is common. A peculiarly Chinese convention is that the characters introduce themselves directly to the audience when they first appear, and sometimes also give a social and psychological description of themselves.

The words are a mixture of soliloquy, dialogue, spoken verse and extended songs, all in the colloquial language, and not the classical style used for most other literary purposes. The arias, like those in Gay's *Beggar's Opera*, are sung to well-known tunes rather than to specially composed music. Their function is to arrest the movement of the story for a moment and to intensify a particular emotion, such as heroic resolution or grief at parting. Sung words in a tonal language like Chinese are difficult to understand (unless you are broadly familiar with them already), and modern theaters nowadays project the texts onto screens on each side of the proscenium.

During the last hundred years or so, the interest of audiences has shifted away from the telling of a story and towards the performance as an exhibition of vocal, mimetic and acrobatic skills. The history of the Chinese theater since Qing times has thus centered on famous actors rather than on playwrights. Programs commonly consist of fragments designed to show off the talents of the stars, rather than complete plays. These remarks of course do not apply to modern Chinese attempts to create "spoken plays" after the Western model, nor to the "revolutionary operas" produced under the Communists.

The musical accompaniment consists of stringed instruments, both bowed and plucked, and percussion, notably wooden clapper-blocks, gongs capable of a peculiarly astringent cutting sound and drums. Sometimes there are also wind instruments like the Chinese oboe, and a flute with rice-paper pasted over one of its holes to give it a slightly edgy timbre. This accompaniment functions like the soundtrack of a film, providing an emotional background of the appropriate type, and not as an

element of artistic interest in its own right. In the hands of ordinary performers it amounts to no more than musical sweet-and-sour sauce.

Chinese physical acting is based on a repertoire of stylized movements expressing particular actions as well as particular emotions and attitudes. They have been brought to an astonishing refinement and possess an evocative power that must be seen to be believed. Scenes of warfare are an occasion for spectacular acrobatics and flag waving that combine elements of gymnastics, the formal routines of the martial arts and circus stunts.

In the past, performances often had a touch of the night-club floorshow. The early theater was closely associated with courtesans, and from Qing times until very recently it has been linked with male prostitution, the practice having become established that women's parts should be played by men, except in a few all-female troupes.

The Chinese theater could also function as a vehicle for implied comment on current affairs, at both the highest and the lowest social levels. This was one of the reasons why the imperial authorities regarded the popular drama with apprehension and tried to suppress plays that seemed to them to be subversive.

The theater took a powerful hold on Chinese popular imagination. Life itself was seen as but a play. Sometimes the plays even left the stage and temporarily invaded reality. During the Boxer uprising of 1899–1900 many Boxers spoke in theatrical fashion, worshiped figures (like Monkey) most familiar from the stage and claimed magical powers that were the stock-in-trade of theatrical fantasy.

Although there was an urban commercial theater, plays were regularly performed for the honor of the gods both in the villages and at the often lavish premises of the city guilds on the anniversaries of deities and other occasions. Such ritually offered plays were often believed to be able to drive away natural calamities, such as plagues of locusts. In the lower Yangzi valley plays were even performed at funerals. The upper classes had a sharply ambivalent attitude towards the theater: as the guardians of Confucian morality they disapproved of it as a source of obscene, criminal and sometimes even rebellious behavior; in their personal capacity almost all of them relished it intensely.

The great Yuan and Ming plays show the themes that most deeply touched the hearts of traditional audiences. One of the most acutely felt was the outrage of injustice inflicted by the law. Perhaps the commonest subject of all, treated in a wide variety of ways, is the power of sexual passion to cause destruction. Bo Renfu's *Rain on the Paulownia* depicts the fatal infatuation of the Tang emperor Minghuang for his concubine Yang Guifei, and how his consequent mishandling of government business led to the rebellion of An Lushan and the lady's brutal death at the insistence of the emperor's own angry troops. In Wang Shifu's *The Western Apartments*, perhaps the most famous of all plays, a youthful student falls into a love sickness when denied the girl he has been promised, but through the wiles of her maid he is able to make love to her and is cured. Loyalty was another paramount theme. Also evident is sheer delight in cunning plotting for good purposes, whether by statesmen, judges or courtesans.

Above These painted masks, the size of eggs, represent various characters who played male roles in traditional Chinese theater, such as warriors, gods or clowns. Both make-up and costume conformed to highly standardized types.

Left Traditional Chinese plays were presented with the minimum of stage properties so that the attention of the audience was focused on the performance of the actors who were immediately recognizable by their make-up and costumes. Part of the highly disciplined training of the actors included applying their own make-up before a performance.

Left The opera *Monkey Creates Havoc in Heaven* is based on an episode from *Pilgrimage to the West*, a 16th-century novel by Wu Cheng'en. According to the novel a monk on pilgrimage was protected by spirit guardians, a monkey and a pig. Of these Monkey was the hero, and has become one of the most lovable figures in Chinese literature and drama. Here he is about to create havoc among the subordinates of the Jade Emperor before being subdued by the Buddha. The Cultural Revolution deemed all traditional drama to be "feudal" propaganda and from 1966 to 1971 only eight model revolutionary operas were performed. The change of leadership in 1976 encouraged the revival of traditional drama and this opera was performed in Shanghai in 1980.

Right A traditional Chinese shadow puppet. Sticks attached to its joints can be manipulated to make it capable of a wide variety of lively movements.

Farming and Food

The way the Chinese farmed in times past was so different from European and American farming today that an effort of imagination is needed to understand it. Even now it remains very unlike most of the farming we know in the West.

Chinese traditional farming was close to gardening. It produced high yields on tiny farms by an immense input of skilled labor. This skill was not based on scientific knowledge, but on a detailed practical understanding of local conditions – soils, weather and types of plant. It was cautious. Too much was at risk for peasants to be very adventurous. But it was not rigidly conservative. There was constant small-scale experimentation and selection of superior strains of plants and animals. Successful innovators were swiftly copied.

During the medieval period, when Inner China was still being opened up to agriculture, large landowners who managed at least part of their farming directly had an important function. They had the resources to act as pioneers. Since the 16th or 17th century small farms were on the whole more productive than large estates. The individual peasant and his family, whether they owned their land or rented it, brought a personal commitment to this garden-type agriculture that hired or servile laborers on large farms could not match. Under premodern technical conditions this commitment more than outweighed the economies of scale available to operators with a managed labor force. With few exceptions, Chinese landlords found it most profitable to lease out their land in parcels that rarely exceeded one and a half or two hectares.

The exception to the dominance of small-scale units was in the use of water. Nearly half of China's grain crop was (and is) rice, which has to be grown in irrigated fields. Using water effectively required collective organization. Channels and reservoirs had to be dug and dredged. Dikes, barrages and sluice-gates had to be built and maintained. Shares of water had to be fairly allocated between different users. Responsibility had to be assigned for the upkeep of the system. Disputes had to be adjudicated. Where very big schemes were involved, the imperial bureaucracy took charge of the work. Examples were the dikes guarding the lands on each side of the river below the Yangzi gorges, the drainage of the lower valley of the Yellow River and the seawalls protecting the southern half of the Yangzi delta. Smaller schemes were run by local officials, members of the gentry and associations of landowners and tenants in a vast variety of combinations. About half of Chinese farming in late traditional times therefore depended on a linking of small-scale private enterprise with large-scale public institutions.

Agriculture as a whole was collectivized in the early 1950s by the Chinese Communist government. Individuals were left with only tiny personal plots. Altogether these amounted to perhaps 5 per cent of the cultivated area. One motive was to destroy the

social and political base of the "old society," but it was also believed that collectivization would increase productivity. In many respects this proved an error. Apart from water control, collectivization only paid where there was enough money to invest extensively in modern methods of production. Since China as a whole was too poor for this to happen except in a few fortunate places, farming methods could not and did not change dramatically under Communism. Motivation and carefully applied local knowledge remained as important as ever for the Chinese garden type of agriculture. Since the early 1960s this has been tacitly recognized by the more realistic Chinese leaders, and it has led to a retreat from large-scale collective management. First the units of day-to-day operation were reduced from what amounted to townships of several tens of thousands of people to units the equivalent of a small village. More recently, under the "responsibility system," the collectives have in effect become landlords renting out small parcels of land to families or small groups of families. Today over a quarter of the total farmland in China is managed under this system, and the percentage is rising. Water-control schemes have, on the other hand, become even larger in modern times. Many of them are now handled by special administrations far larger than their constituent collectives.

Two other general differences between traditional Chinese farming and Western farming are worth noting. One is the small number of large farm animals in China. The other is the virtual absence of common lands. Both can in part be explained by the relentless expansion of the human population until it filled almost every corner that could profitably be cultivated. The result was that the countryside has come to look different from ours. Within Inner China there have been few, if any, common grazing-lands and forests in recent centuries, some lineage

Top Stages in the growing of rice: from left to right, plowing, transplanting rice, harvesting.
Above left The reaping and threshing of rice.
Above center Yaks roaming in the Tibetan grasslands.
Above right Maize being husked on the hilltops of the loess area in Shanxi. The crop was imported from America in the 16th century.
Right Ducks on a commune south of Beijing being reared for the local speciality, "Beijing Duck."
Far right A pig being washed in the Li River near Guilin in southern China before being taken to market.

Left A group of commune members at work on a threshing ground near Lhasa. Barley was the staple crop of Tibet until 1959 when the government of the People's Republic of China replaced it with wheat.

holdings perhaps excepted, nor many great men's private parklands. Instead there developed a relatively monotonous expanse of smallholdings without hedges or enclosures, the imprint of which lies on the collective landscape of today. The typical animals for the last seven centuries have been scavengers – pigs, poultry and ducks. Only in Outer China, beyond the historic confines of traditional Han Chinese culture, have there been large herds in relatively recent times – horses and cattle, goats and sheep, camels and yaks.

It is often thought that Chinese agriculture in times past was in some sense primitive. While it is true that it was not scientific, any more than European agriculture was until the 19th century, the real picture is more complicated. With respect to yields per hectare China probably had the highest levels for any large area in the world before 1800, and they are still high in international terms today. With respect to yields per man hour of labor, however, China's performance is painfully low by the standards of mechanized Western farming. Overpopulation makes it worse. A comparison of the few farms using directly managed hired labor with family farms in northern China in the 1930s indicates that, at least in this area at this time, about *half* the actual rural labor force could have produced the *same* total yield. With respect to the ratio between the energy gained in the form of food compared to the total energy used in producing it, China's simple farms nonetheless do better than North American ones with their heavy reliance on fossil fuels to drive machinery and to manufacture fertilizers and pesticides.

Crops

Ancient China lived on millet. Wheat became important in the middle of the first millennium AD, when better milling machinery was developed. Rice rose to prominence a little later, with the expansion of irrigated farming in the Yangzi valley and the far south. Much later, towards the end of the 16th century, several new crops came to China from the Americas via the Spanish Pacific trading system. These were New World maize, sweet and white potatoes, peanuts and tobacco. By about 1700 Chinese agriculture had assumed its final pattern before modern times. Wheat was the stable cereal north of the Yangzi valley, rice the basic grain south of this line, with a variety of other crops being grown on the poorer soils up the hill slopes and in the mountains.

Until about the 14th century, ordinary Chinese dressed in clothes made of hemp or ramie-grass fiber. The well-to-do also wore silk. After this time most Chinese clothes were of cotton, which was introduced either from India or southeast Asia, or perhaps both. Cotton is warmer than hemp-linen, absorbs moisture better and more of it can be grown per hectare.

In addition to these basic items, the Chinese had a distinctive range of other economic crops. Water-chestnuts, snow-peas, bitter melons and Chinese cabbage are some of the better-known characteristically Chinese vegetables. Lychees and longans (or "dragon's eyes") are examples of fruits not originally grown elsewhere. Other plants of the greatest importance were the tea shrub, the *tong*-tree (the oil of which was used for waterproofing and insecticides), soybeans (which yielded bean-curd, sauce, and oil-cake fertilizer), the lacquer tree and bamboo (of which the tender shoots could be eaten and the stems made into everything from water-pipes to scaffolding).

Tobacco (known as "fire-leaves" or "dry wine") was widely grown after the 17th century. The opium poppy, the juice of which had been used to prepare a painkiller for more than a thousand years, began to be cultivated as a narcotic early in the 18th century. The addiction seems first to have spread as a result of its being smoked together with tobacco. Its high value for weight often made it the only profitable commercial crop in remote regions, and it played an important part in starting the economic development of the Chinese southwest and Manchuria in the 19th and early 20th centuries.

Because arable land was in such short supply, multiple cropping was practiced wherever possible. The use of quick-ripening rice, which originally came from Vietnam, made possible two cereal harvests a year in the warmer regions: rice followed by rice in the far south, rice followed by wheat in the central valley. Vegetables sometimes provided a third crop. Rotations were used to preserve the fertility of the soil and prevent pests establishing themselves. Fallowing was virtually unknown in later centuries. Among the most sophisticated practices used were symbiotic cultivation (for example, growing beans around mulberries to "help" the trees) and intercropping (such as sowing beans between rows of ripening rice, for harvesting at a later date).

Land, fertilizers and cultivation

The greater part of the farmland in China was not given by nature but made by human effort. This is most evident in the terraces used for growing rice, which have to be almost perfectly level, and which sometimes climb up hillsides like giant steps. Continuously farmed land also loses its fertility quickly unless treated with manures and chemicals like lime. Traditional Chinese maintenance of the productive power of the soil was painstaking. At its most laborious it could even involve interchanging, by hand, the soil around mulberry trees with that in the rice fields.

Ideally, fields were prepared for the transplantation of rice shoots by the successive use of a plow, a heavy harrow and a fine-toothed harrow. In practice, the shortage of animal-power often made it necessary to use the heavy hoe instead. There were five main kinds of fertilizers: pressed cakes made from various seeds, green fertilizers like clover that were spaded back directly into the soil, ashes of reeds and grasses, mud scooped from rivers and canals in the course of dredging and the excrement of animals and human beings matured in a variety of ways. One serious consequence of the use of human manure was the spread of certain diseases such as schistosomiasis, passed on through the soles of the peasants' bare feet. This scourge seems to have been largely eliminated in recent years.

High yields depended on repeated weeding, the most unpleasant of all routine tasks. It was sometimes done on hands and knees, with metal tips covering the fingers, though a weeding-rake was also used. The plucked weeds were pushed back into the soil to serve as a sort of green fertilizer.

Right Throughout the ages the Chinese have fertilized the land with human manure. Here the night soil cart is being pulled along the street in Xi'an.

Below Treadmills are still used for raising water, though many have been replaced by electric pumps.

Mechanizing techniques such as these, without reducing output per hectare, is clearly extremely difficult.

Water

Traditional hydraulic works may be broadly divided into irrigation and defense against floods. The type of organization needed varied according to whether water was desired as a precious commodity or feared as an enemy. Some systems combined both elements of irrigation and defense, notably the delta and lakeland polders, low-lying farming and residential areas entirely surround by dikes and below the average water level for at least some parts of the year.

The simplest river irrigation systems need only the digging of distribution channels and some way of controlling the amount of water diverted through each channel. Where the seasonal flow of water is variable, it is also necessary to have retention reservoirs. If a system discharges into the sea, it further requires downstream barrages to prevent salt water backing up into the channels at high tide. All types of system have to be emptied periodically, section by section, through the manipulation of sluice-gates or the building of temporary cross-dikes, so that the accumulated silt can be dredged.

River systems work on gravitational flow. This is also true of those in upland areas where the water has to be lifted a considerable distance to the fields,

Left The design of this simple plow pulled by oxen in the western hills near Beijing has not changed for centuries.

Below The traditional method of cormorant fishing can still be seen on the Li River in southern China. Cormorants attached to boats with ropes catch fish which they are prevented from swallowing by rings around their throats.

Bottom Members of a production team working together on a collective farm.

because the current of the main stream can be used to drive a noria, a huge wheel with canted pots mounted around its circumference. In contrast, polders, and other areas that need to be drained, have to rely on pumps. In traditional times these were mostly the so-called "dragon's bones pumps" – sloping troughs of a rectangular cross-section up which a continuous chain of linked wooden pallets was drawn by human pedaling, by beasts working a turntable or by wind-power. Much of the most impressive progress in modern Chinese farming has been based on replacing these old-fashioned methods with powered pumps, metal pipes and concrete irrigation channels. Here modernization is technically straightforward and more likely to be profitable.

Animals, fish, poultry and insects

Outer China was a world of herds. Meat, milk, fibers, hides and transportation were provided by a range of breeds and hybrids finely adapted to altitude, aridity and other local conditions. By contrast, in Inner China, large animals were kept singly or in small groups. Their chief contribution was power – for plowing, turning machinery and transportation. The "yellow cow" predominated in the north. The Yangzi valley and the far south were the domain of the water buffalo, which not only tolerated but enjoyed mud and wet conditions. Modest numbers of horses, donkeys and mules were used for transportation. Meat was provided by pigs and, in the south and along the Korean border, by pariah-type dogs.

Early in the modern period, crossing with breeds from other countries began to modify traditional Chinese types of livestock. Today many of the old strains have all but vanished in their pure forms. This swift change was the consequence of the same sensitivity to variation and flair for selection that had earlier produced the goldfish from the carp and bred the Pekinese dog to look like the spirit-lion of Buddha. The guess may be hazarded, however, that small herds and fragmented ownership made the systematic breeding of better cattle difficult in the villages of premodern China.

The low level of animal-power was a weak link in the traditional farm economy. How much access a peasant had to such power made a big difference to his productivity and prosperity. It was not just a question of plowing hard soils and clearing new land. Animal-power was essential to many rural industries, such as crushing sugarcane, if water-power was not available. In some areas there were "ox-lords" who hired out cattle in much the same way that a landlord rented out land. Wealth in the form of animals was, however, more precarious than wealth in the form of land. Diseases took a severe toll, partly because of the insanitary conditions in which most beasts were kept. The loss of draft animals could bankrupt a household or even ruin a village.

The old Chinese methods of raising pigs, sheep, poultry, fish and silkworms had in common the creation of a controlled artificial environment for at least a part of the life cycle. In a sense it was a premodern approach to factory farming. Obvious examples are the incubators used for ducks' and hens' eggs. They were earthen jars with double walls, heated by charcoal placed between them. The largest contained over a thousand eggs. Control of the varying temperatures required was a refined skill. Fish farming was another art, in specially prepared pools of different depths and with artificial islands. Most delicate of all was the raising of silkworms. It was done in a house where warmth, humidity and light had all to be controlled, using blinds, vents and braziers. The moths had to be selected and mated. They laid their eggs on heavy sheets of paper that were stored until winter. Then the weaker eggs were killed off by dipping them in brine or exposing them to the weather. When the larvae hatched they were kept in bamboo trays and fed constantly with mulberry leaves. The cocoons were spun on frames covered with straw cocks. Many of them were killed and preserved for later reeling; the rest were plunged into boiling water and reeled immediately before the new moths broke through and tore the silk. There were so many hazards, like disease, rats and a shortage of leaves, that production was surrounded by taboos and superstitions. Today, modern instruments (such as humidity gauges) and electricity have made environment control more precise, and mechanical reeling gives a more even consistency to the thread, but the basic operations are much the same as they have always been.

The peasant family

At the center of traditional Chinese farming was the peasant family. The crucial problem that faced its head was how best to make use of the labor force available to him. All of it had to be fed, whether or not it worked. Unlike the capitalist factory owner he could not lay off employees. If there was nothing better to do, it was still advantageous for the young and the old to work for less than the cost of their keep. It lessened the burden on the others. The wealth or poverty of a peasant household depended to a great extent on the relative numbers of able-bodied adults and of the elderly and very young who depended upon them; this ratio went through more or less regular cyclical changes. A substantial proportion of the farmland rented out to tenants must be seen as a mechanism by means of which families that were temporarily labor-rich and labor-poor reached a mutual adjustment, and made best use of their respective opportunities. For these and other reasons, peasant economics were (and remain) to some extent different from the economics of more developed societies. The economic logic of the commune embracing the entire community is close to that of the peasant family, and one of its functions in Chinese conditions from the late 1950s to the late 1970s may be seen as the sharing of poverty and underemployment.

There was also a variation in the need for manpower around the farming year. Feverish activity took place in May and June, when planting, transplanting, harvesting and silkworm raising were all going on at once. Counterbalancing this was a slack season from November to February. The other months contained an intermediate amount of work. Broadly speaking, the peasant family was caught between two constraints. There was often too little manpower for the key operations in the peak season, and there was too little farmwork for the labor force at other times. For this reason off-season handicrafts and by-employments were of the utmost importance for the economic viability of the old peasant economy.

In recent times, the growth of modern industries and transportation has undermined the profitability of many former by-employments. So has the over-controlled Communist economy with its restrictions on local markets and on unplanned access to materials. The result has been that, while the peasant family has often benefited from the increasing productivity of farming, its total earnings have risen at a much lower rate because of the loss of other forms of income. It is also not easy in a rural society where, at the level of the household, labor-power represents wealth and security in old age, to control the increase in the population. Until quite recently, the government did not take this problem seriously, and the increases in productivity achieved through using more artificial fertilizers, better seeds and the extension of irrigation, have been largely offset by the rising numbers that have had to be fed. Distribution is much fairer than it used to be before the Communist government took power, but until the 1980s the average peasant ate little if any better than he did in the early 1930s.

Food

China's food still exhibits regional varieties and peculiarities because there is neither refrigeration nor nationwide food manufacture. One major difference is that rice is the staple cereal in the south whereas wheat, maize and millet are the staple grains in the north and northeast. There are, however, more nationally known dishes identified with the far south than with any other region. Cantonese food is renowned for its variety and while most of its flavors are mild there are also robuster seasonings based on garlic, black beans, hot peppers and oyster sauce. The texture of dishes is prized, as with shark's fin, and some have such unusual ingredients as snakes. Food here is mostly stir-fried rapidly in oil at a very high temperature. Fujian cuisine is famous for delicately cooked fish and crabs, for soups and for flavorings such as the well-known soy sauce. In the lower Yangzi valley cooking times are longer, and much use is made of a red sauce in which soy is balanced with sugar and wine. Shanghai dishes are heavy with fat and oil.

In the west, Sichuan and Hunan dishes are dry and spicy and make liberal use of the hot chili pepper (a plant that arrived from Central America in the 16th century). The most sophisticated blend several flavors together: hot, fruity, sour and salty for example. Apart from imperial court cuisine in the past, northern food is fairly simple and straightforward, consisting mainly of stir-fried dishes, eaten with steamed rolls, and also noodles and pancakes.

Regional varieties of dishes also depend on whether the raw ingredients can easily be transported. Fruits are in some cases confined to the areas in which they are produced. In the northwest Uighur-style food is similar to that in Iran. Mongolian-style food consists of simple mutton dishes eaten with yoghurt and fermented mare's milk. Tibetan and Mongolian cooking includes much dairy produce, which many Han Chinese find unpalatable. In Tibet barley meal is mixed with a buttered tea for which rancid yak butter is commonly used.

Right This man is cooking noodles in the street in Shanghai. The majority of Chinese derive 85 per cent of their calories from grain and the rest from vegetables such as cabbage and soya beans. Fats and proteins are rare, and meat is only eaten on special occasions.

Far right, above The peasants' minuscule privately owned plots (never more than 5 per cent of the cultivated area) have produced far more proportionately than the collective fields, and have been an invaluable source of extra income for commune members and of fresh vegetables for city-dwellers.

Far right, center These stuffed dumplings are being prepared by expert hands for a special occasion. The dough is carefully folded in a plait-like manner, sealing spiced beef in the center. They are then boiled, and as many as 30 to 40 may be eaten by one person.

Right Wheat bread is the main staple of the northwest. Flat loaves are baked on the sides of ovens such as this one in Turfan. This bread does not differ in type or in method of baking from that made throughout central Asia, as far west as Iran and Egypt.

Far right A typical meal for an individual in this canteen would be several steamed dumplings or two large bowls of rice, stir-fried vegetables and a bowl of soup to finish with. Anything uneatable would be spat onto the floor or table. Brewing was introduced to China by the Germans in Shandong in the late 19th century. Beijing beer is light and thirst quenching.

Family Life

For most Chinese, throughout most of Chinese history, the family has been at the center of their social, psychological and ideological lives. Chinese men, at least, have felt themselves to be part of a male line of descent that stretched back from son to father without limit into the past, and which it was their duty to help continue into the future. It would only be a slight exaggeration to speak of a religious type of belief in the hope for "familial immortality."

In archaic times there was a strong conviction that the living and the dead were interdependent. The ancestors needed sacrificial offerings and their descendants needed the ancestors' protection and goodwill. Ancestors and the supreme religious power (*Di*, later *Di* or *Tian*) were once extremely close. Gradually this linkage weakened. God, or Heaven, became increasingly exalted and the ancestors became correspondingly less powerful. Their ability to interfere in the daily affairs and well-being of their descendants, so evident in the oracles concerning royal ancestors in Shang times, dwindled away over the millennia.

Chinese women were less deeply affected by the descent-line ideal, probably because they were transferred at marriage from their father's line to their husband's. They may often have felt a relatively greater concern for the immediate, if transient, family that they could create around themselves through their children. Nonetheless, devotion to the descent line went deep, as may be seen from the many widows who labored to bring up adopted heirs to husbands who had died sonless.

The conception of an individual personality face-to-face with the universe existed only at certain margins of Chinese society. The Daoist adept or macrobiotic alchemist pursued an individual physical immortality. The Buddhist monk forsook the family and its continuation in order to pursue enlightenment and the ultimate extinction of the self. But even the latter was often justified by Buddhist apologists in familial terms: the monk's accumulation of merits would help his deceased father and mother to better reincarnations.

Many of the most important Chinese virtues were defined with respect to family life. Above all there was *xiao*, the filial obedience owned by a man to his parents and by a wife to her parents-in-law. No one could have even a relatively independent social existence until his parents (or her parents-in-law) had died; and of course women remained subject to their husbands while the latter lived. Deeply felt filial piety could cause miracles, particularly those connected with regrowth, as of withered trees or even lost ears and teeth. It could deflect fires and natural disasters from the virtuous, or so it was popularly believed. The imperial state gave support to filial obedience: an angry father or widowed mother could demand to have a son executed (later on, merely banished) and the magistrate had to comply. There was no appeal. Crimes done by juniors in a family against their seniors were more

heavily punished than were comparable offenses against strangers. Conversely, outstanding practitioners of filial piety were given official recognition, and awards were presented to them so that they became admired models for social imitation.

For a married woman the great virtue was fidelity, even as a widow. It was not illegal to remarry after a husband's death. Indeed, it was the prevailing practice, because of economic pressures. But it was a morally inferior course of action. According to popular belief, a woman who had married into a particular family remained the ghost of that family after her death. Books on the punishments in the Buddhist hells sometimes showed the ghosts of widows who had remarried being sawn vertically in half by the demons, to provide a half for each ghost-husband. After the 11th century the cult of faithful widows grew and grew, giving rise to commemorative poems and inscriptions, hagiography and a vast system of imperial awards in the form of ceremonial arches and inscribed tablets and banners.

Another familial virtue was the cohabitation of all the branches of a family over many generations, with property being held in common and meals being taken together. Such huge households were termed "righteous," and before the Ming dynasty they also qualified for imperial awards. The largest of them were said to include many hundreds of people living in a disciplined, communal fashion. Of one such family legend had it that their virtue had affected even the dogs, all of whom ate together also, and would not start their meal if even one of their number were missing. The founder of the Ming stopped awards for multi-generation co-residence, not wanting to encourage the proliferation of large lineage-groups that were difficult to control. Many of them had their own armies of fellow-kinsmen, fought lineage wars, defied tax-gatherers and were virtually a law to themselves.

The Chinese system may be said to have been based on the subordination of later to earlier generations, of the younger to the older within generations, and of women to men. The intensity of

Above This detail from a Song dynasty painting in the academic court style of the 12th century, executed in ink and color on silk, depicts palace ladies bathing their children.

Right Since the Han dynasty successive Chinese legal codes have reinforced family loyalties, and the family has long been exalted by traditional Confucian ethics. This album painting depicts a family giving thanks before its family shrine. Note that the mother and her little girl do not take part in the proceedings but watch from behind a screen.

Right below A distinctive Chinese term described *every* relationship shown in the diagram, serving to define the appropriate interpersonal behavior required of those so related. Links through females of generations below ego's also had their specific terms. Thus the children of ego's daughter were called "outer grandson" and "outer granddaughter," but these are not shown here for the sake of clarity. Mourning was prescribed for a death within four steps, either vertical or horizontal or in a combination of both, from ego. Thus, vertically, ego had to mourn up to his great-great-grandfather (not shown). Spoken terms of address between two relatives were usually different from those given, varying with dialect, and somewhat simpler, the precise relationships being implicitly understood.

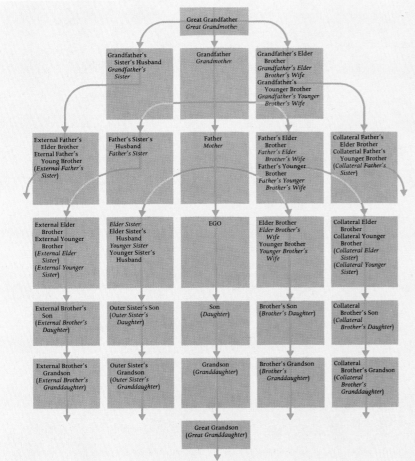

		Great Grandfather *Great Grandmother*		
	Grandfather's Sister's Husband *Grandfather's Sister*	Grandfather *Grandmother*	Grandfather's Elder Brother *Grandfather's Elder Brother's Wife* Grandfather's Younger Brother *Grandfather's Younger Brother's Wife*	
External Father's Elder Brother Eternal Father's Young Brother *(External Father's Sister)*	Father's Sister's Husband *Father's Sister*	Father *Mother*	Father's Elder Brother *Father's Elder Brother's Wife* Father's Younger Brother *Father's Younger Brother's Wife*	Collateral Father's Elder Brother Collaterial Father's Younger Brother *(Collateral Father's Sister)*
External Elder Brother External Younger Brother *(External Elder Sister)* *(External Younger Sister)*	Elder Sister *Elder Sister's Husband* *Younger Sister* *Younger Sister's Husband*	EGO	Elder Brother *Elder Brother's Wife* Younger Brother *Younger Brother's Wife*	Collateral Elder Brother Collateral Younger Brother *(Collateral Elder Sister)* *(Collateral Younger Sister)*
External Brother's Son *(External Brother's Daughter)*	Outer Sister's Son *(Outer Sister's Daughter)*	Son *(Daughter)*	Brother's Son *(Brother's Daughter)*	Collateral Brother's Son *(Collateral Brother's Daughter)*
External Brother's Grandson *(External Brother's Granddaughter)*	Outer Sister's Grandson *(Outer Sister's Granddaughter)*	Grandson *(Granddaughter)*	Brother's Grandson *(Brother's Granddaughter)*	Collateral Brother's Grandson *(Collateral Brother's Granddaughter)*
		Great Grandson *(Great Granddaughter)*		

the relationship, and the associated obligations, were carefully specified in terms of kinship proximity and distance. The basic structure (see figure) shows obligation as extending in graded fashion across four generations in all directions from the person concerned. Relationships were defined with a specificity quite unknown in Western Europe. It made a difference, given the Chinese system of authority and obedience, whether an uncle was (1) your father's brother or your mother's, and (2) whether he was your father's elder brother or his younger brother. To mark these sorts of distinctions, the traditional Chinese kinship nomenclature used 23 basic terms, plus a further 10 basic modifiers to handle variants within these 23.

Naturally, this system did not appear fully fledged at the start of Chinese history. There is some reason to suspect that in Shang times the main emphasis was on groups of brothers. The shift to a primary concern with the father-son relationship took a long time, and was probably only completed by the Eastern Zhou.

There was also competition at times with radically different non-Chinese conceptions. Among some of the "barbarian" dynasties that ruled China in the middle of the first millennium AD, it was quite acceptable to marry the widow of a deceased relative, even across generation lines. This was abhorrent to the Chinese because it destroyed the carefully articulated structure of relationships sketched above.

Generally speaking, "barbarian" women enjoyed more freedom than their Chinese sisters. It was only at times of strong "barbarian" influence, like the early Tang dynasty, that one finds Chinese ladies riding horses and following similarly liberated activities. The reasons for the spread of the horrible practice of female footbinding, from the Southern Song onwards, have yet to be satisfactorily established. It began among the court dancers, and spread through the social imitation of the aristocracy, eventually killing the art of dancing as feet were made progressively tinier. Was this custom, which reached all but the lowest classes and all but the southernmost parts of the country, felt to distinguish the modest Chinese woman from the shameless barbarian? Connoisseurs also alleged that it made sex more exciting by tightening the vagina. Whatever the reasons, it drastically reduced what women could do. In Song and early Yuan times, there were traveling women traders, and even women entrepreneurs like the Daoist nun Huang who pioneered the Lower Yangzi cotton industry. They had few counterparts in later dynasties.

The rise of powerful states in the Springs and Autumns period produced a rival focus of loyalty to the family. Confucius characteristically took the view that devotion to a parent should override devotion to a state, and that a son should shield a father who had committed a crime. The kingdom of Qin under Lord Shang in the middle of the 4th century BC made the only explicit effort to break the cohesiveness of the family in favor of the state. Second and later sons were made to live separately from their fathers once they had grown up, under threat of tax sanctions if they did not. Later ideologues of course regarded this as a typical Qin failure to understand the socially destabilizing effect of such measures. Dynasties from the Han onwards recognized the theoretical primacy of the family by obliging officials to retire for 27 months of mourning when their fathers died. To some extent they derived their right to rule from their role as guarantors of the social order, or, in other words, of the proper familial relationships.

In contrast, Chinese laws of inheritance weakened the family. It was obligatory throughout imperial times that male heirs shared the property more or less equally. This rapidly broke up large accumulations of wealth. To get round this, lineages often created collective property, looked after by managers, but the large and enduring estate in the hands of a sequence of single heirs did not exist.

Rites of passage

Boys were more highly valued than girls. To bring up a girl was to invest in labor-power that would eventually go elsewhere. It was "tilling another man's field," as the proverb had it. A proportion of girl babies were drowned by midwives at birth, and there was always a shortfall of women of marriageable age. Marriage among females was close to 100 per cent. Only the tiniest proportion remained unwed to care for aged parents or to enter a Daoist or Buddhist nunnery. In many parts of China mothers tried to cut down on the costs of a full-scale marriage, to guarantee a wife for their sons and perhaps to ensure more docile daughters-in-law, by taking in and rearing child fiancées, sometimes at a very early age. Sometimes the scarcity of brides enabled a mother who had a daughter but no son to induce a young man to agree to reside at her house as her son-in-law, and to contribute his labor-power to her household.

Females married young. Excluding childbetrothals, where information about the subsequent cursory marriage rites is largely lacking, the average age was not much above 17 and clustered closely around this mean. The age at marriage for men was far more variable, and depended on economic circumstances. Polygamy was practiced by the wealthier classes, and secondary wives and concubines were subordinated to the orders of the principal wife.

Boys and girls were brought up somewhat differently. Up to the age of six, a boy was largely looked after by his mother and female relatives. He was indulged. The excuse for this would be that "he does not understand things yet." Around the age of seven, he would be transferred to the male authority of school and his father, strict discipline being imposed. He would often be rather resentful for the next few years, until he had learned to accept his fate. A certain duality in the Chinese character may perhaps be associated with this upbringing: Daoist dreams of infantile omnipotence and making nature into a sort of benevolent mother on the one hand, and Confucian dutifulness and a strong sense of the need to improve oneself on the other. Young girls were less indulged, and the major shock in their lives came later – at marriage. Marriages were normally arranged by parents, and seen as alliances between families rather than between individuals. Significantly, neither state nor church (in the form of Buddhism or Daoism) played any part in these rites. It was also unusual for a bride to have seen her husband-to-be or her parents-in-law before the day of the wedding ceremony.

Brothers and their wives habitually quarreled. This was the main reason why most Chinese families split up and shared out the estate after the parents had died. Although the extended family remained the ideal, it was rarely long-lived and formed the exception rather than the rule.

Funerals in China were costly, spectacular and noisy affairs, designed in part to assert the social standing of the family of the deceased. Mourners wore types and sometimes colors of dress that symbolized their particular relationship with the dead man. The funeral was thus in part also an occasion for redefining these relationships. This could sometimes be contentious. A mourner who wore a son's mourning, for example, was thereby laying claim to a share of the estate.

In south China burial took place twice: once provisionally and once permanently. Belief in the pseudo-science of geomancy led people to believe that the siting of a forebear's permanent grave had a direct effect on a person's fortunes. Sites allegedly had different effects on different descendants, and so brothers sometimes quarreled over the place to choose.

In contrast to the divisive aspects of this manipulation of the bones of the dead, ancestor-worship stressed what the members of a kin-group had in common. In the home offerings were made to the wooden "soul-tablet" of the deceased for four generations back. At least once a year, in the springtime, the family made a visit to the ancestral graves. More formal worship of the more important members of the ascent line took place in the lineage halls and was performed by males.

All important lineages had genealogical tables in which the recognized lines of descent were listed. If a member behaved in a way thought improper, he

Above The family unit remains strong in China. Families live together and when the parents of a child are away the grandparents naturally act as babysitters.

Left From the Southern Song dynasty onwards the practice of increasingly severe footbinding confined women to the home and its immediate neighborhood by strictly limiting their movements. It was first attacked by the wives of Protestant missionaries and has been abolished. This photograph shows one of the few examples of the custom surviving today.

this being to concentrate the soldiers' minds on victory. Taiping moralistic literature, however, continued to stress the correctness of most traditional familial relationships and the virtues of obedience and chastity in women. There were also some cruel ambiguities. Coming from the far south, the Taipings had no sympathy for those with bound feet, and they set the semi-crippled Yangzi valley women whom they captured at hard labor, under the supervision of their own women, in what amounted to female concentration camps. The rebel leader, Hong Xiuquan, set a bad example with his large harem and addiction to the pleasures of the bed.

In the later 19th century, the Protestant missionaries started movements to abolish bound feet and to give girls a school education. Both caught on quickly among the Chinese themselves. About the same time an unrestrained theoretical attack on the family as an institution was launched by two of China's most radical thinkers. In his *Study of Altruism*, Tan Sitong demanded its complete abolition in the cause of personal liberty and equality among individuals, though he also demanded the fusing of these individual consciousnesses in a total social unity. Kang Youwei's Utopia described in his *The Great Uniformity* featured short-term cohabitation contracts, and the creation of specialized institutions for rearing children and looking after the old. He wished to put devotion and gratitude to the state for its care in the place of filial piety. The only practical efforts to root out family consciousness were made by some of the anarchists, who refused to use surnames.

Since coming to power, the Chinese Communist Party has made efforts to weaken family and kin loyalties. Extravagant weddings and funerals have been forbidden and geomantic burials prohibited, though in none of these cases with total success. At a more extreme level, children have been forced to denounce parents accused of counterrevolutionary crimes. The evidence suggests that family bonds are still extremely strong, though school indoctrination of children has obliged parents to be wary of what they say or do in their presence.

In recent times the Chinese family has moved in contrasting directions. In the countryside of the People's Republic, most of the housing is still in private hands. This confers substantial power on the older generation, as a properly functioning household economy is essential for a tolerable life. The choice of marriage partners still lies mainly with the parents, but the young people have a right of veto. The relationship between mother-in-law and daughter-in-law has subtly changed: the daughter-in-law needs the grandmother to look after her small children if she is to go out and work in the collective economy. Conversely, her greater earning power now gives her an enhanced status relative to the old lady, in comparison with earlier times. Having children brought up by their grandparents is a way, ironically, of filling them with old-fashioned values.

In the urban economy, married couples do not usually live with or near the man's parents, but pay jointly for their own accommodation. Choice of partners tends to be initiated by the young themselves, but is subject to a degree of veto by the parents and cadres in the units in which they work. There is little economic interdependence between

Top This model family eats under the watchful eye of Mao who is flanked by peasant paintings depicting an idealized world of smiling faces and loaded with political content. This photograph predates the campaign for one-child families.

Above This drawing after a woodblock print illustrates a lucky charm promising five male children – healthy, rich and attaining highest honors. In China today families still prefer to have male children. In the rural areas, despite the birth-control campaign, if the first born is a girl, the family will often try for a second child.

could be expelled from the lineage, and his name would be erased from the record.

The status of women and the modern family

A handful of writers in late imperial times pleaded the cause of women as being intellectually and creatively the equals of men. Cao Xueqin, the author of *The Story of the Stone*, is perhaps the most famous. The satirist Li Ruzhen wrote a novel *Flowers in the Mirror* showing an imaginary society in which the conventional sex roles were reversed. There were also scattered literary and social traditions on which the later liberation movements may have drawn, such as the transvestite female knight errant of heroic fiction, and the south China societies of girls who banded together to avoid marriage.

The first attempt to raise the status of women in modern times was made by the Taiping rebels in the 1850s. With their partly Christian ideology they took the view that men and women were of equal value as sons and daughters of God, but their Confucian heritage made them obsessed with lewdness and sexual impropriety as among the most serious sins. They forbade footbinding and prostitution, and gave women much more freedom to move about in public. Their regulations provided in principle for equal rights to land for women and men. There was even a Taiping army composed entirely of female troops. During the early part of their movement, they separated the sexes and temporarily put an end to family life, one purpose of the generations. The children are looked after in collective nurseries. This produces a type of character that places great emotional reliance on the peer-group (rather than elders), and is thus different from that of the rural child. The regimentation in the nursery schools is reported to be awesome, with naps and toilet-training all being taken together at particular times.

There has been growing state pressure over the last decade to limit the number of children. This has culminated in the policy of the one-child family, with reductions in welfare benefits and other sanctions for those who disobey. Women who work in factories are sometimes even assigned the year in which they may have their permitted child. Clearly, if this policy is successful, it will undermine what remains of the male descent-line mystique, since in any generation half the families will have no male heir.

Among overseas Chinese and the Taiwanese, the old family values remain strong, though they have been modified by a belief in the value of female education and careers for women. The impact of modern economic life has not always been to break up traditional kinship links. In a number of cases, the kin network has proved a valuable asset for its members, generating contacts, knowhow, credit and social and economic support. In a few cases the network has even grown stronger as a result.

Domestic architecture

The homes of rich Chinese families, in both city and country, were arranged on a pattern similar to those of the Imperial Palace and temples of the palace style. The number of courtyards decreased with rank and wealth. Within an enclosed space a main building facing south stood to the north of a central north–south axis. Here the head of the family lived. Side-buildings and smaller halls were inhabited by relatives. Servants lived along the southern wall near the entrance. Inside the entrance there was a "spirit wall" to ensure privacy. Today such screens still block the views into courtyards from the lanes of Beijing but large courtyard homes are now lived in by several families or have been turned into public institutions.

The traditional Chinese homes of the less wealthy consist of a single courtyard with one main building positioned to the north. Side-buildings are sometimes used for workshops. The courtyard homes of Beijing and Xi'an as seen today from multi-story buildings are mostly of this type.

Less traditional architecture and that of the ethnic minority groups varies from region to region. In the south, houses of mud walls with thatched or tiled roofs are built in clusters. Houses with white-washed walls and decorated gable ends are built in the mountainous areas of Anhui, while homes are dug into the sandy cliff faces of the loess areas in Shanxi Province. In Tibet houses are built of mud and are whitewashed or painted ocher. In rural areas a flat wooden roof stores hay and fodder for animals and acts as a thatch while the animals are housed on the ground floor, providing warmth for the the occupants who live above. In Mongolia and Xinjiang nomadic herdsmen set up circular tents of stretched skin on collapsible lattice frames, which are lined inside with rugs and felt.

Above A village inhabited by members of the Yi ethnic group near Kunming in Yunnan province.

Right A typical street scene in Guangzhou.

Far right The occupants of this thatched-roof farm dwelling on the outskirts of Kunming in Yunnan have a well-tended private plot.

Below Houses are hewn out of the soft loess soil in Shanxi province.

Below right Flags outside this Tibetan home indicate that part of the house is a shrine. Like many other houses in Tibet it is repainted every year for the Tibetan New Year festival. No nails are used in the wooden roof structure: all joins are dovetailed.

Below center A nomadic herdsman puts the finishing touches to his tent in the Tianshan (Mountains of Heaven) in northwest China.

China and the West

The Chinese traditionally regarded themselves as being at the center of the civilized world. Down to Tang and Song times, however, they remained comparatively open to foreignness and foreign influences, absorbing for example from central Asia both Buddhism and much of what we now think of as characteristically "Chinese" music. It seems to have been the severe shock of the Mongol occupation in the 13th and 14th centuries that produced an element of xenophobia in the Chinese, and led to the closing of the frontiers by the first Ming emperor.

Early contacts with Europeans were mostly with traders (such as the Portuguese, who established themselves at Macao in the 16th century) and with missionaries (above all, the Jesuits, who found a measure of acceptance at Beijing during the 17th and 18th centuries). Mutual attitudes were complex, but by and large Europe at this time was more favorably impressed by China (as a result of the Jesuits' reports) and more influenced by her than the other way round. Two waves of chinoiserie also had a considerable impact on Western art. Outside the Qing court, where the Jesuit painter Castiglione (Lang Shining) exerted some transient influence in the 18th century, there was no comparable reverse artistic flow affecting China.

During the later 18th century and the first half of the 19th mutual incomprehension and hostility grew markedly worse. In part, no doubt, this was because the gap in knowledge and power between China and a swiftly modernizing Europe had grown much wider. Chinese dislike of the West was heightened by the so-called "Opium Wars" that forcibly opened the empire to a freer foreign trade, and by later military humiliations. Christian missionary activity proved a severe cultural irritant at first, though its contribution to Chinese education was eventually to prove substantial and beneficial.

Chinese intellectual and cultural assimilation of the West during the present century has been extremely selective, concentrating almost entirely on the most recent times and showing no interest in the Western Middle Ages and only the most marginal interest in Western antiquity. It has also been punctuated by periods of almost allergic rejection, of which the "Cultural Revolution," with its attacks on Beethoven and Shakespeare, was the most extreme.

Right above The most elaborate and ambitious of the chinoiserie decorations in the Brighton Pavilion, built between 1815 and 1821, were designed by John Nash. Wallpaper and works of art were imported from China. The Pavilion's Indian exterior and Chinese interior do not clash too violently as both were in a sense Western conceptions of the "Orient" as a whole. The chair on the left is made of bamboo and the cabinet on the right is English and made in solid wood carved to simulate bamboo.

Right This engraving illustrates the fountains and garden of the imperial Summer Palace outside Beijing, built to designs by Castiglione. The baroque-style palace and its gardens were destroyed by French and British forces in 1860.

Below left The Chinese figures over Twinings tea shop in the Strand in London date from 1787, long before the theft of Chinese tea plants by Robert Fortune in the 1830s and their cultivation in Calcutta's Botanical Gardens led to the development of a tea industry in India and Ceylon. Hence there is no Indian

figure in the group.

Below right The *Mahonia bealii* depicted in the *Botanical Magazine* in 1855, one of many Chinese plant species brought to the West by missionaries and travelers in the mid-19th century.

Center left This Chinese porcelain figure was made in Benjamin Lund's factory in Bristol in 1750.
Center right European designs of Bristol porcelain were copied in the late Qing dynasty with meticulous precision by Chinese artists in China specifically for the Western export market.

Right Maria Nemeth, dressed for the title role in Puccini's "Chinese" opera *Turandot*, wears a completely Western version of Chinese court robes.

Below The Pekingese, a Chinese toy dog, was the specially bred, exclusive pet of the Chinese imperial family for many centuries. It was introduced to the West by the British after their forces invaded the Forbidden City in Beijing in 1860. It is now popular in the West, but extinct in China.

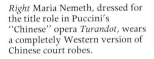

Above The Chinese community in Sydney celebrates the Chinese New Year with a lively dragon dance.

Right A telephone in New York's Chinatown is painted in traditional colors, with red pillars supporting a green Chinese-style roof.

LIST OF ILLUSTRATIONS

BIBLIOGRAPHY

Many of the books with the subtlest insights and the most detailed information on Chinese culture and history are forbiddingly technical to the non-sinologist. A large proportion of the remainder are somewhat out-of-date, or superficial, or in some respect misleading. It has proved impossible not to include some fairly technical items in the selection of titles recommended below for further study but, so far as possible, they have been restricted to those intellectually accessible to the non-specialist, reasonably reliable, and interesting in their own right, not just as quarries for facts.

General Introductions

The best one-volume survey of Chinese history is J. Gernet, *A History of Chinese Civilization* (Cambridge 1982). Possible alternatives are W. Eberhard, *History of China* (rev. ed., London 1977), R. Dawson, *Imperial China* (London 1972), and C. Hucker, *China's Imperial Past* (London 1975). A pithy and attractive introduction to Chinese culture is R. Dawson, ed., *The Legacy of China* (Oxford 1964). M. Elvin, *The Pattern of the Chinese Past* (Stanford, Calif., 1972), is an outline of China's long-term social and economic development. A. Toynbee, ed., *Half the World: the History and Culture of China and Japan* (London 1973), has splendid pictures and a remarkable condensed history of Chinese society by Denis Twitchett. The most compact survey of kinship institutions is H. Baker, *Chinese Family and Kinship* (London 1979). There is no comparable work for class and status structure, but P. T. Ho, *The Ladder of Success in Imperial China: Aspects of Social Mobility, 1368–1911* (New York 1962), is a good introduction to the mandarinate, one of late-traditional China's most distinctive features.

L. Sickmann and A. Soper, *The Art and Architecture of China* (Harmondsworth 1956), and M. Sullivan, *An Introduction to Chinese Art* (Berkeley, Calif., 1961), afford the easiest entry to the arts. W. Willetts, *Chinese Art* (Harmondsworth 1958), is an alternative for those particularly interested in techniques.

There is no satisfactory single-volume introduction to the history of Chinese ideas. If the reader looks at the following sequence of short works, however, he will gain a good notion of the highlights: A Waley, *Three Ways of Thought in Ancient China* (London 1939), H. Wilhelm, *Change* (London 1960), F. Cook, *Hua-yen Buddhism* (Philadelphia, Pa., 1977), A. Graham, *Two Chinese Philosophers* (London 1958), and K. Schipper, *Le Corps taoiste* (Paris 1982). On religion see H. Maspero, *Taoism and Chinese Religion* (Amherst, Mass., 1981).

The vast and much-studied field of Chinese imaginative literature is – surprisingly – in a similar plight, made worse by a scarcity of translations that (to speak honestly) have an appeal in their own right for the non-specialist. For someone who is unfamiliar with the Chinese tradition I would recommend bypassing secondary works at first and beginning with A. Waley, *Chinese Poems* (London 1946), D. Hawkes and J. Minford, trans., *Cao Xueqin, The Story of the Stone*, 5 vols. (Harmondsworth 1973–83), P. Ryckmans, trans., *Shen Fu, Six Recits au fil inconstant des jours* (Bruxelles 1966), and id., trans., *Lu Xun, La Mauvaise Herbe* (Paris 1970). Waley's rendering of Wu Ch'eng-en, *Monkey* (Harmondsworth 1942), is a free adaptation of this serio-comic masterpiece but – rightly – a perennial favorite. Among secondary works, Lu Hsun (Chou Shu-jen), *A Brief History of Chinese Fiction*, trans. H. and G. Yang (Peking 1959), deserves mention as a record of the judgments of 20th-century China's foremost man of letters, as does P. Hanan's *The Chinese Vernacular Story* (Cambridge, Mass. 1982) as possibly the best work of Western scholarship on the subject. J. J. Y. Liu, *The Art of Chinese Poetry* (London 1962), is a little dry, but instructive. C. Gardner, *Chinese Traditional Historiography* (rev. ed., Cambridge, Mass. 1961), is brief, clear and tough going. It should be supplemented by W. Beasley and E. Pulleyblank, eds., *Historians of China and Japan* (London 1961).

Finally, two multi-volume works should be mentioned, both in the course of publication. J. Needham *et al., Science and Civilisation in China* (Cambridge 1954–), and D. Twitchett and J. Fairbank, eds., *The Cambridge History of China* (Cambridge 1978–). Consulting the appropriate volume or section will often be the best way to approach a new subject of interest.

The Land and its Peoples

G. Cressey, *China, The Land of the 500 Million* (New York 1955), is in some respects an aging textbook, but still uniquely lucid and useful. For the first half of the 20th century the British Naval Intelligence Division, *China Proper*, 3 vols. (1945, now derestricted), is invaluable. For the present day, there is no comparable update. Nagel's encyclopedia-guide *China* (Geneva 1973) is the best (almost) contemporary guide, and an astonishing compendium of information, including street plans for many cities. The two densely detailed volumes of the USSR Academy of Science's Institute of Geography, *Physical Geography of China* (New York 1969), based on extensive fieldwork, but unaccompanied by original maps and difficult to read, are nonetheless comprehensive in their coverage of many aspects not usually treated at length in ordinary geographical accounts.

For a historical perspective on the changing nature of life see the three volumes: M. Loewe, *Everyday Life in Early Imperial China* (London 1968); J. Gernet, *Daily Life in China on the Eve of the Mongol Invasion* (London 1962); and A. Watson, *Everyday Life in Communist China* (London 1975). For still greater detail, one possible approach is to read the reports made by foreign travelers in China at various times. Examples are E. Reischauer, *Ennin's Travels in Tang China* (New York 1955), R. Latham, *The Travels of Marco Polo* (Harmondsworth 1958), C. R. Boxer, ed., *South China in the Sixteenth Century* [narratives of Pereira, da Cruz, and de Rada] (London 1953); the 14 volumes of reports from the Jesuits entitled *Mémoires concernant les chinois* (Paris 1776–1814); R. Fortune, *Three Years Wandering in the Northern Provinces of China, including a visit to the tea, silk and cotton countries . . .* (London 1847) and other writings; E. Huc, *A Journey through the Chinese Empire* (New York 1955; reprinted 1971), and 20th-century travelers like O. Lattimore, author of *High Tartary* (Boston, Mass. 1930), *Pivot of Asia* (Boston, Mass. 1950), *The Desert Road to Turkestan* (Boston, Mass., 1929), *Manchuria, Cradle of Conflict* (New York 1932) and others. The descriptive value of R. van Gulik's Judge Dee murder mysteries, such as *The Chinese Maze Murders* (New York 1978), should not be overlooked just because they are fiction. Van Gulik was a master sinologue and his details are fastidiously accurate.

On China's cities see P. Wheatley, *The Pivot of the Four Quarters* (Edinburgh 1971), for the earliest period, and M. Elvin, "Chinese Cities since the Sung," in P. Abrams and E. Wrigley, eds., *Towns in Societies* (Cambridge 1978). For greater detail see the 3-volume series published by Stanford UP: G. W. Skinner, ed., *The City in Late Imperial China* (1978), M. Elvin and G. Skinner, eds., *The Chinese City between Two Worlds* (1974), and J. W. Lewis, ed. *The City in Communist China* (1972). R. Murphey, *The Outsiders* (Ann Arbor, Mich., 1977), is a superb study of the treaty ports in comparative perspective.

On population see H. Bielenstein, "The Census of China during the Period AD 2–742," *Bulletin of the Museum of Far Eastern Antiquities*, 19 (1957), P. T. Ho, "An Estimate of the Population of Sung-Chin China," *Etudes Song* 1 (1970), and id., *Studies on the Population of China, 1368–1953* (Cambridge, Mass., 1959). The problematic nature of the figures for the period around 1600 is demonstrated by S. Y. Yim, "Famine Relief Statistics as a Guide to the Population of 16th-century China," in *Ch'ing-shih wen-t'i*, 3 (1978).

On Han Chinese colonialism see H. Wiens, *China's March towards the Tropics* (Hamden, Conn., 1954), O. Lattimore, *Inner Asian Frontiers of China* (New York 1951), J. Davidson, *The Island of Formosa, Past and Present* (New York 1903), and C. Lombard-Salmon, *Un Example d'acculturation chinoise: la province de Guizhou* (Paris 1972). On more recent times, see A. Whiting, *Sinkiang, Pawn or Pivot?* (East Lansing, Mich., 1958), and G. Moseley, *The Consolidation of the South China Frontier* (Berkeley, Calif., 1973).

On China's overseas trade see G. W. Wang, "The Nanhai Trade," *Journal of the Malayan Branch of the Royal Asiatic Society*, 21 (1958), J. Kuwabara, "On P'u Shou-keng, a Man of the Western Regions," *Memoirs of the Research Department of the Toyo Bunko*, 2 (1928) and 7 (1935), J. Mills, *Ying-yai sheng-lan. Overall Survey of the Ocean's Shores* (Cambridge 1970), and W. Schurz, *The Manila Galleon* (New York 1939). The classic introduction to Chinese migrant communities is V. Purcell, *The Chinese in Southeast Asia* (London 1951). There are now many specialized monographs, of which G. W. Skinner, *Leadership and Power in the Chinese Community of Thailand* (Ithaca, N.Y., 1958), is one of the most interesting.

The Foundation of a Culture

Two short and readable introductions are W. Watson, *China before the Han Dynasty* (London 1961), and C. Li, *The Beginnings of Chinese Civilization* (Seattle, Wash., 1957). More detailed works are K. C. Chang, *The Archaeology of Ancient China* (rev. ed., New Haven, Conn., 1968), and T. K. Cheng, *Archaeology in China*, 3 vols. (Cambridge): 1. *Prehistoric China* (1959), 2. *Shang China* (1960), and 3. *Chou China* (1963). C. Li, *Anyang* (Seattle, Wash., 1977), is a beautifully illustrated account of the birth of archaeology in China. M. Loehr, *Chinese Bronze Age Weapons* (Ann Arbor, Mich., 1956), is of fundamental importance for the study of the new military technology on which early Chinese civilization was based.

For the story from historical sources, H. Maspero, *China in Antiquity* (original ed. in French, 1927); English trans. Amherst, Mass., 1978), though seriously dated in some respects, remains classic. For those with patience and perseverance *The Chronicle of Zuo (or Tso-chuan)* presents a fascinating tapestry of the Springs and Autumns period. There are translations by J. Legge, *The Chinese Classics*, Vol. 5, part 2: *The Ch'un ts'ew with the Tso chuen* (London 1872), and S. Couvreur, *La Chronique de la principauté de Lou, Tch'ouen-ts'iou et Tso-tchouan* (Ho-kien-fou 1914; reprinted Paris 1951). J. Crump, trans., *Chan-kuo-ts'e* (Oxford 1970), is a much more readable compilation of rhetorical anecdotes from the Warring States period. S. B. Griffith, trans., *Sun tzu. The Art of War* (Oxford 1963), is an excellent translation of the most famous of ancient Chinese military treatises.

Neolithic Art

For a general survey see J. Rawson, *Ancient China, Art and Archaeology* (London 1980). Basic technology is discussed in M. Medley, *The Chinese Potter* (Oxford 1976), and a general account is given by M. Sullivan, *The Arts of China* (rev. ed., Berkeley, Calif., 1978). For a more detailed study see T. K. Cheng, *Archaeology in China*, Vol. 1: *Prehistoric China*, and K. C. Chang, *The Archaeology of Ancient China*.

Kinship and Kingship

K. C. Chang, *Shang Civilization* (New Haven, Conn., 1980), is the best point of departure for considering the complex problems of reconstructing the oldest level of Chinese historical society. There is, as yet, no good summary of Japanese scholarship in this field, much of which takes a rather different approach from that of Professor Chang. A useful little addition to the literature is L. Chao, *The Socio-Political Systems of the Shang Dynasty* (Taipei 1982).

On the Zhou period the classic work is H. G. Creel, *The Origins of Statecraft in China*, Vol. 1 (Chicago, Ill., 1970). A massive and technically exacting work of basic importance is L. Vandermeersch, *Wangdao ou la voie royale*, 2 vols. (Paris 1977–80). A basic source for both kinship and kingship is B. Karlgren, trans., *The Book of Odes* (Stockholm 1950), a painstakingly literal translation of the *Scripture of Poetry*.

Bronze Age Art

Excellent illustrations in color can be seen in W. Fong, ed., *The Great Bronze Age of China* (New York 1980). Bronzes from the British Museum are illustrated in a general discussion of the subject in J. Rawson, *Ancient China, Art and Archaeology*. For style see W. Watson, *Ancient Chinese Bronzes* (London 1962), *Style in the Arts of China* (Harmondsworth 1974) and *Art of Dynastic China* (London 1981). For weapons see M. Loehr, *Chinese Bronze Age Weapons*, and W. Watson, *Cultural Frontiers in Ancient East Asia* (Edinburgh 1971). The latter is interesting on China and the nomad heritage. For a detailed study of the excavation of a Shang dynasty site see C. Li, *Anyang*. For jades see T. Lawton, *Chinese Art of the Warring States Period, Change and Continuity, 480–222 B.C.* (Washington, D.C., 1982). For a detailed study of lacquer see Sir H. Garner, *Chinese Lacquer* (London 1979).

The Empire of Qin

A. Cotterell, *The First Emperor of China* (London 1981), is slightly light-weight but lucidly written and elegantly illustrated. Two older works that use a biographical approach are D. Bodde, *China's First Unifier* (Leiden 1938) on Li Si, and id., *Statesman, Patriot, and General in Ancient China* (New Haven, Conn., 1940) on three less important figures.

The Underground Army
Good illustrations in color of the life-sized terracotta army can be seen in W. Fong, ed., *The Great Bronze Age of China* (New York 1980), and in H. Qian, H. Chen and S. Ru, *Out of China's Earth* (London 1981). A more detailed account of the art of the Qin dynasty is given by A. Cotterell, *The First Emperor of China*.

Politics and Power
Books on Chinese politics and political culture differ greatly in the degree of technical expertise they presuppose of the reader. What follows is a list in approximately chronological order of periods covered. H. Bielenstein, *The Bureaucracy of Han Times* (Cambridge 1980), is precise and technical, almost to the point of being a work of reference. M. Loewe, *Crisis and Conflict in Han China* (London 1974), is in contrast an anthology of occasional pieces that give an excellent sense of politics under the Former Han. Y. S. Yü, *Trade and Expansion in Han China* (Berkeley, Calif., 1967), describes foreign relations. For the period of internal fragmentation some of the essays in E. Balazs, *Chinese Civilization and Bureaucracy* (New Haven, Conn., 1964), and in E. T. Z. Sun and J. de Francis, trans., *Chinese Social History* (Washington, D.C., 1956), are illuminating, especially about the growth of large estates. P. Ebrey, *The Aristocratic Families of Early Imperial China* (Cambridge 1978), is a detailed study of one great lineage across a millennium. W. Eberhard, *Das Toba-reich Nord Chinas* (Leiden 1949), is a classic account of a barbarian dynasty that had a major formative effect on later Chinese institutions. For a fascinating picture of politics and literary life under a southern dynasty, read J. Marney, *Liang Chien-Wen ti* (Boston, Mass., 1976). A. Wright, *The Sui Dynasty* (New York 1978), is a clearly written, many-faceted introduction to the architects of imperial reunification. On the first half of the Tang there is still nothing to equal E. Pulleyblank, *The Background to the Rebellion of An Lushan* (London 1955). Valuable detail may be gained from D. Twitchett, *Financial Administration under the Tang* (Cambridge 1963), and the specialized essays in A. Wright and D. Twitchett, eds., *Perspectives on the Tang* (New Haven, Conn., 1973), and in J. Perry and B. Smith, eds., *Essays on Tang Society* (Leiden 1976). On the period of renewed fragmentation following the Tang, G. W. Wang, *The Structure of Power in North China during the Five Dynasties* (Kuala Lumpur 1963), offers a dry·scholarly analysis of the north, while E. Schafer, *The Empire of Min* (Rutland, Vt., 1954), gives a characteristically rich and recherché account of one of the southern kingdoms. An interesting, if controversial, survey of the whole first millennium is W. Eberhard, *Conquerors and Rulers. Social Forces in Medieval China* (rev. ed., Leiden 1965).

For the Song, E. Kracke, *Civil Service in Early Sung China* (Cambridge, Mass., 1953), remains the basic reference on the origins of the examination-based mandarinate. On local-level organization B. McKnight, *Village and Bureaucracy in Southern Sung China* (Chicago, Ill., 1971), shows that changes took place here at this time of almost equal importance. Of the many books on Wang Anshi there is much to be said for the shortest, J. Meskill, ed., *Wang Anshih, Practical Reformer* (Boston, Mass., 1963). On the Song's northern neighbors see K. Wittfogel and C. S. Feng, *History of Chinese Society: Liao* (Philadelphia, Pa., 1949), and J. S. Tao, *The Jurchen in Twelfth-Century China* (Seattle, Wash., 1976). The most incisive account of the Mongol polity in China is J. Dardess, *Conquerors and Confucians* (New York 1973). A charming sketch of the Mongol–Ming transition which touches at countless points on politics and the nature of official life is F. Mote, *The Poet Kao Ch'i* (Princeton, N.J., 1962). C. Hucker, *The Traditional Chinese State in Ming Times* (Tuscon, Ariz., 1961), is a celebrated tour de force of compact exposition. For more detail turn to C. Hucker, ed., *Chinese Government in Ming Times* (New York 1969). R. Huang, *Taxation and Governmental Finance in Sixteenth-Century Ming China* (Cambridge 1974), is unnecessarily tangled but full of useful ideas and information. His *1587, A Year of No Significance: The Ming Dynasty in Decline* (New Haven, Conn., 1981) is however a nice notion – the biography of a year, focused on politics – and elegantly carried out. On the Qing the outstanding work is beyond doubt T. Metzger, *The Internal Organization of the Ch'ing Bureaucracy* (Cambridge, Mass., 1973), which illuminates the professional, ideological and emotional life of the late-imperial official like no other book I know of. Of the several useful studies of local government and the scholar-gentry, T. T. Ch'ü, *Local Government in China under the Ch'ing* (Cambridge, Mass., 1962), is probably the best. There is also much of value in J. Watt, *The District*

Magistrate in Late Imperial China (New York 1972), and C. L. Chang's pioneering *The Chinese Gentry: Studies on their Role in Nineteenth-Century Chinese Society* (Seattle, Wash., 1955). On law see T. T. Ch'ü, *Law and Society in Traditional China* (Paris 1961), and D. Bodde and E. Morris, *Law in Imperial China* (Cambridge, Mass., 1967). For instructive relaxation, the life of the Kangxi emperor, J. Spence, *Emperor of China* (London 1974), is not to be missed, though the author's handling of the sources has attracted some criticism.

Finally mention should be made of F. Kierman and J. Fairbank, eds., *Chinese Ways in Warfare* (Cambridge, Mass., 1974), which spans the entire period covered by this section.

Grand Canals
A. Hoshi, trans. M. Elvin, *The Ming Tribute Grain System* (Ann Arbor, Mich., 1969).

Art of the Imperial Age
An accessible and general account is given by M. Tregear, *Chinese Art* (London 1980), and by M. Sullivan, *The Arts of China*. For a more lavishly illustrated general survey see W. Watson, *Art of Dynastic China*. This book has a useful architectural section at the back and part two consists of the image as document in a series of black-and-white photographs. B. Smith and W. G. Weng, *China, A History in Art* (La Jolla, Calif., 1979), provides a very good visual account of the art of the imperial age. For mural painting see *Murals from the Han to the Tang Dynasty* (Peking 1974) and P. Pelliot, *Les Grottes de Touen-Houang*, 6 vols. (Paris and Brussels 1925). For sculpture see O. Siren, *Sculpture from the Fifth to the Fourteenth Centuries*, 4 vols. (London 1925). For ceramics see the general account by M. Medley, *The Chinese Potter*, and M. Sato, *Chinese Ceramics* (New York and Tokyo 1978). For more detailed studies see M. Medley, *T'ang Pottery and Porcelain* (London 1981), *Yuan Porcelain and Stoneware* (London 1981), and Sir H. Garner *Oriental Blue and White* (London 1954). The most easily accessible and concise account of painting is J. Cahill, *Chinese Painting* (Geneva 1960; New York 1972). His more detailed studies include *Hills beyond a River* (New York and Tokyo 1976), which deals with Chinese painting of the Yuan dynasty, 1279–1368. For a specialized study of Yuan dynasty art see S. E. Lee and W. K. Ho, *Chinese Art under the Mongols: The Yuan Dynasty (1279–1368)* (Cleveland, Ohio, 1968).

The Evolution of Society
Much of the material relevant to this section has already been covered in the works listed under "Politics and Power" above. The distinctive themes treated here are (1) technology, (2) economic relationships and institutions, (3) class and status stratification and (4) kinship relationships and systems, together with the patterns and ideas pertaining to all four of these.

M. Granet, *Chinese Civilization* (London 1930), is based on antiquated scholarship but remains alive with suggestive insights. Another old book still of value is K. Wittfogel, *Wirtschaft and Gesellschaft Chinas* (Leipzig 1931), which is much better than the same author's later *Oriental Despotism* (New Haven, Conn., 1957) with its own overemphasis on hydraulics. For a more objective account of the place of water control in Chinese society see C. T. Chao, *Key Economic Areas in Chinese History as Revealed in the Development of Public Works for Water-Control* (London 1936), and M. Elvin, "On Water Control and Management during the Ming and Ch'ing Dynasties," *Ch'ing-shih wen-t'i* III.3 (Nov. 1975). L. S. Yang, *Les Aspects économiques des travaux publics dans la Chine imperiale* (Paris 1964), is an elegant quartet of lectures on this and related themes. Max Weber's ideas about China are often insecurely based in the historical facts, but are nonetheless stimulating points of departure. See, for examples, his *Religion of China* (London 1964), and "The Chinese Literati" in H. Gerth and C. Mills, trans., *From Max Weber* (New York 1946). For a recent scholarly appraisal, see W. Schluchter, ed., *Max Webers Studie über Konfuzianismus und Taoismus* (Frankfurt 1983).

On the society of the Eastern Zhou, Hsu Cho-yun, *Ancient China in Transition* (Stanford, Calif., 1965), still provides a useful general orientation. T. T. Chü, *Han Social Structure* (Seattle, Wash., 1972), is invaluable and backed by a selection of translated documents. On the Tang, J. Gernet, *Les Aspects économiques du Bouddhisme dans la société chinoise du Ve au Xe siècle* (Saigon 1956), is also a masterly work. Yoshinobu Shiba, trans. M. Elvin, *Commerce and Society in Sung China* (Ann Arbor, Mich., 1970), is a rich collection of documentary sources. On the Yuan, see B. Vladimirtsov, *La Régime sociale des mongoles: le féodalisme nomade* (Paris 1948). On the Ming, E. Rawski, *Agricultural Change and the Peasant Economy of South China* (Cambridge, Mass., 1972), and H. Beattie, *Land and Lineage in China* (Cambridge 1979), are both in some respects inadequate, but full of information. For a brief

indication of some of what is missing, see M. Elvin, "The Last Thousand Years of Chinese History, Changing Patterns in Land Tenure," *Modern Asian Studies* IV.2 (Apr. 1970). On the period of the transition from Ming to Qing see Sung Ying-hsing, trans E. T. Z. and S. C. Sun, *T'ien Kung K'ai Wu. Chinese Technology in the Seventeenth Century* (Philadelphia, Pa., 1966), for a beautifully illustrated translation of a contemporary technical encyclopedia, and J. Dennerline, *The Chia-ting Loyalists: Confucian Leadership and Social Change* (New Haven, Conn., 1981), for a high-quality study of a locality. On the centuries since the Qing, there are two excellent collections of essays: W. Willmott, ed., *Economic Organization in Chinese Society* (Stanford, Calif., 1972), and D. Perkins, ed., *China's Modern Economy in Historical Perspective* (Stanford, Calif., 1975).

On special topics mention may be made of the following: L. Lanciotti, ed., *La donna nella Cina imperiale e nella Cina repubblicana* (Firenze 1980), about half of which is in English; W. Eberhard, *Social Mobility in Traditional China* (Leiden 1962), scrappy but full of interesting items and ideas; J. de Groot, *Sectarianism and Religious Persecution in China* (Leiden 1901), fairly criticized by the Japanese scholar Suzuki Chusei for underestimating the political element in Chinese religious persecution, but nonetheless interesting; E. Ahern, *Chinese Ritual and Politics* (Cambridge 1981), intermittently opaque but highly original; M. Freedman, *Lineage Organization in Southeastern China* and *Chinese Lineage and Society* (London 1958, 1966), two basic works by the late doyen of Chinese anthropology, many of whose occasional pieces may further be found in his *Study of Chinese Society* (Stanford, Calif., 1979); and G. W. Skinner, "Marketing and Social Structure in Rural China," 2 parts, *Journal of Asian Studies* XXIV.1 and 2 (Nov. 1964 and Feb. 1965), now recognized even by their author as somewhat oversimple in their analysis but probably (and not unjustifiably) the most celebrated articles in the history of Chinese studies.

Art of the Late Empire
An architectural account of Peking is given by O. Siren, *The Walls and Gates of Peking* (London 1924) and *The Imperial Palaces of Peking*, 3 vols. (Paris and Brussels 1926). These comprise mainly plates with a short historical account by the author. The former is illustrated with 109 photogravures after photographs by the author and 50 architectural drawings by Chinese artists. It gives a good picture of Peking before the walls were demolished. A more up-to-date picture of the Ming tombs is given by A. Paludan, *The Imperial Ming Tombs* (New Haven, Conn., and London 1981), which is beautifully illustrated with black-and-white and color photographs. For gardens see O. Siren, *Gardens of China* (New York 1949), which is illustrated in black and white, and M. Keswick, *The Chinese Garden, History, Art and Architecture* (London 1978), which is well illustrated in color. For painting in the late empire see R. Whitfield, *In Pursuit of Antiquity* (Princeton, N.J., and Tokyo 1972), J. Cahill, *Painting at the Shore, Chinese Painting of the Early and Middle Ming Dynasty, 1368–1558* (New York and Tokyo 1978), *The Distant Mountains, Chinese Painting of the Late Ming Dynasty, 1570–1644* (New York and Tokyo 1982) and *The Compelling Image* (Cambridge, Mass., and London 1982), which deals with nature and style in 17th-century Chinese painting. A general introduction to the aesthetics and techniques of calligraphy is given by Y. Chiang, *Chinese Calligraphy* (London 1938). An interesting work on the Jesuit painter who painted at the Chinese court in the 18th century is C. and M. Beurdeley, trans. M. Bullock, *Giuseppe Castiglione* (London 1972). The impact of Oriental styles on Western art and decoration is discussed by O. Impey, *Chinoiserie* (London 1977). The decorative arts are well covered in the general books already mentioned.

Prospect and Retrospect
On the perfection and stasis of art, see M. M. Sze *The Tao of Painting . . . with a translation of the "Mustard Seed Garden Manual of Painting"* (New York 1956). Of the subtlety of aesthetic philosophy P. Ryckmans, *Les "Propos sur la peinture" de Shitao* (Bruxelles 1970), is the supreme example. On the limits of originality in painting in mid-19th-century China, Ryckmans's *Su Renshan* (Hong Kong 1970) is a pioneering study of an individual artist. The difficulties of heterodoxy are well brought out in J. Billeter, *Li Zhi, philosophe maudit* (Geneva 1979). The classic account of the Manchu suppression of works thought politically subversive is L. C. Goodrich, *The Literary Inquisition of Ch'ien-lung* (Baltimore, Md., 1935). On the high-level equilibrium trap in the economy, see M. Elvin, *The Pattern of the Chinese Past*.

The Film of Events
No general history of modern China fully rises to the challenges of its subject matter. J. Chen, *China and the*

West (London 1979), is one of the most nearly adequate. For reference, J. Fairbank, E. Reischauer and A. Craig, *East Asia, The Modern Transformation* (London 1965), remains invaluable, if a little solid.

On the opening of China J. Fairbank, *Trade and Diplomacy on the China Coast* (Cambridge, Mass., 1953), is a classic. The main mid-century rebellions are covered by F. Michael and C. L. Chang, *The Taiping Rebellion*, 3 vols. (Seattle, Wash., 1966–71), S. Y. Teng, *The Nien Army and their Guerrilla Warfare* (Paris 1961), and W. D. Chu, *The Moslem Rebellion in Northwest China* (The Hague 1966).

On the introduction of institutional reforms, and the obstacles in their way, see S. Y. Teng and J. Fairbank, *China's Response to the West* (Cambridge, Mass., 1954), for a general survey, and on specific periods M. Wright, *The Last Stand of Chinese Conservatism: The T'ung-chih Restoration, 1862–1874* (Stanford, Calif., 1957), Lloyd Eastman, *Throne and Mandarins* (Cambridge, Mass., 1967), M. Cameron, *The Reform Movement in China 1898–1912* (Stanford, Calif., 1931), and J. Fincher, *Chinese Democracy* (London 1981). P. Cohen, *China and Christianity* (Cambridge, Mass., 1963), describes the problems caused by the missionaries. On ultra-conservatism, M. Elvin, ''Mandarins and Millenarians,'' *Journal of the Anthropological Society of Oxford* X.3 (Michaelmas 1979), punctures some of the accepted myths. The best introduction to the recent reappraisal of the 1911 revolution is M. Wright, ed., *China in Revolution. The First Phase 1900–1913* (New Haven, Conn., 1968). A glimpse of the vast volume of scholarship now devoted to this subject may be had from the lopsidedly polemical but stimulating special issue of *Modern China* (II.2, Apr. 1976) devoted to it. Excellent complementary studies of the great reform polemicist Liang Qichao are H. Chang, *Liang Ch'i-ch'ao and the Intellectual Transition in China, 1890–1907* (Cambridge, Mass., 1971), and P. Huang, *Liang Ch'i-ch'ao and Modern Chinese Liberalism* (Seattle, Wash., 1972). A compact overview of some of the deeper intellectual currents of this time is M. Elvin, *Self-Liberation and Self-Immolation in Modern Chinese Thought* (Canberra 1978). There are two biographies of China's first president: J. Chen, *Yuan Shih-k'ai* (London 1961), and E. Young, *The Presidency of Yuan Shih-k'ai* (Ann Arbor, Mich., 1977). The warlords may be approached through D. Gillin, *Warlord: Yen Hsi-shan in Shansi Province, 1911–1949* (Princeton, N.J., 1967), and J. Sheridan, *Chinese Warlord: The Career of Feng Yü-hsiang* (Stanford, Calif., 1966). On the mass movements see J. Chesneaux, *The Chinese Labor Movement* (Stanford, Calif., 1968), and R. Hofheinz, *The Broken Wave. The Chinese Communist Peasant Movement, 1922–1928* (Cambridge, Mass., 1977). R. Myers, *The Chinese Peasant Economy* (Cambridge, Mass., 1970), deflates popular myths about landlordism, and C.M. Hou, *Foreign Investment and Economic Development in China* (Cambridge, Mass., 1965), does a similar demolition job on economic ''imperialism.'' On the intertwined rise of the Nationalist and Communist parties, D. Jacobs, *Borodin* (Cambridge, Mass., 1981), is an outstanding recent work, while H. Isaacs's Trotskyist *The Tragedy of the Chinese Revolution* (Stanford, Calif., 1951) has a compelling eloquence. On the Nationalist government Lloyd Eastman, *The Abortive Revolution* (Cambridge, Mass., 1974), is a sharp-eyed and disenchanted survey, while the two articles by P. Cavendish, ''The 'New China' of the Kuomintang,'' in J. Gray, *Modern China's Search for a Political Form* (London 1969), and ''Anti-Imperialism in the Kuomintang 1923–8,'' in J. Chen and N. Tarling, eds.,

Studies in the Social History of China and South-East Asia (Cambridge 1970), are unusually incisive analyses.

J. Harrison, *The Long March to Power. A History of the Chinese Communist Party 1921–1972* (London 1972), is stylistically heavy going but incomparably complete and dependable. Insights may be more easily gained from C. Johnson, *Peasant Nationalism and Communist Power* (Stanford, Calif., 1963), L. van Slyke, *Enemies and Friends. The United Front in Chinese Communist History* (Stanford, Calif., 1967), and J. W. Lewis, *Leadership in Communist China* (Ithaca, N.Y., 1963). There are two good biographies of Mao: S. Schram, *Mao Tse-tung* (London 1967), and J. Chen, *Mao and the Chinese Revolution* (London 1965). On Mao's thought the indispensable primer is S. Schram, *The Political Thought of Mao Tse-tung* (London 1963), and this may be supplemented by R. Wylie, *The Emergence of Maoism* (Standord, Calif., 1980), on the circumstances surrounding the creation of the ''Thought.'' E. Snow, *Red Star over China* (New York 1938), is a masterpiece of eyewitness reportage on the heroic days of Chinese Communism at Yan'an. The enthusiasm underpinning the early Communist revolution is evoked from personal experience in W. Hinton, *Fanshen. A Documentary of Revolution is a Chinese Village* (New York 1967). There is no space here to explore the almost endless literature on the People's Republic, but no one interested in the events of the last 20 years should fail to read the books by ''Simon Leys'' (Pierre Ryckmans), especially *The Chairman's New Clothes* (London 1977) and *Chinese Shadows* (Harmondsworth 1978), which broke the spell of the illusions gripping so many Western intellectuals. Chen Jo-hsi's short stories, trans. N. Ing and H. Goldblatt, *The Execution of Major Yin* (Bloomington, Ind., 1978), are a remarkable literary evocation of life under the Cultural Revolution. Perhaps the best book on China today is F. Butterfield, *Alive in the Bitter Sea* (London 1983).

Art of the Modern Age

Art of the modern age is briefly introduced in the general works previously mentioned. A comprehensive study of 20th-century art is yet to be produced.

Symbols and Society

Many of the topics in this section have already been covered bibliographically elsewhere. Only a few further items of particular interest are therefore given below.

Language: P. Kratochvil, *The Chinese Language Today* (London 1968), is a non-technical outline of modern Chinese. B. Karlgren, *The Chinese Language* (New York 1949), does a similar job for its historical development.

Writing: Y. Chiang, *Chinese Calligraphy*, is both beautiful and instructive.

Medicine: F. Mann, *Acupuncture. The Ancient Chinese Art of Healing* (London 1962), is a simple introduction by a practitioner. J. Needham, *Celestial Lancets* (Cambridge 1980), is a detailed historical and scientific treatment.

Geomancy: S. Feuchtwang, *An Anthropological Interpretation of Chinese Geomancy* (Vietiane 1974).

Mathematics: U. Libbrecht, *Chinese Mathematics in the 13th Century* (Cambridge, Mass., 1973).

Ingenuity: In addition to J. Needham's *Science and Civilisation* (cited above), R. Hommel, *China at Work* (Cambridge, Mass., 1969), is a detailed illustrated survey of tools and machinery.

Music: L. Picken, ''Music of Far Eastern Asia-1: China,'' in *New Oxford History of Music*, vol. 1 (London 1957).

Theater: A. C. Scott, *The Classical Theater of China* (Westport, Conn., 1957), is a handbook of actors, roles, costumes and technique. W. Dolby, *A History of Chinese Drama* (London 1970), is an introduction to the plays.

Farming: the essays in R. Barker and R. Sinha, eds., *The Chinese Agricultural Economy* (Boulder, Colo., 1982), cover almost every aspect of the subject.

Food: Everyone has their own favorite Chinese cookbook. Ours is C. and A. Lee, *The Gourmet Chinese Regional Cookbook* (Secaucus, N.J., 1980). K. C. Chang, ed., *Food in Chinese Culture* (New Haven, Conn., 1977), is a fascinating miscellany.

Family Life: M. Wolf, *Women and Family in Rural Taiwan* (Stanford, Calif., 1972), argues that Chinese women see the family differently from men. A. Wolf and C. S. Huang, *Marriage and Adoption in China* (Stanford, Calif., 1980), is the best technical study in the field, combining anthropology and demography.

China and the West: W. Franke, *China and the West* (Oxford 1967), is an introduction to this vast subject. D. Lach, *Asia in the Making of Europe*, 3 vols. (Chicago, Ill., 1965, 1970, 1978), is a widely acclaimed work of great range.

Miscellaneous: A. H. Smith, *Chinese Characteristics* (New York 1894) is a tour de force of sharp-eyed observation by a Victorian missionary.

Reference Works

Though dating fast, C. Hucker, *China: A Critical Bibliography* (Tucson, Ariz., 1962), is the most accessible introduction to the scholarly literature on China. For the period after the mid-17th century, G. W. Skinner, ed., *Modern Chinese Society. An Analytical Bibliography*, Vol. 1: *Publications in Western Languages* (Stanford, Calif., 1973), is indispensable. For recent work, the *Journal of Asian Studies* carries an annual bibliographical survey.

The atlas on which all others have to a great degree built is A. Herrmann, *Historical and Commercial Atlas of China* (Cambridge, Mass., 1935; numerous reprints). P. Geelan and D. Twitchett, *The Times Atlas of China* (London 1974), is solid, if a little unenterprising. The Central Intelligence Agency, *People's Republic of China, Atlas* (Washington, D.C., 1971), gives excellent coverage of present-day China. Specialists will turn for guidance on source maps to J. F. Williams, *China in Maps ... A Selective and Annotated Cartobibliography* (East Lansins, Mich., 1974).

For general handy reference B. Hook, ed., *The Cambridge Encyclopedia of China* (Cambridge 1982), is a useful first resort.

Biographical dictionaries are: H. Giles, *A Chinese Biographical Dictionary* (London 1898); H. Franke, ed., *Sung Biographies* (Wiesbaden 1976); L. Goodrich and C. Fang, eds., *Dictionary of Ming Biography* (New York 1976); A. Hummel, ed., *Eminent Chinese of the Ch'ing Period* (Washington, D.C., 1943); H. Boorman and R. Howard, eds., *Biographical Dictionary of Republican China* (New York 1967–71); and D. Klein and A. Clark, eds., *Biographic Dictionary of Chinese Communism* (Cambridge, Mass., 1971).

Of the many journals wholly or partly devoted to China, among the most accessible are the *Journal of Asian Studies*, the *Harvard Journal of Asiatic Studies*, *T'oung Pao*, the *Bulletin of the School of Oriental and African Studies*, the *China Quarterly* (devoted mostly to current affairs), *Philosophy East and West* and *Modern China*.

GAZETTEER

Names in *italics* represent the Wade-Giles equivalent of the preceding Pinyin transcription.

Acapulco (Mexico) 16°51′N 99°56′E, 38
Aden (S Yemen) 12°47′N 45°03′E, 34
Aigun/*Ai-kun* 50°16′N 127°25′E, 32, 33, 34
Aiyang Gate/*Ai-yang* 40°57′N 124°30′E, 33
Aizhou/*Ai-chou* (Vietnam) 19°50′N 105°55′E, 30
Aksu 41°10′N 80°20′E, 34, 41, 150
Alakol L (USSR) 41
Alchuka 45°27′N 126°59′E, 33
Alma Ata (USSR) 43°19′N 76°55′E, 34
Almaliq 43°55′N 81°10′E, 150
Altai Mts, 11
Altun Mts, 11
Alu/*A-lu* see Deli
Amman (Jordan) 31°57′N 35°56′E, 34
Amoy see Xiamen
Amu Darya R/Oxus (USSR), 34, 92
Amul (USSR) 39°10′N 63°20′E, 92
Amur R see Heilong
An/*An* see Anlu
Anbianbao/*An-pien-pao* 37°36′N 108°11′E, 41
Andaman (Isls) (India), 34, 38
Andijan (USSR) 40°48′N 72°22′E, 41
Anding/*An-ting* 39°38′N 116°29′E, 41
Andong/*An-tung* 40°08′N 124°20′E, 32, 34
Angangqi/*An-kang-ch'i* 47°09′N 123°47′E, 32
Anjara R (USSR), 15, 34
Anhui Province/*An-hui*, 27, 150, 152, 158
Ankang/*An-k'ang* see Xing'an
Ankara (Turkey) 39°55′N 32°50′E, 34
Anlu/*An-lu*/An/Anzhou/Anlufu/De'an 31°18′N 113°40′E, 26, 27, 31, 158
Anlu/*An-lu* see Chengtian
Anlufu/*An-lu-fu* see Anlu
Annam Province/Annan, 25, 26, 27, 150
Anping/*An-p'ing* 41°13′N 123°26′E, 33
Anping/*An-p'ing* (Taiwan) 23°01′N 120°08′E, 33
Anqing/*An-ch'ing* 30°31′N 117°02′E, 27, 123, 149, 150, 158
Anqing/*An-ch'ing*/Shu 30°46′N 119°40′E, 24, 31
Ansai/*An-sai* 36°51′N 109°17′E, 164
Anshan/*An-shan* 41°05′N 122°58′E, 24
Anshun/*An-shun* 26°19′N 105°50′E, 27, 36, 149, 150
Anxi/*An-hsi*/Guazhou 40°32′N 95°45′E, 41, 92, 158
Anyang/*An-yang*/Dayi Shang/Zhangde 36°04′N 114°20′E, 24, 27, 52, 54, 164
Anyi/*An-i* 35°07′N 111°16′E, 30, 54, 71, 164
Anzhou/*An-chou* see Anlu
Anzhou/*An-chou* 38°51′N 115°48′E, 152
Ao/*Ao* see Zhengzhou
Arkhangelsk (USSR) 64°32′N 40°40′E, 34
Astrakhan (USSR) 46°22′N 48°04′E, 34
Athens (Greece) 38°00′N 23°44′E, 34

Ba/*Pa* see Bazhou
Ba/*Pa* see Chongqing
Badakhshan (Afghanistan) 36°25′N 70°05′E, 92
Baghdad (Iraq) 33°20′N 44°26′E, 34
Bai R/*Pai*, 103
Baicheng/*Pai-ch'eng* 41°48′N 81°50′E, 41
Baituahang Gate/*Pai-t'u-a-hang* 41°49′N 121°50′E, 33
Balkh (Afghanistan) 36°40′N 66°50′E, 92
Balkhash L (USSR), 11, 15, 41, 92
Bam'kin-seng (Taiwan) 22°35′N 120°43′E, 33
Bamyan (Afghanistan) 35°05′N 67°50′E, 92
Bandjarmasin/Wenlangmashen (Indonesia) 03°22′S 114°33′E, 38
Bangkok (Thailand) 13°44′N 100°30′E, 34
Banpo/*Pan-p'o* 34°00′N 109°00′E, 52
Banqiao/*Pan-ch'iao* (Taiwan) 25°03′N 121°28′E, 33
Banqiaozhen/*Pan-ch'iao-chen* 36°30′N 120°25′E, 31, 123
Banten/Shunta (Indonesia) 06°00′S 106°09′E, 38
Banzhu/*Pan-chu* 34°48′N 113°10′E, 105
Bao/*Pao* see Baoding
Baoan/*Pao-an* 36°45′N 108°47′E, 31, 164
Baode/*Pao-te* 39°02′N 111°05′E, 164
Baodi/*Pao-ti* 39°43′N 117°18′E, 152
Baoding/*Pao-ting*/Bao/Qingyuan 38°54′N 115°26′E, 16, 26, 27, 31, 123, 149, 150, 152, 164
Baodu/*Pao-tu* 37°50′N 115°35′E, 110
Baofeng/*Pao-feng* 39°03′N 106°45′E, 41
Baoji/*Pao-chi* 34°21′N 107°23′E, 41, 52
Baoning/*Pao-ning* 31°30′N 105°55′E, 27
Baoqing/*Pao-ch'ing*/Shao 27°22′N 111°29′E, 27, 31, 123
Baotou/*Pao-t'ou* 40°33′N 110°01′E, 11, 41, 164
Baoxin/*Pao-hsin* 32°33′N 114°58′E, 103
Barkol 43°46′N 93°02′E, 41
Bayan Har Mts/*Pa-yen*, 11
Bayanrongge/*Pa-yen-jung-ko* 36°30′N 102°10′E, 41
Baykal L (USSR), 11, 15, 33, 34, 98
Bazhou/*Pa-chou*/Ba 31°50′N 106°49′E, 98, 102
Bazhou/*Pa-chou*/Ba 39°05′N 116°23′E, 31, 152
Bei R/*Pei*, 11, 123
Beihai/*Pei-hai* 21°29′N 109°10′E, 34
Beijing/*Pei-ching*/Peking/Yu/Ji/Dadu/Jojun/Khanbaliq 39°55′N 116°26′E, 11, 15, 16, 23, 24, 25, 26, 27, 28, 30, 32, 33, 34, 38, 94, 98, 104, 105, 149, 150, 164
Beijing/*Pei-ching* 34°20′N 112°12′E, 95
Beipan R/*Pei-p'an*, 36
Beipiao/*Pei-p'iao* 41°48′N 120°44′E, 32
Beiru R/*Pei-ju*, 103
Beiting/*Pei-t'ing* see Tingzhou
Beixu/*Pei-hsü* 35°15N 118°12′E, 95
Beiyu/*Pei-yü* see Chenggao
Bei Zhili Province/*Pei Chih-li* see Zhili
Belgrade (Yugoslavia) 44°50′N 20°30′E, 34
Bengbu/*Peng-pu* 32°55′N 117°23′E, 11
Beruwala/*Bieluoli* (Sri Lanka) 06°29′N 79°59′E, 38
Beshbaliq see Tingzhou
Bian/*Pien* see Kaifeng
Bian Canal/*Pien*, 103, 105
Bianliang/*Pien-liang* see Kaifeng
Bianzhou/*Pien-chou* see Kaifeng
Bieluoli/*Pieh-lo-li* see Beruwala
Bijie/*Pi-chieh* 27°18′N 105°20′E, 27, 36, 94
Bijing/*Pi-ching* (Vietnam) 17°30′N 106°20′E, 92
Bikar (Isl) (USA Trust Territory) 12°13′N 170°05′E, 38
Bikini (Isl) (USA Trust Territory) 11°35′N 165°20′E, 38
Bin/*Pin* 23°21′N 108°46′E, 31
Bin/*Pin* see Binxian
Bi'nan/*Pi-nan*/Pilan (Taiwan) 22°45′N 121°10′E, 33
Binchuan/*Pin-ch'uan* 25°49′N 100°34′E, 149
Bing/*Ping* see Taiyuan
Bingkujiang/*Ping-k'u-chiang*/Kobe (Japan) 34°40′N 135°12′E, 38
Binglu/*Ping-lu* (Tang "province"), 103
Bingmei/*Ping-mei* 26°42′N 108°52′E, 36
Binning/*Pin-ning* (Tang "province"), 26
Binxian/*Pin-hsien*/Bin/Binzhou/Zhou 34°59′N 108°04′E, 31, 41, 52, 54, 62
Binzhou/*Pin-chou* see Binxian
Biya R (USSR), 15
Biyang/*Pi-yang* 32°49′N 113°21′E, 103
Blagoveschchensk (USSR) 50°19′N 127°30′E, 32
Bo/*Po* 27°43′N 106°58′E, 31, 98
Bo/*Po* see Boxian
Bogda Feng (Mt) 43°45′N 88°32′E, 11
Boluo/*Po-lo* 23°10′N 114°16′E, 158
Bombay (India) 18°56′N 72°51′E, 34
Borneo (Isl) (Indonesia), 34, 38
Boshan/*Po-shan* 36°23′N 117°50′E, 164
Bosten L, 11, 41
Boxian/*Po-hsien*/Bo/Bozhou 33°52′N 115°45′E, 31, 54, 102, 149
Boyang/*Po-yang* 29°00′N 116°38′E, 24
Bozhou/*Po-chou* see Boxian
Brahmaputra R see Yarlung Zangbo
Brava (Somalia) 01°02′N 44°02′E, 38
Budapest (Hungary) 47°30′N 19°03′E, 34
Bukhara (USSR) 39°47′N 64°26′E, 34, 92
Bukou/*Pu-k'ou* 32°21′N 112°26′E, 158
Bulongjier/*Pu-lung-chi-erh* 40°15′N 95°28′E, 41

Cai/*Ts'ai* see Runan
Cairo (Egypt) 30°03′N 31°15′E, 34
Caizhou/*Ts'ai-chou* see Runan
Calcutta (India) 22°30′N 88°20′E, 11, 34
Calicut/Guli (India) 11°15′N 75°45′E, 34, 38
Camp Dingyuan/*Ting-yüan* 38°45′N 106°00′E, 41
Cang/*Ts'ang* see Cangxian
Cangwu/*Ts'ang-wu* 23°29′N 111°42′E, 30
Cangxian/*Ts'ang-hsien*/Cang 38°19′N 116°51′E, 26, 31, 95, 98, 123, 150, 152, 164
Cangyuan/*Ts'ang-yüan* 34°50′N 113°10′E, 110
Canton see Guangzhou
Cao/*Ts'ao* see Caoxian
Caohe/*Ts'ao-ho* 40°55′N 124°02′E, 33
Caoxian/*Ts'ao-hsien*/Cao/Caozhou 34°50′N 115°35′E, 30, 54, 62, 98, 152, 164
Caozhou/*Ts'ao-chou* see Caoxian
Celebes (Isl) (Indonesia), 34, 38
Ceylon/Sri Lanka, 34
Chaghanian (USSR) 38°05′N 67°40′E, 92
Chahannaoer/*Ch'a-han-nao-erh* 38°03′N 109°42′E, 150
Chaling/*Ch'a-ling* 27°03′N 113°49′E, 31
Chang/*Ch'ang* 29°25′N 105°34′E, 31, 102
Chang/*Ch'ang* see Changzhou
Chang R/*Ch'ang* see Yangzi
Chang'an/*Ch'ang-an* see Xi'an
Changbai Mts/*Ch'ang-pai*, 11
Changchun/*Ch'ang-ch'un*/Kuanchengzi 43°53′N 125°18′E, 11, 32, 34
Changde/*Ch'ang-te*/Ding 29°03′N 111°35′E, 24, 26, 27, 31, 34, 94, 123
Changdian/*Ch'ang-tien* 40°38′N 125°09′E, 33
Changge/*Ch'ang-ko* 34°12′N 113°46′E, 54
Changji/*Ch'ang-chi* 44°00′N 87°20′E, 41
Changle/*Ch'ang-le* 25°55′N 119°31′E, 38, 94
Changqing/*Ch'ang-ch'ing* 36°32′N 116°43′E, 152
Changsha/*Ch'ang-sha*/Tan/Tanzhou 28°15′N 112°59′E, 11, 24, 25, 26, 27, 30, 31, 34, 92, 94, 98, 102, 123, 149, 158
Changshou/*Ch'ang-shou* 29°50′N 107°03′E, 158
Changting/*Ch'ang-t'ing*/Ting/Tingzhou 25°51′N 116°22′E, 26, 27, 31, 98, 102, 123
Changwu/*Ch'ang-wu* 35°09′N 107°42′E, 41
Changye/*Ch'ang-yeh* 38°57′N 100°41′E, 30
Changzhi/*Ch'ang-chih*/Lu/Lu'an/Longde 36°09′N 113°08′E, 26, 31, 54, 164
Changzhou/*Ch'ang-chou*/Chang 31°47′N 119°57′E, 27, 30, 31, 98, 102, 105
Chao/*Ch'ao* 44°58′N 126°12′E, 98
Chao/*Ch'ao* see Chao'an
Chao'an/*Ch'ao-an*/Chao/Chaoqing/Chaozhou 23°42′N 116°36′E, 24, 26, 27, 30, 31, 94, 98, 123, 149, 150
Chaoge/*Ch'ao-ko* 35°23′N 114°04′E, 54
Chaoqing/*Ch'ao-ch'ing* see Chao'an
Chaozhou/*Ch'ao-chou* see Chao'an
Charchan 37°55′N 85°45′E, 150
Chen/*Ch'en* 28°02′N 110°12′E, 31, 98, 123
Chen/*Ch'en* 33°40′N 115°25′E, 71
Chen/*Ch'en* see Chenxian
Chen/*Ch'en* see Huaiyang
Cheng/*Ch'eng* see Chengzhou
Chengde/*Ch'eng-te* 40°50′N 117°55′E, 164
Chengde/*Ch'eng-te* (Tang "province"), 26
Chengdu/*Ch'eng-tu*/Chengdufu/Yizhou 30°39′N 104°04′E, 11, 15, 24, 26, 27, 28, 30, 31, 34, 71, 92, 94, 98, 102, 110, 123, 156, 158
Chengdu/*Ch'eng-tu* (Song "route"), 26
Chengdufu/*Ch'eng-tu-fu* see Chengdu
Chenggao/*Ch'eng-kao*/Beiyu 34°47′N 113°14′E, 71, 95
Chengtian/*Ch'eng-t'ien*/Anlu/Ying 31°15′N 112°46′E, 26, 27, 31, 94
Chengzhou/*Ch'eng-chou*/Cheng 33°42′N 105°36′E, 31, 98, 102
Chenliu/*Ch'en-liu*/Liang 34°39′N 114°35′E, 95, 110
Chenqiu/*Ch'en-ch'iu* 33°21′N 115°10′E, 103
Chenxian/*Ch'en-hsien*/Chen/Chenzhou 25°48′N 113°02′E, 24, 30, 92, 98, 102, 123, 149
Chenzhou/*Ch'en-chou* 28°15′N 110°05′E, 27, 36, 102, 149
Chenzhou/*Ch'en-chou* see Chenxian
Chenzhou/*Ch'en-chou* see Huaiyang
Cheribon/Zheliwen (Indonesia) 06°46′S 108°33′E, 38
Chi/*Ch'ih* see Chizhou
Chijin/*Ch'ih-chin* 40°45′N 95°55′E, 150
Chishui/*Ch'ih-shui* 28°29′N 105°44′E, 36
Chizhou/*Ch'ih-chou*/Chi/Guichi 30°40′N 117°28′E, 26, 27, 31, 98, 102, 123
Chongde/*Ch'ung-te* 30°55′N 120°25′E, 150
Chongqing/*Ch'ung-ch'ing* 30°38′N 103°40′E, 11, 15, 23, 24, 26, 28, 34, 149
Chongqing/*Ch'ung-ch'ing*/Yu/Yuzhou/Gong/Ba 29°39′N 106°34′E, 27, 30, 31, 62, 71, 94, 98, 102, 123, 158
Choujiakou/*Ch'ou-chia-k'ou* 32°58′N 114°36′E, 149
Christmas (Island) (Kiribati) 02°00′N 157°30′W, 38
Chu/*Ch'u* 32°19′N 118°21′E, 31, 98, 123
Chu/*Ch'u* 28°30′N 120°10′E, 26, 31, 98
Chu/*Ch'u* 32°55′N 117°43′E, 95
Chu/*Ch'u* see Huai'an
Chu State/*Ch'u*, 71
Chujialing/*Ch'u-chia-ling* 31°00′N 113°00′E, 52
Chuxiong/*Ch'u-hsiung* 25°00′N 101°25′E, 27, 149
Chuya R (USSR), 15
Chuzhou/*Ch'u-chou* 28°25′N 119°50′E, 26, 27, 102
Chuzhou/*Ch'u-chou* 33°38′N 119°01′E, 102
Ci/*Tz'u* see Cizhou
Cixian/*Tz'u-hsien* 36°20′N 114°23′E, 54
Cizhou/*Tz'u-chou*/Ci 36°02′N 110°48′E, 31, 102
Cochin (India) 09°56′N 76°15′E, 38
Colombo (Sri Lanka) 06°55′N 79°52′E, 34
Crete (Isl) (Greece), 34
Cua Hoi/Jichangmen (Vietnam) 18°25′N 105°58′E, 38
Cu Lao Re (Isl) (Vietnam) 15°56′N 108°28′E, 38
Cyprus (Isl), 34

Da/*Ta* 31°08′N 107°32′E, 31, 98, 123
Da'an/*Ta-an* 32°53′N 106°22′E, 31
Daba Mts/*Ta-pa*, 11, 22
Dabie Mts/*Ta-pieh*, 103
Dacca (Bangladesh) 23°42′N 90°22′E, 11, 34
Dacheng/*Ta-ch'eng* 42°06′N 124°02′E, 33
Dading/*Ta-ting* 27°10′N 105°31′E, 36
Dading/*Ta-ting* 41°39′N 118°41′E, 98
Dadonggou/*Ta-tung-kou* 39°52′N 124°08′E, 34
Dadu/*Ta-tu* see Beijing
Dadu R/*Ta-tu*, 41, 149
Dai/*Tai* see Daizhou
Daijun/*Tai-chun* 39°40′N 113°17′E, 71
Dairen see Lüda
Daizhou/*Tai-chou*/Dai 39°04′N 112°56′E, 26, 31, 94, 98, 102, 123, 158
Dajiang/*Ta-chiang* see San Vicente
Dajianlu/*Ta-chien-lu*/Kangding 30°00′N 102°50′E, 150
Dalachi/*Ta-la-ch'ih* 36°36′N 105°36′E, 41
Dali/*Ta-li* 25°50′N 100°10′E, 25, 27, 98, 149, 150
Dali/*Ta-li*/Tong/Tongzhou 34°47′N 109°55′E, 24, 30, 31, 41, 92, 98, 102, 164
Dalian/*Ta-lien* see Lüda
Daliang/*Ta-liang* 34°20′N 114°43′E, 71
Daling R/*Ta-ling*, 33
Dalny see Lüda
Dalou Mts/*Ta-lou*, 11
Daluo/*Ta-lo* see Hanoi
Damascus (Syria) 33°30′N 36°19′E, 34
Daming/*Ta-ming*/Da'ning 36°19′N 115°06′E, 27, 31, 98, 123, 150, 152, 164
Dan/*Tan* 34°54′N 116°31′E, 31
Dan/*Tan* 36°02′N 110°12′E, 31
Dangaer/*Tan-ka-erh* 36°40′N 101°27′E, 41, 149
Dangshan/*Tang-shan* 34°24′N 116°21′E, 152
Dani/*Ta-ni* see Pattani
Da'ning/*Ta-ning* 41°43′N 119°03′E, 26, 27
Da'ningjian/*Ta-ning-chien* 31°28′N 109°39′E, 31
Danjiang/*Tan-chiang* 26°03′N 108°22′E, 36
Danmu/*Tan-mu* see Demak
Danshui/*Tan-shui*/Tamshui (Taiwan) 25°13′N 121°29′E, 33, 34, 149
Dantu/*Tan-t'u* 31°50′N 119°55′E, 150
Danube R (Central Europe), 34
Danyang/*Tan-yang* 31°55′N 119°50′E, 110, 150
Danyang/*Tan-yang* 31°07′N 111°04′E, 71
Dao/*Tao* see Daozhou
Daozhou/*Tao-chou*/Dao 25°31′N 111°27′E, 31, 102, 123
Dapu/*Ta-p'u* 34°41′N 119°12′E, 164
Daquan/*Ta-ch'üan* 41°18′N 95°22′E, 41
Dashiquao/*Ta-shih-ch'iao* 40°37′N 122°30′E, 32, 164
Datai/*Ta-t'ai* 39°55′N 115°49′E, 164
Datong/*Ta-t'ung*/Xijing 40°05′N 113°17′E, 11, 27, 94, 98, 102, 150, 164
Datong/*Ta-t'ung* 36°56′N 101°40′E, 41
Daxingcheng/*Ta-hsing-ch'eng* 34°06′N 108°38′E, 105
De'an/*Te-an* see Anlu
Da Xing'an Mts/*Ta Hsing-an*, 11
Daxue Mts/*Ta-hsüeh*, 11
Daybul (Pakistan) 24°58′N 67°10′E, 92
Daye Swamp/*Ta-yeh* 35°10′N 115°10′E, 16
Dayi Shang/*Ta-i Shang* see Anyang
Da Yunhe/*Ta-Yün-ho*/Grand Canal, 105
Dazhu/*Ta-chu* 30°43′N 107°12′E, 158
De/*Te* see Dezhou
Dejiang/*Te-chiang* 28°15′N 108°10′E, 36
Delhi (India) 28°40′N 77°14′E, 34
Deli/Alu (Indonesia) 03°58′N 98°30′E, 38
Demak/Danmu (Indonesia) 06°53′S 110°40′E, 38
Deng/*Teng* see Dengzhou
Deng/*Teng* see Penglai
Dengfeng/*Teng-feng*/Songzhou 30, 34°27′N 113°03′E, 54
Dengyue/*Teng-yüeh* 24°50′N 100°50′E, 34
Dengzhou/*Teng-chou*/Deng 32°41′N 112°07′E, 30, 31, 62, 92, 98, 103, 123
Dengzhou/*Teng-chou* see Penglai
Deqing/*Te-ch'ing* 23°11′N 111°49′E, 31
Dexian/*Te-hsien* see Dezhou
Dexun/*Te-hsün* 35°29′N 105°37′E, 31
Dezhou/*Te-chou*/De/Dexian 37°29′N 116°11′E, 24, 31, 94, 123, 149, 150, 152, 164
Di/*Ti*/Huimin 37°29′N 117°29′E, 31, 123
Dianjiang/*Tien-chiang* 30°19′N 107°20′E, 158
Dihua/*Ti-hua* see Urumqi
Ding/*Ting* see Changde
Ding/*Ting* see Changting
Ding/*Ting* see Dingxian
Ding/*Ting* see Zhongshan
Dingbian/*Ting-pien* 37°39′N 107°40′E, 27, 41, 149
Dingfan/*Ting-fan* 26°03′N 106°49′E, 36
Dingjialu/*Ting-chia-lu* see Trengganu
Dingliao/*Ting-liao*/Liaoyang 41°16′N 123°06′E, 26, 33, 98
Dingxian/*Ting-hsien*/Ding/Dingzhou 38°28′N 114°57′E, 30, 102, 123, 150, 164
Dingxiang (N Korea) 39°05′N 125°54′E, 33
Dingxing/*Ting-hsing* 39°12′N 115°50′E, 150
Dingzhou/*Ting-chou* (N Korea) 39°18′N 127°11′E, 98
Dingzhou/*Ting-chou* see Dingxian
Djakarta/Jiaoliuba (Indonesia) 06°08′S 106°45′E, 34, 38
Dolon-Nor 42°36′N 114°11′E, 33
Dong R/*Tung*, 11, 23
Donga/*Tung-a* 36°06′N 116°16′E, 105
Dongchang/*Tung-ch'ang* see Liaocheng
Dongchuan/*Tung-ch'uan* 30°54′N 105°00′E, 98
Dongchuan/*Tung-ch'uan* 26°10′N 103°10′E, 24, 27, 149
Dongguan/*Tung-kuan* 37°21′N 112°27′E, 164
Donghai/*Tung-hai* 36°52′N 118°22′E, 30
Dongji/*Tung-chi* (Tang "province"), 26
Dongjiang/*Tung-chiang* (Taiwan) 22°28′N 120°28′E, 33
Dongjing/*Tung-ching* see Kaifeng
Dongliao/*Tung-liao* see Xing'an
Dongliao R/*Tung-liao*, 33
Dongping/*Tung-p'ing* 35°53′N 116°19′E, 105, 150
Dongsha/*Tung-sha* (Isls) 20°45′N 116°43′E, 34
Dongting L/*Tung-t'ing*, 11, 15, 22, 23, 30, 31, 34, 62, 71, 94, 98, 102, 123, 149
Dongyan/*Tung-yen* 40°02′N 118°49′E, 95
Dongzhou/*Tung-chou* 41°41′N 123°57′E, 33
Douliu/*Tou-liu* (Taiwan) 23°42′N 120°32′E, 149
Duban/*Tu-pan* see Tuban
Duji/*Tu-chi* (Tang circuit), 26
Dukang/*Tu-k'ang* 39°07′N 115°13′E, 71
Dunhua/*Tun-hua* 43°21′N 128°12′E, 32
Dunhuang/*Tun-huang*/Shazhou/Gua 40°10′N 94°45′E, 27, 41, 92, 95, 98, 110, 150
Dushan/*Tu-shan* 25°49′N 107°32′E, 36, 149
Duyun/*Tu-yün* 26°16′N 107°29′E, 24, 27, 36, 149

E/*O* see Ezhou
Ebi Nor, 41
Edo/Tokyo (Japan) 35°25′N 137°12′E, 33, 34, 38
Ejin/*O-chin* 41°50′N 101°04′E, 41
Emei/*O-mei* 29°36′N 103°29′E, 110
Eniwetok (Isl) (USA Trust Territory) 11°30′N 162°15′E, 38
Enshi/*En-shih* 30°20′N 108°57′E, 24
Enxian/*En-hsien* 37°10′N 116°16′E, 152
Ergun R/*Erh-kun*, 11, 23, 33
Etzina/Juyan 41°58′N 101°05′E, 150
Euphrates R (Iraq), 34
Eyu/*O-yü* 37°30′N 113°33′E, 71
Eyue/*O-yüeh* (Tang "province"), 26, 103
Ezhou/*O-chou*/E/Shouchang 30°23′N 114°50′E, 26, 30, 31, 103

Faku Gate/*Fa-k'u* 42°32′N 123°22′E, 33
Fancheng/*Fan-ch'eng* see Xiangfan
Fang/*Fang* 32°10′N 110°52′E, 31, 98
Fang/*Fang* 35°31′N 109°18′E, 31
Fangliao/*Feng-liao* (Taiwan) 22°22′N 120°36′E, 33
Fanhe/*Fan-ho* 42°12′N 123°48′E, 33
Farghana (USSR) 39°00′N 71°50′E, 92
Feicheng/*Fei-ch'eng* 36°13′N 116°47′E, 152
Feilong/*Fei-lung* 31°00′N 115°00′E, 110
Feixian/*Fei-hsien* 35°15′N 117°58′E, 152
Fen/*Fen* see Fenyang
Fen R/*Fen*, 11, 16, 41, 62, 103, 105, 123, 149
Feng/*Feng* 23°30′N 111°33′E, 31
Feng/*Feng* 40°54′N 111°35′E 26, 98
Feng/*Feng* see Fengxian
Feng/*Feng* see Fengzhou
Fengbituo/*Feng-pi-t'o* (Taiwan) 22°30′N 120°30′E, 52
Fengdu/*Feng-tu* 29°58′N 107°42′E, 123
Fenghuang/*Feng-huang* 27°58′N 109°35′E, 36
Fenghuangcheng/*Feng-huang-ch'eng* 40°24′N 123°57′E, 33, 158
Fengjiang/*Feng-chiang* (Taiwan) 22°12′N 120°41′E, 33
Fengjibao/*Feng-chi-pao* 41°41′N 123°31′E, 33
Fengrun/*Feng-jun* 39°50′N 118°10′E, 164
Fengshan/*Feng-shan* (Taiwan) 22°32′N 120°25′E, 33

Jingkou/*Ching-k'ou* 32°00'N 119°25'E, 105
Jingmen/*Ching-men* 31°06'N 112°13'E, 31, 98, 102
Jingnan/*Ching-nan* (Tang "province"), 26, 103
Jingning/*Ching-ning* 35°25'N 105°56'E, 41
Jingshan/*Ching-shan* 31°01'N 113°05'E, 158
Jinguantai Gate/*Chin-kuan-t'ai* 41°36'N 120°43'E, 33
Jingxi Bei/*Ching-hsi Pei* (Song "route"), 26
Jingxi Nan/*Ching-hsi Nan* (Song "route"), 26
Jingyang/*Ching-yang* 34°27'N 108°46'E, 41
Jingyuan/*Ching-yüan* 36°34'N 104°46'E, 41
Jingyuan/*Ching-yüan* (Tang "province"), 26
Jingyuanbao/*Ching-yüan-pao* 41°57'N 123°23'E, 33
Jingzhou/*Ching-chou*/Jing 35°20'N 107°20'E, 30, 31, 41
Jingzhou/*Ching-chou* 26°35'N 109°36'E, 36
Jingzhou/*Ching-chou see* Jiangling
Jinhua/*Chin-hua*/Wu 29°06'N 119°40'E, 24, 26, 27, 31, 123
Jining/*Chi-ning*/Jizhou 35°23'N 116°34'E, 54, 149, 150, 152, 164
Jining/*Chi-ning* 37°41'N 112°24'E, 26
Jinjiang/*Chin-chiang* 29°41N 116°03'E, 24
Jinjibao/*Chin-chi-pao* 37°57'N 106°10'E, 41, 149
Jinling/*Chin-ling see* Nanjing
Jinning/*Chin-ning* 36°14'N 111°37'E, 26
Jinsha *R*/*Chin-sha*, 11, 30, 36, 149
Jinshang/*Chin-shang* (Tang "province"), 26
Jintan/*Chin-t'an* 31°45'N 119°30'E, 150
Jintang/*Chin-t'ang* 31°06'N 104°06'E, 102
Jintian/*Chin-t'ien* 23°27'N 111°28'E, 149
Jinxian/*Chin-hsien*/Yuzhong 35°47'N 104°00'E, 41
Jinxiang/*Chin-hsiang* 35°04'N 116°19'E, 152
Jinyang/*Chin-yang see* Taiyuan
Jinyang/*Chin-yang*/Jinzhou 31°30'N 104°50'E, 94
Jinzhou/*Chin-chou*/Kaiping 39°10'N 121°31'E, 27, 33, 94
Jinzhou/*Chin-chou* 35°50'N 111°46'E, 30, 102
Jinzhou/*Chin-chou*/Jin/Guangning zhongtun 41°07'N 121°07'E, 11, 27, 32, 105, 164
Jiqing/*Chi-ch'ing see* Nanjing
Jiubang/*Chiu-pang see* Koepang
Jiuji/*Chiu-chi* 25°00'N 112°00'E, 110
Jiujiang/*Chiu-chiang*/Jiang/ Jiangzhou 29°41'N 116°03'E, 26, 27, 30, 31, 34, 102, 123, 149, 158
Jiujiang/Chiu-chiang *see* Palembang
Jiuquan/*Chiu-ch'üan see* Suzhou
Jiuzhen/*Chiu-chen* (Vietnam) 18°55'N 105°44'E, 30
Jixian/*Chi-hsien*/Ji/Jizhou 37°35'N 115°30'E, 24, 31, 102, 164
Jizhou/*Chi-chou see* Ji'an
Jizhou/*Chi-chou see* Jining
Jizhou/*Chi-chou see* Jixian
Jizhou Canal/*Chi-chou*, 105
Jojun *see* Beijing
Ju/*Chü see* Juzhou
Juliuhe/*Chü-liu-ho* 41°55'N 122°53'E, 33
Julu/*Chü-lu* 36°52'N 115°20'E, 30
Jun/*Chün* 32°50'N 111°15'E, 31, 98
Juyang/*Chü-yang* 32°47'N 116°14'E, 71
Juye/*Chü-yeh* 35°23'N 116°06'E, 152
Juzhou/*Chü-chou*/Ju 35°27'N 118°48'E, 62, 71, 152
Juzijie/*Chü-tzu-chieh*/Yanji 42°53'N 129°30'E, 32
Juzjan (Afghanistan) 36°09'N 66°05'E, 92

Kabul (Afghanistan) 34°30'N 69°10'E, 34, 92
Kai/*K'ai* 31°13'N 108°30'E, 31
Kaicheng/*K'ai-ch'eng* (N Korea) 37°54'N 126°30'E, 25, 98
Kaifeng/*K'ai-feng*/Dongjing/Bian/Bianliang/ Bianzhou 34°47'N 114°20'E, 15, 16, 23, 24, 25, 26, 27, 30, 31, 92, 94, 98, 102, 103, 105, 123, 149, 150, 158, 164
Kaili/*K'ai-li* 26°34'N 107°58'E, 36, 149
Kailu/*K'ai-lu* 43°36'N 121°15'E, 32
Kaiyuan/*K'ai-yüan*/Sanwan 42°31'N 124°02'E, 27, 32, 33, 94
Kaizhou/*K'ai-chou* 27°02'N 106°59'E, 36
Kaizhou/*K'ai-chou* 30°58'N 108°58'E, 102
Kalgan *see* Zhangjiakou
Kandahar (Afghanistan) 31°36'N 65°47'E, 92
Kandy (Sri Lanka) 07°17'N 80°40'E, 34
Kanko/Xianxing (N Korea) 39°54'N 127°35'E, 32
Kapisa (Afghanistan) 34°25'N 69°55'E, 92
Karachi (Pakistan) 24°51'N 67°02'E, 34
Karakorum/Helin (Mongolia) 47°10'N 102°50'E, 26, 150
Karashahr/Yanqi 42°04'N 86°34'E, 41, 92
Karategin (Afghanistan) 38°15'N 70°10'E, 92
Karikal (India) 10°58'N 79°50'E, 34
Kashgar/Sule 39°28'N 75°58'E, 15, 34, 41, 92, 150
Kashgar R, 41
Kathmandu (Nepal) 27°42'N 85°19'E, 11, 34
Katun R (USSR), 15
Kelanjun/*K'o-lan-chün* 38°42'N 111°34'E, 102
Kelantan/Jilandan (Malaysia) 06°13'N 103°10'E, 38
Kerulen R (USSR/China), 33, 41, 98
Keshan/*K'o-shan* 48°01'N 125°53'E, 32
Khabarovsk (USSR) 48°32'N 135°08'E, 32, 34
Kharkov (USSR) 50°00'N 36°15'E, 34
Khiva (USSR) 41°25'N 60°49'E, 34
Khocho/Gaochang 43°30'N 91°05'E, 150
Khosanya (USSR) 40°05'N, 66°15'E, 92
Khotan/Yutian 37°07'N 79°57'E, 34, 41, 150
Khulm (Afghanistan) 36°15'N 68°10'E, 92
Kiakhta (USSR) 50°08'N 106°32'E, 33
Kiev (USSR) 50°25'N 30°30'E, 34
Kimpaoli (Taiwan) 25°15'N 121°38'E, 33
Kish (USSR) 38°40'N 66°10'E, 92
Kobdo/Jargalant (Mongolia) 48°00'N 91°43'E, 41
Koepang/Jiubang (Indonesia) 10°13'S 123°38'E, 38
Koko Nor *see* Qinghai
Kokonor R, 98
Kota Kinabalu (Malaysia) 05°59'N 116°04'E, 34
Kouquan/*K'ou-ch'üan* 40°03'N 113°07'E, 164
Kousia/K'ou-ssu-a (Taiwan) 22°38'N 120°19'E, 33
Kuai R/*K'uai*, 103
Kuala Lumpur (Malaysia) 03°08'N 101°42'E, 34
Kuandian/*K'uan-tien* 40°45'N 124°41'E, 33
Kucha/*K'u-ch'a*/Anxi 41°43'N 82°58'E, 41, 92, 150
Kuching (Malaysia) 01°32'N 110°20'E, 34
Kui/*K'uei see* Kuizhou
Kui R/*K'uei*, 23
Kuizhou/*K'uei-chou*/Kui 31°05'N 109°37'E, 26, 27, 30, 31, 98, 102, 123, 158
Kulkaraussu 44°27'N 84°37'E, 41
Kulun/*K'u-lun see Ulaan Baatar*
Kunlun/*K'un-lun* 37°00'N 121°50'E, 110
Kunlun Mts/*K'un-lun*, 11
Kunming/*K'un-ming*/Yunnan/Yunnanfu 25°02'N 102°42'E, 11, 27, 28, 36, 94, 149, 150, 158
Kunyang/*K'un-yang* 24°39'N 102°35'E, 149
Kuo/*K'uo* 35°57'N 102°17'E, 31
Kuoxian/*K'uo-hsien* 38°52'N 112°48'E, 164
Kuo cang/*K'uo-ts'ang* 28°49N 120°58'E, 110
Kuril (Isls) (USSR), 34
Kurla 41°48'N 86°10'E, 41
Kuye (Isl) *see* Sakhalin (Isl)
Kuyu/*K'u-yü* 45°40'N 96°35'E, 150
Kyoto (Japan) 35°02'N 135°45'E, 33, 34

Laccadive Islands (India), 34
Lahore (Pakistan) 31°34'N 74°22'E, 34
Lai/*Lai see* Laizhou
Laishui/*Lai-shui* 39°23'N 115°41'E, 152
Laisu/*Lai-su* 32°18'N 105°46'E, 102
Laiyang/*Lai-yang* 36°58'N 120°41'E, 164
Laizhou/*Lai-chou*/Lai 37°13'N 120°04'E, 27, 31, 71, 98, 102, 105, 152, 164
Lamuri/Nanwuli (Indonesia) 05°55'N 95°18'E, 38
Lan/*Lan see* Lanzhou
Lancang R/*Lan-ts'ang*/Mekong, 11, 15, 27, 34, 41, 98
Lang/*Lang* 31°44'N 105°55'E, 31
Langdai/*Lang-tai* 26°06'N 105°20'E, 36
Langshan/*Lang-shan*/Queshan 32°50'N 114°02'E, 103
Langya/*Lang-ya* 35°40'N 119°53'E, 30, 71, 110
Langzhou/*Lang-chou* 29°01'N 111°32'E, 30, 102
Lanqi/*Lan-ch'i* 29°25'N 120°50'E, 94
Lanzhou/*Lan-chou*/Lan 36°01'N 103°47'E, 11, 15, 24, 25, 26, 27, 30, 31, 34, 41, 52, 92, 94, 149, 150, 158
Lanzhou/*Lan-chou* 38°16'N 111°37'E, 102
Lao/*Lao* 36°30'N 121°00'E, 110
Lao'an/*Lao-an* (Taiwan) 23°05'N 121°09'E, 33
Laopi/*Lao-p'i* (Taiwan) 22°38'N 120°41'E, 33
La'sa (S Yemen) 14°34'N 49°07'E, 38
Le/*Le* 36°32'N 102°36'E, 31
Lei'Lei 20°48'N 110°06'E, 31, 98
Leizhou/*Lei-chou see* Zhanjiang
Leling/*Le-ling* 37°43'N 117°13'E, 152
Lend R (USSR), 15
Leping/*Le-p'ing*/Pingjinjun 37°19'N 113°32'E, 102
Lhasa/Ra-sa 29°39'N 91°07'E, 11, 15, 28, 34, 92, 98
Li/*Li* 41°12'N 119°11'E, 98
Li/*Li* 34°30'N 108°13'E, 31
Li/*Li see* Guangyuan
Li/*Li see* Lizhou
Lian/*Lien see* Lianzhou
Liang/*Liang see* Chenliu
Liang/*Liang see* Wuwei
Liang/*Liang see* Yang
Liangchengzhen/*Liang-ch'eng-chen* 36°00'N 119°00'E, 52
Liangdong/*Liang-tung* 33°52'N 106°18'E, 41
Liangshan/*Liang-shan* 30°43'N 127°56'E, 31
Liangzhe/*Liang-che* (Song "route"), 26
Liangzhou/*Liang-chou see* Wuwei
Lianghzu/*Liang-chu* 30°23'N 120°03'E, 52
Lianhua/*Lien-hua* 35°47'N 103°00'E, 41, 149
Lianhuashan/*Lien-hua-shan* 24°43'N 113°35'E, 102
Lianshan/*Lien-shan* 40°59'N 123°41'E, 33
Lianshui/*Lien-shui* 33°47'N 119°16'E, 123
Lianyun/*Lien-yün see* Lianyungang
Lianyungang/*Lien-yün-kang*/Lianyun 34°42'N 119°26'E, 11, 164
Lianzhou/*Lien-chou*/Lian 24°48'N 112°26'E, 30, 31, 102, 123
Lianzhou/*Lien-chou*/Lian 21°45'N 109°10'E, 27, 31, 149
Liao R/*Liao*, 11, 15, 23, 24, 27, 33, 34
Liacheng/*Liao-ch'eng*/Dongchang 36°26'N 115°58'E, 27, 105, 150, 152, 164
Liaodong/*Liao-tung* (Ming province), 27
Liaolin/*Liao-lin* 39°26'N 116°40'E, 150
Liaoyang/*Liao-yang see* Dingliao
Liaoyang/*Liao-yang* (Mongol province), 26
Liaozhou/*Liao-chou* 37°03'N 113°22'E, 31, 102
Lidai/*Li-tai see* Meureudai
Lijiang/*Li-chiang* 26°57'N 100°15'E, 27
Lima (Peru) 12°06'S 77°03'W, 38
Lin/*Lin* 38°07'N 111°05'E, 71
Lin/*Lin* 44°29'N 119°58'E, 98
Lin'an/*Lin-an* 23°20'N 103°10'E, 27, 149
Lin'an/*Lin-an see* Hangzhou
Lincheng/*Lin-ch'eng* 34°43'N 117°13'E, 164
Linfen/*Lin-fen see* Pingyang
Ling/*Ling* 37°54'N 106°40'E, 95, 98
Lingbao/*Ling-pao* 31°31'N 110°53'E, 54
Lingjiu/*Ling-chiu*/Vulture Peak 24°00'N 113°00'E, 110
Lingling/*Ling-ling* 26°04'N 111°28'E, 30
Lingnan/*Ling-nan* (Tang "province"), 26
Lingshou/*Ling-shou* 38°16'N 114°22'E, 54
Lingtai/*Ling-t'ai* 35°05'N 107°46'E, 41
Lingwu/*Ling-wu* 37°00'N 102°54'E, 26
Lingyan/*Ling-yen* (Tang "province"), 26
Lingyunzha/*Ling-yün-cha* 33°35'N 114°10'E, 103
Lingzhou/*Ling-chou* 38°06'N 106°21'E, 41
Linhai/*Lin-hai*/Tai/Taizhou 28°54'N 121°08'E, 24, 26, 27, 31, 98, 123
Linhuai/*Lin-huai* 32°20'N 116°16'E, 149
Linjiang/*Lin-chiang* 28°02'N 115°20'E, 27, 31
Linqing/*Lin-ch'ing* 36°51'N 115°42'E, 24, 105, 150, 152, 164
Linru/*Lin-ju*/Ruzhou 34°09'N 112°55'E, 54, 102, 103, 164
Lintan/*Lin-t'an*/Tao/Taozhou 34°41'N 103°25'E, 27, 31, 41, 150
Lintao/*Lin-t'ao*/Didaozhou 35°19'N 103°50'E, 27, 41
Lintong/*Lin-t'ung* 34°25'N 109°10'E, 41
Linyi/*Lin-i*/Yi/Yizhou 34°03'N 118°20'E, 31, 98, 102, 149, 152, 164
Linying/*Lin-ying* 33°48'N 113°58'E, 103
Linzi/*Lin-tzu* 36°43'N 118°20'E, 62, 71
Liping/*Li-p'ing* 26°16'N 109°08'E, 24, 36
Liquan/*Li-ch'üan* 34°23'N 108°40'E, 41
Lishi/*Li-shih*/Yongning 37°33'N 111°10'E, 71, 164
Liu/*Liu* 24°36'N 109°34'E, 31, 98
Liu R/*Liu*, 11, 23
Liuhe Harbor/*Liu-ho* 31°28'N 121°16'E, 105
Liukun/*Liu-k'un see* Nakhon
Liuqiu/*Liu-ch'iu see* Taiwan
Liuqiu (Isls)/Ryukyu (Japan) 34, 38
Liuzhou/*Liu-chou* 24°17'N 109°15'E, 27, 36, 102, 149
Lixian/*Li-hsien* 34°05'N 105°00'E, 41
Lizhou/*Li-chou*/Li 29°41'N 111°51'E, 31, 98, 102, 123
Lizhou/*Li-chou*/Li 29°10'N 102°20'E, 26, 30, 31
Lizhou/*Li-chou see* Guangyuan
Lizhou/*Li-chou* (Song "route"), 26
Lolang (N Korea) 58°52'N 125°17'E, 30
Long/*Lung* 44°30'N 125°00'E, 98
Long/*Lung see* Long'an
Long/*Lung see* Longxian
Long R/*Lung*, 36
Long'an/*Lung-an*/Long 32°40'N 104°20'E, 26, 27
Longde/*Lung-te* 35°38'N 106°06'E, 41
Longhu/*Lung-hu* 28°30'N 116°45'E, 110
Longkou/*Lung-k'ou* 37°41'N 120°18'E, 34
Longli/*Lung-li* 26°23'N 106°57'E, 36
Longmen/*Lung-men* 35°40'N 110°38'E, 110
Longquan/*Lung-ch'üan* 30°52'N 105°48'E, 158
Longtian/*Lung-t'ien* (Vietnam) 21°03'N 106°21'E, 150
Longtou/*Lung-t'ou* 23°41'N 113°24'E, 102
Longweiguan/*Lung-wei-kuan* 25°30'N 110°10'E, 30
Longxi/*Lung-hsi*/Gongchang/Wei 34°58'N 104°43'E, 27, 41, 95, 149, 150
Longxian/*Lung-hsien*/Long 34°48'N 106°53'E, 31, 123
Longxing/*Lung-hsing see* Nanchang
Longyou/*Lung-yu* (Tang circuit), 26
Longyu/*Lung-yü* 25°40'N 100°15'E, 92
Longzhou/*Lung-chou* 22°24'N 106°59'E, 34, 158
Longzhou/*Lung-chou* 34°50'N 107°20'E, 41
Lop 39°55'N 89°50'E, 150
Lop L, 11, 34, 41, 92
Lu/*Lu* 28°52'N 105°20'E, 31, 98
Lu/*Lu* 35°34'N 116°22'E, 30
Lu/*Lu* 29°20'N 115°00'E, 110
Lu/*Lu see* Changzhi
Lu/*Lu see* Hefei
Lu/*Lu see* Luzhou
Lu State/*Lu*, 71
Lu'an/*Lu-an*/Dongsheng 31°48'N 116°30'E, 27, 123
Lu'an/*Lu-an see* Changzhi
Luan R/*Luan*, 11, 24, 105, 149
Luang Prabang (Laos) 19°53'N 102°10'E, 34
Luanxian/*Luan-hsien* 39°43'N 118°44'E, 32, 164
Lüda/*Lü-ta*/Dalny/Dairen/Dalian 38°53'N 121°37'E, 11, 32, 34, 152, 158, 164
Luhun/*Lu-hun* 33°00'N 111°30'E, 110
Lujiang/*Lu-chiang* 31°50'N 117°41'E, 30
Lüliang Mts/*Lü-liang*, 11
Luo R/*Lo*, 41, 62, 71
Luochuan/*Lo-ch'uan* 35°55'N 109°28'E, 41, 164
Luoding/*Lo-ting* 33°32'N 114°01'E, 149
Luofou/*Lo-fou*/Panyu 22°54'N 113°18'E, 110
Luohu/*Lo-hu* 25°23'N 106°45'E, 36
Luolang/*Lo-lang* (N Korea) 58°52'N 125°17'E, 30
Luoning/*Lo-ning* 34°24'N 111°39'E, 54
Luoyang/*Lo-yang*/Xijing/Honan/He'nan/ He'nanfu/Zhou 34°47'N 112°26'E, 16, 23, 25, 26, 27, 30, 31, 52, 54, 62, 71, 92, 94, 95, 98, 102, 103, 105, 110, 123, 164
Lüshun/*Lü-shun*/Port Arthur/Ryojun 38°46'N 121°15'E, 32, 152, 158, 164
Lüsong/*Lü-sung see* Manila
Lutai/*Lu-t'ai* 39°20'N 117°48'E, 152
Luyi/*Lu-i* 33°50'N 115°28'E, 54
Luzhou/*Lu-chou*/Lu 31°45'N 116°35'E, 26, 27, 30
Lüzhou/*Lü-chou*/Lü 28°55'N 105°25'E, 24, 26, 30, 36, 123, 149, 158
Lüzhou/*Lü-chou see* Hefei

Macao (Portugal) 22°16'N 113°30'E, 11, 24, 34, 38, 158
Machang/*Ma-ch'ang* 36°00'N 102°00'E, 52
Macheng/*Ma-ch'eng* 31°11'N 115°02'E, 103
Madras (India) 13°05'N 80°18'E, 34
Magendan/*Ma-ken-tan* 41°33'N 123°56'E, 33
Mahu/*Ma-hu* 28°15'N 103°45'E, 27
Maimaicheng/*Mai-mai-ch'eng* 49°29'N 106°19'E, 33
Maimana (Afghanistan) 35°54'N 64°43'E, 92
Maimurgh (USSR) 38°35'N 65°30'E, 92
Majing/*Ma-ching* 23°12'N 113°06'E, 102
Malacca/Manlajia (Malaysia) 02°14'N 102°14'E, 38
Malden (Isl) (UK) 04°00'S 155°00'W, 38
Maldive Islands, 34, 38
Malindi (Kenya) 03°14'S 40°05'E, 38
Manas 44°16'N 86°02'E, 41
Mandalay (Burma) 21°57'N 96°04'E, 11, 34
Manila/Lüsong (Philippines) 14°37'N 120°58'E, 34, 38
Manlajia/*Man-la-chia see* Malacca
Manus (Isls) (Papua New Guinea) 2°00'S 147°00'E, 38
Manzhouli/*Man-chou-li* 49°34'N 117°30'E, 32, 34
Mao/Mao 31°36'N 103°52'E, 31, 98
Mao/Mao 30°10'N 120°22'E, 110
Maoming/*Mao-ming* 21°50'N 110°56'E, 24
Maomucheng/*Mao-mu-ch'eng*/Dingxing 40°21'N 99°42'E, 41
Maqi/*Ma-ch'i* 28°00'N 114°00'E, 110
Marianas (Isls) (USA Trust Territory), 38
Marquesas (Isls) (France), 38
Marshall (Isls) (USA Trust Territory), 38
Mary (USSR) 37°42'N 61°54'E, 92
Mecca (Saudi Arabia) 21°26'N 39°49'E, 34, 38
Mei/*Mei* 24°21'N 116°20'E, 31
Mei/*Mei see* Meizhou
Meijiang/*Mei-chiang* 24°25'N 102°20'E, 27
Meizhou/*Mei-chou*/Mei 30°02'N 103°43'E, 30, 31, 98, 102, 123
Mekong R/Lancang, 11, 15, 27, 34, 41, 98
Meng/*Meng see* Mengxian
Mengcheng/*Meng-ch'eng* 33°16'N 116°32'E, 149
Menghua/*Meng-hua* 25°20'N 100°25'E, 27, 150
Mengxian/*Meng-hsien*/Meng 35°05'N 112°41'E, 31, 54
Mengzi/*Meng-tzu* 23°20'N 103°21'E, 34
Mergen 49°10'N 125°15'E, 32 33
Meureudai/Lidai (Indonesia) 05°14'N 96°14'E, 38
Mexico City (Mexico) 19°25'N 99°10'W, 38
Mi/Mi *see* Mizhou
Mian/*Mien* 31°12'N 104°33'E, 31, 98
Mian/*Mien see* Mianzhou
Mianchi/*Mien-ch'ih* 34°45'N 111°45'E, 54
Mianning/*Mien-ning* 28°33'N 102°09'E, 149
Mianyang/*Mien-yang* 30°22'N 113°27'E, 158
Mianzhou/*Mien-chou* 30°33'N 114°20'E, 30, 92
Mianzhou/*Mien-chou*/Mian 31°29'N 104°45'E, 30, 123
Miaodigou/*Miao-ti-kou* 34°30'N 111°50'E, 52
Midway (Isls) (USA), 38
Mile/*Mi-le* 24°10'N 102°42'E, 36, 149
Min/*Min see* Minzhou
Min R/*Min*, 11, 15, 23, 71, 123, 149
Min R/*Min*, 11, 23, 31, 123
Ming/*Ming see* Ningbo
Mingshan/*Ming-shan* 30°04'N 103°05'E, 149
Mingzhou/*Ming-chou see* Ningbo
Minzhou/*Min-chou*/Min 34°20'N 104°09'E, 27, 31, 41, 94, 98, 102
Miyun/*Mi-yün* 40°23'N 116°47'E, 164
Mizhi/*Mi-chih* 37°50'N 110°03'E, 41, 164
Mizhou/*Mi-chou*/Mi/Zhucheng 36°06'N 119°24'E, 27, 31, 62, 102, 123
Mo/*Mo see* Renqiu
Mogadishu (Somalia) 02°02'N 45°21'E, 38
Mohei/*Mo-hei* 23°10'N 101°12'E, 149
Mombasa (Kenya) 04°04'S 39°40'E, 38
Moscow (USSR) 55°45'N 37°42'E, 34
Mozhou/*Mo-chou see* Renqiu
Mu/Mu *see* Jiande
Mudanjiang/*Mu-tan-chiang* 44°34'N 129°36'E, 11
Mukden *see* Shenyang
Multan (Pakistan) 30°10'N 71°36'E, 92
Muzhou/*Mu-chou* 29°11'N 119°26'E, 30, 102
Muztag Mt 36°28'N 87°29'E, 11
Muztagata Mt 38°15'N 75°05'E, 11
Nagapattinam (India) 10°46'N 79°51'E, 38
Nagasaki (Japan) 32°45'N 129°52'E, 34, 38
Nagur/*Naguer* (Indonesia) 05°11'N 96°00'E, 38
Naha/Haobajiang (Japan) 26°10'N 127°40'E, 38
Nakhon/Liukun (Thailand) 08°24'N 99°58'E, 38
Nan Mts/*Nan*, 11
Nan'an/*Nan-an* 24°57'N 118°25'E, 24, 27, 31
Nan'an/*Nan-an* 25°36'N 114°24'E, 31
Nanchang/*Nan-ch'ang*/Hong/Hongzhou/ Longxing/Yuzhang 28°40'N 115°52'E, 11, 24, 26, 27, 30, 31, 94, 102, 123, 150, 158
Nandongwan/*Nan-tung-wan see* Wuxi
Nan'en/*Nan-en* 21°51'N 111°56'E, 31, 123
Nangong/*Nan-kung* 37°21'N 115°23'E, 152
Nanhai/*Nan-hai* 23°00'N 113°03'E, 30, 110
Nanjian/*Nan-chien* 26°38'N 118°05'E, 26, 31, 98, 123
Nanjing/*Nan-ching*/Nankang/Jinling/ Jiqing/Tianjing/Yang/Jiangning 32°02'N 118°47'E, 11, 15, 23, 24, 26, 27, 28, 34, 38, 94, 102, 149, 150, 158
Nanjing/*Nan-ching*/Xijin 40°03'N 115°53'E, 102
Nanjing/*Nan-ching see* Shangqiu
Nanjun/*Nan-chün* 30°11'N 112°47'E, 30
Nankang/*Nan-k'ang* 29°10'N 116°01'E, 27, 31, 123
Nanlanling/*Nan-lan-ling* 31°52'N 120°15'E, 95
Nanliang/*Nan-liang* 30°35'N 106°31'E, 95
Nanning/*Nan-ning* 22°50'N 108°19'E, 11, 24, 27, 34, 94, 149, 158
Nan-pan R/*Nan-p'an*, 11, 30, 31, 98, 149
Nanpi/*Nan-p'i* 38°01'N 116°44'E, 152
Nanping/*Nan-p'ing* 29°05'N 107°11'E, 31
Nansha/*Nan-sha* (Isls) 34
Nantong/*Nan-t'ung* 32°00'N 120°53'E, 158
Nanwuli/*Nan-wu-li see* Lamuri
Nanxiang/*Nan-hsiang* 23°21'N 112°17'E, 102
Nanxiong/*Nan-hsiung* 25°10'N 114°20'E, 27, 31, 123, 149
Nanxu/*Nan-hsü* 32°15'N 119°39'E, 95
Nanyan/*Nan-yen* 32°27'N 119°41'E, 95
Nanyang/*Nan-yang*/Wan 33°06'N 112°31'E, 24, 27, 30, 54, 71, 105, 164
Nanying/*Nan-ying* 39°19'N 116°11'E, 95
Nanyu/*Nan-yü* 31°42'N 118°21'E, 95
Nanzhao Province/*Nan-chao*, 26, 27, 92
Nanzheng/*Nan-cheng see* Hanzhong
Nan Zhili/*Nan chih-li*/Ming province, 27
Nauru 00°31'S 166°56'E, 38
Nen R/*Nen*, 11
Nerchinsk/Nibuchu (USSR) 52°02'N 116°38'E, 32, 33
New Delhi (India) 28°37'N 77°13'E, 11
New Guinea (Isls) (Papua New Guinea/Indonesia), 38
Nianbo/*Nien-po*/Ledu 36°32'N, 102°25'E, 41
Nicobar (Isls) (India), 34
Ning/*Ning see* Ningzhou
Ning'an/*Ning-an* 44°21'N 129°28'E, 32, 33
Ningbo/*Ning-po*/Ming/Mingzhou 29°54'N 121°33'E, 24, 26, 27, 34, 38, 94, 98, 102, 123, 149, 150, 158
Ningfan/*Ning-fan* 28°40'N 102°00'E, 27
Ningguo/*Ning-kuo*/Xuan 30°38'N 118°58'E, 27, 31, 123, 149
Ningjiang/*Ning-chiang* 45°05'N 126°15'E, 98
Ningnian/*Ning-nien*/Fuyu 47°46'N 124°21'E, 32
Ningtiaoliang/*Ning-t'iao-liang* 37°42'N 108°19'E, 41
Ningwu/*Ning-wu* 39°00'N 112°18'E, 158
Ningxi/*Ning-hsi* 38°40'N 106°20'E, 94
Ningxia/*Ning-hsia*/Egrigaia (Chinese city) 38°30'N 106°18'E, 26, 27, 41, 150
Ningxia/*Ning-hsia* (Manchu city) 38°20'N 106°17'E, 41
Ningxia/*Ning-hsia* 44°25'N 129°15'E, 33
Ningxia-hou/*Ning-hsia-hou see* Huamachi
Ningxia-zhong/*Ning-hsia-chung see* Zhongwei
Ningyang/*Ning-yang* 35°45'N 116°47'E, 152
Ningyuan/*Ning-yüan*/Ningyuanzhou 40°38'N 120°46'E, 27, 33, 158
Ningyuan/*Ning-yüan* 34°28'N 104°51'E, 41
Ningyuan/*Ning-yüan* 28°13'N 102°12'E, 158
Ningyuanzhou/*Ning-yüan-chou see* Ningyuan
Ningzhou/*Ning-chou*/Ning 35°30'N 108°05'E, 31, 41
Niuzhuang/*Niu-chuan*/Yingkou 40°39'N 122°13'E, 32, 33, 34, 164
Nizhniy Novgorod (USSR) 56°20'N 44°00'E, 34
Nu R/*Nu*/Salween R, 11, 15, 34, 41, 98
Nyainqêntanglha Mts, 11

Ob R (USSR), 11, 15, 34
Odessa (USSR) 47°19'N 118°40'E, 34
Omsk (USSR) 55°00'N 73°22'E, 34
Orchon R, 11, 98

Pagan (Burma) 21°12'N 95°19'E, 98
Pahang/Pengheng (Malaysia) 03°50'N 103°19'E, 38
Palembang/Jiujiang (Indonesia) 02°59'S 104°45'E, 38
Pangasinan/Pengjiashilan (Philippines) 15°59'N 120°22'E, 38
Pao-ki-choui (Taiwan) 23°21'N 120°07'E, 33
Pataliputra (India) 25°20'N 85°35'E, 92
Pattani/Dani (Thailand) 06°50'N 101°20'E, 38

Tongnan/*T'ung-nan*, 30°10'N 105°49'E, 41
Tongren/*T'ung-jen* 27°38'N 109°03'E, 27, 36
Tongshan/*T'ung-shan* 31°10'N 106°24'E, 102
Tongshan/*T'ung-shan see* Xuzhou
Tongxian/*T'ung-hsien*/Tongzhou 39°43'N 116°32'E, 105, 150, 152, 164
Tongxin/*T'ung-hsin* 37°01'N 106°08'E, 41
Tongyuan/*T'ung-yüan*/Gong 35°10'N 104°40'E, 31
Tongzhou/*T'ung-chou see* Dali
Tongzhou/*T'ung-chou see* Tongxian
Torres (Isls) (UK/France) 13°15'S 166°37'E, 38
Touatoutia (Taiwan) 25°07'N 121°30'E, 33
Trengganu/Dingjialu (Malaysia) 05°20'N 103°07'E, 38
Truk (Isls) (USA Trust Territory), 38
Tsazitsyn (USSR) 48°44'N 44°24'E, 34
Tuanbogu/*T'uan-po-ku* 37°24'N 112°10'E, 102
Tuanfeng/*T'uan-feng* 30°38'N 114°51'E, 94
Tuban/*Duban* (Indonesia) 06°55'S 112°01'E, 38
Tuo R/*T'o*, 41, 103
Turfan/Karakhoja/Xizhou 42°55'N 89°06'E, 41, 92, 150
Turfan Depression, 11
Tyumen (USSR) 57°09'N 65°32'E, 34

Uch-Turfan/Wushi 41°11'N 79°15'E, 41
Ulaan Baatar/Kulun/Urga (Mongolia) 47°54'N 106°52'E, 11, 34, 41
Ulan Ude (USSR) 51°50'N 107°37'E, 34
Uliassutai (Mongolia) 47°42'N 96°52'E, 41
Ulungur L, 41
Unggi/Xiongji (N Korea) 42°19'N 130°24'E, 32
Ural Mts (USSR), 34
Urga *see* Ulaan Baatar
Urumqi/*Wu-lu-mu-ch'i*/Dihua/Luntai 43°49'N 87°34'E, 11, 28, 34, 150
Uvs L (Mongolia), 11, 15

Vanuatu 14°00'S 165°00'E, 38
Vienna (Austria) 48°13'N 16°20'E, 34
Vientiane (Laos) 17°59'N 102°38'E, 11
Vladivostok (USSR) 43°09'N 131°53'E, 32, 34
Volga R (USSR), 34

Waifang Mts/*Wai-fang*, 103
Wake (Isl) (USA) 19°17'N 166°37'E, 38
Wan/*Wan see* Nanyang
Wan/*Wan see* Wanxian
Wan'an/*Wan-an* 18°44'N 110°19'E, 98
Wanggecun/*Wang-ko-ts'un* 34°47'N 110°08'E, 41, 149
Wangqing Gate/*Wang'ch'ing* 41°42'N 125°26'E, 33
Wanjinyou/*Wan-chin-yu* 40°26'N 113°32'E, 27
Wankou/*Wan-k'ou* 30°22'N 117°02'E, 102
Wanquan/*Wan-ch'üan* 40°52'N 114°45'E, 94
Wanxian/*Wan-hsien*/Wan/Wanzhou 30°54'N 108°20'E, 24, 31, 102, 123, 158
Wanzhou/*Wan-chou see* Wanxian
Warsaw (Poland) 52°15'N 21°00'E, 34
Washington (Isl) (Kiribati) 04°43'N 160°24'W, 38
Wei/*Wei* 31°24'N 103°25'E, 31, 62, 98
Wei/*Wei* 35°26'N 106°30'E, 31
Wei/*Wei see* Longxi
Wei/*Wei see* Weifang
Wei/*Wei see* Weixian
Wei R/*Wei*, 11, 16, 23, 24, 27, 30, 31, 41, 52, 62, 95, 98, 102, 105, 123, 149
Wei State/*Wei*, 71
Weibo/*Wei-po* (Tang "province"), 26
Weicheng/*Wei-ch'eng* 31°38'N 105°42'E, 102
Wei'ercheng/*Wei-erh-ch'eng* 27°00'N 106°28'E, 36
Weifang/*Wei-fang*/Wei/Weixian 36°43'N 119°08'E, 24, 31, 123, 152, 164
Weihaiwei/*Wei-hai-wei* 37°28'N 122°07'E, 34, 152, 158
Weihui/*Wei-hui* 35°30'N 114°18'E, 26, 27, 30, 31
Weinan/*Wei-nan* 34°30'N 109°30'E, 41, 149, 164
Weining/*Wei-ning* 26°52'N 104°12'E, 36, 149
Weiningying/*Wei-ning-ying* 41°19'N 123°52'E, 33
Weishan L/*Wei-shan*, 105
Weixian/*Wei-hsien*/Wei/Weizhou 36°21'N 114°57'E, 26, 30, 152
Weixian/*Wei-hsien see* Weifang
Weiyuan/*Wei-yüan* 36°50'N 101°59'E, 41
Weiyuanbao Gate/*Wei-yüan-pao* 42 38'N 124°12'E, 33
Weizhou/*Wei-chou* 35°08'N 104°10'E, 102
Weizhou/*Wei-chou see* Weihui
Weizhou/*Wei-chou see* Weixian
Wen/*Wen* 32°54'N 104°46'E, 31, 98
Wen/*Wen see* Wenzhou
Wenchang/*Wen-ch'ang* 33°02'N 113°48'E, 103
Wenlangmashen *see* Bandjarmasin
Wenshang/*Wen-shang* 35°44'N 116°29'E, 94, 152
Wenxi/*Wen-hsi* 35°21'N 111°13'E, 54
Wenzhou/*Wen-chou*/Wen/Rui'an 28°00'N 120°37'E, 11, 24, 26, 27, 30, 31, 34, 94, 98, 102, 158
Western Samoa, 38
Wu/*Wu* 31°13'N 120°30'E, 71
Wu/*Wu see* Jinhua
Wu/*Wu see* Qi
Wu/*Wu see* Suzhou
Wu/*Wu see* Wuxi
Wu/*Wu see* Wuzhou
Wu Pass/*Wu* 33°27'N 110°00'E, 71
Wu R/*Wu*, 11, 31, 41, 102, 123, 149
Wubao/*Wu-pao* 37°36'N 110°16'E, 164
Wuchang/*Wu-ch'ang*/Jiangxia 30°20'N 114°17'E, 26, 27, 94, 110, 123, 150, 158
Wucheng/*Wu-ch'eng* 37°11'N 116°05'E, 152
Wuchuan/*Wu-ch'uan* 28°25'N 108°05'E, 36
Wudang/*Wu-tang* 32°30'N 110°50'E, 110
Wudi/*Wu-ti* 37°58'N 117°39'E, 62, 123
Wuding/*Wu-ting* 25°35'N 102°15'E, 27, 149
Wuding/*Wu-ting see* Huimin
Wuding R/*Wu-ting*, 41
Wufang/*Wu-fang*/Suiping 33°08'N 113°59'E, 103
Wugang/*Wu-kang* 26°50'N 110°49'E, 31
Wuguocheng/*Wu-kuo-ch'eng* 46°18'N 130°00'E, 98
Wuhan/*Wu-han* 30°33'N 114°17'E, 11, 15, 24, 28, 149, 158
Wuhu/*Wu-hu* 31°23'N 118°25'E, 24, 34, 149, 150, 158
Wuliang Mts/*Wu-liang*, 11
Wumeng/*Wu-meng* 27°15'N 103°40'E, 27, 150
Wuning/*Wu-ning* (Tang "province"), 26
Wuqing/*Wu-ch'ing* 39°22'N 117°04'E, 152
Wusa/*Wu-sa* 27°00'N 104°33'E, 27
Wushan/*Wu-shan* 31°05'N 109°48'E, 94
Wusong/*Wu-sung* 31°22'N 121°27'E, 158
Wusuli R/*Wu-su-li*, 11, 33
Wutahe (USSR) 38°45'N 63°45'E, 92
Wutai/*Wu-t'ai* 38°42'N 113°11'E, 110
Wuwei/*Wu-wei*/Liang/Liangzhou/Xiliang/Erginul 37°55'N 102°50'E, 25, 26, 27, 30, 41, 92, 95, 98, 110, 150
Wuwei/*Wu-wei* 31°20'N 117°50'E, 31, 123
Wuxi/*Wu-hsi*/Wu/Nandongwan 31°35'N 120°19'E, 24, 95, 105, 158
Wuyang/*Wu-yang* 33°25'N 113°35'E, 103
Wuyi/*Wu-i* 37°47'N 115°54'E, 110, 149
Wuyi/*Wu-i* 27°00'N 117°20'E, 110
Wuyi Mts/*Wu-i*, 11
Wuyuan/*Wu-yüan* 40°32'N 110°21'E, 30
Wuzhou/*Wu-chou*/Wu 23°32'N 111°20'E, 11, 24, 27, 30, 31, 34, 98, 102, 149
Wuzhou/*Wu-chou* 29°10'N 120°05'E, 30

Xi/*Hsi*/Zhentao 35°24'N 103°51'E, 31
Xi/*Hsi* 28°30'N 115°10'E, 110
Xi/*Hsi* (Song "route"), 26
Xi R/*Hsi* 11, 15, 23, 24, 27, 30, 31, 34, 94, 98, 102, 149, 150
Xia/*Hsia see* Xiazhou
Xiajin/*Hsia-chin* 36°56'N 116°00'E, 152
Xiakou/*Hsia-k'ou* 38°45'N 101°12'E, 41
Xiamen/*Hsia-men*/ Amoy 24°26'N 118°05'E, 11, 24, 34, 38, 149, 158
Xi'an/*Hsi-an*/Chang'an/Jingchao/Yong 34°12'N 108°57'E, 11, 15, 16, 23, 24, 26, 27, 28, 30, 31, 34, 41, 52, 54, 92, 94, 95, 98, 102, 110, 123, 150, 164
Xi'an/*Hsi-an* 42°28'N 125°10'E, 32
Xi'an/*Hsi-an* 33°30'N 105°31'E, 31
Xiang/*Hsiang* 36°07'N 114°18'N, 31, 54, 98
Xiang/*Hsiang* 24°00'N 109°44'E, 31
Xiang/*Hsiang see* Xiangfan
Xiang R/*Hsiang* 11, 23, 30, 31, 98, 102, 110, 123, 149
Xiangfan/*Hsiang-fan*/Xiang/Xiangyang/Xiangzhou/Fancheng/Yong 31°59'N 112°09'E, 26, 27, 30, 31, 92, 95, 102, 103, 110, 123, 149, 150, 158
Xiangguo/*Hsiang-kuo* 36°30'N 113°50'E, 110
Xiangping/*Hsiang-p'ing* 41°13'N 122°50'E, 71
Xiangshan/*Hsiang-shan* 22°25'N 113°14'E, 158
Xiangtan/*Hsiang-t'an* 27°51'N 112°54'E, 94
Xiangyang/*Hsiang-yang see* Xiangfan
Xiangzhou/*Hsiang-chou* 36°42'N 113°44'E, 30, 31
Xiangzhou/*Hsiang-chou* 24°00'N 110°05'E, 102
Xiangzhou/*Hsiang-chou* 25°13'N 114°21'E, 102
Xiangzhou/*Hsiang-chou see* Xiangfan
Xianping/*Hsien-p'ing* 40°03'N 124°11'E, 95
Xianping/*Hsien-p'ing* 42°30'N 124°13'E, 98
Xianxian/*Hsien-hsien* 38°10'N 116°07'E, 152
Xianyang/*Hsien-yang* 34°22'N 108°42'E, 41, 71
Xianzhou/*Hsien-chou* 38°27'N 111°06'E, 102
Xiaoheishan/*Hsiao-hei-shan* 41°42'N 122°09'E, 33
Xiaoling R/*Hsiao-ling*, 33
Xiaolinghe/*Hsiao-ling-ho* 41°00'N 121°19'E, 33
Xiao Xing'an Mts/*Hsiao-hsing-an* 11
Xiaoyizhen/*Hsiao-i-chen* 34°32'N 109°35'E, 41
Xiapei/*Hsia-p'ei* 34°10'N 118°10'E, 110
Xiasui/*Hsia-sui* (Tang "province") 26
Xiazhou/*Hsia-chou*/Xia 30°46'N 111°24'E, 26, 31, 98, 102
Xiazhou/*Hsia-chou*/Xia 38°09'N 109°08'E, 30, 95, 98
Xie/*Hsieh*/Jiezhou 35°10'N 111°06'E, 31, 150
Xie/*Hsieh* 34°53'N 116°46'E, 62, 71
Xie State/*Hsieh*, 71
Xifei R/*Hsi-fei* 103
Xihe/*Hsi-ho see* Fenyang
Xijing/*Hsi-ching*/Yalufu 41°58'N, 122°49'E, 25
Xijing/*Hsi-ching see* Datong
Xijing/*Hsi-ching see* Luoyang
Xiliang/*Hsi-liang see* Wuwei
Xiliao R/*Hsi-liao* 33
Xin/*Hsin* 44°00'N 124°28'E, 98
Xin/*Hsin* 22°45'N 112°13'E, 31
Xin/*Hsin see* Xinzhou
Xin'an/*Hsin-an* 23°00'N 115°07'E, 158
Xincai/*Hsin-ts'ai* 32°42'N 114°55'E, 62, 103, 150
Xinchang/*Hsin-ch'ang* 29°32'N 120°50'E, 150
Xincun/*Hsin-ts'un see* Gresik
Xindian/*Hsin-tien* (Taiwan) 24°58'N 121°31'E, 33
Xindu/*Hsin-tu* 30°50'N 104°11'E, 150, 158
Xinfan/*Hsin-fan* 31°06'N 103°48'E, 102
Xing/*Hsing see* Hanzhong
Xing/*Hsing see* Xingtai
Xing/*Hsing see* Xingzhou
Xing'an/*Hsing-an*/Ankang/Dongliao 32°38'N 109°03'E, 95, 150, 158
Xingguo/*Hsing-kuo* 30°05'N 115°06'E, 31
Xinghua/*Hsing-hua* 25°20'N 118°40'E, 26, 27, 31
Xingjing/*Hsing-ching* 41°41'N 124°53'E, 33
Xingkai L/*Hsing-k'ai* 11, 33
Xingqing/*Hsing-ch'ing* 38°24'N 108°20'E, 98
Xingtai/*Hsing-t'ai*/Xing/Xingzhou/Geng 37°03'N 114°30'E, 26, 31, 54, 62, 102
Xingxian/*Hsing-hsien* 38°26'N 111°09'E, 164
Xingyi/*Hsing-i* 25°08'N 104°52'E, 36
Xingyuang/*Hsing-yüan* 33°15'N 107°35'E, 26, 30, 31, 98
Xingzhong/*Hsing-chung* 41°36'N 120°32'E, 98
Xingzhou/*Hsing-chou*/Xing 33°10'N 105°58'E, 31, 102
Xingzhou/*Hsing-chou see* Xingtai
Xingzizhen/*Hsing-tzu-chen* 29°40'N 115°45'E, 150
Xining/*Hsi-ning*/Sinju 36°35'N 101°46'E, 11, 27, 31, 41, 149, 150
Xinjiang/*Hsin-chiang* 35°32'N 111°11'E, 164
Xintai/*Hsin-t'ai* 35°52'N 117°45'E, 164
Xinxian/*Hsin-hsien*/Xinzhou 38°23'N 112°42'E, 54, 102, 164
Xinxiang/*Hsin-hsiang* 35°12'N 113°49'E, 54, 164
Xinyang/*Hsin-yang* 32°06'N 114°03'E, 54, 103, 123
Xinye/*Hsin-yeh* 32°29'N 112°20'E, 150
Xinzhen/*Hsin-chen* 39°00'N 116°22'E, 152
Xinzheng/*Hsin-cheng* 34°10'N 113°40'E, 71, 164
Xinzhou/*Hsin-chou*/Xin 28°23'N 117°57'E, 26, 30, 31, 98, 102
Xinzhou/*Hsin-chou see* Xinxian
Xinzhou/*Hsin-chou* 23°00'N 113°00'E, 30
Xinzhoujiang/*Hsin-chou-chiang see* Qui Nhon
Xinzhu/*Hsin-chu* (Taiwan) 24°48'N 120°59'E, 33
Xiong/*Hsiung see* Xiongxian
Xiongxian/*Hsiung-hsien* 38°58'N 116°05'E, 31, 152
Xiongyue/*Hsiung-yüeh* 40°12'N 122°10'E, 33
Xiping/*Hsi-p'ing* 33°21'N 113°59'E, 103
Xisha (Isls)/*Hsi-sha* 18°00'N 112°00'E, 34
Xiu/*Hsiu* 30°49'N 120°43'E, 31, 98
Xiushan/*Hsiu-shan* 28°27'N 108°58'E, 36
Xiuyan/*Hsiu-yen* 40°15'N 123°13'E, 33
Xixiabangma Feng (Mt)/*Hsi-hsia-pang-ma* 28°21'N 85°47'E, 11
Xu/*Hsü*/Yingchang 34°06'N 117°50'E, 26, 31
Xu/*Hsü see* Xuzhou
Xu/*Hsü see* Yibin
Xuan/*Hsüan see* Ningguo
Xuanfu/*Hsüan-fu* 40°28'N 113°29'E, 27, 150
Xuanshe/*Hsüan-she* (Tang "province") 26
Xuanwei/*Hsüan-wei* 26°13'N 104°06'E, 149
Xuanwu/*Hsüan-wu* (Tang "province") 26, 103
Xuanzhou/*Hsüan-chou* 31°15'N 118°45'E, 30
Xuchang/*Hsü-ch'ang*/Xuzhou 34°03'N 113°48'E, 62, 103, 110, 164
Xun/*Hsün* 24°08'N 115°15'E, 31, 98
Xun/*Hsün see* Guiping
Xundian/*Hsün-tien* 25°40'N 103°20'E, 27
Xunhua/*Hsün-hua* 35°48'N 102°35'E, 41
Xunmalin/*Hsün-ma-lin* 41°20'N 113°54'E, 150
Xunzhou/*Hsün-cho see* Guiping
Xuyi/*Hsü-i* 33°02'N 118°22'E, 105
Xuzhou/*Hsü-chou*/Xu/Tongshan 34°15'N 117°11'E, 11, 24, 26, 30, 31, 94, 95, 98, 102, 105, 123, 149, 152
Xuzhou/*Hsü-chou see* Xuchang
Xuzhou/*Hsü-chou see* Yibin

Ya/*Ya see* Yazhou
Yablonovy Mts, 11
Yaishan/*Yai-shan* 21°36'N 113°24'E, 98
Yakesa /Albazin 53°23'N 123°16'E, 33
Yakutsk (USSR) 62°13'N 129°49'E, 34
Yalong R/*Ya-lung*, 11, 15, 27, 30, 41, 94, 98, 149
Yalu R/*Ya-lu*, 11, 24, 33
Yan/*Yen* 37°24'N 107°34'E, 26, 98
Yan/*Yen see* Yan'an
Yan/*Yen see* Yanzhou
Yan State/*Yen*, 71
Yan'an/*Yen-an*/Yan/Yanzhou/Fushi 36°35'N 109°27'E, 11, 26, 27, 30, 31, 41, 98, 102, 123, 149, 150, 164
Yancha/*Yen-ch'a*/Haiyuan 36°32'N 104°52'E, 41
Yanchang/*Yen-ch'ang* 36°31'N 110°04'E, 41, 164
Yancheng/*Yen-ch'eng* 33°32'N 114°02'E, 54, 98, 103
Yanchuan/*Yen-ch'uan* 36°52'N 110°09'E, 164
Yang/*Yang*/Liang 33°14'N 107°35'E, 31, 95
Yang/*Yang* 32°33'N 116°31'E, 95
Yang/*Yang see* Nanjing
Yang/*Yang see* Yangzhou
Yang/*Yang see* Yiyang
Yanggu/*Yang-ku* 36°06'N 115°46'E, 152
Yanghe/*Yang-ho* 40°10'N 113°30'E, 27
Yangishahr 42°50'N 89°10'E, 41
Yanguan/*Yen-kuan* 34°17'N 105°27'E, 41, 149
Yangzhou/*Yang-chou*/Yang/Jiangchu 32°24'N 119°26'E, 26, 27, 30, 31, 98, 102, 105, 123, 150, 158
Yangzhou/*Yang-chou*/Yang 33°02'N 108°10'E, 30, 98, 123
Yangzhou/*Yang-chou* 26°20'N 111°45'E, 27
Yangzhou Canal/*Yang-chou*, 105
Yangzi R/*Yang-tzu*/Chang/Jiang, 11
Yangzi Gorges/*Yang-tzu*, 24
Yanhai/*Yen-hai* (Tang "province"), 26
Yanjing/*Yen-ching* 27°40'N 101°55'E, 27
Yanmen/*Yen-men* 38°42'N 113°11'E, 30, 158
Yanmen/*Yen-men* 40°04'N 112°14'E, 71
Yanping/*Yen-p'ing* 26°40'N 117°50'E, 27
Yanshan/*Yen-shan* 38°01'N 117°14'E, 150, 152
Yanshi/*Yen-shih* 34°43'N 112°48'E, 54
Yantai/*Yen-t'ai*/Chefoo/Zhefu 37°31'N 121°23'E, 11, 34, 152, 158
Yanying/*Yen-ying*/Ruo 32°03'N 111°55'E, 62, 71
Yanzhou/*Yen-chou*/Yan 35°33'N 116°50'E, 26, 27, 30, 31, 95, 98, 102, 152, 164
Yanzhou/*Yen-chou* 29°30'N 119°30'E, 27
Yanzhou/*Yen-chou see* Yan'an
Yao/*Yao* 34°46'N 109°13'E, 31
Yao'an/*Yao-an* 25°40'N 101°10'E, 27
Yaozhou/*Yao-chou* 26°40'N 101°45'E, 92
Yaozhou/*Yao-chou* 40°32'N 122°27'E, 33
Yarkand/Soju/Souche 38°27'N 77°16'E, 41, 92, 150
Yarkant R, 11
Yarlung Zangbo R/Brahmaputra, 11, 15, 34, 41
Yasin (Pakistan) 36°23'N 72°23'E, 92
Yazhou/*Ya-chou*/Ya 30°03'N 103°02'E, 26, 31, 102
Ye/*Yeh* 33°40'N 113°26'E, 71
Ye/*Yeh* 35°10'N 114°10'E, 110
Yehe/*Yeh-ho* 43°01'N 124°19'E, 33
Yenisey R (USSR), 15
Yerevan (USSR) 40°11'N 44°30'E, 34
Yezhou/*Yeh-chou* 36°08'N 114°12'E, 102
Yi/*I*/Qingyuan 24°46'N 108°43'E, 31
Yi/*I see* Linyi
Yi/*I see* Shu
Yibin/*I-pin*/Rong/Rongzhou/Xu/Xuzhou 28°46'N 104°34'E, 11, 27, 30, 31, 92, 102
Yichang/*I-ch'ang* 30°40'N 111°19'E, 11, 24, 34, 158
Yicheng/*I-ch'eng* 31°43'N 112°07'E, 94
Yicheng/*I-ch'eng* (Tang "province") 26, 103
Yichuan/*I-ch'uan* 36°04'N 110°05'E, 41, 54, 149, 164
Yidu/*I-tu*/Qing/Qingzhou 36°41'N 118°29'E, 26, 27, 30, 31, 54, 95, 98, 102, 123, 152
Yiguang/*I-kuang* 32°22'N 105°48'E, 102
Yijun/*I-chün* 35°20'N 109°00'E, 41
Yili/*I-li*/Huiyuan/Kulja 43°50'N 81°28'E, 41
Yiliang/*I-liang* 24°55'N 103°07'E, 149
Yilu/*I-lu* 42°06'N 123°45'E, 33
Yin/*Yin* 38°01'N 115°03'E, 95
Yimucheng/*I-mu-ch'eng* 40°32'N 122°28'E, 33
Yincheng/*Yin-ch'eng* 31°58'N 115°10'E, 103
Yinchuan/*Yin-ch'uan* 38°27'N 106°17'E, 11
Ying/*Ying* 30°10'N 112°24'E, 62, 71
Ying/*Ying* 21°42'N 120°50'E, 26
Ying/*Ying see* Chengtian
Ying/*Ying see* Fuyang
Ying/*Ying see* Yingde
Ying/*Ying see* Yingzhou
Ying R/*Ying*, 11, 23, 71, 103, 105
Yingchuan/*Ying-ch'uan see* Zhengzhou
Yingde/*Ying-te*/Ying 24°12'N 113°24'E, 31, 98, 123
Yingkou/*Ying-k'ou see* Niuzhuang
Yingle Gate/*Ying-le* 42°14'N 125°14'E, 33
Yingluanzhen/*Ying-luan-chen* 32°16'N 119°11'E, 102
Yingshang/*Ying-shan*/Ying 32°38'N 116°15'E, 95, 103, 123
Yingtian/*Ying-t'ien* 34°29'N 115°32'E, 31
Yingzhou/*Ying-chou see* Fuyang
Yingzhou/*Ying-chou*/Ying 38°10'N 116°04'E, 31, 102
Yingzhou/*Ying-chou* 23°52'N 113°24'E, 102
Yi'ning/*I-ning* 25°25'N 109°50'E, 36
Yinshui/*Yin-shui*/Shangshui 33°30'N 114°40'E, 103
Yishi/*I-shih* 35°22'N 110°52'E, 150
Yishui/*I-shui* 35°46'N 118°37'E, 152
Yiwu/*I-wu* (Tang "province"), 26
Yixian/*I-hsien* 39°18'N 115°28'E, 164
Yixing/*I-hsing* 31°22'N 119°49'E, 102
Yiyang/*I-yang*/Yang 34°13'N 112°15'E, 71, 95, 149
Yizhang/*I-chang* 25°22'N 113°02'E, 149
Yizhou/*I-chou* 39°32'N 115°07'E, 30
Yizhou/*I-chou* 24°45'N 103°07'E, 30
Yizhou/*I-chou* 41°33'N 121°14'E, 33
Yizhou/*I-chou* 24°35'N 108°35'E, 102
Yizhou/*I-chou see* Chengdu
Yizhou/*I-chou see* Linyi
Yo *see* Yueyang
Yong/*Yung* 22°42'N 108°22'E, 26, 31, 98, 123
Yong/*Yung*/Qin 34°23'N 107°58'E, 62, 71
Yong/*Yung* 29°34'N 104°22'E, 31
Yong/*Yung see* Xi'an
Yong/*Yung see* Xiangfan
Yong/*Yung see* Yongzhou
Yongchang/*Yung-ch'ang*/Jinchi 25°15'N 99°00'E, 27
Yongchang/*Yung-ch'ang* 28°15'N 103°24'E, 27
Yongchang/*Yung-ch'ang* 39°15'N 102°09'E, 94
Yongcheng/*Yung-ch'eng* 33°54'N 116°23'E, 54
Yongcong/*Yung-ts'ong* 26°05'N 109°08'E, 36
Yongding R/*Yung-ting*, 11, 30, 31, 105
Yongfeng/*Yung-feng* 27°18'N 115°25'E, 149
Yongguan/*Yung-kuan* (Tang "province"), 26
Yongji/*Yung-chi*/Puzhou 34°51'N 110°32'E, 164
Yongji Canal/*Yung-chi*, 105
Yongjing/*Yung-ching* 39°05'N 115°52'E, 152
Yongjing/*Yung-ching see* Yongjingjun
Yongjingjun/*Yung-ching-chün*/Yongjing/Dongguang 37°53'N 116°30'E, 31, 123
Yongkang/*Yung-k'ang* 31°32'N 103°35'E, 31
Yongning/*Yung-ning* 27°47'N 100°38'E, 27
Yongning/*Yung-ning* 28°14'N 105°25'E, 36
Yongning/*Yung-ning* 25°53'N 105°29'E, 36
Yongning/*Yung-ning* 38°48'N 103°20'E, 98
Yongningjian/*Yung-ning-chien* 39°56'N 121°53'E, 33
Yongping/*Yung-p'ing* 39°55'N 119°28'E, 27, 150
Yongsui/*Yung-sui* 28°36'N 109°36'E, 36
Yongxing/*Yung-hsing* (Song "route"), 26
Yongzhou/*Yung-chou*/Yong 26°15'N 111°33'E, 26, 30, 31, 98, 102
You/*Yu see* Youzhou
You R/*Yu*, 23
Youbeiping/*Yu-pei-p'ing* 40°47'N 119°17'E, 30
Youyang/*Yu-yang* 28°48'N 108°45'E, 36
Youzhou/*Yu-chou*/You 21°13'N 117°24'E, 30, 95
Youzhou/*Yu-chou* (Tang "province"), 26
Yu/*Yü see* Beijing
Yu/*Yü see* Chongqing
Yu R/*Yü*, 123, 149
Yuan/*Yüan* 27°46'N 109°35'E, 31, 98
Yuan/*Yüan see* Yuanzhou
Yuan R/*Yüan*, 11, 27, 31, 36, 94, 102, 149
Yuan R/*Yüan*/Red R, 11, 23, 98
Yuanjiang/*Yüan-chiang* 23°30'N 101°59'E, 27
Yuanmou/*Yüan-mou* 25°42'N 101°52'E, 149
Yuanping/*Yüan-p'ing* 38°41'N 112°46'E, 164
Yuanqu/*Yüan-chü* 35°17'N 111°39'E, 149
Yuanzhou/*Yüan-chou* 27°51'N 114°28'E, 27, 94, 98, 102
Yuanzhou/*Yüan-chou*/Yuan 35°46'N 106°08'E, 26, 31, 95, 102
Yucheng/*Yü-ch'eng* 36°54'N 116°38'E, 54, 152
Yuci/*Yü-tz'u* 37°39'N 112°45'E, 164
Yue/*Yüeh see* Yuezhou
Yue/*Yüeh see* Yueyang
Yuechi/*Yüeh-ch'ih* 30°31'N 106°25'E, 158
Yuesui/*Yüeh-sui* 28°46'N 102°10'E, 27
Yueyang/*Yüeh-yang*/Yue/Yuezhou/Yo 29°21'N 113°07'E, 11, 24, 27, 30, 31, 34, 92, 98, 102, 123, 149, 158
Yuezhou/*Yüeh-chou*/Yue 29°50'N 121°10'E, 26, 30, 31
Yuezhou/*Yüeh-chou see* Yueyang
Yuhang/*Yü-hang* 30°30'N 120°22'E, 105, 110
Yulin/*Yü-lin* 38°16'N 109°49'E, 27, 41, 94, 149, 164
Yulin/*Yü-lin* 22°37'N 110°07'E, 30, 31
Yulin/*Yü-lin* 39°22'N 112°41'E, 164
Yuling/*Yü-ling* 29°43'N 119°09'E, 123
Yun/*Yün*/Dongping 35°55'N 116°18'E, 31, 62, 123
Yun/*Yün see* Yunzhou
Yun R/*Yün*, 103
Yu'nan/*Yü-nan* 31°01'N 108°58'E, 31, 123
Yuncheng/*Yün-ch'eng* 35°32'N 115°54'E, 123
Yunnan/*Yün-nan see* Kunming
Yunnan Province/*Yün-nan*, 26, 27, 36, 150, 158
Yunnanfu/*Yün-nan-fu see* Kunming
Yuntai/*Yün-t'ai* 31°00'N 107°10'E, 110
Yunyang/*Yün-yang* 32°03'N 112°01'E, 27
Yunyang/*Yün-yang* 30°58'N 108°53'E, 158
Yunzhou/*Yün-chou*/Yun 39°55'N 113°00'E, 30, 92
Yunzhou/*Yün-chou* 36°06'N 115°50'E, 30
Yuxian/*Yü-hsien* 39°50'N 114°32'E, 164
Yuzhang/*Yü-chang* 24°39'N 115°36'E, 30, 110
Yuzhang/*Yü-chang* 28°00'N 117°30'E, 110
Yuzhang/*Yü-chang see* Nanchang
Yuzhou/*Yü-chou see* Chongqing

Zai/*Tsai* 33°07'N 114°24'E, 31
Zanzibar (Isl) (Tanzania), 38
Zarang (Afghanistan) 36°06'N 61°53'E, 92
Zaysan L (USSR), 41
Ze/*Tse see* Jincheng
Zelu/*Tse-lu* (Tang "province"), 26
Zezhou/*Tse-chou see* Jincheng
Zhande/*Chan-te* 44°05'N 80°42'E, 41
Zhang/*Chang see* Zhangzhou
Zhangde/*Chang-te see* Anyang
Zhanghua/*Chang-hua* (Taiwan) 24°06'N 120°31'E, 33, 149

Zhangjiachuan/*Chang-chia-ch'uan* 34°55'N
  106°26'E, 41
Zhangjiakou/*Chang-chia-k'ou*/Kalgan
  40°46'N 114°52'E, 150, 158, 164
Zhangye/*Chang-yeh* 38°51'N 100°22'E, 95
Zhangyizhan/*Chang-i-chan* 41°40'N
  123°07'E, 33
Zhangzhou/*Chang-chou*/Zhang 24°31'N
  117°40'E, 26, 27, 30, 31, 98, 102, 123, 150,
  158
Zhangzhou/*Chang-chou* 31°36'N 120°21'E,
  26
Zhanjiang/*Chan-chiang*/Leizhou 21°11'N
  110°22'E, 11, 27, 30
Zhanwutai Gate/*Chan-wu-t'ai* 42°22'N
  122°46'E, 33
Zhanyi/*Chan-i* 25°39'N 103°45'E, 36
Zhao/*Chao* 24°06'N 110°45'E, 98
Zhao/*Chao see* Zhaozhou
Zhao State/*Chao*, 71
Zhaoqing/*Chao-ch'ing* 23°05'N 112°20'E, 27,
  31, 149
Zhaotong/*Chao-t'ung* 26°48'N 103°52'E, 150
Zhaotong/*Chao-t'ung* 27°12'N 103°40'E, 150
Zhaoyankou/*Chao-yen-k'ou*/Jiyang 36°59'N
  117°11'E, 123
Zhaoyi/*Chao-i* 35°00'N 110°09'E, 41

Zhaozhou/*Chao-chou*/Zhao 37°44'N
  114°47'E, 30, 31, 123
Zhaozhou/*Chao-chou* 24°36'N 110°28'E, 102
Zhedijiang/*Che-ti-chiang*/Chittagong
  (Bangladesh) 22°20'N 91°48'E, 38
Zhedong/*Che-tung* (Tang "province"), 26
Zhefu/*Che-fu see* Yantai
Zhejiang Province/*Che-chiang*/Jiangzhe, 27,
  150, 158
Zheliwen/*Che-li-wen see* Cheribon
Zhen/*Chen*/Yizheng 32°16'N 119°12'E, 26,
  123
Zhen/*Chen see* Hengzhou
Zhen'an/*Chen-an* 23°15'N 106°45'E, 27
Zhending/*Chen-ting*/Zhengding 38°15'N
  114°39'E, 26, 27, 30, 31, 94, 98, 123, 150,
  164
Zhenfeng/*Chen-feng* 25°22'N 105°32'E, 36
Zheng/*Cheng see* Zhengzhou
Zheng'an/*Cheng-an* 28°25'N 107°28'E, 36
Zhengding/*Cheng-ting see* Zhending
Zhengning/*Cheng-ning* 35°25'N 108°19'E, 41
Zhengxian/*Cheng-hsien see* Zhengzhou
Zhengzhou/*Cheng-chou*/Zheng/Zhengxian/
  Ao/Yingchuan 34°44'N 113°41'E, 11, 16,
  24, 31, 52, 54, 94, 95, 102, 103, 110, 150,
  164

Zhenjiang/*Chen-chiang*/Run/Runzhou
  32°08'N 119°30'E, 24, 26, 27, 30, 34, 98,
  102, 105, 123, 150, 158
Zhenjiang/*Chen-chiang* 40°17'N 124°24'E, 33
Zhenshuo/*Chen-shuo* 37°34'N 107°40'E, 27
Zhenwu/*Chen-wu* 37°36'N 102°30'E, 31
Zhenwu/*Chen-wu* (Tang "province"), 26
Zhenxiong/*Chen-hsiung*/Mangbu 27°25'N
  104°55'E, 27
Zhenyuan/*Chen-yüan* 26°53'N 108°19'E, 27,
  36
Zhenyuan/*Chen-yüan* 23°55'N 100°55'E, 27
Zhenyuan/*Chen-yüan* 35°44'N 107°41'E, 41
Zhenzhou/*Chen-chou*/Yizheng 32°15'N
  119°10'E, 105
Zhenzhou/*Chen-chou* 38°08'N 114°33'E, 102
Zherzong/*Chen-tsung* 36°02'N 106°16'E, 31
Zhexi/*Che-hsi* (Tang "province"), 26
Zhifu/*Chih-fu* 37°31'N 121°22'E, 164
Zhigu/*Chih-ku* 39°08'N 117°10'E, 105
Zhihe/*Chih-ho*/Woyang 33°32'N 116°18'E,
  149
Zhili Province/*Chih-li*/Bei Zhili 27, 150, 152,
  158
Zhongbu/*Chung-pu* 35°40'N 109°20'E, 41,
  149, 164
Zhongdu/*Chung-tu* 39°48'N 116°32'E, 98

Zhonghou-suo/*Chung-hou-so* 40°24'N
  120°31'E, 33
Zhongjing/*Chung-ching* 30°40'N 103°29'E, 31
Zhongluan/*Chung-luan* 34°41'N 113°55'E,
  105
Zhongmou/*Chung-mou* 35°43'N 114°01'E, 71
Zhongnan/*Chung-nan* 35°10'N 119°30'E, 110
Zhongning/*Chung-ning* 37°00'N 105°23'E, 98
Zhongshan/*Chung-shan*/Ding 38°20'N
  114°40'E, 31, 62, 95, 110
Zhongshan State/*Chung-shan*, 71
Zhongshu/*Chung-shu* (Mongol province), 26
Zhongwei/*Chung-wei*/Ningxia-zhong
  37°31'N 105°13'E, 27, 41, 149
Zhongwu/*Chung-wu* (Tang "province"), 26
Zhongxing/*Chung-hsing* 30 18'N 112°00'E,
  26
Zhongzhou/*Chung-chou*/Xianchun 30°20'N
  108°01'E, 31, 102
Zhuangliang/*Chuang-liang* 36°26'N
  102°59'E, 27
Zhugedanlan/*Chu-ko-tan-lan see* Sukadana
Zhuo/*Chou see* Zhuoxian
Zhuoxian/*Chou-hsien*/Zhuo 39°27'N
  115°58'E, 94, 150, 152, 164
Zhuxu/*Chu-hsü* (Thailand) 13°12'N 99°59'E,
  38

Zhuyai/*Chu-yai see* Haikou
Zi/*Tzu*/Santai/Tongchuan 31°04'N 105°03'E,
  26, 31, 102, 123
Zi/*Tzu* 36°42'N 118°00'E, 31
Zi/*Tzu see* Zizhou
Zichuan/*Tzu-ch'uan* 36°45'N 119°40'E, 30
Zihe/*Tzu-ho* 42°20'N 124°06'E, 33
Ziliujing/*Tzu-liu-ching* 29°19'N 104°46'E,
  158
Ziqing/*Tzu-ch'ing* (Tang "province"), 26
Ziya R/*Tzu-ya*, 23, 105
Ziyang/*Tzu-yang* 30°07'N 104°38'E, 158
Zizhou/*Tzu-chou*/Zi 29°50'N 104°57'E, 31,
  158
Zizhou/*Tzu-chou* 36°46'N 118°03'E, 102
Zouping/*Tsou-p'ing* 36°51'N 117°45'E, 152
Zouxian/*Tsou-hsien* 35°20'N 116°58'E, 54,
  149, 164
Zufaer/*Tsu-fa-erh see* Salala
Zunghaer Basin, 11
Zunhua/*Tsun-hua* 40°11'N 117°57'E, 152,
  164
Zunyi/*Tsun-i* 27°39'N 106°57'E, 27, 36
Zuo R/*Tso*, 11

INDEX